Reliable Knowledge Discovery

Honghua Dai • James N.K. Liu • Evgueni Smirnov
Editors

Reliable Knowledge
Discovery

 Springer

Editors
Honghua Dai
Deakin University
Burwood, Victoria, Australia

James N.K. Liu
The Hong Kong Polytechnic University
Hong Kong

Evgueni Smirnov
Maastricht University
Maastricht, The Netherlands

ISBN 978-1-4899-9532-2   ISBN 978-1-4614-1903-7 (eBook)
DOI 10.1007/978-1-4614-1903-7
Springer New York Dordrecht Heidelberg London

Springer is part of Springer Science+Business Media (www.springer.com)

Preface

1 Description

With the rapid development of the data mining and knowledge discovery, a key issue which could significantly affect the real world applications of data mining is the reliability issues of knowledge discovery. It is natural that people will ask if the discovered knowledge is reliable. Why do we trust the discovered knowledge? How much can we trust the discovered knowledge? When it could go wrong. All these questions are very essential to data mining. It is especial crucial to the real world applications.

One of the essential requirements of data mining is validity. This means both the discovery process itself and the discovered knowledge should be valid. Reliability is a necessary but not sufficient condition for validity. Reliability could be viewed as stability, equivalence and consistency in some ways.

This special volume of the book on the reliability issues of Data Mining and Knowledge Discovery will focus on the theory and techniques that can ensure the discovered knowledge is reliable and to identify under which conditions the discovered knowledge is reliable or in which cases the discovery process is robust. In the last 20 years, many data mining algorithms have been developed for the discovery of knowledge from given data bases. However in some cases, the discovery process is not robust or the discovered knowledge is not reliable or even incorrect in certain cases. We could also find that in some cases, the discovered knowledge may not necessary be the real reflection of the data. Why does this happen? What are the major factors that affect the discovery process? How can we make sure that the discovered knowledge is reliable? What are the conditions under which a reliable discovery can be assured? These are some interesting questions to be investigated in this book.

2 Scope and Topics of this Book

The topics of this book covers the following:

- The theories on reliable knowledge discovery
- Reliable knowledge discovery methods
- Reliability measurement criteria of knowledge discovery
- Reliability estimation methods
- General reliability issues on knowledge discovery
- Domain specific reliability issues on knowledge discovery
- The criteria that can be used to assess the reliability of discovered knowledge.
- The conditions under which we can confidently say that the discovered knowledge is reliable.
- The techniques which can improve reliability of knowledge discovery
- Practical approaches that can be used to solve reliability problems of data mining systems.
- The theoretical work on data mining reliability
- The practical approaches which can be used to assess if the discovered knowledge is reliable.
- The analysis of the factors that affect data mining reliability
- How reliability can be assessed
- In which condition, the reliability of the discovered knowledge is assured.

3 The Theme and Related Resources

The main purpose of this book is to encourage the use of Reliable Knowledge Discovery from Databases (RKDD) in critical-domain applications related to society, science, and technology. The book is intended for practitioners, researchers, and advanced-level students. It can be employed primarily as a reference work and it is a good compliment to the excellent book on reliable prediction Algorithmic learning in a random world by Vladimir Vovk, Alex Gammerman, and Glenn Shafer (New York: Springer, 2005). Extra information sources are the proceedings of the workshops Reliability Issues in Knowledge Discovery held in conjunction with the IEEE International Conferences on Data Mining. Other relevant conferences are the Annual ACM SIGKDD Conference on Knowledge Discovery and Data Mining (KDD), the International Conference on Machine Learning (ICML), The pacific-Asia Conference on Knowledge Discovery (PAKDD), and the European Conference on Machine Learning and Principles and Practice of Knowledge Discovery in Databases (ECML PKDD). Many AI-related journals regularly publish work in RKDD. Among others it is worth mentioning the Journal of Data Mining and Knowledge Discovery, the Journal of Machine Learning Research, and the Journal of Intelligent Data Analysis.

4 An Overview of the Book

This book presents the recent advances in the emerging field of **Reliable Knowledge Discovery from Data (RKDD)**. In this filed the knowledge is considered as reliable in the sense that its generalization performance can be set in advance. Hence, RKDD has a potential for a broad spectrum of applications, especially in critical domains like medicine, finance, military etc. The main material presented in the book is based on three consequent workshops Reliability Issues in Knowledge Discovery held in conjunction with the IEEE International Conferences on Data Mining (ICDM) in 2006, 2008, and 2010, respectively. In addition we provided an opportunity to authors to publish the results of their newest research related to RKDD.

This book is organized in seventeen chapters divided into four parts.

Part I includes three chapters on Reliability Estimation.

Chapter 1 provides an overview of typicalness and transductive reliability estimation frameworks. The overview is employed for introducing an approach for accessing reliability of individual classifications called joint confidence machine. Chapter 1 describes an approach that compensates the weaknesses of typicalness-based confidence estimation and transductive reliability estimation by integrating them into a joint confidence machine. It provides better interpretation of the performance of any classifiers. Experimental results performed with different machine learning algorithms in several problem domains show that there is no reduction of discrimination performance and is more suitable for applications with risk-sensitive problems with strict confidence limits.

Chapter 2 introduces new approaches to estimating and correcting individual predictions in the context of stream mining. It investigates the online reliability estimation of individual predictions. It proposes different strategies and explores techniques based on local variance and local bias, of local sensitivity analysis and online bagging of predictors. Comparison results on benchmark data are given to demonstrate the improvement of prediction accuracy.

Chapter 3 deals with the problem of quantifying the reliability in the context of neural networks. It elaborates on new approaches to estimation of confidence and prediction intervals for polynomial neural networks.

Part II includes seven chapters on Reliable Knowledge Discovery Methods.

Chapter 4 investigates outliers in regression targeting robust diagnostic regression. The chapter discusses both robust regression and regression diagnostics, presents several contemporary methods through numerical examples in linear regression.

Chapter 5 presents a conventional view on the definition of reliability; points out the three major categories of factors that affect the reliability of knowledge discovery, examined the impact of model complexity, weak links, varying sample sizes and the ability of different learners to the reliability of graphical model discovery, proposed reliable graph discovery approaches.

Chapter 6 provides a generalization of version spaces for reliable classification implemented using support vector machines.

Chapter 7 presents a unified generative model ONM which characterizes the life cycle of a ticket. The model uses maximum likelihood estimation to capture reliable ticket transfer profiles which can reflect how the information contained in a ticket is used by human experts to make reliable ticket routing decisions.

Chapter 8 applies the methods of aggregation functions for the reliable web based knowledge discovery from network trafic data.

Chapter 9 gives two new versions of SVM for the regression study of features in the problem domain. It provides means for feature selection and weighting based on the correlation analysis to give better and reliable result.

Chapter 10 describes in detail an application of transductive confidence machines for reliable handwriting recognition. It introduces a TCM framework which can enhance classifiers to reduce the computational costs and memory consumption required for updating the non-conformity scores in the offline learning setup of TCMs. Results are found to have outperformed previous methods on both relatively easy data and on difficult test samples.

PART III includes four Chapters on Reliability Analysis.

Chapter 11 addresses the problem of reliable feature selection. It introduces a generic-feature-selection measure together with a new search approach for globally optimal feature-subset selection. It discusses the reliability in the feature-selection process of a real pattern-recognition system, provides formal measurements and allows consistent search for relevant features in order to attain global optimal solution.

Chapter 12 provides three detailed case studies to show how the reliability of an induced classifier can be influenced. The case study results reveal the impact of data-oriented factors to the relaibility of the discovered knowledge.

Chapter 13 analyzes recently-introduced instance-based penalization techniques capable of providing more accurate predictions.

Chapter 14 investigates subsequence frequency measurement and its impact on the reliability of knowledge discovery in single sequences.

PART IV includes three chapters on Reliability Improvement Methods.

Chapter 15 proposed to use the inexact field learning method and parameter optimized one-class classifiers to improving reliability of unbalanced text mining by reducing performance bias.

Chapter 16 proposes a formal description technique for ontology representation and verification using a high level Petri net approach. It provides the capability of detection and identification of potential anomalies in ontology for the improvement of the discovered knolwedge.

Chapter 17 presents an UGDSS framework to provide reliable support for multi-criteria decision making in uncertainty problem domain. It gives the system design and architecture.

5 Acknowledgement

We would like to thank many people that made this book possible. We start with the organizers of the workshops held in conjunction with the IEEE International Conferences on Data Mining (ICDM): Shusaku Tsumoto, Francesco Bonchi, Bettina Berendt, Wei Fan and Wynne Hsu. We express our gratitude to the authors whose contributions can be found in the book. Finally, we thank our colleagues from Springer that made the publication process possible in a short period.

Burwood Victoria (Australia),   *Honghua Dai*
Hong Kong (China),   *James Liu*
Maastricht (The Netherlands),   *Evgueni Smirnov*
                             August 2011

Contents

Part IV Reliability Improvement Methods

Part I
Reliability Estimation

Chapter 1
Transductive Reliability Estimation for Individual Classifications in Machine Learning and Data Mining

Matjaž Kukar

Abstract Machine learning and data mining approaches are nowadays being used in many fields as valuable data analysis tools. However, their serious practical use is affected by the fact, that more often than not, they cannot produce reliable and unbiased assessments of their predictions' quality. In last years, several approaches for estimating reliability or confidence of individual classifiers have emerged, many of them building upon the algorithmic theory of randomness, such as (historically ordered) transduction-based confidence estimation, typicalness-based confidence estimation, and transductive reliability estimation. In the chapter we describe typicalness and transductive reliability estimation frameworks and propose a joint approach that compensates their weaknesses by integrating typicalness-based confidence estimation and transductive reliability estimation into a joint confidence machine. The resulting confidence machine produces confidence values in the statistical sense (e.g., a confidence level of 95% means that in 95% the predicted class is also a true class), as well as provides us with a general principle that is independent of to the particular underlying classifier

1.1 Introduction

Usually machine learning algorithms output only bare predictions (classifications) for the new unclassified examples. While there are ways for almost all machine learning algorithms to at least partially provide quantitative assessment of the particular classification, so far there is no general method to assess the quality (confidence, reliability) of a single classification. We are interested in the assessment of classifier's performance on a *single example* and not in average performance on an

Matjaž Kukar
University of Ljubljana, Faculty of Computer and Information Science,
Tržaška 25, SI-1001 Ljubljana, Slovenia,
e-mail: matjaz.kukar@fri.uni-lj.si

independent dataset. Such assessments are very useful, especially in risk-sensitive applications (medical diagnosis, financial and critical control applications) because there it often matters, how much one can rely upon a given prediction. In such cases an overall quality measure of a classifier (e.g. classification accuracy, mean squared error, ...) with respect to the whole input distribution would not provide the desired value. Another possible use of quality assessment of single classifications is in ensembles of machine learning algorithms for selecting or combining answers from different classifiers [24].

There have been numerous attempts to assign probabilities to machine learning classifiers' (decision trees and rules, Bayesian classifiers, neural networks, nearest neighbour classifiers, ...) in order to interpret their decision as a probability distribution over all possible classes. In fact, we can trivially convert every machine learning classifier's output to a probability distribution by assigning the predicted class the probability 1, and 0 to all other possible classes. The posterior probability of the predicted class can be viewed as a classifier's confidence (reliability) of its prediction. However, such estimations may in general not be good due to inherent applied algorithm's biases.[1]

1.2 Related work

In statistics, estimation for individual predictions is assessed by confidence values and intervals. On the same basis, the reliability estimation was implemented in machine learning methods, where properties of predictive models were utilized to endow predictions with corresponding reliability estimates. Although these approaches are specific for a particular predictive model and cannot be generalized, they provide favorable results to the general approaches. Such reliability estimates were developed for the Support Vector Machines [10, 33] the ridge regression model [28], the multilayer perceptron [27], the ensembles of neural networks [15, 7] and others.

In contrast to the former group of methods, general (model-independent) methods utilize approaches, such as local modeling of prediction error based on input space properties and local learning [2, 11], meta-predicting the leave-one-out error of a single example [39], transductive reasoning [31, 24], and sensitivity analysis [6, 18, 19, 5, 4].

Sensitivity analysis aims at determining how much the variation of input can influence the output of a system. The idea for putting the reliability estimation in the context of the sensitivity analysis framework is, therefore, in observing the changes in model outputs by modifying its inputs. Treating the predictive model as a black box, the sensitivity analysis approach, therefore, indirectly analyzes qualitatively describable aspects of the model, such as generalization ability, bias, resistance to noise, avoidance of overfitting, and so on. The motivation came from the related

---

[1] An extreme case of inherent bias can be found in a trivial constant classifier that blindly labels any example with a predetermined class with self-proclaimed confidence 1.

fields of data perturbation [9] and co-learning (using unlabeled examples in supervised learning) [3]. Transductive reliability estimation can be viewed as an intersection of these two fields, as it perturbs the training set with as single unlabelled example.

1.2.1 Transduction

Several methods for inducing probabilistic descriptions from training data, figuring the use of density estimation algorithms, are emerging as an alternative to more established approaches for machine learning. Frequently kernel density estimation [43] is used for density estimation of input data using diverse machine learning paradigm such as probabilistic neural networks [37], Bayesian networks and classifiers [17], decision trees [36]. By this approach a chosen paradigm, coupled with kernel density estimation, is used for modelling the probability distribution of input data. Alternatively, stochastically changing class labels in the training dataset is proposed [13] in order to estimate conditionally class probability.

There is some ongoing work for constructing classifiers that divide the data space into reliable and unreliable regions [1]. Such meta-learning approaches have also been used for picking the most reliable prediction from the outputs of an ensemble of classifiers [35].

Meta learning community is partially dealing with predicting the right machine learning algorithm for a particular problem [30] based on performance and characteristics of other, simpler learning algorithms. In our problem of confidence estimation such an approach would result in learning to predict confidence value based on characteristics of single examples.

A lot of work has been done in applications of the transduction methodology [33], in connection with algorithmic theory of randomness. Here, approximations of randomness deficiency for different methods (SVMs, ridge regression) have been constructed in order to estimate confidence of single predictions. The drawback of this approach is that confidence estimations need to be specifically designed for each particular method and cannot be applied to other methods.

Another approach to reliability estimation, similarly based on the transduction principle, has been proposed in [24]. While it is general and independent of the underlying classifier, interpretation of its results isn't always possible in the statistical sense of confidence levels.

A few years ago typicalness has emerged as a complementary approach to transduction [26, 31, 16]. By this approach, a "strangeness" measure of a single example is used to calculate its typicalness, and consequently a confidence in classifier's prediction. The main drawback of this approach is that for each machine learning algorithm it needs an appropriately constructed strangeness measure.

In the chapter we present a further development of the latter two approaches where transductive reliability estimation serves as a generic strangeness measure in the typicalness framework. We compare the experimental results to that of kernel density estimation and show that the proposed method significantly outperforms it. We also suggest how basic transduction principle can be used to significantly improve results of kernel density estimation so it almost reaches results of transductive typicalness.

The chapter is organized as follows. In Sec. 1.3 we describe the basic ideas of typicalness and transduction, outline the process of their integration, and review kernel density estimation methods used for comparison. In Sec. 1.4 we evaluate how our methodology compares to other approaches in 15 domains with 6 machine learning algorithms. In Sec. 1.5 we present some conclusions and directions for future work.

1.3 Methods and materials

Reliability estimation of a classification ($\tilde{y}$) of a single example (x), given its true class (y) should have the following property:

$$Rel(\tilde{y}\|x) = t \Rightarrow P(\tilde{y} \neq y) \leq 1 - t \tag{1.1}$$

If Eq. 1.1 holds, or even better, if it approaches equality, a reliability measure can be treated as a confidence value [26].

The produced confidence values should be valid in the following sense. Given some possible label space $\tilde{Y}$, if an algorithm predicts some set of labels $Y \subseteq \tilde{Y}$ with confidence t for a new example which is truly labelled by $y \in \tilde{Y}$, then we would expect the following to hold over randomization of the training set and the new example:

$$P(y \notin Y) \leq 1 - t \tag{1.2}$$

Note that Eq. 1.2 is very general and valid for both classification (Y is predicted set of classes) and regression problems (Y is a predicted interval). As we deal only with single predictions in this chapter, Eq. 1.2 can be simplified to a single predicted class value ($Y = \{\tilde{y}\}$):

$$P(y \neq \tilde{y}) \leq 1 - t \tag{1.3}$$

1.3.1 Typicalness

In the typicalness framework [26, 28, 33] we consider a sequence of examples $(z_1, \ldots, z_n) = ((x_1, y_1), \ldots, (x_n, y_n))$, together with a new example x_{n+1} with unknown label $\tilde{y}_{n+1}$, all drawn independently from the same distribution over $\mathcal{Z} = \mathcal{X} \times \mathcal{Y}$ where $\mathcal{X}$ is an attribute space and $\mathcal{Y}$ is a label space. Our only assumption is therefore that the training as well as new (unlabelled) examples are independently and identically distributed (*iid* assumption).

We can use the typicalness framework to gain confidence information for each possible labelling for a new example x_{n+1}. We postulate some labels $\tilde{y}_{n+1}$ and for each one we examine how likely (typical) it is that all elements of the extended sequence $((x_1, y_1), \ldots, (x_{n+1}, \tilde{y}_{n+1}))$ might have been drawn independently from the same distribution or how typically *iid* the sequence is. The more typical the sequence, the more confident we are in $\tilde{y}_{n+1}$. To measure the typicalness of sequences, we define, for every $n \in \mathbb{N}$, a typicalness function $t : \mathcal{Z}^n \to [0, 1]$ which, for any $r \in [0, 1]$ has the property

$$P((z_1, \ldots, z_n) : t(z_1, \ldots, z_n) \leq r) \leq r \tag{1.4}$$

If a typicalness function returns 0.05 for a given sequence, we know that the sequence is unusual because it will be produced at most 5% of the time by any *iid* process. It has been shown [26] that we can construct such functions by considering the "strangeness" of individual examples. If we have some family of functions

$$f : \mathcal{Z}^n \times \{1, 2, \ldots, n\} \to \mathbb{R}, \ n \in \mathbb{N} \ldots, \tag{1.5}$$

then we can associate a strangeness value

$$\alpha(z_i) = f(\{z_1, \ldots, z_n\}; i), i = 1, 2, \ldots n \tag{1.6}$$

with each example and define the following typicalness function

$$t((z_1, \ldots, z_n)) = \frac{\#\{\alpha(z_i) : \alpha(z_i) \geq \alpha(z_n)\}}{n} \tag{1.7}$$

We group individual strangeness functions α_i into a family of functions $A_n : n \in \mathbb{N}$, where $A_n : \mathcal{Z}^n \to \mathbb{R}^n$ for all n. This is called an individual strangeness measure if, for any n, any permutation $\pi : \{1, \ldots, n\} \to \{1, \ldots, n\}$, any sequence $(z_1, \ldots, z_n) \in \mathcal{Z}^n$, and any $(\alpha_{\pi(1)}, \ldots, \alpha_{\pi(n)}) \in \mathbb{R}^n)$ it satisfies the following criterion [26]:

$$(\alpha_1, \ldots, \alpha_n) = A_n(z_1, \ldots, z_n) \implies (\alpha_{\pi(1)}, \ldots, \alpha_{\pi(n)}) = A_n(z_{\pi(1)}, \ldots, z_{\pi(n)}) \tag{1.8}$$

The meaning of this criterion is that the same value should be produced for each individual element in sequence, regardless of the order in which their individual strangeness values are calculated. This is a very important criterion, because it can be proven [26] that the constructed typicalness function (1.7) satisfies the condition from (1.4), provided that the individual strangeness measure satisfies the criterion (1.8).

From a practical point of view it is advisable [26] to use positive strangeness measures, ranging between 0 for most typical examples, and some positive upper bound, (up to $+\infty$), for most untypical examples.

1.3.1.1 Typicalness in machine learning

In the machine learning setup, for calculating the typicalness of a new example $z_{n+1} = (x_{n+1}, \widetilde{y}_{n+1})$ described with attribute values x_{n+1} and labelled with $\widetilde{y}_{n+1}$, given the training set $(z_1, \ldots, z_n)$, Eq. 1.7 changes to

$$t((z_1, \ldots, z_{n+1})) = \frac{\#\{\alpha(z_i) : \alpha(z_i) \geq \alpha(z_{n+1})\}}{n+1} \qquad (1.9)$$

Note that on the right-hand side of Eq. 1.9, z_i belongs to the extended sequence, i.e. $z_i \in \{z_1, \ldots, z_{n+1}\}$. For a given machine learning algorithm, first we need to construct an appropriate strangeness measure and modify the algorithm accordingly.[2] Then, for each new unlabelled example x, all possible labels $\widetilde{y} \in Y$ are considered. For each label $\widetilde{y}$ a typicalness of labelled example $t((x, \widetilde{y})) = t((z_1, \ldots, z_n, (x, \widetilde{y})))$ is calculated. Finally, the example is labelled with "most typical" class, that is the one that maximizes $\{t((x, \widetilde{y}))\}$. By Eq. 1.7 the second largest typicalness is an upper bound on the probability that the excluded classifications are correct [31]. Consequently, the confidence is calculated as follows:

$$\text{confidence}((x, \widetilde{y})) = 1 - \text{typicalness of second most typical label.} \qquad (1.10)$$

1.3.2 Transductive reliability estimation

Transduction is an inference principle that takes a training sample and aims at estimating the values of a discrete or continuous function only at given unlabelled points of interest from input space, as opposed to the whole input space for induction. In the learning process the unlabelled points are suitably labelled and included into the training sample. The usefulness of unlabelled data has also been advocated in the context of co-training. It has been shown [3] that for every better-than-random classifier its performance can be significantly boosted by utilizing only additional unlabelled data.

It has been suggested [40] that when solving a given problem one should avoid solving a more general problem as an intermediate step. The reasoning behind this principle is that, in order to solve a more general task, resources may be wasted or compromises made which would not have been necessary for solving only the problem at hand (i.e. function estimation only on given points). This common-sense principle reduces a more general problem of inferring a functional dependency on the whole input space (inductive inference) to the problem of estimating the values of a function only at given points (transductive inference).

---

[2] This is the main problem of the typicalness approach, as the algorithms need do be considerably changed.

1.3.2.1 A formal background

Let $\mathcal{X}$ be a space of attribute descriptions of points (examples) in a training sample (dataset), and $\mathcal{Y}$ a space of labels (continuous or discrete) assigned to each point. Given a probability distribution $\mathcal{P}$, defined on the input space $\mathcal{X} \times \mathcal{Y}$, a training sample

$$S = \{(x_1, y_1), \ldots, (x_l, y_l)\} \qquad (1.11)$$

consisting of l points, is drawn *iid* (identically independently distributed) according to $\mathcal{P}$. Additional m data points (working sample)

$$W = \{x_{l+1}, \ldots, x_{l+m}\} \qquad (1.12)$$

with unknown labels are drawn in the same manner. The goal of transductive inference is to label all the points from the sample W using a fixed set $\mathcal{H}$ of functions $f : \mathcal{X} \mapsto \mathcal{Y}$ in order to minimize an error functional both in the training sample S and in the working sample W (effectively, in $S \cup W$). In contrast, inductive inference aims at choosing a single function $f \in \mathcal{H}$ that is best suited to the unknown probability distribution $\mathcal{P}$.

At this point there arises a question how to calculate labels of points from a working sample. This can be done by labelling every point from a working sample with every possible label value; however given m working points this leads to a combinatorial explosion yielding n^m possible labellings. For each possible labelling, an induction process on $S \cup W$ is run, and an error functional (error rate) is calculated.

By leveraging the *iid* sampling assumption and transductive inference, one can for each labelling estimate its reliability (also referred to as confidence, a probability that it is correct). If the *iid* assumption holds, the training sample S as well as the joint correctly labelled sample $S \cup W$ should both reflect the same underlying probability distribution $\mathcal{P}$.

If one could measure a degree of similarity between probability distributions $\mathcal{P}(S)$ and $\mathcal{P}(S \cup W)$, this could be used as a measure of reliability of the particular labelling. Unfortunately, this problem in general belongs to the non-computable class [25], so approximation methods have to be used [42, 22].

Evaluation of prediction reliability for single points in data space has many uses. In risk-sensitive applications (medical diagnosis, financial and critical control applications) it often matters, how much one can rely upon a given prediction. In such a case a general reliability measure of a classifier (e.g. classification accuracy, mean, squared error, ...) with respect to the whole input distribution would not provide the desired warranty. Another use of reliability estimations is in combining answers from different predictors, weighed according to their reliability.

1.3.2.2 Why is transduction supposed to work?

There is a strong connection between the transduction principle and the algorithmic (Kolmogorov) complexity. Let the sets S and $S \cup W$ be represented as binary strings

u and v, respectively. Let $l(v)$ be the length of the string v and $C(v)$ its Kolmogorov complexity, both measured in bits. We define the *randomness deficiency* of the string v as following [25, 42]:

$$\delta(v) = l(v) - C(v) \tag{1.13}$$

Randomness deficiency measures how random is the respective binary string and therefore the set it represents. The larger it is, more regular is the string (and the set). If we could calculate the randomness deficiency (but we cannot, since it is not computable), we could do it for all possible labellings of the set $S \cup W$ and select the labelling of W with largest randomness deficiency as the most probable one [42]. That is, we would select the most regular one. We can also construct a universal Martin-Löf's test for randomness [25]:

$$\sum \{P(x|l(x) = n) : \delta(x) \geq m\} \leq 2^{-m} \tag{1.14}$$

That is, for all binary strings of fixed length n, the probability of their randomness deficiency δ being greater than m is less than 2^{-m}. The value $2^{-\delta(x)}$ is therefore a p-value function for our randomness test [42].

Unfortunately, as the definition of randomness deficiency is based on the Kolmogorov complexity, it is not computable. Therefore we need feasible approximations to use this principle in practice. Extensive work has been done by using Support Vector Machines [10, 33, 42], however no general approach exists so far.

1.3.2.3 A machine learning interpretation

In machine learning terms, the sets S and $S \cup W$ are represented by the induced models M_S and $M_{S \cup W}$. The randomness of the sets reflects in the (Kolmogorov) complexity of the respective models. If for the set $S \cup W$ the labelling of W with largest randomness deficiency is selected, it follows from our definition of randomness deficiency (Eq. 1.13) that since the length $l(v)$ is constant, the Kolmogorov complexity $C(M_{S \cup W})$ is minimal. Therefore the model $M_{S \cup W}$ is most similar to the M_S.

This greatly simplifies our view on the problem, namely it suffices to compare the (finite) models M_S and $M_{S \cup W}$. Greater difference between them means that the set $S \cup W$ is more random than the set S and (under the assumption that S is sufficient for learning effective model) that W consist of (at least some) improperly labelled, untypical examples.

Although the problem seems easier now, it is still a computational burden to calculate changes between model descriptions (assuming that they can be efficiently coded; black-box methods are thus out of question). However, there exists another way.

Since transduction is an inference principle that aims at estimating the values of a function only at given points of interest from input space (the set W), we are interested only in model change considering this examples. Therefore we can compare the classifications (or even better, probability distributions) of models M_S and models $M_{S \cup W}$. Obviously, the labelling of W that would minimally change the model M_S is as given by M_S. We will examine this approach in more detail in the next section.

The transductive reliability estimation process and its theoretical foundations originating from Kolmogorov complexity are described in more detail in [24]. Basically, we have a two-step process, featuring an *inductive step* followed by a *transductive step*.

- An *inductive step* is just like an ordinary inductive learning process in machine learning. A machine learning algorithm is run on the training set, *inducing* a classifier. A selected example is taken from an independent dataset and classified using the induced classifier. An example, labelled with the classified class is temporarily included into the training set.
- A *transductive step* is almost a repetition of an inductive step. A machine learning algorithm is run on the changed training set, *transducing* a classifier. The same example as before is taken from the independent dataset and and classified using the transduced classifier. Both classifications of the same example are compared and their difference (distance) is calculated, thus approximating the randomness deficiency.
- After the reliability is calculated, the example in question is removed from the training set.

In practice the inductive step is performed only once, namely on the original training set. New examples are not permanently included in the training set; this would be improper since the correct class is at this point still unknown. Although retraining for each new example seems to be highly time consuming, it is not such a problem in practice, especially if incremental learners (such as naive Bayesian classifier) are used.

A brief algorithmic sketch is given in Fig. 1.1. An intuitive explanation of transductive reliability estimation is that we disturb a classifier by inserting a new example in a training set. A magnitude of this disturbance is an estimation of classifier's instability (unreliability) in a given region of its problem space.

Since a prerequisite for a machine learning algorithm is to represent its classifications as a probability distribution over all possible classes, we need a method to measure the difference between two probability distributions. The difference measure D should ideally satisfy all requirements for a distance (i.e. nonnegativity, triangle nonequality and symmetry), however in practice nonnegativity suffices. For calculating the difference between probability distributions, a *Kullback-Leibler divergence* is frequently used [12, 38]. Kullback-Leibler divergence, sometimes referred to as a relative entropy or I-divergence, is defined between probability distributions P and Q

$$I(P,Q) = -\sum_{i=1}^{n} p_i \log_2 \frac{p_i}{q_i} \tag{1.16}$$

In our experiments we use a symmetric Kullback-Leibler divergence, or J-divergence, which is defined as follows:

$$J(P,Q) = (I(P,Q) + I(Q,P)) = \sum_{i=1}^{n} (p_i - q_i) \log_2 \frac{p_i}{q_i} \qquad (1.17)$$

$J(P,Q)$ is limited to the interval $[0,\infty]$, where $J(P,P) = 0$. Since in this context we require the values to be from the $[0,1]$ interval we normalize it in the spirit of Martin-Löf's test for randomness.

$$J_N(P,Q) = 1 - 2^{-J(P,Q)} \qquad (1.18)$$

However, measuring the difference between probability distributions does not always perform well. There are at least a few exceptional classifiers (albeit trivial ones) where the original approach utterly fails.

1.3.2.4 Assessing the classifier's quality: the curse of trivial models

So far we have implicitly assumed that the model used by the classifier is good (at the very least better than random). Unsurprisingly, our approach works very well with random classifiers (probability distributions are randomly calculated) by effectively labelling their classifications as unreliable [22, 23].

$Input$: $machine learning classifier, a training set and an unlabelled test$
            $example$ (1.15)
$Output$: $Estimation of test example's classification reliability$

Inductive step:

- train a classifier from the provided training set
- select an unlabelled test example
- classify this example with an induced classifier
- label this example with a predicted class
- temporarily add the newly labelled example to the training set

Transductive step:

- train a classifier from the extended training set
- select the same unlabelled test example as above
- classify this example with a transduced classifier

Calculate a randomness deficiency approximation as a *normalized difference* $J_N(P,Q)$ between inductive (P) and transductive (Q) classification.

Calculate the reliability of classification as in a universal Martin-Löf's test for randomness 1-*normalized difference*

–

Fig. 1.1: The algorithm for transductive reliability estimation

On the other hand, there also exist simple *constant* and *majority* classifiers. A *constant classifier* is such that it classifies all examples into the same class C_k with probability 1. In such cases our approach always yields reliability 1 since there is no change in probability distribution. A *majority classifier* is such that it classifies all examples into the same class C_k that is the majority class in the training set. Probability distribution is always the same and corresponds to the distribution of classes in the training set. In such cases our approach yields reliability very close to 1 since there is almost no change in probability distribution (only for the example in question), that is at most for $1/N$, where N is number of training examples. In large datasets this change is negligible.

Note that such extreme cases do occur in practice and even in real life. For example, a physician that always diagnoses an incoming patient as ill is a constant classifier. On the other hand, a degenerated – overpruned – decision tree (one leaf only) is a typical majority classifier.

In both cases all classifications are seemingly completely reliable. Obviously we also need to take in account the quality of classifier's underlying model and appropriately change our definition of reliability.

Obviously we assume that the learnt (induced) data model is good. Our reliability estimations actually estimate the conditional reliability with respect to the model M

$$\text{Rel}(y_i|M) = P(y_i \text{ is a true class of } x_i \mid \text{model M is good}) \quad (1.19)$$

To calculate required unconditional reliability we apply the conditional probability theorem for the whole model

$$\text{Rel}'(y_i) = P(\text{model M is good}) * P(y_i \text{ is true class of } x_i \mid \text{model M is good}) \quad (1.20)$$

or even better for the partial models for each class y_i

$$\text{Rel}'(y_i) = P(\text{model M is good for } y_i) * P(y_i \text{ is true class of } x_i \mid \text{model M is good for } y_i) \quad (1.21)$$

Now we only need to estimate the unconditional probabilities

$$P(\text{model is good}) \quad \text{or} \quad \forall i : P(\text{model is good for } y_i) \quad (1.22)$$

In machine learning we have many methods to estimate the quality of the induced model, e.g. a cross-validation computation of classification accuracy is suitable for estimation of Eq. 1.22. However it may be better to calculate it in a less coarse way, since at this point we already know the predicted class value (y_i).

We propose a (Bayesian) calculation of probability that the classification in a certain class is correct. Our approach is closely related to the calculation of post-test probabilities in medical diagnostics [8, 29]. Required factors can be easily estimated from the confusion matrix (Def. 1.1) with internal testing.

Definition 1.1. A *confusion matrix (CM)* is a matrix of classification errors obtained with an internal cross validation or leave-one-out testing on the training dataset. The ij-th element c_{ij} stands for the number of classifications to the class i that should belong to the class j.

$$CM = \begin{pmatrix} c_{11} & c_{12} & c_{13} & \cdots & c_{1N} \\ c_{21} & c_{22} & c_{23} & \cdots & c_{2N} \\ c_{31} & c_{32} & c_{33} & \cdots & c_{3N} \\ \vdots & \vdots & \vdots & \ddots & \vdots \\ c_{N1} & c_{N2} & c_{N3} & \cdots & c_{NN} \end{pmatrix}$$

$$c_{ij} = \text{number of classifications to class i that belong to class j} \qquad (1.23)$$

Definition 1.2. Class sensitivity and specificity are a generalization of sensitivity (true positives ratio) and specificity (true negatives ratio) values for multi-class problems. Basically, for N classes we have N two-class problems. Let C_p be a correct class in certain case, and C a class, predicted by the classifier in the same case. For each of possible classes C_i, $i \in \{1..N\}$, we define its *class sensitivity* $Se(C_i) = P(C = C_i | C_p = C_i)$ and its *class specificity* $Sp(C_i) = P(C \neq C_i | C_p \neq C_i)$ as follows:

$$Se(C_i) = P(C = C_i | C_p = C_i) = \frac{c_{ii}}{\sum_j c_{ij}} \qquad (1.24)$$

$$Sp(C_i) = P(C \neq C_i | C_p \neq C_i) = \frac{\sum_{j \neq i} c_{ji}}{\sum_{j \neq i} \sum_k c_{jk}} \qquad (1.25)$$

Class conditional probability is calculated for each class C_i, given its prior probability $P(C_i)$, approximated with the prevalence of C_i in the training set, its class specificity (Sp) and sensitivity (Se):

$$P_{\text{cond}}(C_i) = \frac{P(C_i)Se(C_i)}{P(C_i)Se(C_i) + (1 - P(C_i))(1 - Sp(C_i))} \qquad (1.26)$$

To calculate the reliability estimation we therefore need the probability distributions P and Q, and index $i = \text{argmax } P$ that determines the class with max. probability (C_i). According to the Eq. 1.21 we calculate the reliability estimations by

$$Rel(P, Q; C_i) = P_{\text{cond}}(C_i) \times J_N(P, Q) \qquad (1.27)$$

Multiplication by class conditional probabilities accounts for basic domain characteristics (prevalence of classes) as well as classifier's performance. This includes class sensitivity and specificity, and it is especially useful in an automatic setting for detecting possible anomalies such as default (either majority or constant classifiers) that – of course – cannot be trusted. It is easy to see that in this case we have one class with sensitivity 1 and specificity 0, whereas for all other classes we have sensitivity 0 and nonzero specificity. In the first case, the class post-test probability is equal to its prior probability, whereas in the second case it is 0.

1.3.3 Merging the typicalness and transduction frameworks

There is a very good reason for merging typicalness and transductive reliability estimation frameworks together. While transduction gives good reliability estimations, they are often hard to interpret in the statistical sense. On the other hand, the typicalness framework gives clear confidence values, however in order to achieve this a good strangeness measure $\alpha(z_i)$ needs to be constructed.

Of course, there is a trivial solution to it, namely a uniform strangeness measure $\alpha_i = C$, where C is some constant value. Unfortunately, this does us no good, since it treats all examples as equally strange and can be considered as most conservative strangeness measure. It is therefore necessary to construct a sensible strangeness measure. In [26, 34, 31] some ideas on how to construct strangeness measures for different machine learning algorithms are presented.

On the other hand, as we shall see later, for a strangeness measure we can always use transductive reliability estimation. We may speculate that most reliable examples are also least strange. Therefore we define the strangeness measure for a new example $z_{n+1} = (x_{n+1}, \widetilde{y}_{n+1})$, described with attribute values x_{n+1} and labelled with $\widetilde{y}_{n+1}$, given the training set $(z_1, \ldots, z_n)$ as follows:

$$\alpha(z_{n+1}) = f(z_1, \ldots, z_{n+1}; n+1) = 1 - \text{Rel}(z_{n+1}) \in [0,1] \qquad (1.28)$$

It can be shown that such a strangeness function satisfies the criterion from Eq. 1.8 and therefore has the property required by Eq. 1.7.

Theorem 1.1. *The strangeness measure* $\alpha(z_i) = 1 - \text{Rel}((x_i, \widetilde{y}_i))$ *is independent of the order in which the examples' strangeness values are calculated.*

Proof. The training set is only temporarily changed by including a suitably labelled new example in a transductive step (Fig. 1.1. It is restored back to the initial training set as soon as the reliability estimation is calculated. Therefore the training set remains invariant for all new examples for which the reliability estimation needs to be calculated. It follows that it is irrelevant in which order the examples are presented and the criterion for Eq. 1.8 is therefore satisfied. Note that Eq. 1.8 does not require that examples are ordered in any particular way, but only that any permutation of the order of their evaluations produces the same result for each example.

Consequently we can, for any machine learning classifier, universally use a strangeness measure $\alpha((x, \widetilde{y})) = 1 - Rel((x, \widetilde{y}))$ (although, as we shall see later, in the typicalness setting this expression can be even more simplified). It is positive, and the "more strange" examples have higher strangeness values, as suggested in [26].

1.3.3.1 Simplification of transductive reliability estimation for application within the typicalness framework

Alternatively, the calculation of the strangeness measure can, in the context of typicalness and reliability estimation, be much simplified. Simplifications are twofold.

1. Since the only requirement for strangeness measure is that is is positive, no transformations to $[0,1]$ interval are necessary. The transformation is actually performed by Eq. 1.9.
2. Since typicalness framework efficiently deals with extremely deviant classifiers (such as those from Sec. 1.3.2.4). As an example, let us consider the most "pathological" case, the constant classifier. Therefore all strangeness values are equal (i.e. all examples are equally – maximally – strange). Note that in this case magnitudes of strangeness values are irrelevant as they are all the same. By Eq. 1.9 it follows that for all possible classifications of every (new) example the typicalness is therefore 1.0. By Eq. 1.10 this yields confidence of 0. Such trivial classifiers are therefore maximally distrusted.

Let between $P_{(x,\widetilde{y})}$ and $Q_{(x,\widetilde{y})}$ be the probability distributions obtained after the inductive step ($P_{(x,\widetilde{y})}$) and transductive step ($Q_{(x,\widetilde{y})}$) of the algorithm from Fig. 1.1. It can easily be shown that Theorem 1.1 holds also for $\alpha((x,\widetilde{y})) = J(P_{(x,\widetilde{y})}, Q_{(x,\widetilde{y})})$ (symmetric Kullback-Leibler divergence) as well as for $\alpha((x,\widetilde{y})) = I(P_{(x,\widetilde{y})}, Q_{(x,\widetilde{y})})$ (asymmetric Kullback-Leibler divergence).

An implementation of transductive reliability estimation in typicalness framework is straightforward. For all training examples, reliability estimation is calculated by leave-one-out testing, and they are labelled as correctly or incorrectly classified. For each new example x with classification $\widetilde{y}$ its confidence $\text{conf}((x,\widetilde{y}))$ is calculated as in Sec. 1.3.1, Eq. 1.10. Regardless of the number of classes in original problem, there are only two possibilities (meta-classes) for each classification. It is either correct or incorrect. Therefore only that we always deal with exactly two meta-classes that represent correct classifications and incorrect classifications. As we want the confidence to reflect the probability of a correct classification, we need to invert the confidence values for incorrect meta-class:

$$\text{confidence}((x,\widetilde{y})) = \begin{cases} \text{conf}((x,\widetilde{y})) & \text{"correct" meta-class,} \\ 1 - \text{conf}((x,\widetilde{y})) & \text{"incorrect" meta-class.} \end{cases} \tag{1.29}$$

1.3.4 Meta learning and kernel density estimation

The problem of estimating a confidence value can also be viewed as a meta learning problem where the original class value is replaced by correctness of its prediction. Let $\widehat{y}$ be a meta-class for training examples obtained with internal leave-one-out testing (i.e. $\widehat{y} = 1$ for correct and $\widehat{y} = 0$ for incorrect classifications). We can calculate the confidence in a given prediction of a new, previously unseen example x by estimating the function $\widehat{y}(x)$ with a nearest neighbour classifier:

$$\widehat{y}(x) = \frac{1}{K} \sum_{x_i \in N_K(x)} \widehat{y}_i(x_i) \tag{1.30}$$

Here $N_K(x)$ is the set of K points nearest to x according to some distance measure. However, such simple estimations may be problematic when the attribute space is large (lots of multi-valued, possibly correlated, attributes), and sparsely populated (relatively small number of training examples). Our experimental results (Tab. 1.2) also shows this problem, as using a nearest neighbour meta-learner results in lowest performance of all methods[3]. Therefore, a transformation of input space is necessary to reduce the dimensionality of input space. We have chosen the principal component analysis (PCA) methodology on the training data, and two components with largest variances were selected as data descriptors. On average, the sum of the two components' relative variances is about 0.7. This means, that the two principal components describe about 70% of data variability.

Rather than giving the nearest neighbours equal weights, we can assign them weights that decrease smoothly with distance from the target point. This leads us to kernel density estimation [41] in reduced and uncorrelated data space. It can be estimated by using the Nadaraya-Watson kernel weighted average:

$$\widehat{y}(x) = \frac{\sum_{i=i}^{N} K_\lambda(x, x_i) \widehat{y}_i(x_i)}{\sum_{i=i}^{N} K_\lambda(x, x_i)} \tag{1.31}$$

where $\lambda = [\lambda_1, \lambda_2]$ is a vector of kernel parameters (bandwidths), and $K_\lambda(x, x_i)$ is a simplified (uncorrelated) bivariate gaussian kernel:

$$K_{\lambda_1, \lambda_2}(x, x_i) = \frac{1}{2\pi \lambda_1 \lambda_2} e^{-\frac{1}{2}\left(\frac{(x[1] - x_i[1])^2}{\lambda_1^2} + \frac{(x[2] - x_i[2])^2}{\lambda_1^2}\right)} \tag{1.32}$$

As the principal component analysis involves a numerical procedure that transforms a number of possibly correlated input variables (attributes) into a (smaller) number of uncorrelated variables (principal components), it is therefore perfectly justified to use a simplified bivariate gaussian kernel for density estimation on uncorrelated variables. Our experiments have shown, that indeed in all cases the correlation between the largest two principal components was less than 10^{-14}, also negligible. For the bivariate gaussian kernels, appropriate bandwidths were calculated from training data according to the rule of thumb as described by Wand [43, p. 98].

For each dataset and algorithm the following procedure was performed. For each training example, a correctness of its classification was determined by the leave-one-out testing methodology. Training examples were partitioned in sets of correctly and

---

[3] To be fair, one must say that other more advanced meta-learners could have been used. However, this was not the aim of the chapter.

incorrectly classified examples, and used for kernel density estimations of correct and incorrect classifications. For each new examples, principal components were calculated and used to calculate the density of correct classifications (cd) as well as the density of incorrect classifications (id) at respective coordinates. The confidence value of a new example was calculated as $cd/(cd+id)$ [14].

1.3.5 Improving kernel density estimation by transduction principle

The procedure described in Sec. 1.3.4 is computationally fast when applying to new examples as it involves only calculating the principal components (scaling and one matrix multiplication), and two fast uncorrelated density estimations. Unfortunately, its performance (Tab. 1.2) compared to transductive confidence estimation is rather uninspiring. The performance, however, can be easily improved by using some ideas from meta learning and transduction frameworks. Namely, we can easily extend the original data description by including the predicted class as well as class probability distributions. They may be obtained with internal leave-one-out testing on the training set.

On extended data the principal components are calculated. A new example's class and class distribution is predicted by the original classifier, and the example's description is enhanced by the classifier's prediction. An enhanced example description is then used in density estimation procedure as described in Sec. 1.3.4.

1.3.6 Testing methodology

To validate the proposed methodology we performed extensive experiments with 6 different machine learning algorithms – naive and semi naive Bayesian classifier [21], backpropagation neural network [32], K-nearest neighbour, locally naive Bayesian classifier (a combination KNN of and naive Bayesian classifier) [24], two kinds of Assistant (ID3-like decision trees) [20] on 14 well-known benchmark datasets from the UCI repository (Mesh, Breast cancer, Diabetes, Heart, Hepatitis, Iris, Chess endgame (king-rook vs. king), LED, Lymphography, Primary tumor, Rheumatology, Soybean, Voting), and on a real-life problem of nuclear cardiology diagnostics (Nuclear).

For each dataset and algorithm we determined for each training example by internal leave-one-out testing its correctness – whether it was correctly (1) or incorrectly (0) classified. For reliability estimations, confidence values and density estimations, we calculated their correlation with correctness. In an ideal case (each correct example has value 1, each incorrect 0), the result would be 1.

We also measured how well a method discriminates between correctly and incorrectly classified examples. For each method (reliability estimations, confidence values, and density estimations) we calculated the boundary b that maximizes the purity (information gain) of the discriminated examples. The boundary b is calculated by maximizing Eq. 1.33.

$$H(S) = -\frac{|S_1|}{|S|} \log_2 \frac{|S_1|}{|S|} - \frac{|S_2|}{|S|} \log_2 \frac{|S_2|}{|S|} \qquad \text{(entropy before split)}$$

$$H(S;b) = \frac{|S_1|}{|S|} H(S_1) + \frac{|S_2|}{|S|} H(S_2) \qquad \text{(entropy after split)}$$

$$\text{Gain}(S,b) = H(S) - H(S;b) \qquad (1.33)$$

Here, S is the set consisting of all examples, in the set S_1 there are unreliable examples $\{z_i : \text{Rel}(z_i) < b\}$ whereas in the set S_2 there are reliable examples $\{z_i : \text{Rel}(z_i) \geq b\}$. In an ideal case when both splits are pure, the result would be equal to the entropy of classifications $H(S)$.

All experiments were performed by leave-one-out testing. In this setup, one example was reserved, while learning and preparatory calculations were performed on the rest, in many cases two nested leave-one-out testings were carried out. Final results are averages of leave-one-out experiments on all examples from the dataset.

Finally, we also applied our approach to a real-world application on a large database of 600.000 customers of a large local corporation. Here, due to large quantities of data testing methodology was slightly different. While leave-one out testing was still used for obtaining strangeness values for the training set (50%) of data, the remaining data was used as an independet testing set.

Table 1.1: Comparison of confidence estimation on KNN with the algorithm-specific TCM-NN, both with 10 nearest neighbours. Accurracy was obtained with standard 10-NN algorithm.

	Accuracy	Correlation with correctness		Information gain (in bit)	
		KNN	TCM-NN	KNN	TCM-NN	KNN
Mesh	64.7%	0.49	0.40	0.26	0.19
Brest cancer	80.2%	0.09	0.14	0.02	0.03
Nuclear	81.0%	0.35	0.28	0.12	0.07
Diabetes	73.7%	0.26	0.19	0.06	0.05
Heart	79.3%	0.34	0.18	0.11	0.09
Hepatitis	85.2%	0.28	0.25	0.07	0.07
Iris	94.7%	0.23	0.36	0.12	0.12
Chess end.	92.0%	0.43	0.33	0.21	0.12
LED	73.2%	0.20	0.19	0.04	0.05
Lymphography	83.1%	0.50	0.22	0.32	0.18
Primary tumor	41.3%	0.10	0.37	0.00	0.19
Rheumatology	61.3%	0.42	0.42	0.17	0.16
Soybean	92.1%	0.32	0.38	0.12	0.12
Voting	94.0%	0.42	0.26	0.18	0.09
Average	78.3%	0.32	0.28	0.13	0.11

1.4 Results

Experimental results were obtained with two different setups. The first one consists of series of experiments on well-known (UCI) problem domains. These results were used to validate our approach and compare it with existing ones. The second experimental setup consists of applications in a real-life commercial data mining system. It also presents some valuable practical considerations.

1.4.1 Experiments on benchmark problems

Results of confidence estimation on KNN (nearest neighbour) algorithm are compared with the TCM-NN nearest neighbour confidence machine [31], where a tailor-made strangeness measure for confidence estimation in typicalness framework was constructed. In Tab. 1.1 experimental results in 15 domains are shown. Results of TCM-NN are slightly better, as could be expected from the tailor-made method, though the differences are not significant with two-tailed, paired t-test).

1.4.1.1 Reliability, confidence and density estimation

The obtained confidence values are compared with transductive reliability estimations and density estimations. Our first goal was to evaluate the performance of confidence values in terms of correlation with correctness, and its ability to separate correct and incorrect classifications in terms of information gain. Our second goal was to see whether confidence values are more easily interpretable than transductive reliability estimations.

Figures 1.3(a) and 1.3(b) depict how reliability estimations in are transformed to confidence levels. This is a typical example and probably the most important result of our work, as it makes them easily statistically interpretable. On average, the best decision boundary for reliability estimations is 0.74, on the other hand, for confidence it is about 0.45. Also, the mass of correct and incorrect classification has shifted towards 1 and 0, respectively.

In Tab. 1.2 experimental results are presented. We see that confidence values significantly ($p < 0.05$ with two-tailed, paired t-test) outperform reliability estimations in terms of correlation with correctness. From Fig. 1.3 it is clear that this is because of the shift towards 1 and 0. Information gains do not differ significantly.

Comparing confidence values and density estimations shows a slightly different picture. Here, in terms of correlation with correctness as well as for for information gain criterion, the differences are significant ($p < 0.01$ with two-tailed, paired t-test). Fig. 1.2 depicts typical density estimations for both correct and incorrect classifications. On average, the best decision boundary for density estimations is 0.52.

In Tab. 1.2 we can also see that meta-learning with 10 nearest neighbours (10-NN) performed worst (although 10 was a tuned parameter). This was expected, since it was used in the whole – sparsely populated – attribute space. Density estimations (Den.) performed on a reduced attribute space significantly better ($p < 0.01$ with two-tailed, paired t-test). We can also see that transductive attributes improve the performance of density estimation (Tr. den.) quite significantly ($p < 0.05$ with two-tailed, paired t-test). While it does not reach performance of transductive reliability or confidence estimations, it is much easier to compute as it does not require re-learning of a classifier.

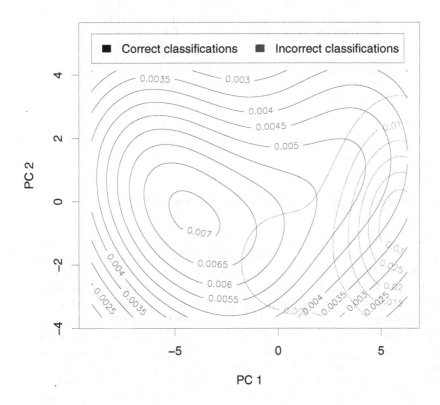

Fig. 1.2: Densities of correct and incorrect classification in Soybean dataset using neural networks.

Table 1.2: Experimental results with confidence values, reliability and density estimations with 6 machine learning algorithm in 15 datasets. Accuracy was calculated as an average of all 6 base classifiers.

Domain	Accu-racy	Correlation with correctness			Information gain (in bit)		
		Relia-bility	Confi-dence	Den-sity	Relia-bility	Confi-dence	Den-sity
Mesh	65.7%	0.51	0.46	0.10	0.25	0.25	0.12
Brest cancer	77.4%	0.28	0.22	0.09	0.10	0.10	0.07
Nuclear	88.0%	0.21	0.21	0.09	0.07	0.08	0.07
Diabetes	74.3%	0.26	0.33	0.08	0.18	0.18	0.05
Heart	80.7%	0.26	0.27	0.08	0.11	0.11	0.11
Hepatitis	86.6%	0.25	0.30	0.12	0.12	0.11	0.14
Iris	93.8%	0.23	0.42	0.08	0.13	0.13	0.09
Chess endgame	95.5%	0.09	0.27	0.08	0.11	0.11	0.05
Chess endgame	71.1%	0.11	0.12	0.07	0.10	0.10	0.05
LED	73.0%	0.16	0.18	0.04	0.05	0.05	0.03
Lymphography	81.9%	0.20	0.27	0.13	0.13	0.13	0.17
Primary tumor	44.8%	0.39	0.38	0.07	0.16	0.16	0.07
Rheumatology	58.0%	0.47	0.48	0.10	0.22	0.22	0.10
Soybean	89.4%	0.35	0.37	0.08	0.14	0.13	0.09
Voting	94.0%	0.17	0.22	0.09	0.08	0.08	0.07
Average	78.3%	0.26	0.30	0.09	0.13	0.13	0.08

1.4.2 Real-life application and practical considerations

We also did a practical application of integration of decision support system with data mining methods working with data from extensive customer relationship management (CRM) survey for a large local corporation. It turned out that immense quantities of raw data had been collected and needed to be assessed. Thus the use of data mining methods was called for. The system was implemented in Oracle application framework using Oracle's Data Mining (ODM) database extension. An Adaptive Bayesian Network classifier was used. The database consisted of about 600.000 customers' records consisting of up to 100 attributes. The preparatory calculations (leave-one-out testing on training dataset) were quite lengthy as they took more than a week. However, producing a confidence estimation for a single customer was much more acceptable; depending on system use it took about a minute.

Produced confidence values were much better (on average by 0.2 bit of gained information) than the probability estimations of the applied Adaptive Bayesian Network classifier. There was also improvement of more than 10% of confident classification (confidence $\geq$ 95%). In practice this could (and in near future probably will) save significant amounts of CRM campaign money.

The main drawback of our approach in this practical problem is its relative slowness. It needs more than a week to perform preparatory calculations and it took again more than a week to calculate confidence values for all testing examples (customer records from independent set). It may therefore not be suitable for quick on-line analysis of an overall situation, but is perfectly suited for assessment of individual customers. A great advantage of typicalness/transduction approach over other approaches (such as kernel density estimation) is that it can be easily implemented even with relatively closed (no source code available for modifications) commercial data mining systems.

1.5 Discussion

We propose an approach that compensates the weaknesses of typicalness-based confidence estimation and transductive reliability estimation by integrating them into a joint confidence machine.

The resulting values are true confidence levels, and this makes them much easier to interpret. Contrary to the basic typicalness and transductive confidence estimation, the described approach is not bound to the particular underlying classifier. This is an important improvement since this makes possible to calculate confidence values for almost any classifier, no matter how complex it is.

Experimental comparison on comparable unmodified and modified algorithms (confidence estimation on k-nearest neighbour algorithm and TCM-NN nearest neighbour confidence machine) show that the proposed approach performs similarly to the specially modified algorithm. There is no significant reduction in performance while there is a huge gain in generality.

Comparisons with kernel density estimation show that the computed confidence values significantly outperform density estimations. However, this does not mean that density estimations should not be used as they are much easier to compute and do not require re-learning of a classifier. Their performance can also be significantly improved by using additional transductive attributes.

Experimental results performed with different machine learning algorithms in several problem domains show that there is no reduction of discrimination performance with respect to transductive reliability estimation. More important than this, statistical interpretability of confidence values makes possible for applications in risk-sensitive problems with strict confidence limits.

The main drawback of our approach is computational complexity, as it needs to perform the leave-one-out testing in advance, and requires temporary re-learning of a classifier for each new example. However, this may not be a problem if incremental learners (such as naive Bayesian classifier) are used. In other cases, density estimation with included transductive attributes may also be used.

In the near future we are planning several experiments in risk-sensitive problems in business problems as well as in medical diagnostics and prognostics.

Acknowledgement

This work was supported by the Slovenian Ministry of Higher Education.

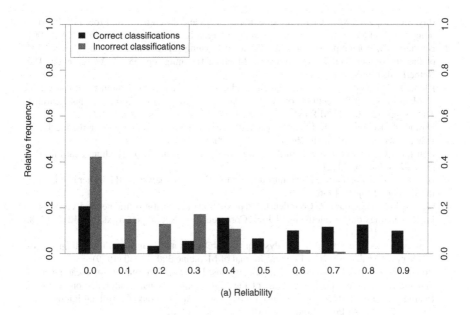

(a) Reliability

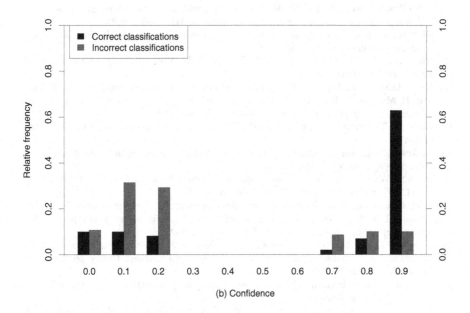

(b) Confidence

Fig. 1.3: Relative frequencies of reliability estimations and confidence levels in Soybean dataset using neural networks.

References

1. Bay, S.D., Pazzani, M.J.: Characterizing model errors and differences. In: Proc. 17th International Conf. on Machine Learning, pp. 49–56. Morgan Kaufmann, San Francisco, CA (2000)
2. Birattari, M., Bontempi, H., Bersini, H.: Local learning for data analysis. In: Proceedings of the 8th Belgian-Dutch Conference on Machine Learning, pp. 55–61. Wageningen, The Netherlands (1998)
3. Blum, A., Mitchell, T.: Combining labeled and unlabeled data with co-training. In: P. Bartlett, Y. Mansour (eds.) Proceedings of the 11th Annual Conference on Computational Learning Theory, pp. 92–100. ACM Press, New York, USA, Madison, Wisconsin (1998)
4. Bosnić, Z., Kononenko, I.: Estimation of individual prediction reliability using the local sensitivity analysis. Appl. intell. **29(3)**, 187–203 (2008)
5. Bousquet, O., Elisseeff, A.: Stability and generalization. Journal of Machine Learning Research **2**, 499–526 (2002)
6. Breierova, L., Choudhari, M.: An introduction to sensitivity analysis. MIT System Dynamics in Education Project (1996)
7. Carney, J., Cunningham, P.: Confidence and prediction intervals for neural network ensembles. In: Proceedings of the International Joint Conference on Neural Networks, pp. 1215–1218. Washington, USA (1999)
8. Diamond, G.A., Forester, J.S.: Analysis of probability as an aid in the clinical diagnosis of coronary artery disease. New England Journal of Medicine **300**, 13–50 (1979)
9. Elidan, G., Ninio, M., Friedman, N., Schuurmans, D.: Data perturbation for escaping local maxima in learning. In: Proceedings of the Eighteenth National Conference on Artificial Intelligence and Fourteenth Conference on Innovative Applications of Artificial Intelligence, pp. 132–139. AAAI Press, Edmonton, Alberta, Canada (2002)
10. Gammerman, A., Vovk, V., Vapnik, V.: Learning by transduction. In: G.F. Cooper, S. Moral (eds.) Proceedings of the 14th Conference on Uncertainty in Artificial Intelligence, pp. 148–155. Morgan Kaufmann, San Francisco, USA, Madison, Wisconsin (1998)
11. Giacinto, G., Roli, F.: Dynamic classifier selection based on multiple classifier behaviour. Pattern Recognition **34**, 1879–1881 (2001)
12. Gibbs, A.L., Su, F.E.: On choosing and bounding probability metrics. International Statistical Review **70(3)**, 419–435 (2002)
13. Halck, O.M.: Using hard classifiers to estimate conditional class probabilities. In: T. Elomaa, H. Mannila, H. Toivonen (eds.) Proceedings of the Thirteenth European Conference on Machine Learning, pp. 124–134. Springer-Verlag, Berlin (2002)
14. Hastie, T., Tibisharani, R., Friedman, J.: The Elements of Statistical Learning. Springer-Verlag (2001)
15. Heskes, T.: Practical confidence and prediction intervals. Advances in Neural Information Processing Systems **9**, 176–182 (1997)
16. Ho, S.S., Wechsler, H.: Transductive confidence machine for active learning. In: Proc. Int. Joint Conf. on Neural Networks'03. Portland, OR. (2003)
17. John, G.H., Langley, P.: Estimating continuous distributions in Bayesian classifiers. In: P. Besnard, S. Hanks (eds.) Proceedings of the Eleventh Conference on Uncertainty in Artificial Intelligence. Morgan Kaufmann, San Francisco, USA (1995)
18. Kearns, M.J., Ron, D.: Algorithmic stability and sanity-check bounds for leave-one-out cross-validation. In: Y. Freund, R. Shapire (eds.) Computational Learning Theory, pp. 152–162. Morgan Kaufmann (1997)
19. Kleijnen, J.: Experimental designs for sensitivity analysis of simulation models, tutorial at the Eurosim 2001 Conference (2001)
20. Kononenko, I., Šimec, E., Robnik-Šikonja, M.: Overcoming the myopia of inductive learning algorithms with ReliefF. Applied Intelligence **7**, 39–55 (1997)
21. Kononenko, I.: Semi-naive Bayesian classifier. In: Y. Kodratoff (ed.) Proc. European Working Session on Learning-91, pp. 206–219. Springer-Verlag, Berlin-Heidelberg-New York, Porto, Potrugal (1991)

22. Kukar, M.: Transductive reliability estimation for medical diagnosis. Artif. intell. med. pp. 81–106 (2003)
23. Kukar, M.: Quality assessment of individual classifications in machine learning and data mining. Knowledge and information systems **9**(3), 364–384 (2006)
24. Kukar, M., Kononenko, I.: Reliable classifications with Machine Learning. In: T. Elomaa, H. Mannila, H. Toivonen (eds.) Proceedings of 13th European Conference on Machine Learning, ECML 2002, pp. 219–231. Springer-Verlag, Berlin (2002)
25. Li, M., Vitányi, P.: An introduction to Kolmogorov complexity and its applications, 2nd edn. Springer-Verlag, New York (1997)
26. Melluish, T., Saunders, C., Nouretdinov, I., Vovk, V.: Comparing the Bayes and typicalness frameworks. In: Proc. ECML 2001, vol. 2167, pp. 350–357 (2001)
27. Nouretdinov, I., Melluish, T., Vovk, V.: Predictions with confidence intervals (local error bars). In: Proceedings of the International Conference on Neural Information Processing, pp. 847–852. Seoul, Korea (1994)
28. Nouretdinov, I., Melluish, T., Vovk, V.: Ridge regression confidence machine. In: Proc. 18th International Conf. on Machine Learning, pp. 385–392. Morgan Kaufmann, San Francisco (2001)
29. Olona-Cabases, M.: The probability of a correct diagnosis. In: J. Candell-Riera, D. Ortega-Alcalde (eds.) Nuclear Cardiology in Everyday Practice, pp. 348–357. Kluwer, Dordrecht, NL (1994)
30. Pfahringer, B., Bensuasan, H., Giraud-Carrier, C.: Meta-learning by landmarking various learning algorithms. In: Proc. 17th International Conf. on Machine Learning. Morgan Kaufmann, San Francisco, CA (2000)
31. Proedrou, K., Nouretdinov, I., Vovk, V., Gammerman, A.: Transductive confidence machines for pattern recognition. In: Proc. ECML 2002, pp. 381–390. Springer, Berlin (2002)
32. Rumelhart, D., McClelland, J.L.: Parallel Distributed Processing, vol. 1: Foundations. MIT Press, Cambridge (1986)
33. Saunders, C., Gammerman, A., Vovk., V.: Transduction with confidence and credibility. In: T. Dean (ed.) Proceedings of the International Joint Conference on Artificial Intelligence. Morgan Kaufmann, San Francisco, USA, Stockholm, Sweden (1999)
34. Saunders, C., Gammerman, A., Vovk, V.: Computationally efficient transductive machines. In: Algorithmic Learning Theory, 11th International Conference, ALT 2000, Sydney, Australia, December 2000, Proceedings, vol. 1968, pp. 325–333. Springer, Berlin (2000)
35. Seewald, A., Furnkranz, J.: An evaluation of grading classifiers. In: Proc. 4th International Symposium on Advances in Intelligent Data Analysis, pp. 115–124 (2001)
36. Smyth, P., Gray, A., Fayyad, U.: Retrofitting decision tree classifiers using kernel density estimation. In: A. Prieditis, S.J. Russell (eds.) Proceedings of the Twelvth International Conference on Machine Learning, pp. 506–514. Morgan Kaufmann, San Francisco, USA, Tahoe City, California, USA (1995)
37. Specht, D.F., Romsdahl, H.: Experience with adaptive pobabilistic neural networks and adaptive general regression neural networks. In: S.K. Rogers (ed.) Proceedings of IEEE International Conference on Neural Networks. IEEE Press, Piscataway, USA, Orlando, USA (1994)
38. Taneja, I.J.: On generalized information measures and their applications. Adv. Electron. and Elect. Physics **76**, 327–416 (1995)
39. Tsuda, K., Raetsch, M., Mika, S., Mueller, K.: Learning to predict the leave-one-out error of kernel based classifiers. In: Lecture Notes in Computer Science, pp. 227–331. Springer, Berlin/Heidelberg (2001)
40. Vapnik, V.: Statistical Learning Theory. John Wiley, New York, USA (1998)
41. Venables, W.N., Ripley, B.D.: Modern Applied Statistics with S-PLUS. Fourth edition. Springer-Verlag (2002)
42. Vovk, V., Gammerman, A., Saunders, C.: Machine learning application of algorithmic randomness. In: I. Bratko, S. Dzeroski (eds.) Proceedings of the 16th International Conference on Machine Learning (ICML'99). Morgan Kaufmann, San Francisco, USA, Bled, Slovenija (1999)
43. Wand, M.P., Jones, M.C.: Kernel Smoothing. Chapman and Hall, London (1995)

Chapter 2
Estimating Reliability for Assessing and Correcting Individual Streaming Predictions

Pedro Pereira Rodrigues, Zoran Bosnić, João Gama, and Igor Kononenko

Abstract Several predictive systems are nowadays vital for operations and decision support. The quality of these systems is most of the time defined by their average accuracy which has low or no information at all about the estimated error of each individual prediction. In these cases, users should be allowed to associate a measure of reliability to each prediction. However, with the advent of data streams, batch state-of-the-art reliability estimates need to be redefined. In this chapter we adapt and evaluate five empirical measures for online reliability estimation of individual predictions: similarity-based (k-NN) error, local sensitivity (bias and variance) and online bagging predictions (bias and variance). Evaluation is performed with a neural network base model on two different problems, with results showing that online bagging and k-NN estimates are consistently correlated with the error of the base model. Furthermore, we propose an approach for correcting individual predictions based on the CNK reliability estimate. Evaluation is done on a real-world problem (prediction of the electricity load for a selected European geographical region), using two different regression models: neural network and the k nearest neighbors algorithm. Comparison is performed with corrections based on the Kalman filter. The results show that our method performs better than the Kalman filter, significantly improving the original predictions to more accurate values.

Pedro Pereira Rodrigues
University of Porto, Faculty of Medicine & LIAAD - INESC Porto, L.A.
Rua de Ceuta, 118 - 6, 4050-190 Porto, Portugal, e-mail: pprodrigues@med.up.pt

Zoran Bosnić
University of Ljubljana, Faculty of Computer and Information Science
Tržaška cesta 25, 1000 Ljubljana, Slovenia, e-mail: zoran.bosnic@fri.uni-lj.si

João Gama
University of Porto, Faculty of Economics & LIAAD - INESC Porto, L.A
Rua de Ceuta, 118 - 6, 4050-190 Porto, Portugal, e-mail: jgama@fep.up.pt

Igor Kononenko
University of Ljubljana, Faculty of Computer and Information Science
Tržaška cesta 25, 1000 Ljubljana, Slovenia, e-mail: igor.kononenko@fri.uni-lj.si

2.1 Introduction

The main goal of the supervised learning models is to model the learning data the most accurately while also achieving the best possible prediction accuracy for the unseen examples that were not included in the learning process. Motivated by this goal, the field of machine learning is continually striving to propose new and to improve existing predictions models in order to achieve the best possible predictions.

Supervised machine learning systems are usually evaluated by their average accuracy on test examples. Measures such as the mean squared error (MSE), the relative mean squared error (RMSE) or the mean absolute percentage deviation (MAPE) are common tools for assessing global model quality. However, these measures give no information whatsoever about the expected quality of an individual prediction for a given unseen example.

The expected error of a prediction is a very relevant point in many sensitive applications, such as medical diagnosis or industrial applications for forecast and control. Users seem more comfortable with both a prediction and an error estimate for that prediction. Since the prediction quality can be evaluated through its different quality aspects (accuracy, error, availability, computational complexity, etc.) we use the term "reliability" in the context of its accuracy [4]. The *prediction-reliability* pair is seen as a more robust output and with deeper information about the prediction.

The field of online learning from data streams is particularly challenging, since the sources of the data are characterized as being open-ended, flowing at high-speed, and generated by non stationary distributions. Online learning algorithms should process examples at the rate they arrive, using a single scan of data and fixed memory, maintaining a decision model at any time and being able to adapt the model to the most recent data [14]. In streaming scenarios, the estimation of prediction reliability takes increased importance as faster decisions are many times required. In such demand-intensive environment, one does not have a luxury (in terms of time) of online testing and choosing among different models or iteratively optimizing them. The described situations may call for an alternative approach which can be applying a corrective mechanism to improve the accuracy of the predictions.

In this chapter we focus on utilization of reliability estimates in data streaming scenarios as follows. Section 2 presents some related work on reliability estimation, prediction correction and data stream analysis. In section 3 we present and evaluate (on real-world scenarios) the various reliability estimation strategies. In Section 4 we propose an approach for correcting individual predictions using reliability estimates, also experimentally evaluated on a real-world scenario. Section 5 finalizes the exposition with conclusion and future work.

2.2 Background

In this section we review the areas strongly connected to the problem of reliability estimation for individual predictions. Such areas are: data perturbation towards better predictive accuracy, reliability estimates for individual predictions used with batch learners, and online learning for data stream mining.

2.2.1 Computation and utilization of prediction reliability estimates

Research has followed the path of a group of approaches that generate perturbations of initial learning set to improve accuracy of final aggregated prediction. *Bagging* [7] and *boosting* [10] are well-known and possibly the most popular in this field. They have been show to improve generalization performance compared to individual models. While *bagging* works by learning different models in different regions of the input space (by sampling original data set), *boosting* focus on those regions which are not so well covered by the learned model. These techniques perturb the entire learning data set that is fed to individual models, thus operating by creating different learning models.

When changing the model is inapplicable, performing several simple perturbations of an individual example, obtaining their predictions using the learned model, and aggregating these predictions has been proved to improve results by reducing the variance of predictions. This simple but efficient variance reduction method is the *Dual Perturb and Combine (DPC)* method [15]. It consists on perturbing each test example several times, adding white noise to the attribute values, and predicting each perturbed version of the test example. The final prediction is obtained by aggregating (usually by averaging) the different predictions. The method is directly applicable in the streaming setting because multiple predictions only involve test examples. This strategy has been successfully used in real-world applications [23]. However, previous experimental work has proven this method as a bad reliability estimator [24].

A traditional approach to the estimation of the prediction confidence/reliability is based on distribution of learning examples. The density-based estimation of prediction error assumes that error is lower for predictions which are made in denser problem subspaces (i.e. contain more information about the problem), and higher for predictions which are made in sparser subspaces. A typical use of this approach is, for example, with decision and regression trees, where we trust each prediction according to proportion of learning examples that fall in the same leaf of a tree as the predicted example.

Conformal prediction [27] is a recent strategy to define prediction regions which contain the true label with a given error probability, using the base predictor and a nonconformity measure for each example. The main drawback when applying this technique to data streams is that it assumes that examples are either drawn independently from a unknown stable distribution, or exchangeable. In usual streaming applications this is not the case. Nevertheless, further work should investigate the applicability of this technique to open-ended data streams.

Yet another approach to reliability estimation is the local sensitivity analysis, which focuses on observing the magnitudes of changes in model output as a result of inducing changes in it's input [6]. The approach is to locally modify the learning set in a controlled manner in order to explore the sensitivity of the regression model in a particular part of the problem space. By doing so, the technique adapts the reliability estimate to the local particularities of data distribution and noise [3].

Definitions of reliability estimates based on the sensitivity analysis technique have been proposed for classification [20] and regression [3]. However, streams produce huge loads of data over time, disabling the application of techniques based on transformation of the entire data set.

2.2.2 Correcting individual regression predictions

In the previous work, Bosnić and Kononenko [3, 2] proposed and evaluated several different reliability estimates for regression predictions. All these reliability estimates are model-independent, i.e. they treat model as a black box, and are based on several approaches: sensitivity analysis, bagging variance, density estimation, and local error estimation. The greater value of the estimate for a particular example is to be interpreted as the indicator of the greater estimated prediction error for that example. The experimental evaluation has confirmed the significance of the latter correlation, however, its significance can depend on the used regression model and the domain. The succeeding work [5] presented some initial experiments which indicated that these reliability estimates can be used to correct the initial predictions of regression models.

Among nine proposed reliability estimates, the estimate CNK, which estimates the prediction error by modeling it locally, is particularly interesting, since it is very efficient to compute and can take positive as negative values (whereas seven other estimates can take only positive values). This means that besides providing the degree of confidence in the predictions, it also provides the information about the direction of the error (whether the prediction was too high or too low). Among the evaluated estimates, there is also another such estimate (named SAbias), however, the computational complexity of its approach is much higher compared to the one for computation of CNK.

2.2.3 Reliable machine learning from data streams

A data stream is an ordered sequence of instances that can be read only once or a small number of times using limited computing and storage capabilities. The data elements in the stream arrive online, being potentially unbounded in size. Once an element from a data stream has been processed it is discarded or archived. It cannot be retrieved easily unless it is explicitly stored in memory, which is small relative to the size of the data streams. These sources of data are characterized by being open-ended, flowing at high-speed, and generated by non stationary distributions [12, 14].

In online streaming scenarios, predictions are usually followed by the real label value in a short future (e.g., prediction of next value of a time series). Nevertheless, there are also scenarios where the real label value is only available after a long term, such as predicting one week ahead electrical power consumption [23]. Learning techniques which operate through fixed training sets and generate static models are obsolete in these contexts. Faster answers are usually required, keeping an anytime data model and enabling better decisions, possibly forgetting older information.

The sequences of data points are not independent, and are not generated by stationary distributions. We need dynamic models that evolve over time and are able to adapt to changes in the distribution generating examples [12]. If the process is not strictly stationary (as most of real-world applications), the target concept may gradually change over time. Hence data stream mining is an incremental task that requires incremental learning algorithms that take drift into account [11].

Hulten et al. [16] presented desirable properties for data stream learning systems. Overall, they should process examples at the rate they arrive, use a single scan of data and fixed memory, maintain a decision model at any time and be able to adapt the model to the most recent data. Successful data stream learning systems were already proposed for both prediction [23] and clustering [8, 25, 13]. All of them share the aim to produce reliable predictions or clustering structures.

The flexibility of the representational power of online learning systems implies error variance. In stationary data streams the variance shrinks when the number of examples goes to infinity. In a dynamic environment where the target function changes smoothly, and where even abrupt changes can occur, the variance of predictions is problematic. Given this, one way to estimate the reliability of the prediction is to test the instability of the model, by means of its sensitivity (i.e., the effect on the prediction) when small changes are applied in the predictive setting. There are three variance-enforcing properties of data stream learning:

1. There is uncertainty in the information provided by the previously known input data (e.g., if a sensor reads 100, most of times the real-value is around 100: it could be 99 or 101);
   a reliable predictor should be robust to slight changes in the *input vector*.
2. The same uncertainty in the data can also be present in the objective output value;
   a reliable predictor should be robust to slight changes in the *learned output value*.
3. As online systems learn with time, in dynamic settings, and without strict convergence measures, predictions may be produced by unstable models;
   a reliable predictor should be robust to slight changes in the *model's parameters*.

There are several possible ways to modify the learning model/data in order to assess instability, and the next section will try to address the three mentioned issues.

2.3 Estimating reliability of individual streaming predictions

Some of the estimates designed for batch reliability are inapplicable to the data stream scenario, given the restriction of using each example once or a small number of times. We now address online learning and reliability estimates for individual predictions, using restricted resources.

2.3.1 Preliminaries

Let x represent an input example and let y be its label. Therefore, with (x,y) we denote a learning example with known/assigned label y and with $(x, \_)$ we denote an example with unknown label. Let $(x, \_)$ be the unlabeled example for which we wish to estimate the reliability of prediction. The prediction $\hat{y}$, which we are estimating, is made by regression model M, therefore $f_M(x) = \hat{y}$. The quality of this prediction is given by a qualitative reliability estimate $\hat{r}$ until the real value y is available. Hence, for each prediction $\hat{y}$ generated by model M with example x, we should associate a reliability estimate $\hat{r}$ produced by a given reliability estimator R, therefore $f_R(M,x) = \hat{r}$.

The setting which we are trying to address is the following. At a given time t, an unlabelled example $(x^t, \_)$ is available to the system, which should produce as output the *prediction-reliability* pair, $(\hat{y}^t, \hat{r}^t)$. The system can then temporarily store the triplet $(x^t, \hat{y}^t, \hat{r}^t)$, waiting for the real output value y to be available. As soon as this occurs, which may actually be only at time $t + u$, the system can finally learn the real example (x^t, y^t). In local terms, the key point in regression is to approximate each $\hat{y}^t$ to y^t. As we will see in further explanations, the reliability estimate $\hat{r}^t$ of prediction $\hat{y}^t$ should somehow give an indication on how close y^t and $\hat{y}^t$ are from each other, exploiting the importance of good reliability estimators in online regression analysis.

We define different instability detectors, motivated by the three properties, and inspect their ability to present good online reliability estimates for individual predictions. We need to define a estimator to estimate reliability for each individual prediction $\hat{y}$. As previously stated, in reliable models, small changes in the input data/model should yield small changes in the output value. This way, a simple way to detect model's instability is to monitor the variability of k output predictions $\hat{Y}_\delta = \{\hat{y}_1, \hat{y}_2, ..., \hat{y}_k\}$ for example $(x, \_)$, each one made after perturbing the corresponding predictive setup by a certain modifier δ. Since we assumed that the zero-difference between predictions represents the maximum reliability, we also define the reliability measures so that value 0 indicates the most reliable prediction. We therefore approach reliability estimation by estimating the prediction error. As different instability detectors produce perturbed predictions in different ways, we shall formally define the reliability estimators in each corresponding section.

2.3.2 Reliability estimates for individual streaming predictions

In this section we present approaches to online reliability estimation using three reliability estimation frameworks: similarity-based estimation (for input uncertainty), local sensitivity analysis (for output uncertainty), and online bagging (for model's parameters uncertainty).

2.3.2.1 Reliability based on input similarity

A simple strategy to estimate the reliability of a given prediction is to consider the error of previous predictions of the same model in similar examples in the input space. In data streams, given the ordered arrival of examples, we can argue that a new example $(x, \_)$ should be more similar to recent examples than to older examples. Hence, we can inspect the mean squared error (MSE) of the model in the last b examples, and consider this an estimate of the error for the next prediction:

$$R_{MSE} = \frac{\sum_{t \in B}(\hat{y}^t - y^t)^2}{|B|}$$

where B is the buffer of $|B|$ most recent examples.

However, this naive approach can be refined with actual similarity of examples. Instead of computing the MSE for *all* most recent examples, we can consider only the k *nearest neighbors* of the objective example. This way, the reliability estimate would become:
$$R_{kNN} = \frac{\sum_{t \in K}(\hat{y}^t - y^t)^2}{k}$$
where $K \in B$ is the set of most recent examples which are the k nearest neighbors of $(x, \_)$ in B.

2.3.2.2 Reliability based on the local sensitivity analysis

To address the second property (uncertainty in output values), we decided to adjust the *Local Sensitivity Analysis* strategy proposed by Bosnić and Kononenko [3] in order to make it applicable to online learning. *Local variance* estimates represent the wideness of the intervals between various sensitivity predictions (see further subsections) and *local bias* estimates the model's affinity to predicting higher or lower prediction values for the local point in question.

In the original proposal, a learning set is expanded with additional learning examples with perturbed output values. To expand a learning set with example $(x, \_)$ it is first labeled with $\hat{y}_\varepsilon = \hat{y}_0 + \delta$, where $\hat{y}_0$ denotes the initial prediction modified by some small change δ. Note, that the initial prediction $\hat{y}_0$ is used as a central value for $\hat{y}_\varepsilon$, which is afterwards incremented by term δ (which may be either positive or negative), proportional to known bounds of label values. In particular, if the interval of learning example labels is denoted by $[a, b]$ and if ε denotes a value that expresses the relative portion of this interval, then $\delta = \varepsilon(b - a)$.

After selecting ε and labeling the new example, a learning data set is expanded with example $(x, \hat{y}_\varepsilon)$. Based on this modified learning set with $n + 1$ examples a new model is built, referred to as the *sensitivity regression model M'*. M' is used to predict $(x, \_)$, thus having $f_{M'}(x) = \hat{y}_\varepsilon$. Let us refer to $\hat{y}_\varepsilon$ as the *sensitivity prediction*. By selecting different ε_i with $i \in \{1, 2, ..., m\}$ to obtain $\hat{y}$, the process iteratively obtains a set of sensitivity predictions

$$\hat{Y}_\varepsilon = \{\hat{y}_{\varepsilon_1}, \hat{y}_{-\varepsilon_1}, \hat{y}_{\varepsilon_2}, \hat{y}_{-\varepsilon_2}, ..., \hat{y}_{\varepsilon_m}, \hat{y}_{-\varepsilon_m}\}$$

with $|\hat{Y}_\varepsilon| = 2m$. The obtained differences $\hat{y}_\varepsilon - \hat{y}_0$ serve to observe the model stability and can be combined into different reliability measures.

The application of this procedure in the online setting is straightforwardly derived from offline learning and is as follows. As soon as a new unlabeled example $(x, \_)$ is available, the system makes the *initial prediction* $\hat{y}_0 = f_M(x)$. Afterwards, the examples $(x, \hat{y}_{\varepsilon_i})$ are fed only once, separately to each copy M_i of the model M. Then, each *sensitivity regression model* M_i is used to compute the prediction $\hat{y}_{\varepsilon_i} = f_{M_i}(x)$, resulting in the final set of *sensitivity predictions*. Sensitivity regression models are discarded after the example is processed. To avoid selecting a particular ε, we define measures to use an arbitrary number of sensitivity predictions (defined by using different ε parameters). The number of used ε parameters therefore represents a trade-off between gaining more stable reliability estimates and the total computational time.

In the case of reliable predictions we expect that the change in sensitivity model for $\hat{y}_\varepsilon$ and $\hat{y}_{-\varepsilon}$ would be minimal (0 for the most reliable predictions). We define this reliability measure using both, $\hat{y}_\varepsilon$ and $\hat{y}_{-\varepsilon}$, to capture the model instabilities not regarding the sign of ε.

Let us assume we have a set of non-negative ε values $E = \{\varepsilon_1, \varepsilon_2, ..., \varepsilon_{|E|}\}$. The set of *sensitivity predictions* $\hat{Y}_\varepsilon$ will be computed as previous, with $|\hat{Y}_\varepsilon| = 2|E|$.

The estimates are defined as follows:

- *Local Variance*: $LV_{LSA} = \frac{\sum_{\varepsilon \in E}(\hat{y}_\varepsilon - \hat{y}_{-\varepsilon})}{|E|}$

- *Local Bias*: $LB_{LSA} = \frac{\sum_{\hat{y}_i \in \hat{Y}_\varepsilon} \hat{y}_i}{|\hat{Y}_\varepsilon|} - \hat{y}_0$

For the batch setting, the authors conclude that estimates LV_{LSA} and LB_{LSA} are more suitable for estimation of the prediction error than density estimates [3].

2.3.2.3 Reliability based on online bagging sensitivity analysis

Sometimes, the uncertainty in predictions is not easily derivable from current data. This way, techniques may be used which try to explore multiple versions of a base model in different regions of the data space. The variability of these models should give some information about the reliability of individual predictions. Online bagging is a relatively new technique which applies the same principle of bagging [7] to massive data sets with comparable results with its batch pair. To preserve the idea behind bagging, which stands for an ensemble of homogeneous models learned with different samples of the existing data, online processing needs to be redefined.

Let m be the number of base models we will consider for the final prediction. Bagging works by sampling a data set with replacement, thus creating a different data set with the same length, and learning a base model with this data set. This process is repeated for each of the m base models. In the online setting, we never have access to the entire data set. This way, at each new example arrival we should estimate if this example should be included in each of the base online models. Oza and Russel [22] proposed an online bagging algorithm which feeds each example to a base model k times, where k is randomly taken from a Poisson distribution with $\lambda = 1$ expected number of feeds. Online bagging is a good approximation to batch bagging since their base model learning algorithms produce similar hypotheses when trained with similar distributions of training examples [22]. However, this strategy allows a given example to be fed more than once to the same base model. In the streaming setting, this is often not possible. A simple approximation has been proved elsewhere to work well where, instead of taking $k \sim Poisson(1)$, we take uniformly distributed $p \sim U(0,1)$ and define $k = 1$ if $p > \tau$, and $k = 0$ otherwise. For suitable τ, the system should converge to the same base hypotheses when the data set grows to infinity.

Let $(x, \_)$ be the most recent available example. A prediction is made by each base model M_i, $\hat{y}_i = f_{M_i}(x)$, creating a set of predictions $\hat{Y} = \{\hat{y}_1, \hat{y}_2, ..., \hat{y}_m\}$. As soon as there is a true label value for the example, (x, y) is fed to each base model according to the rules previously defined. This ensembling technique was proved to improve results, both for regression and classification problems [7].

It seems reasonable to infer that the dispersion of the predictions should give some indication about the reliability of the ensemble prediction. However, our goal is to assess online bagging as a reliability estimator for single model predictions. This way, the reliability estimates are defined as:

- *Local Variance*:
$$LV_{BAG} = \frac{\sum_{i \in \{1,...,k\}} (\hat{y}_i - y_0)^2}{k}$$

- *Local Bias*:
$$LB_{BAG} = \frac{\sum_{i \in \{1,...,k\}} \hat{y}_i - \hat{y}_0}{k}$$

where $\hat{y}_0$ is the simple prediction that the same base model would give if fed with all the data.

2.3.3 Evaluation of reliability estimates

A key point in any intelligent system is the evaluation methodology. Learning systems generate compact representations of what is being observable. They should be able to improve with experience and continuously self-modify their internal state. From the previous section, several reliability estimates arise, which they all consider predictions with reliability values close to zero as more reliable (they are therefore estimates of prediction error). This way, the comparison between them is straightforward. We shall investigate if, and to which extent, they are correlated with the error, using statistical correlation measures.

Given the online setting of learning from data streams, the quality of a learning model is difficult to condense in a single value of loss or performance, since data is being produced with evolving concepts and the model itself is being continuously updated. Even in recent works, evaluation of online learners has been sidestepped, assuming either hold-out or fixed test set at the end of the learning process, computing average losses in time windows.

In this experimental section we try a slightly different approach. We are interested in reliability estimates for individual predictions of a base model (search for better ensembles of predictors is not the scope of this chapter). We want to compute the correlation between a reliability estimate of a prediction and the corresponding error of that prediction. Computing correlation of thousands of examples with online learning can be misleading. Therefore, we define overlapping time windows, where correlation is computed, supported by a statistical test on this correlation. This setting creates a new data set where each variable is a reliability estimate and each observation is the correlation between that estimate and the prediction error, for the current time window. Afterwards, to assess the quality of each estimate, we compute the cumulative sum of the significant (according to the statistical test) correlations. Non-significant correlations add zero to the cumulative sum. Estimates with higher correlation with error should present higher slopes in the plot of this cumulative sum. Namely, the perfect estimate, with correlation 1 all the time, should lay on the diagonal of the graph.

Craven and Shavlik [9] argue that the inductive bias of neural networks is the most appropriate for sequential and temporal prediction tasks. For the first assessment of the soundness of the proposed measures as reliability estimates, we will use neural networks, trained online, applied to two different problems: predicting the number of rings abalone to assess their age, using the *abalone* data set [21] from the UCI Machine Learning Repository [1], and predicting the electrical *load* for a given horizon given the date and previous values of the electricity demand stream, already addressed in previous works [23]. Experiments with more learning methods and other data sets are in progress.

For all the experiments described in this section, a neural network is trained online, with each example being fed only once. During the learning process, all reliability estimates are also computed online. Overlapping time windows are defined with 500 examples, and a step of 50 examples. Finally, results of correlations between reliability estimates and error are gathered as previously stated, and averaged over 10 runs. Significance of resulting correlations is assessed using Kendall's rank correlation test [18] and evaluated using *t-test* for correlation coefficients, with confidence level of 95%. This choice was mainly motivated by the fact that other coefficients (e.g. Spearman's correlation) are not so well interpreted when the null hypotheses is rejected. As we produce a cumulative sum of significant coefficients, we need these to have a interpretable meaning. Given their non-negative characteristic, *local variance* estimators' correlation is tested against absolute error of corresponding predictions.

The setup includes three results for the *online bagging* framework ($\tau = 0.33$ and $m = \{3, 6, 10\}$ base models); one result for *local sensitivity analysis* (using $E =$

Table 2.1: Final cumulative significant correlations between each reliability estimate (k-NN MSE, local sensitivity and online bagging) and the base model error, for the *abalone* data set, and the three problems of electricity load demand (bold values are the best estimate for each problem).

Strategy	Parameters	Abalone	Electricity Load Demand		
			next hour	*next day*	*next week*
		MSE	MSE	MSE	MSE
Similarity-based	*1-NN*	2.26	13.94	9.73	2.64
	3-NN	3.47	**22.60**	**16.33**	10.66
	5-NN	3.68	19.24	14.95	10.13
	500-NN	0.50	-0.76	0.26	1.20
		Bias Var	Bias Var	Bias Var	Bias Var
Local Sensitivity		1.95 6.91	-1.06 -0.07	-1.41 -1.14	-2.29 -1.22
Online Bagging	*3 models*	9.26 6.52	4.43 1.63	7.74 4.89	6.76 4.94
	6 models	10.72 11.21	12.90 7.39	14.27 10.00	12.86 9.11
	10 models	**14.69** 13.24	13.83 13.81	15.38 14.98	**13.78** 13.42

$\{0.01, 0.1, 0.5, 1.0, 2.0\}$); and four results for the *similarity-based* approach (number of nearest neighbors $k = \{1, 3, 5, 500\}$). Such parameter values were selected due to simple empirical analysis of acceptable values. Further work will extend these experiments with a wider range of values.

2.3.4 Abalone data set

The task presented in this problem is to predict age of an abalone shell from its physical measurements. The age of an abalone is determined by counting the number of rings after cutting the shell, so the task is to predict the number of rings without cutting the shell. The data set has 8 attributes with 4177 observations. We use an online neural network with 8 inputs, one hidden layer and one linear output.

Table 2.2 presents the final values of the cumulative significant correlations for all problems. As for the current problem, and With respect to the *online bagging* approach, higher number of base models produced better correlations with the error, for both estimates. For the *local sensitivity analysis* approach, we observe higher correlation of the *local variance* estimator, while for the *similarity-based* approach, it is unclear whether using the MSE of the buffered data is a profitable option. Apparently, *online bagging* and *local sensitivity analysis* estimates present better reliability estimations for individual predictions using a base model.

2.3.5 Electricity load demand data stream

Considering a time series representing electricity load demand of a given geographical region, the goal is to have an incremental system to continuously predict in real time the electricity load demand. The system must predict with a given temporal horizon, that is, if at moment t we receive an observation, the system must execute a prediction for the value for the moment $t + k$. This is a real-world problem where online learning systems are useful, and where predictions should be supplemented with reliability estimates, especially in scenarios where the real value is not available for a long while (e.g. predicting the load demand for one week ahead).

We use the online neural network setup defined in [23], for the next hour, next day and next week predictions, separately, and apply it to a time series containing one value every 15 minutes. Data is standardized using only data from the current buffer of the most recent examples. The structure of the neural network consists of 10 inputs, one hidden layer (*tanh*-activated) and a linear output. The input vector for next hour prediction at time t is t minus $\{1,2,3,4\}$ hours and t minus $\{7,14\}$ days. For the next day predictor, the historical inputs are t minus $\{24,(168-24),168,169,(168+24),336\}$ hours. The next week predictor takes as input t minus $\{168,169,(336-24),336,(336+24),(336+168)\}$ hours. As usual [19], we consider also 4 cyclic variables, for hourly and weekly periods (*sin* and *cos*).

After several experiments, with empirical sensitivity analysis of different predictive methods, and as expected, the *next hour* prediction revealed to be a fairly easy task, with *3-NN* prediction even better than the neural network. Therefore, we concentrate on the *next day* and *next week* problems, which usually require better reliability as the actual value is observed for only several hours in the future.

An example of the evolution of such reliability estimates over time in a stream is sketched in Figure 2.1, where the consistency of the used estimates can be confirmed. Final correlation results are presented in Table 2.2. Overall, *online bagging* and *similarity-based* estimators present better correlation with the error of the base model predictions. Surprisingly, in these problems the *local sensitivity analysis* presented low correlation with the error, which could be motivated by the model being extremely stable. Such stable models in also stable concepts should produce prediction errors quite similar to those produced preciously in similar examples. Hence the benefits of using the *k-NN* estimators in these settings.

2.4 Correcting individual streaming predictions

Given the benefits of using k-NN estimators presented in the previous section, in the following we will describe an approach for correcting predictions using the locality-based reliability estimate CNK [2] and compare it with correcting predictions using the Kalman filter [17].

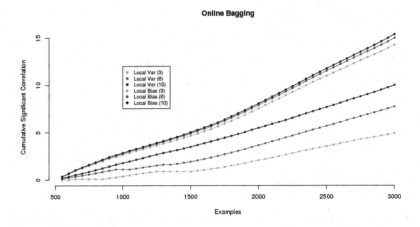

Fig. 2.1: Cumulative significant correlation of online bagging reliability estimates with the corresponding base model prediction error, for the 'next day' problem. Online bagging estimates are consistently correlated with error (as not shown similarity-based estimates also are).

2.4.1 Correcting predictions using the CNK reliability estimate

The reliability estimate CNK for estimation of regression prediction error for a given example is defined as a local estimate of error. Let us denote with CNK the general reliability estimate (i.e. the concept of the reliability estimation approach) and with CNK_i an estimate value for some particular i-th example. For offline learning setting, the estimate CNK was defined as follows. Suppose we are given a learning set of n examples $L = \{(x_1, C_1), \ldots, (x_n, C_n)\}$ where $x_i, i = 1 \ldots n$ denote the attribute vectors and $C_i, i = 1 \ldots n$ denote the true target values of the examples (their labels). In our scenario, we are given an unseen example $(x_u, \_)$ for which we wish to compute a prediction and supplement it with the reliability estimate CNK_u.

First, we induce a regression model on L and output the prediction K_u for the example $(x_u, \_)$. To compute CNK_u, we first localize the set of the k nearest neighbors $N = \{(x_{u1}, C_{u1}), \ldots, (x_{uk}, C_{uk})\}$ of the example, $N \subseteq L$. CNK_u is then defined as the difference between the average label of the nearest neighbors and the example's prediction K_u, as follows:

$$CNK_u = \frac{\sum_{i=1}^{k} C_{ui}}{k} - K_u \qquad (2.1)$$

hence the name CNK (average $\underline{C}$ of $\underline{N}$eighbors minus $\underline{K}$ of the example). In the above equation, k denotes the number of neighbors, C_{ui} denotes the neighbors' labels and K_u denotes the example's prediction. The construction of the estimate CNK is illustrated in Figure 2.2 (left).

In our work we adapt this definition of CNK to the online learning scenario, i.e. we use an incremental online model instead of the model which learns from the the

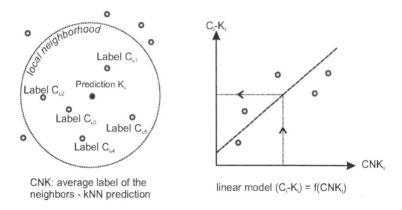

CNK: average label of the
neighbors - kNN prediction

linear model $(C_i\text{-}K_i) = f(CNK_i)$

Fig. 2.2: Construction of the reliability estimate CNK (left) and linear model through the nearest neighbors from the buffer (right): the model is used to predict unknown prediction error for the unseen examples using their value of the estimate CNK.

stationary learning set L. Since the storage of examples is of a limited size, only the most recent examples in the buffer B can participate as the nearest neighbors (either for computation of CNK or for predicting with the k nearest neighbors model), therefore $N \subseteq B$.

Note, that CNK is a reliability estimate that can be easily influenced by local noise and subject to local bias. To robustly transform the value of CNK_u to the value of predicted error $C_u - K_u$, we apply a linear regression model for this task. The linear model $f(CNK_i) = (C_i - K_i)$ is built using the estimate values and the prediction error values of all examples in the buffer, of which the true target outcomes are already known (required for computation of the prediction error). The use of this linear model is illustrated in Fig. 2.2(right). The corrected prediction is finally computed as $K_{CNK_u} = K_u + f(CNK_u)$.

2.4.2 Correcting predictions using the Kalman filter

The Kalman filter [17] is a general and the most widely used in engineering for two main purposes: for combining measurements of the same variables but from different sensors, and for combining an inexact forecast of the system's state with an inexact measurement of the state [23]. We use the Kalman filter to combine the prediction K_u for an example $(x_u, \_)$ with the expected most correlated value $\overline{K}_u$ from the previous time point (depends on the prediction problem variant) and gain a corrected prediction K_{Kalman_u}:

$$K_{Kalman_u} = \overline{K}_u + F_u \cdot (K_u - \overline{K}_u) \tag{2.2}$$

where F_u is the filter transition weight which controls the influence of the past prediction [17].

2.4.3 Experimental evaluation

Our data is a real-world and risk-sensitive problem where the decisions based on the online learning systems influence the financial outcomes. Since the prediction accuracy is of a critical importance, this makes the problem interesting for evaluation of our corrective strategies. In the following subsections, we describe the data, the used regression models, the evaluation approach and we present the testing results.

2.4.3.1 Electricity load data and predictive models

For the purpose of experimental evaluation, the streaming data was converted into the relational form, which is appropriate for supervised learning. The examples of data represent the electricity load values for a points in time with a resolution of 1 hour. The data consists of 10 attributes which include 4 cyclic variables (couples of *sin* and *cos* values which denote the hourly and weekly periods) and 6 historical load attributes. These attributes are specific to three variations of the problem, as described previously in Sect. 2.3.5. The *next hour* and *next day* prediction problems consist of 16200 examples and the *next week* prediction problem consists of 15528 examples. For all three problem variations, a buffer size of 336 was used, which corresponds to last 14 days of examples. For computation of the CNK estimate, 2 nearest neighbors were used (in the buffer of 14 days, the 2 examples from the same days in previous weeks are expected to have the most correlated prediction error). Following the previous work [23], the expected most correlated value used in the Kalman filter was the example from the last hour for the first problem and the example from the previous week (168 hours) for the last two variants of the problem.

Our correction approach was tested using two different online learning models:

- **neural network**: consisting of 10 input neurons, a hidden layer of 5 neurons and 1 output neuron. The *tansig* activation function was used in the hidden neurons and the linear activation function in the output neuron,
- k **nearest neighbors**: k was chosen as 336 (all the examples in the buffer), the examples were inversely weighted by their distance to the query example.

2.4.3.2 Model evaluation using fading statistics

In the online learning setting, the typical definitions of the averaged accuracy measures over all examples (such as the mean squared error - MSE) cease to be appropriate. Namely, when averaged across the increasing number of examples, the measure becomes increasingly stable (each new example represents increasingly small proportional contribution) and as such it provides no information about the current model accuracy which corresponds to the current model adaptation to the data.

A possible approach to measuring how model accuracy evolves over time is to use the fading statistic which is recursively updated and emphasizes the model behavior on the most recent data [26]. Such is the *alpha*-fading mean squared error (αMSE), which, for being computed over i historical examples, is defined using the recursive definitions for the sum of the prediction errors s_i and the counter of examples n_i as:

$$s_i = (K_i - C_i)^2 + \alpha \cdot s_{i-1} \tag{2.3}$$
$$n_i = 1 + \alpha \cdot n_{i-1}$$
$$\alpha MSE_i = \frac{s_i}{n_i}$$

In the above equations, K_i and C_i denote the prediction and the true value of the i-th example, respectively, and α denotes the weight factor for consideration of the historical part of the estimate. The initial recursion values are $n_0 = 0$ and $s_0 = 1$ and the weight α is set to $0.01^{1/\text{buffer\_size}} = 0.01^{1/336} \sim 0.9864$, following the elsewhere proposed error-bounded strategy [26].

For comparative performance assessment of two algorithms A and B on a stream, a Q statistic should be used [14]:

$$Q_i(A,B) = \log \left(\frac{\alpha MSE_i^A}{\alpha MSE_i^B} \right) = \log \left(\frac{(K_i^A - C_i)^2 + \alpha \cdot s_{i-1}^A}{(K_i^B - C_i)^2 + \alpha \cdot s_{i-1}^B} \right) \tag{2.4}$$

where the superscripts A and B refer to the models. Note that, like the αMSE, the Q statistic can be computed for all examples in a stream, thus providing a comparison of two algorithms over time. The value of the Q statistic is easy to interpret: its negative values denote the better performance of the algorithm A (lower αMSE_i^A) and its positive values denote the better performance of the algorithm B (lower αMSE_i^B).

2.4.4 Performance of the corrective approaches

In our experiments, we have computed the electricity load predictions for three variations of the problem (load prediction for the next hour, next day and next week). The online learning scenario was simulated on the data described in Sect. 2.4.3.1 by implementing a sliding window over the examples (i.e., a buffer) and by iteratively updating an incremental model with a single new example. When the sliding window passed all the examples, the electricity load predictions were calculated for every example in the dataset. Fig. 2.3(top) shows a sample data segment of a *next day* problem for a period of three weeks. Along with the true load values, predictions using the neural network are shown.

In parallel with predicting the electricity load, both described approaches for correction of the predictions were applied, as well. Fig. 2.3(middle) shows a short sample segment of the data, which visualizes the true load values and all three computed predictions for the *next day* problem: the original neural network prediction, the CNK-corrected prediction and the prediction that was corrected using the Kalman filter (only a short segment of data is shown due to impaired possibility to compare all curves on the larger segments of the data). The comparison of curves reveal that in many cases, both corrected predictions are closer to the true value than the original prediction. However, in some cases this is not the rule, e.g. for the last day in a figure. Therefore a more thorough statistical evaluation is required and is performed in the following.

Along with computing the original prediction and producing its two corrected versions, the evolution of the model's performance was evaluated using the fading αMSE measure. Three estimates were computed, αMSE, αMSE$_{CNK}$ and αMSE$_{Kalman}$, for three versions of predictions, i.e. the original prediction, the corrected prediction using the estimate CNK, and the prediction, corrected with the Kalman filter, respectively. Based on the computed performance measures, a Q statistic was computed for comparing the performance of the original model (αMSE) with the accuracy of each of the corrective approaches. The computed values of the Q statistic for neural network (for the *next day* problem) are shown in Fig. 2.3 (bottom). The figure reveals the dominantly positive values of the Q statistic for corrected predictions with the reliability estimate CNK, which clearly speaks in favor of this approach. The picture for correction using the Kalman filter is not as clear as is the previous case. In the following we statistically evaluate both approaches, as well as present the results for the k nearest neighbors model.

2.4.5 Statistical comparison of the predictions' accuracy

We used the t-test to test the null hypothesis (H_0) that the mean value of the Q statistic equals zero (i.e. that the accuracies of the original and the corrected predictions are not significantly different). A variant of t-test, which compares the mean of the data to an expected value, was used. The results for three problem variants and for two model types are shown in Table 2.2.

The results show that all means of the Q statistics are positive if we compare the original predictions with the predictions, corrected with the estimate CNK. All the means are different from zero with a high level of significance (p<0.001); the gain in accuracy with this type of correction (CNK) was always significant. On the other hand, a gain in accuracy with the referential method (the Kalman filter) was mixed. Namely, the results show that the statistical accuracy improvement with the Kalman filter correction was achieved only with neural network and in the *next day* and the *next week* problem. The remaining results indicate either that the original model was better ($\mu < 0$ and $p < 0.001$) or that the predictions are statistically equally accurate ($p = 0.106$).

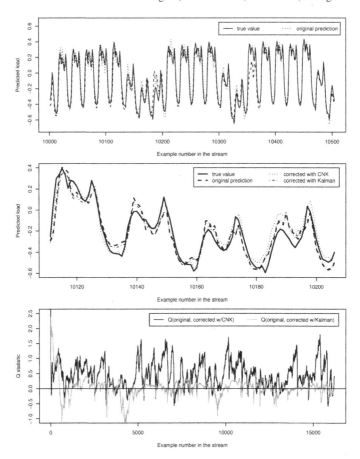

Fig. 2.3: A sample of the true and predicted electricity load for the period of three weeks using the neural network (only a segment of the whole data stream is shown); the predictions clearly reflect the daily and weekly cycles in the predicted load (top). Comparison of the original and both corrected predictions on a data segment of four days (middle). Values of the Q statistic for comparing accuracy of the original predictions with both two versions of corrected predictions: using the estimate CNK and the Kalman filter (bottom).

2.5 Conclusions

Human experts usually feel more comfortable when they are present with a prediction and a reliability estimate for that prediction. Moreover, actual learning processes could improve themselves using this reliability information. Hence the need to define reliability estimates for individual predictions in streaming scenarios. Therefore, focus is now given to this estimates in real-world applications, especially those where predictions imply decision on the control process. Better reliability es-

Table 2.2: Results of the t-test for testing the equality of the Q statistic (for comparison of the original and the corrected predictions) to the value 0. The table cells show the average values of the Q statistic for the three problem variants and for two regression models. The average values of the Q statistic and the p-values for H_0 are given.

problem	model	t-test for H_0 : Q(original, corr.w/CNK)=0	t-test for H_0 : Q(original, corr.w/Kalman)=0
next hour	nn	$\mu = 0.617, p < 0.001$	$\mu = -0.012, p < 0.001$
	knn	$\mu = 0.438, p < 0.001$	$\mu = -0.109, p < 0.001$
next day	nn	$\mu = 0.463, p < 0.001$	$\mu = 0.021, p < 0.001$
	knn	$\mu = 0.575, p < 0.001$	$\mu = -0.007, p = 0.106$
next week	nn	$\mu = 0.575, p < 0.001$	$\mu = 0.337, p < 0.001$
	knn	$\mu = 0.596, p < 0.001$	$\mu = -0.046, p < 0.001$

timates would yield better decision support tools, especially in applications where thousands of predictions are fed to users.

In this chapter we propose different strategies to estimate the reliability of individual predictions, exploring techniques based on *local variance* and *local bias*, of *local sensitivity analysis* and *online bagging* of predictors. We also consider *similarity-based k-NN* estimations. Given the preliminary results on the *abalone* age prediction and the electricity load demand prediction, we tend to consider that *online bagging* and *similarity-based* estimators are more connected with the error of simple base model predictions. Nevertheless, *local sensitivity analysis* presents promising results in less stable concepts, where models keep intrinsic instability.

Furthermore, we have explained the motivation to apply a corrective mechanism to predictions of the data streams in contrast to more extensive online model comparisons and selection. We have tested two such corrective approaches: using the reliability estimate CNK and using a referential method - the Kalman filter. The testing results on the electricity load prediction domain show that our method performs better than the Kalman filter, significantly improving the original predictions towards more accurate values.

Current and future work is concentrated on exploring different base models (e.g. linear regression or regression trees). Also, the application of the estimations to different problems, with artificial and real-world data is also necessary to assess the overall quality of the proposed estimators. The third correction approach (using a sensitivity analysis based reliability estimate [3]) shall be implemented as well.

Acknowledgements This work has been developed under the scope of bilateral project agreement between the governments of Portugal and Slovenia. P.P. Rodrigues and J. Gama thank FCT's Pluri-anual financial support attributed to LIAAD and the participation of project KDUS under FCT's contract PTDC/EIA-EIA/098355/2008.

References

1. Asuncion, A., Newman, D.: UCI machine learning repository (2007). URL http://www.ics.uci.edu/$\sim$mlearn/{MLR}epository.html
2. Bosnić, Z., Kononenko, I.: Comparison of approaches for estimating reliability of individual regression prediction. Data and Knowledge Engineering **67**(3), 504–516 (2008)
3. Bosnić, Z., Kononenko, I.: Estimation of individual prediction reliability using the local sensitivity analysis. Applied Intelligence **29**(3), 187–203 (2008)
4. Bosnić, Z., Kononenko, I.: An overview of advances in reliability estimation of individual predictions in machine learning. Intelligent Data Analysis **13**(2) (2009)
5. Bosnić, Z., Kononenko, I.: Correction of regression predictions using the secondary learner on the sensitivitiy analysis outputs. Computing and Informatics (in press) pp. 1–17 (2010)
6. Bousquet, O., Elisseeff, A.: Stability and generalization. Journal of Machine Learning Research **2**, 499–526 (2002)
7. Breiman, L.: Bagging predictors. Machine Learning **24**, 123–140 (1996)
8. Cormode, G., Muthukrishnan, S., Zhuang, W.: Conquering the divide: Continuous clustering of distributed data streams. In: Proceedings of the 23rd International Conference on Data Engineering (ICDE 2007), pp. 1036–1045 (2007)
9. Craven, M., Shavlik, J.W.: Understanding time-series networks: a case study in rule extraction. International Journal of Neural Systems **8**(4), 373–384 (1997)
10. Drucker, H.: Improving regressors using boosting techniques. In: Machine Learning: Proceedings of the Fourteenth International Conference, pp. 107–115 (1997)
11. Gama, J., Medas, P., Castillo, G., Rodrigues, P.P.: Learning with drift detection. In: Proceedings of the 17th Brazilian Symposium on Artificial Intelligence (SBIA 2004), pp. 286–295. Springer Verlag, São Luiz, Maranhão, Brazil (2004)
12. Gama, J., Rodrigues, P.P.: Data stream processing. In: Learning from Data Streams - Processing Techniques in Sensor Networks, chap. 3, pp. 25–39. Springer Verlag (2007)
13. Gama, J., Rodrigues, P.P., Lopes, L.: Clustering distributed sensor data streams using local processing and reduced communication. Intelligent Data Analysis **15**(1), 3–28 (2011)
14. Gama, J., Sebastião, R., Rodrigues, P.P.: Issues in evaluation of stream learning algorithms. In: Proceedings of the 15th ACM SIGKDD International Conference on Knowledge Discovery and Data Mining (KDD 2009), pp. 329–337. ACM Press, Paris, France (2009)
15. Geurts, P.: Dual perturb and combine algorithm. In: Proc. of the Eighth International Workshop on Artificial Intelligence and Statistics, AI+STATS2001, pp. 196–201. Florida (2001)
16. Hulten, G., Spencer, L., Domingos, P.: Mining time-changing data streams. In: Proceedings of the Seventh ACM SIGKDD International Conference on Knowledge Discovery and Data Mining, pp. 97–106. ACM Press (2001)
17. Kalman, R.E.: A new approach to linear filtering and prediction problems. Transaction of ASME - Journal of Basic Engineering pp. 35–45 (1960)
18. Kendall, M.: A new measure of rank correlation. Biometrika **30**, 81–89 (1938)
19. Khotanzad, A., Afkhami-Rohani, R., Lu, T.L., Abaye, A., Davis, M., Maratukulam, D.J.: Annstlf–a neural-network-based electric load forecasting system. IEEE Transactions on Neural Networks **8**(4), 835–846 (1997)
20. Kukar, M., Kononenko, I.: Reliable classifications with machine learning. In: Proceedings of the 13th European Conference on Machine Learning, pp. 219–231. Springer Verlag (2002)
21. Nash, W.J., Sellers, T.L., Talbot, S.R., Cawthorn, A.J., Ford, W.B.: The population biology of abalone (_haliotis_ species) in tasmania. i. blacklip abalone (_h. rubra_) from the north coast and islands of bass strait. Tech. Rep. 48, Sea Fisheries Division (1994)
22. Oza, N.C., Russell, S.J.: Experimental comparisons of online and batch versions of bagging and boosting. In: Proceedings of the seventh ACM SIGKDD international conference on Knowledge discovery and data mining, pp. 359–364 (2001)
23. Rodrigues, P.P., Gama, J.: A system for analysis and prediction of electricity load streams. Intelligent Data Analysis **13**(3), 477–496 (2009)

24. Rodrigues, P.P., Gama, J., Bosnić, Z.: Online reliability estimates for individual predictions in data streams. In: ICDM Workshops, pp. 36–45. IEEE (2008)
25. Rodrigues, P.P., Gama, J., Pedroso, J.P.: Hierarchical clustering of time-series data streams. IEEE Transactions on Knowledge and Data Engineering **20**(5), 615–627 (2008)
26. Rodrigues, P.P., Gama, J., Sebastião, R.: Memoryless fading windows in ubiquitous settings. In: Proceedings of the Ubiquitous Data Mining Workshop, pp. 23–27. Lisboa, Portugal (2010)
27. Shafer, G., Vovk, V.: A tutorial on conformal prediction. Journal of Machine Learning Research **9**, 371–421 (2008)

Chapter 3
Error Bars for Polynomial Neural Networks

Nikolay Nikolaev, and Evgueni Smirnov

Abstract Recent research in genetically programmed polynomial neural networks demonstrates that they are successful in time-series modelling. Currently, an important issue is how to quantify the reliability of the inferred polynomial networks, that is how to evaluate their uncertainty in order to obtain evidence for their usefulness. This paper elaborates on approaches to estimation of error bars (confidence and prediction intervals) for polynomial neural networks including: 1) the analytical delta method, implemented using a neural network technique; 2) the empirical bootstrap method; and 3) an empirical network training method. We present results on empirical data which show that the delta method may lead to more unstable intervals and thus favour the bootstrap for practical applications.

3.1 Introduction

The Genetic Programming (GP) [12] is a contemporary paradigm suitable for finding well performing non-linear polynomials. Well performing are considered such polynomials that exhibit good accuracy on training data, parsimonious structure, and good predictability. Recent research shows that genetically programmed polynomials, represented as Polynomial Neural Networks (PNN), perform especially well on practical environmental and financial time series as they capture the intrinsic non-linearities in them [10], [13], [14].

When learning models from data it is important to quantify the belief in them in order to become confident in their usefulness. The model uncertainties can be

Nikolay Nikolaev
Department of Computing, Goldsmiths College, University of London, London SE14 6NW, United Kingdom. e-mail: n.nikolaev@gold.ac.uk

Evgueni Smirnov
Department of Knowledge Engineering, Maastricht University, P.O.BOX 616, 6200 MD Maastricht, The Netherlands. e-mail: smirnov@maastrichtuniversity.nl

evaluated using statistical means such as the error bars. The research in error bars for non-linear regression models [20] has influenced the studies on error bars for neural network models [4], [5], [6], [7], [9], [11], [16], [18].

This chapter elaborates on approaches to estimation of error bars (confidence and prediction intervals) for non-linear PNN models. Confidence intervals are generated according to: 1) the analytical delta method [8], which is implemented using a neural network technique, and 2) the empirical residual bootstrap method [21]. Prediction intervals are generated following: 1) the analytical delta method, and 2) the empirical backprop network training method [15]. The GP is taken to find the structure and weights of polynomials from given training data. After that, the confidence and prediction intervals of the best PNN are evaluated.

This chapter is organised as follows. Section two presents the PNN and the GP mechanisms for their manipulation. The sources of PNN deviations from the unknown regression function are analysed in section three. Section four describes the methods for estimating confidence intervals of PNN, and section five presents the methods for prediction intervals. Finally, a brief conclusion is given.

3.2 Genetic Programming of PNN

3.2.1 Polynomial Regression

The polynomial regression problem arises in many applications. It is defined as follows: given examples $E = \{(\mathbf{x}_n, y_n)\}_{n=1}^{N}$ of input vectors $\mathbf{x}_n = (x_{n1}, x_{n2}, ..., x_{nd}) \in \mathcal{R}^d$, and corresponding targets $y_n \in \mathcal{R}$, the goal is to find the best polynomial approximation $P(\mathbf{x})$ of the true regression $\tilde{f}(\mathbf{x})$ of y on $\mathbf{x}$. We consider polynomials $P(\mathbf{x})$ written in *block format* as follows:

$$P(\mathbf{x}) = b_0 + \sum_{i=1}^{d} b_1(i) T_i + \sum_{i=1}^{d}\sum_{j=1}^{d} b_2(i,j) T_i T_j + \sum_{i=1}^{d}\sum_{j=1}^{d}\sum_{k=1}^{d} b_3(i,j,k) T_i T_j T_k + ... \quad (3.1)$$

where b_i are weights, and T are terminals defined using summation blocks s or variables x_i:

$$T = \begin{cases} x_0, \ x_0 = \sum_{i=1}^{d} x_i \\ x_i \ \ otherwise \ (1 \leq i \leq d) \end{cases} \quad (3.2)$$

The key idea is that such polynomials can be represented as tree-structured PNN. Having tree-structured PNN means that the GP mechanisms can be used to search for the relevant model structure and weights, and there could be applied neural network techniques for estimating error bounds.

3.2.2 Tree-structured PNN

The GP system used in this research performs stochastic search with a population of PNN represented as *binary trees* [14]. The trees compose complex models from easy to process low-order bivariate polynomials (see Figure 3.1). The outcomes of activation polynomials, allocated in the tree nodes, are fed forward to their parent nodes, where partial models are built of received outcomes from the activation polynomials below and/or input variables. The output at the tree root is a high-order, high-dimensional multinomial.

The GP system uses a set of activation polynomials with which the nonlinear interactions among the explanatory variables are identified more precisely. This allows the GP mechanisms to discard overfitting terms. A set $\{p_i\}_{i=1}^{16}$ of activation polynomials (Table 3.1) is derived from the complete bivariate polynomial after the elimination of terms. This set contains low-order polynomials since higher-order polynomials rapidly increase the order of the overall polynomial, which unfortunately causes overfitting.

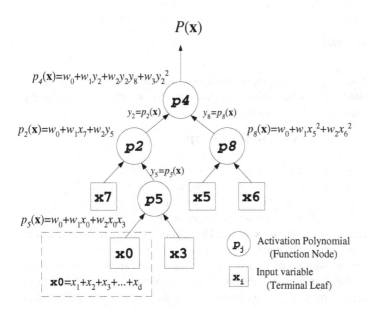

$P(\mathbf{x})$

$p_4(\mathbf{x})=w_0+w_1y_2+w_2y_2y_8+w_3y_2^2$

p4

$y_2=p_2(\mathbf{x})$ $y_8=p_8(\mathbf{x})$

$p_2(\mathbf{x})=w_0+w_1x_7+w_2y_5$ $p_8(\mathbf{x})=w_0+w_1x_5^2+w_2x_6^2$

p2   **p8**

$y_5=p_5(\mathbf{x})$

x7   **p5**   **x5**   **x6**

$p_5(\mathbf{x})=w_0+w_1x_0+w_2x_0x_3$

x0   **x3**

$\mathbf{x0}=x_1+x_2+x_3+...+x_d$

$\mathbf{p_j}$ Activation Polynomial (Function Node)

$\mathbf{x_i}$ Input variable (Terminal Leaf)

Fig. 3.1: A tree-structured representation of a polynomial model composed of different activation polynomials $p_j(\mathbf{x}), 1 \leq j \leq 16$, $\mathbf{x} = (x_1, x_2)$ in the internal tree nodes, applied with variables: $x_i, 0 \leq i \leq 10$ passed through the leaves. This tree builds the polynomial $P(\mathbf{x}) = p_4(p_2(x_7, p_5(x_0, x_3)), p_8(x_5, x_6))$.

Table 3.1: The set of bivariate activation polynomials.

$p_1(\mathbf{x}) = w_0 + w_1 x_1 + w_2 x_2 + w_3 x_1 x_2$
$p_2(\mathbf{x}) = w_0 + w_1 x_1 + w_2 x_2$
$p_3(\mathbf{x}) = w_0 + w_1 x_1 + w_2 x_2 + w_3 x_1^2 + w_4 x_2^2$
$p_4(\mathbf{x}) = w_0 + w_1 x_1 + w_2 x_1 x_2 + w_3 x_1^2$
$p_5(\mathbf{x}) = w_0 + w_1 x_1 + w_2 x_1 x_2$
$p_6(\mathbf{x}) = w_0 + w_1 x_1 + w_2 x_2 + w_3 x_1^2$
$p_7(\mathbf{x}) = w_0 + w_1 x_1 + w_2 x_1^2 + w_3 x_2^2$
$p_8(\mathbf{x}) = w_0 + w_1 x_1^2 + w_2 x_2^2$
$p_9(\mathbf{x}) = w_0 + w_1 x_1 + w_2 x_2 + w_3 x_1 x_2 + w_4 x_1^2 + w_5 x_2^2$
$p_{10}(\mathbf{x}) = w_0 + w_1 x_1 + w_2 x_2 + w_3 x_1 x_2 + w_4 x_1^2$
$p_{11}(\mathbf{x}) = w_0 + w_1 x_1 + w_2 x_1 x_2 + w_3 x_1^2 + w_4 x_2^2$
$p_{12}(\mathbf{x}) = w_0 + w_1 x_1 x_2 + w_2 x_1^2 + w_3 x_2^2$
$p_{13}(\mathbf{x}) = w_0 + w_1 x_1 + w_2 x_1 x_2 + w_3 x_2^2$
$p_{14}(\mathbf{x}) = w_0 + w_1 x_1 + w_2 x_2^2$
$p_{15}(\mathbf{x}) = w_0 + w_1 x_1 x_2$
$p_{16}(\mathbf{x}) = w_0 + w_1 x_1 x_2 + w_2 x_1^2$

3.2.3 Weight Learning

The use of simple activation polynomials allows us to learn their weights by ordinary least squares training. We use individual regularization parameters in the following *regularized least squares* (RLS) formula:

$$\mathbf{w} = (\mathbf{H}^T \mathbf{H} + \mathbf{L})^{-1} \mathbf{H}^T \mathbf{y} \qquad (3.3)$$

where $\mathbf{w}$ is the column weights vector $\mathbf{w} = (w_0, w_1, ..., w_m)$, $\mathbf{H}$ is a $N \times (m+1), 1 \leq m \leq 5$, design matrix of row vectors $\mathbf{h}(\mathbf{x}_n) = (h_0(\mathbf{x}_n), ..., h_m(\mathbf{x}_n))$, $n = 1..N$, $\mathbf{y}$ is a $N \times 1$ output vector, and $\mathbf{L}$ is the $(m+1) \times (m+1)$ diagonal matrix with the individual regularizers λ_j. The basis functions h are: $h_0(\mathbf{x}) = 1, h_1(\mathbf{x}) = x_1, h_2(\mathbf{x}) = x_2, h_3(\mathbf{x}) = x_1 x_2, h_4(\mathbf{x}) = x_1^2$, and $h_5(\mathbf{x}) = x_2^2$. The regularizers λ_j are determined in advance using a statistical technique [3] (page 2360).

After estimating the weights of a particular activation polynomial, subset selection of weights greater than a predefined threshold is performed. Then, the remaining weights are pruned by setting them to zero, since they have a negligible effect on the mapping.

3.2.4 Mechanisms of the GP System

The GP system organizes evolutionary search with a population of tree-like PNN. The search is navigated by random selection of good PNN that are picked from the population according to their fitness. The chosen elite PNNs are modified by either crossover or mutation operators and, after that, allocated over the worst PNNs in the population. The initial population is randomly generated.

Fitness Function. The fitness function should control the evolutionary search so as to avoid overfitting, and to learn well performing polynomials. Well performing are considered polynomials which are accurate, predictive, and parsimonious. We design a *statistical fitness function* with three ingredients: 1) an accuracy measurement that favors highly fit models; 2) a regularization factor that tolerates smoother mappings with higher generalization potential; and, 3) a complexity penalty that prefers short size models.

The generalization capacity of a PNN is measured using the *regularized prediction error (RPE)* which is a leave-one-out estimate plus regularization:

$$RPE = \frac{1}{N} \left(\sum_{i=1}^{N} \left(\frac{y_i - P(\mathbf{x}_i)}{1 - R_{jj}} \right)^2 + \sum_{j=1}^{W} \lambda_j w_j^2 \right) \tag{3.4}$$

where W is the number of the polynomial weights.

GP search navigation is performed using the *final prediction error* [1] as a statistical fitness function, which scales this *RPE* by the model complexity:

$$FPE = \left(\frac{N+W}{N-W} \right) RPE \tag{3.5}$$

where N is the number of the data, and W is the number of the weights.

This *FPE* polynomial fitness is calculated only once at the tree root (PNN output) and should be minimized.

Genetic Operators and Selection. The *crossover* operator randomly chooses a cut point node in each tree, and swaps the subtrees rooted in the cut-point nodes. This crossover is restricted by a predefined maximum tree size so if there is an offspring tree of larger size it is discarded.

The *mutation* operator selects a tree node, and performs one of the following transformations: 1) replacement of the selected node by another randomly chosen node; 2) deletion of the selected node, and replacing it by one of its children nodes (a terminal leaf or a subtree rooted at a functional node); and 3) insertion of a randomly chosen node before the selected one, so that the selected becomes an immediate child of the new one, and the other child is a random terminal. If the tree size exceeds the predefined maximum it is trimmed.

These genetic operators are applied to selected promising models with good fitness. *Fitness proportional selection* is used to choose randomly 40% from the population elite to generate offspring. The fitness proportional selection scheme requires to rank the PNN in the population according to their fitnesses in order to enable selection of the fittest to reproduce in the next generation. The offspring models are allocated over the worst population members.

3.3 Sources of PNN Deviations

There are various reasons that disturb in practice the model identification process, thus leading to model deviations from the true underlying regression function (i.e. the mean $E[y|\mathbf{x}]$). In our case of learning PNN the main reasons that influence the uncertainty in the models are: a) the sampling variations of the data, b) the model characteristics, and c) the neural network learning approach.

Data Influences. First, there are usually inherent uncertainties in the given training data, like measurement and noise errors, which hinder the search for models. Second, it depends whether the input data are evenly distributed, or they have different densities in different regions of the true function. The learning algorithms are unfortunately sensitive to the variations of the data samples.

Model Influences. First, the embedding dimension and the model structure may not be convenient for the task. That is, the input variables that should be in the model may not have been chosen properly, it may be mistaken how many of them are sufficient, and which they should be. Second, the maximal order (degree) of the polynomial may have not been determined correctly.

Learning Algorithm Influences. First, the application of network growing and/or pruning techniques may cause model misspecification due to overgrowing, undergrowing, overpruning, and underpruning. Second, even if the model complexity is relatively accurate, the learning process still may be unable to converge to an acceptable solution, for example due to early stopping. There are many local optima on the error surface arising from linear models, and many are unlikely to possess the desired characteristics.

3.4 Estimating Confidence Intervals

The GP is suitable for inferring PNN from data. The question is to what degree one can be certain in the approximation qualities of the PNN models. In order to quantify the belief in the learned best PNN, it is necessary to determine how reliably it models the data under certain assumptions. Our assumptions are that the data are contaminated by noise ε which is normally distributed with zero mean and unit variance, there are given a finite number of data, and the PNN has been trained to convergence. The model is described as:

$$y = P(\mathbf{x}, \mathbf{w}) + \varepsilon \qquad (3.6)$$

where $P(\mathbf{x}, \mathbf{w})$ is the PNN model with weights $\mathbf{w} = (w_1, w_2, ..., w_W)$, $w \in \mathcal{R}^W$.

The model reliability is defined by the probability with which it contains the true regressor. In statistical parlance the task of measuring the model uncertainty involves finding the *confidence interval* in which one has $(1 - \alpha)\%$ (i.e. 95%) belief that randomly drawn data will be captured correctly by the model.

Two approaches are elaborated here for PNN confidence interval estimation: analytical based on the delta method, and empirical based on the residual bootstrap method. These methods are applied to the best PNN model discovered by GP using the benchmark *Airline series* [2]. The GP system was run over the normalized data series. We used 12 input variables: $x_{t-1}, x_{t-2}, ..., x_{t-12}$. The system settings were kept constant in all runs: *PopulationSize* $= 100$, *Generations* $= 300$, *MaxTreeSize* $= 40$ (sum of nodes and leaves). The GP system was made using *SteadyStateReproduction* $= 50\%$, that is, half of the good models were chosen by fitness proportional selection, modified by either crossover or mutation and, after that, allocated over the worst 50% network in the population. The local regularizers were predetermined using $\lambda_0 = 0.001$, and the selection threshold was $z = 0.01$. Approximately 100 runs were conducted.

3.4.1 Delta Method for Confidence Intervals

The analytical delta method [8] yields estimates of the standard error according to the maximum likelihood theory. The standard error of the model is given by:

$$\hat{se}_{delta}(P(\mathbf{x}, \mathbf{w})) = \sqrt{\sigma^2 \mathbf{g}^T(\mathbf{x}) \mathbf{H}^{-1} \mathbf{g}(\mathbf{x})} \tag{3.7}$$

where σ^2 is the variance of the error term ε, $\mathbf{g}(\mathbf{x})$ contains the first-order derivatives of the model output $P(\mathbf{x}, \mathbf{w})$ with respect to the weights $\mathbf{g}(\mathbf{x}) = \partial P(\mathbf{x}, \mathbf{w})/\partial \mathbf{w}$, and $\mathbf{H}$ is the is the Hessian matrix with the second-order partial derivatives of the output with respect to the combinations of weights:

$$H = \sum_{i=1}^{N} \left\{ \frac{\partial P(\mathbf{x}_n, \mathbf{w})}{\partial w_i} \frac{\partial P(\mathbf{x}_n, \mathbf{w})}{\partial w_j} - (y_n - P(\mathbf{x}_n, \mathbf{w})) \frac{\partial^2 P(\mathbf{x}_n, \mathbf{w})}{\partial w_i \partial w_j} \right\} \tag{3.8}$$

and N is the number of observations, and i, j are the weight indices.

In practice formula (3.7) can be implemented by replacing the error variance σ^2 by the mean squared error of the model: $\hat{\sigma}^2 = (1/N) \sum_{n=1}^{N} (y_n - P(\mathbf{x}_n, \mathbf{w}))^2$. Another practical concern is to incorporate the influence of weight decay regularization factors λ_j, applied when training PNN, on the diagonal elements of the Hessian matrix (3.8). the *confidence interval of a PNN model* becomes:

$$P(\mathbf{x}, \mathbf{w}) \pm z_{.025} \hat{\sigma} \sqrt{\mathbf{g}^T(\mathbf{x})(\mathbf{H} + \mathbf{L})^{-1} \mathbf{g}(\mathbf{x})} \tag{3.9}$$

where $z_{.025}$ is the critical value of the normal distribution.

This formula (3.9) provides a general estimate of neural network models, like the PNN. A simplified version of this estimate was recently derived directly from nonlinear regression models, and, more precisely, using a linear Taylor expansion of the nonlinear model output [18]. However, this simplified version (3.9) uses only a diagonal approximation of the Hessian matrix by elements $[\mathbf{H}]_{ij} =$

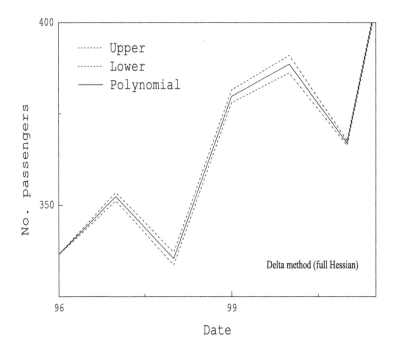

Fig. 3.2: Confidence intervals of fitting the *Airline series* by the best PNN from GP estimated by the delta method using the complete Hessian matrix.

$(\partial P(\mathbf{x}, \mathbf{w}) / \partial w_i)(\partial P(\mathbf{x}, \mathbf{w}) / \partial w_j)$. Since there are available very precise contemporary techniques for evaluating the full Hessian matrix (3.8), we prefer formula (3.8) which leads to more accurate results.

The backpropagation technique for multilayer networks enable us to find both the first-order $\mathbf{g}(\mathbf{x})$ and second-order $\mathbf{H}$ derivatives of the model output with respect to the weights [19]. We developed a backpropagation version and the $\mathcal{R}$-propagation [17] algorithms especially for PNN with polynomial activation functions. The estimated confidence intervals of PNN using the Airline series are plotted within an arbitrary interval in Figures 3.2 and 3.3.

An important clarification concerning the estimation of the PNN confidence intervals by the delta method should be made. The GP learns PNN using normalized input data, here the normalized Airline series. In order to produce error bouns in their original magnitude formula (3.9) should be modified to reflect the fact that the input and output data are normalized. More precisely, realistic confidence intervals can be obtained by multiplying the quantity under the square root in (3.9) by $z_{.025}\hat{\sigma}^* y_{std}$, where $\hat{\sigma}^*$ is the mean squared error of the normalized model, and

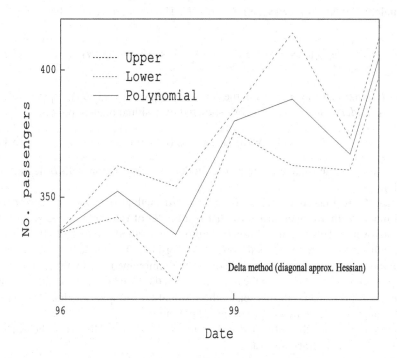

Fig. 3.3: Confidence intervals of fitting the *Airline series* by the best PNN from GP estimated by the delta method using a diagonal approximation of the Hessian matrix.

y_{std} is the standard deviation of the original outputs y. The standard deviation of the original outputs is computed as follows: $y_{std} = \sqrt{(1/(N-1)) \sum_{n=1}^{N} (y_n - \bar{y})^2}$. The Hessian **H** and the gradient $\mathbf{g}(\mathbf{x})$ are calculated only with the normalized data since in the way in which we find the PNN it becomes a model of the normalized series.

3.4.2 Residual Bootstrap for Confidence Intervals

The residual bootstrap [21] is an alternative method for estimating the standard error, which generates a number, B, of different models from a selected one $P(\mathbf{x}, \mathbf{w})$ by estimating it with replicates of the original data sample $D = \{(\mathbf{x}_n, y_n)\}_{n=1}^{N}$. Every model $P(\mathbf{x}, \mathbf{w}^b)$, $1 \le b \le B$, is made by reestimating $P(\mathbf{x}, \mathbf{w})$ with its output deliberately contaminated by a randomly drawn residual error: $P(\mathbf{x}_n, \mathbf{w}^b) = P(\mathbf{x}_n, \mathbf{w}) + e_n^b$, $1 \le n \le N$, where e_n^b is the n-th residual from the b-th error series: $\mathbf{e}^b = (e_1^b, e_2^b, ..., e_N^b)$, $1 \le b \le B$. In order to make the models $P(\mathbf{x}, \mathbf{w}^b)$ an error series

$\mathbf{e}^b$ is produced by independently resampling the residuals $(e_1, e_2, ..., e_N)$ from the original model: $e_n = y_n - P(\mathbf{x}_n, \mathbf{w})$, $1 \le n \le N$. The standard error is therefore:

$$\hat{se}_{boot}(P(\mathbf{x}, \mathbf{w})) = \sqrt{\frac{1}{B-1} \sum_{b=1}^{B} \left(P(\mathbf{x}, \mathbf{w}^b) - \bar{P}(\mathbf{x}, \mathbf{w}) \right)^2} \qquad (3.10)$$

where $\bar{P}(\mathbf{x}, \mathbf{w})$ is the average from the B models: $\bar{P}(\mathbf{x}, \mathbf{w}) = (1/B) \sum_{b=1}^{B} P(\mathbf{x}, \mathbf{w}^b)$.

The *confidence interval of a PNN* estimated by residual bootstraping is:

$$P(\mathbf{x}, \mathbf{w}) \pm t_{.025[B]} \hat{se}_{boot}(P(\mathbf{x}, \mathbf{w})) \qquad (3.11)$$

where $t_{.025[B]}$ is the critical value of the Student's t-distribution with B degrees of freedom.

Since the residual bootstrap is a model-based method it requires to consider a good model with a proper structure, that is a model of relevant complexity which does not overfit. This is a motivation to employ this method, as we study PNN models produced by inductive genetic programming [14]. The inductive genetic programming offers a contemporary paradigm that simultaneously identifies the relevant polynomial structure from the data, discovers the variables that should enter the model, and the weights. In this sense, the residual bootstraping method is suitable for the analysis of genetically programmed polynomials.

Figure 3.4 shows the estimated confidence intervals of PNN using the Airline series within an arbitrary interval.

The problem again is how to find the error bars in their realistic original magnitude. When implementing the bootstrap method we computed the error variance $\hat{\sigma}$ using the original outputs y and the estimated realistic $P(\mathbf{x}, \mathbf{w})$, and next we normalized this error variance into $\hat{\sigma}^*$ in order to make the normalized error series $\mathbf{e}^b$ necessary for the estimation of the the bootstrap sample models $P(\mathbf{x}, \mathbf{w}^b)$. Next, realistic differences $P(\mathbf{x}, \mathbf{w}^b) - \bar{P}(\mathbf{x}, \mathbf{w})$ were calculated according to (3.10) using restored to their original magnitude model outputs $P(\mathbf{x}, \mathbf{w}^b)$ and the corresponding mean output $\bar{P}(\mathbf{x}, \mathbf{w})$.

3.5 Estimating Prediction Intervals

When performing statistical diagnosis of forecasting models it is necessary to evaluate also the uncertainty in their prediction. Although PNN infer the mean of the data distribution, whose variation from one sample to another can be estimated by confidence intervals, it is also important to quantify what is the belief that a future PNN output will belong to the distribution of the given sample. In statistical parlance the task of measuring the model reliability is to find the prediction interval in which one has $(1 - \alpha)\%$ (i.e. 95%) belief the model output will belong to this interval. *Prediction interval* for a randomly drawn value are two limits: from above and from below, which with a certain probability contain this unseen value. While

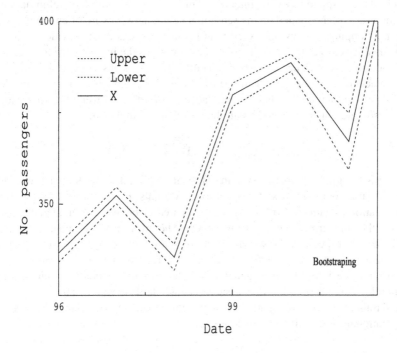

Fig. 3.4: Confidence intervals of fitting the *Airline series* by the best PNN from GP estimated by the bootstrapping method.

the confidence intervals account for the model variance due to its biasedness, that is improper structure, the prediction intervals account for the model variance from the data. The prediction bars are estimates of the input dependent target noise, and they should be expected to be broader, larger than the confidence error bars.

The prediction intervals for PNN are determined according to the hypothesis that their output error varies as a function of the inputs:

$$P(\mathbf{x}, \mathbf{w}) \pm z_{.025} \sigma(\mathbf{x}) \tag{3.12}$$

where $\sigma(\mathbf{x})$ is the noise variance which in the general case is unknown.

3.5.1 Delta Method for Prediction Intervals

Asymptotic prediction bands can be estimated following the theory of nonlinear regression in a similar way as the confidence bands using the delta method. The straightforward modification of the delta method, discussed in Section 4.1, however often leads to suspiciously wide intervals. This happens because the preliminary assumptions are often violated, in the sense that neural networks are often trained with the early stopping strategy not exactly until convergence and the provided data sets are of small size. In cases of such violated assumptions the intervals are found unreliable because the variance is unstable to compute. These observations inspired the development of a precise analytical formula for evaluating prediction error bars. Analytical prediction intervals that take into account the effect of weight regularization can be estimated in case of PNN with the following formula [6]:

$$P(\mathbf{x}, \mathbf{w}) \pm z_{.025} \hat{\sigma}^* y_{std} \sqrt{1 + \mathbf{g}^T (\mathbf{H} + \mathbf{L})^{-1} \mathbf{J}^T \mathbf{J} (\mathbf{H} + \mathbf{L})^{-1} \mathbf{g}} \qquad (3.13)$$

where $\mathbf{g}$ is the gradient vector, $\mathbf{H}$ is the Hessian matrix, $\mathbf{J}$ is the Jacobian with the network output derivatives with respect to the weights, $\mathbf{L}$ is a matrix with the local regularization parameters, $\hat{\sigma}^*$ is the mean squared error of the normalized model, and y_{std} the standard deviation of the targets. The error variance under the square root is derived especially for weight decay regularization as $\sum_{i=1}^{W} w_i^2$, so if another regularization is appliedanother formula has to be rederived.

This formula is designed to generate prediction bars restored in their original magnitude. This restoration is necessary because the PNN are usually evolved by GP and trained by backpropagation using the normalized input data in order to avoid computational instabilities and inaccuracies.

3.5.2 Training Method for Prediction Bars

The function of the latent noise variance can be determined empirically using a neural network training method obtained from a maximum likelihood perespective [15]. This method offers the idea to extend the polynomial network so that it learns not only the mean of the data distribution, but also the variance of this mean around the desired targets. Since the standard PNN output generates the mean $P(\mathbf{x}) \simeq E[y|\mathbf{x}]$, we install another output node to generate the noise variance $\hat{\sigma}^2(\mathbf{x})$ assuming that it is not constant but conditioned on the inputs. Thus, we infer the moments of the conditional probability density of the outputs as a function of the input data.

The second output node in the variance network extention should accept signals from all nodes through a separate layer in order to capture the characteristics of the studied original PNN. An additional separate hidden layer is installed whose nodes have incoming connections from all input (terminal) and hidden (functional) nodes. The extension is fully connected: every input and hidden node output feeds via a corresponding link every node in the additional hidden layer, whose outputs next feed the second output node.

The variance network uses the same activation polynomials as these in the original PNN part. The second output node transforms the weighted summation of the signals from the extended hidden nodes by the exponential function:

$$\hat{\sigma}^2(\mathbf{x}) = \exp\left(\sum_{j=1}^{J} v_{kj}u_j + v_{k0}\right) \tag{3.14}$$

where v_{kj} are the weights on connections feeding the second output node, v_{k0} is bias term, and u_j are the outputs of the additional hidden nodes whose number is J. The exponent function is necessary to generate positive values.

There are sigmoidal activation functions in the additional hidden layer which serve to filter out the weighted summations of the incoming signals:

$$u_j = sig\left(\sum_{i=1}^{I} v_{ji}x_i + v_{j0}\right) \tag{3.15}$$

where x_i are the outputs from the activation polynomials in the PNN part of the extended network, v_{ji} are the weights from the PNN nodes to the extended hidden nodes, and sig is the sigmoid function: $sig(z) = 1/(1+\exp(-z))$.

3.5.2.1 PNN Learning of Error Variance

The derivation of the error variance learning algorithm follows the maximal likelihood principle [15] and requires to make two assumptions: 1) that the noise is normally distributed, and 2) that the errors are statistically independent. This allows us to introduce a common criterion for coherent training of both the first and the second output nodes.

The following negative log likelihood criterion is considered for both parts of the polynomial network:

$$C = \frac{1}{2}\sum_{n=1}^{N}\left(\frac{[y_n - P(\mathbf{x}_n, \mathbf{w})]^2}{\hat{\sigma}^2(\mathbf{x}_n)} + \ln(\hat{\sigma}^2(\mathbf{x}_n))\right) \tag{3.16}$$

where y_n is the given target, $P(\mathbf{x}_n, \mathbf{w})$ is the network output from the n-th input, and $\hat{\sigma}^2(\mathbf{x}_n)$ is the sensitivity of the error variance on the n-th input.

Training of the extended PNN is performed using weight training rules obtained by finding the minimum of this criterion. It is differentiated with respect to the weights, the result is equated to zero, and solved for the free variables. This is performed for both the first PNN output producing the mean, as well as for the second output producing the variance because they are mutually dependent. The mathematical derivations yield two different training rules.

Training of the Second Output Node Weights. Suppose that the second output node producing the variance $\hat{\sigma}^2(\mathbf{x})$ is indexed by k and the hidden nodes whose outgoing connections feed it are indexed by j. The *training rule for the second output node* is:

$$\Delta v_{kj} = \eta\left(\frac{[y_n - P(\mathbf{x}_n, \mathbf{w})]^2 - \hat{\sigma}^2(\mathbf{x}_n)}{2\hat{\sigma}^2(\mathbf{x}_n)}\right)u_j \tag{3.17}$$

where η is the learning rate, v_{kj} are the hidden to output weights that enter the second output node, and the signals on their connections from the additional hidden nodes are u_j. Note that this rule uses the squared error $[y_n - P(\mathbf{x}_n, \mathbf{w})]^2$ produced at the output of the first node when the original PNN is estimated with the same n-th input.

Training of the First Output Node Weights. Suppose that the first PNN output node modeling the mean $P(\mathbf{x}) \simeq E[y|\mathbf{x}]$ is also indexed by k, let its children nodes are at level j, and the weights on the links between them are specified by w_{kj}. The *training rule for the first output node* that prescribes how to modify the weights associated with its incoming connections is:

$$\Delta w_{kj} = \eta \delta'_k x'_{kj} = \eta \left(\frac{[y_n - P(\mathbf{x}_n, \mathbf{w})]^2}{\hat{\sigma}^2(\mathbf{x}_n)} \right) x'_{kj} \qquad (3.18)$$

where w_{kj} are the hidden to first output weights, and x'_{kj} are the derivatives of the output activation polynomial with respect to its weights. This rule uses the variance $\hat{\sigma}^2(\mathbf{x}_n)$ emitted from the the second output node.

The remaining weights below are updated as follows: 1) the network weights in the original PNN part are adjusted using the backpropagation rules for high-order networks; and 2) the weights on links to the nodes in the additional hidden layer are adjusted according to the standard delta rules for gradient descent search in multilayer neural networks using sigmoidal activations.

Training of the Extended Hidden Node Weights. Suppose that the hidden nodes in the extended layer are indexed by j as above and the PNN nodes that feed them are indexed by i. The *training rule for the additional hidden nodes* is:

$$\Delta v_{ji} = \eta [u_j (1 - u_j)(-\delta'_k) w_{kj}] x_i \qquad (3.19)$$

where the signals x_i are either inputs or outputs from the activation polynomials in the PNN network, u_j are the outputs from the hidden nodes in the additional layer, and δ'_k is the backpropagated error down from the second output.

3.5.2.2 Training Algorithm for Extended PNN

The extended PNN can be trained with the backpropagation algorithm for gradient descent search in the weight space using the above training rules. In order to avoid early entrapment at suboptimal local optima, due to the mutual dependence of the learning rules for the hidden to output node connections in both parts of the extended network, the training process is divided in three consequtive phases.

The first phase performs training of the original PNN so as to minimize the mean squared error $E_n = (1/N) \sum_{n=1}^{N} (y_n - P(\mathbf{x}_n, \mathbf{w}))^2$, using the backpropagation technique for networks with polynomial activation functions. In this phase the extended part of the network is not trained at all. The training should be made only with a subset from the given data so as to avoid overfitting.

During the second phase a different subset from the data is taken to train the extended part of the network aiming also at minimization of the mean squared error. The training is conducted using the backpropagation algorithm with the learning rule for the second output node (3.17) without dividing it by $2\hat{\sigma}^2(\mathbf{x}_n)$, and the training rules for the hidden nodes in the additional layer (3.19). In the second phase the weights in the original PNN part remain unchanged.

The training objective in the third phase is to minimize the log likelihood criterion (4.16). In the third phase the hidden to root node weights in the original PNN part are tuned according to the novel learning rule (3.18), while the remaining weights below are tuned with the learning rules for high-order networks with activation polynomials. The weights in the second extended part of the network are adjusted using the rules (3.17) and (3.19). The training proceeds till reaching the minimum of the log likelihood criterion.

3.6 Conclusion

After conducting experiments with the above analytical and empirical methods for error bar estimation, it was found that the bootstrapping provides on average more stable confidence intervals. The delta method yields either too pessimistic or too optimistic confidence intervals.

Further investigations are carried out to understand how the confidence and prediction intervals are affected by different data distributions, how they are influenced by the weight convergence of PNN.

References

1. Akaike, H.: Power Spectrum Estimation through Autoregression Model Fitting. Annals Inst. Stat. Math. 21, 407–419 (1969)
2. Box, G.E.P. and Jenkins, G.M.: Time Series Analysis Forecasting and Control. Holden-Day, San Francisco (1970)
3. Breiman, L.: Heuristics of Instability and Stabilization in Model Selection. The Annals of Statistics 24, N:6, 2350–2383 (1996)
4. Cawley, G.C. and Janacek, G.J.: Predictive Uncertainty in Environmental Modelling. Neural Networks 20, N:4, 537–549 (2007)
5. Chryssolouris, G., Lee, M. and Ramsey, A.: Confidence Interval Prediction for Neural Network Models. IEEE Trans. on Neural Networks 7, N:1, 229–232 (1996)
6. De Veaux, R.D., Schumi, J., Schweinsberg, J. and Lyle, H.U.: Prediction Intervals for Neural Networks via Nonlinear Regression. Technometrics 40, N:4, 273–282 (1998)
7. Dybovski, R. and Roberts, S.J.: Confidence Intervals and Prediction Intervals for Feedforward Neural Network Models, In: Dybovski,R. and Gant,V. (eds.) Clinical Applications of Artificial Neural Networks. pp.298-326. Cambidge University Press, UK, (2001)
8. Efron, B. and Tibshirani, R.J.: An Introduction to the Bootstrap. Chapman and Hall, New York, NY (1989)
9. Hwang, J.T.G. and Ding, A.A.: Prediction intervals for artificial neural networks. Journal of the American Statistical Association 92, N:438, 748–757 (1997)

10. Iba, H., Paul, T.K. and Hasegawa, Y.: Applied Genetic Programming and Machine Learning. CRC Press, Boca Raton, FL (2010)

11. Khosravi, A., Nahavandi, S., Creighton, D. and Atiya, A.F.: A Comprehensive Review of Neural Network-based Prediction Intervals and New Advances. IEEE Trans. on Neural Networks, (2011)

12. Koza, J.R.: Genetic Programming: On the Programming of Computers by Means of Natural Selection. The MIT Press, Cambridge, MA (1992)

13. Lauretto, M.S., Nakano, F., Pereira, C.A.B. and Stern, J.M.: Hierarchical Forecasting with Polynomial Nets, In: Nakamatsu,K. et al. (eds.) Proc. New Advances in Intelligent Decision Technologies, pp.305–315, Springer, Berlin (2009)

14. Nikolaev, N.Y. and Iba, H.: Adaptive Learning of Polynomial Networks: Genetic Programming, Backpropagation and Bayesian Learning. Springer, New York (2006)

15. Nix, D.A. and Weigend, A.S.: Estimating the Mean and Variance of the Target Probability Distribution. In: Proc. of the IEEE Int. Conf. on Neural Networks (IEEE-ICNN'94). pp.55–60. IEEE Press (1994)

16. Papadopoulos, G., Edwards, P.J. and Murray, A.F.: Confidence Estimation Methods for Neural Networks: A Practical Comparison. IEEE Trans. on Neural Networks 12, N:6, 1278–1287 (2001)

17. Pearlmutter, B.A.: Fast Exact Multiplication by the Hessian. Neural Computation 6, N:2, 147–160 (1994)

18. Rivals, I. and Personnaz, L.: Construction of Confidence Intervals for Neural Networks Based on Least Squares Estimation. Neural Networks 13, 463–484 (2000)

19. Rumelhart, D.E., Hinton, G.E., and Williams, R.J.: Learning Internal Representations by Error Propagation, In: Rumelhart, D., and McClelland, J. (eds.) Parallel Distributed Processing: Explorations in the Microstructure of Cognition. vol.1, 318–362 The MIT Press, Cambridge, MA (1986)

20. Seber, G.A.F. and Wild, C.: Nonlinear Regression. Wiley, New York, NY (1989)

21. Tibshirani, R.: A Comparison of Some Error Estimates for Neural Network Models. Neural Computation 8, N:1, 152–163 (1996)

Part II
Reliable Knowledge Discovery Methods

Chapter 4
Robust-Diagnostic Regression: A Prelude for Inducing Reliable Knowledge from Regression

Abdul Awal Md. Nurunnabi, and Honghua Dai

Abstract Regression lies heart in statistics, it is the one of the most important branch of multivariate techniques available for extracting knowledge in almost every field of study and research. Nowadays, it has drawn a huge interest to perform the tasks with different fields like machine learning, pattern recognition and data mining. Investigating outlier (exceptional) is a century long problem to the data analyst and researchers. Blind application of data could have dangerous consequences and leading to discovery of meaningless patterns and carrying to the imperfect knowledge. As a result of digital revolution and the growth of the Internet and Intranet data continues to be accumulated at an exponential rate and thereby importance of detecting outliers and study their costs and benefits as a tool for reliable knowledge discovery claims perfect attention. Investigating outliers in regression has been paid great value for the last few decades within two frames of thoughts in the name of robust regression and regression diagnostics. Robust regression first wants to fit a regression to the majority of the data and then to discover outliers as those points that possess large residuals from the robust output whereas in regression diagnostics one first finds the outliers, delete/correct them and then fit the regular data by classical (usual) methods. At the beginning there seems to be much confusion but now the researchers reach to the consensus, robustness and diagnostics are two complementary approaches to the analysis of data and any one is not good enough. In this chapter, we discuss both of them under the unique spectrum of regression diagnostics. Chapter expresses the necessity and views of regression diagnostics as well as presents several contemporary methods through numerical examples in linear regression within each aforesaid category together with current challenges and

Abdul Awal Md. Nurunnabi
SLG, Department of Statistics, University of Rajshahi, Rajshahi-6205, Bangladesh
e-mail: pyal1471@yahoo.com

Honghua Dai
Deakin University, 221 Burwood Highway, Burwood, Melbourne, VIC 3125, Australia,
email: honghua.dai@deakin.edu.au

possible future research directions. Our aim is to make the chapter self-explained maintaining its general accessibility.

4.1 Introduction

Out of the myriad of multivariate techniques available for the investigation of knowledge in almost every branch of study, regression analysis is an important statistical technique that is routinely applied. Chatterjee and Hadi (2006) mentioned, It is appealing because it provides a conceptually simple method for investigating functional relationship among observed variables. The standard approach in regression analysis is to take data, fit a model, and then evaluating the fit using various statistics. Ordinary least squares (OLS) method is the most popular estimation technique in regression, but the presence of unusual observations could make huge interactive problems in estimation and inference from OLS. Unusual observations may unduly influence the results of the analysis, and their presence may be a signal that a regression model fails to capture important characteristics of the data. These unusual observations are known by many names: abnormal data, anomaly, intrusion, irregular observation, misuse, noise, novelty, outlier, rarity, surprise, unusual event, etc. to the scientific community. We choose outlier in this chapter for its wide range of acceptance. There are a numerous definitions for outlier that differ in words but indicate the same. Most of the works on outlier detection lies in the field of statistics (Hawkins, 1980; Barnett and Lewis, 1995; Chatterjee and Hadi, 2006); Cook and Weisberg, 1982). Hawkins (1980) definition captures the sprit well, An outlier is an observation that deviates so much from other observations as to arouse suspicions that it was generated by a different mechanism. Knorr et al. (2000) pointed out, Outlier detection is a meaningful and important knowledge discovery task. Robust regression and regression diagnostics are two branches in regression analysis that investigate, detect and deal outliers. According to Huber (1991), Robustness and diagnostics are complementary approaches to the analysis of data, and any one of the two is not good enough. Each views the same problem from the opposite sites with the same objectives. Rousseeuw and Leroy (2003) mentioned that the purpose of robustness is to safeguard against deviations from the assumption and the purpose of diagnostics is to find and identify deviation from the assumptions. In this chapter, we give a meaningful short description of robust regression and regression diagnostics methods, and their importance for inducing reliable knowledge discovery through several numerical demonstrations.

The materials of the chapter are arranged as follows. Section 2 presents some background information of reliable knowledge discovery; Section 3 gives the basic ideas about linear regression, OLS and outliers; in Section 4, we make short description about robustness and on several popular robust regression methods with a numerical demonstration. Section 5 contains the idea of regression diagnostics, and some popular diagnostic methods, it demonstrates the performance of the methods through two well-referred datasets. Section 6 concludes this chapter and presents directions for further work.

4.2 Background of Reliable Knowledge Discovery

Berry et al. (1997) defined, Data mining is the exploration and analysis, by automatic or semiautomatic means, of large quantities of data in order to discover meaningful patterns and rules. It involves interdisciplinary research encompassing diverse domains (e. g., machine learning, statistics, and databases (Elder and Pregibon, 1995; Mannila, 1996). As the evolution of data mining has matured, it is widely accepted to be a single phase in a larger life cycle known as Knowledge Discovery in Databases (KDD). The KDD in databases process was defined by many, for instance, Fayyad et al. (1996) expressed it as "the nontrivial process of identifying valid, novel, potentially useful, and ultimately understandable patterns in data". The goal of knowledge discovery is to obtain useful knowledge from large collections of data. This task is inherently interactive and iterative: one can not expect to extract useful knowledge simply by putting a huge amount of data into a black box. Data mining can be considered as the central step of the overall KDD process. The additional steps (see Figure 17.1) in the KDD process, such as data preparation, data selection, data cleaning, incorporation of appropriate prior knowledge, and proper interpretation of the results of mining ensure that useful knowledge is derived from the data. Fayyad et al. (1996) pointed out Blind application of data mining methods can be dangerous activity leading to discovery of meaningless patterns.

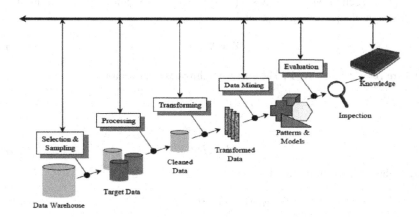

Fig. 4.1: The traditional KDD paradigm (Collier et al., 1998)

Over the last two decades, a multitude of data mining techniques has been devised for the discovery of knowledge in databases. A big question is; can we always rely on the knowledge that are discovered by a data mining system unconditionally? It is evident that the answer is obviously not; even in certain cases the discovered knowledge is incorrect and misleading. To achieve a successful application of data mining, it is essential to make sure that the discovered knowledge is valid (Dai. 2006). Therefore, it is necessary to find out and study the reliability issues: (see Berka, 1997; Dai, 2006, 2008, 2010; Feng et al., 2006) (i) when we can trust the discovered knowledge? (ii) what are the factors that affect the reliability of the discovery? (iii) how the factors affect the reliability? (iv) how can we make sure that the discovered knowledge is reliable? and (v) what are the conditions under which a discovered knowledge is assured as reliable? Researchers, developers and practitioners are interested in these reliability issues have been meeting since the first international workshop on reliability issues in knowledge discovery (RIKD) in 2006.

4.3 Linear Regression, OLS and Outliers

The customary linear regression model is

$$Y = X\beta + \varepsilon \tag{4.1}$$

where Y is an $n \times 1$ vector of response (continuous) variable, X is an $n \times k (k = p + 1)$ full rank matrix formed by p explanatory variables with a constant term, β is a $k \times 1$ unknown vector of finite parameters and ε is an $n \times 1$ vector of i.i.d. random disturbances each of which follows $N(0, \sigma^2)$. The OLS method wants to minimize the error sum of squares via the model

$$\hat{Y} = X\hat{\beta} \tag{4.2}$$

where $\hat{\beta} = (X^T X)^{-1} X^T Y$. The corresponding residual vector,

$$e = Y - \hat{Y} = (I - H)Y \tag{4.3}$$

$$= (I - H)\varepsilon \tag{4.4}$$

with the variance of e given by

$$var(e) = \sigma^2 (I - H) \tag{4.5}$$

where

$$H = X(X^T X)^{-1} X^T Y \tag{4.6}$$

is the leverage/prediction matrix. In scalar form, i-th residual is

$$e_i = \varepsilon_i - \sum_{j=1}^{n} h_{ij}\varepsilon_j, i = 1, 2, ..., n \qquad (4.7)$$

where h_{ij} is the ij-th element of H. Clearly if the h_{ij} are sufficiently small, e_i will serve as a reasonable alternative of ε_i. The OLS is traditionally used for fitting linear regression models mainly because of its computational simplicity and for having some optimal properties under certain underlying assumptions. Violation of these assumptions, particularly the so called implicit assumption that all observations are equally reliable and should have an equal role in determining the least squares results and influencing conclusions (Chatterjee and Hadi, 1988), destroys the OLS results. Researchers often see some observations in a dataset are atypical from the majority of the data and consider as unusual. It is well-showed in literature that unusual observations are often considered as errors, they may carry important information. In regression, generally unusual observations categorize into three: outliers, high leverage points and influential observations. Outliers can deviate as follows: (see Figure 17.2), (i) the change in the direction of response variable (outlier in y-direction but not a leverage point is called vertical outlier) generally measured by absolute magnitude of scaled residuals of the observation, (ii) the deviation in the space of explanatory variable(s), deviated points in x-direction called high leverage points (leverage points are two types: (a) good leverage points, if (x_i, y_i) does fit the linear relation, it improves the precession of the regression coefficient and (b) bad leverage points, cases for which an x_i is far away from the bulk of the x_i, do not fit linear relationship) (iii) the other is change in both the directions (direction of the explanatory variable(s) and the direction of the response variable). According to Belsley et al. (1980), Influential observation is one which either individual or together with several other observations has a demonstrably larger impact on the calculated values of various estimates (coefficients, standard errors, t-values, etc.) than is the case for most of the other observations.

4.4 Robustness and Robust Regression

Box (1953) coined the technical term robust only in 1950s, and the subject matter acquired recognition as a legitimate topic for investigation only in mid-sixties, mainly due to the pioneer works of Tukey (1960, 1962), Huber (1964, 1981), Hampel (1968), Hampel et al. (1986) and Maronna et al. (2006). Many assumptions commonly made in statistics (such as normality, linearity, and independence) are at most approximations to reality. A minor error in the mathematical model should cause only a small error in the final conclusions, but it does not always true. Some of the most common statistical procedures are excessively sensitive to seemingly minor deviations from the assumptions. One reason is the occurrence of gross errors, such as copying or keypunch errors. They usually show up as outliers and are dangerous for many statistical procedures. Other reasons behind deviations from initialized model assumptions include the empirical characters of many models and the

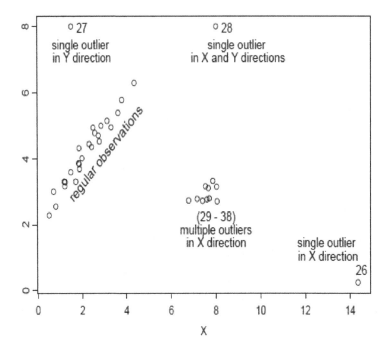

Fig. 4.2: Scatter plot of the simulated dataset (Table 1); assigned outliers in different locations

approximate characters of many theoretical models. The problem with the theories of classical parametric statistics is that they derive optimal procedures under exact parametric models, but say nothing about their behaviors (e. g., stability) when the models are only approximately valid. In this regards, robust statistics try to study with optimality and stability both the mutually complementary characteristics in the same study. It is concerned with evaluating and improving the stability of estimation techniques when data points are deviated from assumptions. Hampel et al. (1986) expressed, Robust statistics, as a collection of related theories, is the statistics of approximate parametric models. In a broad informal sense, robust statistics is a body of knowledge, partly formalized into theories of robustness, relating to deviations from idealized assumptions in statistics. In regression, lack of stability of the least squares (LS) estimation is not the only serious problem for estimating the parameters but also for the lack of normality assumptions on error terms, we cannot test the reliability of the estimated parameters by using the common test procedures like t, F or chi-squares and therefore, we cannot check the model adequacy. That is why we depend on robust regression that possesses some stability in variance and bias under deviation from the regression model. In robust statistics one seeks new estimation and test techniques that are rather insensitive to, or robust against, certain type of failures in the parametric model. So good estimates are obtained even in some assumptions are only approximately true. A robust regression first wants to fit a regression to the majority of the data and then to discover the outliers as those points that possess large residuals from the robust output. Hence, the goal of robust regression is to safeguard against deviation from the assumptions of the classical least squares. A number of software packages like S-plus, R, SAS, PROGRESS are available for performing different types of robust regression. Several most commonly used robust regression methods are as follows.

4.4.1 Least Median of Squares Regression

Least median of squares (LMS) was proposed by Hampel (1975) and further developed by Rousseeuw (1984). Instead of minimizing the sum of squared residuals, Rousseeuw proposed minimizing their median as follows:

$$minimize_\beta\, med_i e_i^2. \tag{4.8}$$

This estimator effectively trims almost the $n/2$ observations having the largest residuals, and uses the maximal residual value in the remaining set as the criterion to be minimized. Its breakdown point is $((\lfloor n/2 \rfloor - p + 2)/n)$ for p-dimensional dataset i.e. it attains maximum possible breakdown point (Huber, 1981) $1/n$ at usual models, but unfortunately it possesses poor asymptotic efficiency. In spite of that the family of LMS has excellent global robustness.

4.4.2 Least Trimmed Squares Regression

Least trimmed squares (LTS) regression was introduced by Rousseeuw (1984) and is given by

$$minimize_\beta \sum_i^k e_{i:n}^2. \tag{4.9}$$

where $e_{k:n}^2 \leq ... \leq e_{n:n}^2$ denotes the ordered squared residuals and h is to be chosen between $n/2$ and n. The LTS estimators search for the optimal subset of size h whose least squares fit has the smallest sum of squares residuals. Hence, the LTS estimate of β is then the least square estimate of that subset of size . For the data come from continuous distribution, breakdown point of LTS is equal to $minimum(n - h + 1, h - p + 1)/n$, we have $h = (n + p + 1)/2$, yields the maximum breakdown point, whereas $h = n$ gives the ordinary least squares with breakdown point $= 1/n$. LTS has the properties: affine equivariance and asymptotic normality. Its influence function (Hampel et al., 1986) is bounded for both (response and

explanatory variables) the vertical outliers and bad leverage points. LTS has better statistical efficiency than LMS, because of its asymptotically normal property
(Hossjer, 1994), whereas LMS has a lower convergence rate (Rousseeuw, 1984).
This also makes the LTS more suitable than the LMS as a starting point for two-step
estimators such as the MM-estimators (Yohai, 1987) and generalized M-estimators
(Simpson et al., 1992, Cookley and Hettmansperger, 1993). It also fails to fit a correct model when large number of clustered outliers exits and with more than 50%
outliers in the data. The performance of this method has recently been improved by
the FAST-LTS (Rousseeuw and Van Driessen, 1999) and Fast and robust bootstrap
for LTS (Willems and Aelst, 2004).

4.4.3 Reweighted Least Squares Regression

Reweighted least squares (RLS) regression was developed by Rousseeuw and Leroy
(2003) in order to improve on the crude LMS and LTS solutions, and to obtain
standard quantities like $t-$values, confidence intervals, and the like. We can apply
a weighted least squares analysis based on the identification of the outliers. For
instance, we could make use of the following weights:

$$w_i = \begin{cases} 0 \ if |e_i/\hat{\sigma}| > 2.5 \\ 1 \ if |e_i/\hat{\sigma}| \leq 2.5 \end{cases} \tag{4.10}$$

This means simply that case-i will be retained in the weighted LS, if its LMS
residual is small to moderate. The bound 2.5 is, of course, arbitrary, but quite reasonable because in a Gaussian situation xthere will be very few residuals larger than
2.5 $\hat{\sigma}$. We then apply weighted least squares defined by

$$minimum \sum_{i=1}^{n} w_i e_i^2 \tag{4.11}$$

4.4.4 Robust M (GM)- Estimator

In regression, Huber (1973) introduced M-estimator that he developed in 1964 to
estimate location parameter robustly. Robust M-estimators attempt to limit the influence of outliers and based on the idea of replacing the squared residuals (e_i^2) used
in OLS estimation with less rapidly increasing loss-function (Huber, 1981; Hampel
et al., 1986) of the data value and parameter estimate, yielding minimize $\sum_{i=1}^{n} \rho(e_i)$,
where ρ is a symmetric, positive-definite function generally with a unique minimum
at zero. Differentiating this expression with respect to the regression coefficients,

$$\sum_{i=1}^{n} \psi(e_i)x_i = 0 \tag{4.12}$$

where ψ is the derivative of ρ, whose normalized form is called the influence function that measures the influence of an observation on the value of the parameter estimate. It has two drawbacks: (i) estimators are not equivariant (in many cases the nature of the observations is such that changing the units of measurement should have the conclusion unaltered) and (ii) finite breakdown point is $1/n$ due to outlying x_i. To remove these demerits Mallows (1975) suggested,

$$\sum_{i=1}^{n} w(x_i)\psi(e_i/\hat{S})x_i = 0. \tag{4.13}$$

where σ is estimated simultaneously by $\hat{S}$ and later some authors proposed some variants of this form, but nobody was able to attain maximum possible breakdown point.

4.4.5 Example

We simulate a dataset in simple linear regression for the understanding about outliers and to see the consequences of outlier on OLS fit. We generate 25 observations from the model

$$Y = \beta_0 + \beta_1 X + \varepsilon. \tag{4.14}$$

where $x_i \sim$ Uniform $(0.5, 4.5)$ and $y_i = 2 + x_i + \varepsilon_i$, where $\varepsilon_i \sim N(0,0.2); i = 1,2,...,25$. To create outliers, we generate cases 26 (14.345, 0.243), 27 (1.5, 8.0) and 28 (8, 8) as single outliers, and 10 multiple outliers (cases 29-38) in X-direction, where $X \sim N(7.5, 0.3)$ and $Y \sim N(3.0, 0.3)$. Figure 1(scatter plot, Y versus X) shows the indications of outliers (single and multiple) and regular observations in different locations. We now apply the OLS method for the cases (126), where case 26 is the only outlier and we get the fitted model

$$\hat{Y} = 4.357 - 0.137X. \tag{4.15}$$

Validations of the parameters are shown in Table 2. Coefficient of determination, $R^2 = 0.0798 \approx 8\%$ (approximately) that sufficiently proves the insignificant performance of the OLS method in presence of just a single outlier. Moreover, residuals normal quantile-quantile (QQ) plot (Gnanadesikan and Wilk, 1968; Figure 3) shows residuals are non-normal, which means one of the OLS assumptions is violated and this method is not suitable for the dataset until the outlier is eliminated or refitted (if necessary). We know in prior, observation 26 is an outlier; we discard the observation and again apply OLS method. Now, we have the fitted model of the regular 25 cases

$$\hat{Y} = 2.044 + 0.975X. \tag{4.16}$$

It shows finds that the estimated parameters in Eq. (4.15) with case 26 (outlier) and in Eq. (4.16) without outlier are significantly different (justifications are in Table 2). We get the value of the coefficient of determination, $R^2 = 0.9502 \approx 95\%$ in absence of the outlier. Figure 2 shows that the OLS lines are in reverse directions in presence of outlier and without the outlier. We apply here robust LTS method for all 26 cases and see that (Figure 17.3) the LTS (robust) fitted line is almost similar as OLS without the outlying case 26. Hence the demonstration of using robust regression proves that typical LS method is not fit for finding reliable knowledge and to make proper decision.

Index	Y	X	Index	Y	X	Index	Y	X
1	3.680859	1.8748195	14	5.381036	3.6301985	27	8.000000	1.5000000
2	2.282518	0.5066858	15	6.290366	4.3419400	28	8.000000	8.0000000
3	4.991353	2.8542301	16	4.517831	2.7760444	29	2.700177	8.0512198
4	3.587328	1.4827927	17	3.000189	0.6998121	30	3.314881	7.8576621
5	3.298528	1.1900892	18	4.005830	1.9888573	31	3.152737	7.5295289
6	2.547192	0.8071130	19	4.931645	2.4862063	32	3.138253	8.0276155
7	3.854897	1.8313971	20	3.286396	1.2316987	33	2.722638	6.7764856
8	5.775769	3.7972150	21	3.834744	1.8572683	34	2.785257	7.7028700
9	3.157755	1.2113028	22	4.772236	2.5719365	35	2.758155	7.5938326
10	4.941136	3.3149569	23	4.313283	1.8537475	36	2.714485	7.3922135
11	4.698342	2.7280090	24	5.138678	3.1375774	37	3.095817	7.6601113
12	4.349434	2.4213998	25	4.437982	2.3044582	38	2.771519	7.1580103
13	3.298488	1.7095037	26	0.243000	14.345000			

Table 4.1: Simulated dataset

	OLS results with outlier				OLS results without outlier			
Variables	Coefficients	Std. error	t-value	p-value	Coefficients	Std. error	t-value	p-value
Intercept	4.387	0.347	12.651	0.000	2.044	0.112	18.342	0.000
X	-0.137	0.095	-1.442	0.162	0.975	0.047	20.944	0.000
	R2=0.0798; F=2.081				R2=0.9502; F=438.6			

Table 4.2: OLS results (with and without outlier)

Hence the demonstration of using robust regression proves that typical LS method is not fit for finding reliable knowledge and to make proper decision. Though robust regression techniques give us better results as an alternative of OLS,

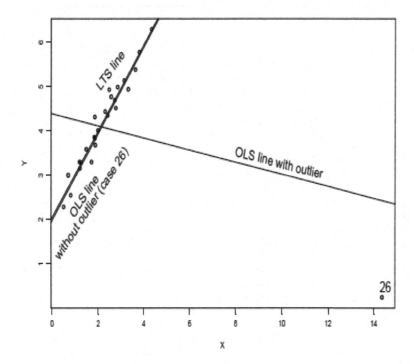

Fig. 4.3: Scatter plot Y versus X, OLS fitted lines with and without outliers, and LTS (robust) line in presence of outlier

they have some major drawbacks. The diversity of estimator types and the necessary choices of tuning constants are combined with a lack of guidance for these decisions. The lack of simple procedures for inference or reluctance to use the straight forward inference based on asymptotic procedure. We need to take some necessary help from the re-sampling techniques like bootstrapping (Efron and Tibshirani, 1993) especially for small samples. Robust techniques have unfamiliarity with interpretation of results from a robust analysis.

4.5 Regression Diagnostics

Regression diagnostics is more popular because it is relatively easy to interpret results than robust regression that is a complementary approach to deal with unusual cases in regression. Fox (1993) mentioned, Regression diagnostics are techniques for exploring problems that compromise a regression analysis and for determining whether certain assumptions appear reasonable. Field diagnostics is a combination

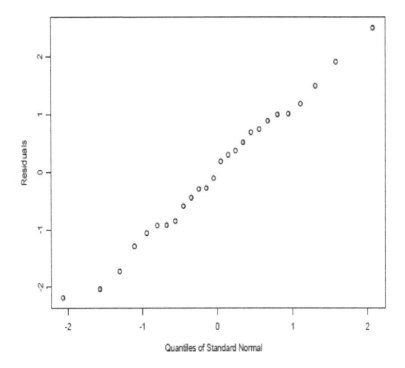

Fig. 4.4: Residuals normal QQ plot

of graphical and numerical tools. It is designed to detect and delete/refit (if necessary) the outliers first and then to fit the good data by classical (least squares) methods. The basic building blocks of regression diagnostics are different versions of residuals and leverage values. The usual regression outputs clearly do not tell the whole story about the cause and/or effect of deviations from the assumptions of the model building process. Regression diagnostic can serve as the identification purpose of the deviations from the assumptions. So that basic need of regression diagnostics is to identify the unusual observations in a data set. Outliers are generally identified by measuring the residual vector. Chatterjee and Hadi (1988) pointed that the ordinary residuals are not appropriate for diagnostic purpose and a transformed/scaled version of them is preferable. Since the approximate average variance of a residual is estimated by MSres (mean squared residuals), a logical scaling for the residuals is the standardized residuals

$$e_i^* = \frac{e_i}{\sqrt{MS_{res}}}, i = 1, 2, ..., n \tag{4.17}$$

which have mean zero and approximate variance equal to one, consequently a large standardized residual potentially indicate an outlier. Since the residuals have different variances and are correlated, the variance of the i-th residual is

$$V(e_i) = \sigma^2(1 - h_{ii}) \tag{4.18}$$

where σ is an estimate of MS_{res} and

$$h_{ii} = x_i^T(X^TX)^{-1}x_i, i = 1, 2, ..., n. \tag{4.19}$$

is the i-th diagonal element of H. Daniel and Wood (1971) introduced a type of (*i*-th internally Studentized) residual

$$r_i = \frac{e_i}{\hat{\sigma}\sqrt{1 - h_{ii}}}, i = 1, 2, ..., n \tag{4.20}$$

where $\sigma = \hat{\sigma}_{(-i)}\sqrt{1 - h_{ii}}$. This is also known as Pearsons standardized residual. Many authors think that internally Studentized residuals are over estimated by the extreme observations and they suggested the i-th externally Studentized residuals as the better choice (e.g. Atkinson, 1981),

$$r_i^* = \frac{e_i}{\hat{\sigma}_{(-i)}\sqrt{1 - h_{ii}}}, i = 1, 2, ..., n \tag{4.21}$$

where $\sigma_i = \hat{\sigma}_{-i}\sqrt{1 - h_{ii}}$, $\hat{\sigma}_{-i}$ is the residual mean squared error estimate when the i-th observation is omitted. Ellenberg (1976) stated that i-th observation to be declared as outlier if

$$r_i^* \geq t_{n-k-1}^{\alpha/2}, i = 1, 2, ..., n \tag{4.22}$$

where $t_{n-k-1}^{\alpha/2}$ is the upper $\alpha/2$ quantile of the t-distribution with $n - k - 1$ degrees of freedom. The scaled residuals, especially externally Studentized residual overall performs well, but it is well-evident that (Chatterjee and Hadi, 2006; Nurunnabi 2008) none of them can successfully identify multiple outliers due to masking and swamping phenomena. According to Hadi and Simonoff (1993), masking occurs when an outlying subset goes undetected because of the presence of another, usually adjacent, subset. Swamping occurs when good observations are incorrectly identified as outliers because of the presence of another, usually remote, subset of observations. We need group deleted version of residuals which are not affected by masking and swamping problems. In general, observations corresponding to excessively large values of h_{ii} are treated as high leverage points (outliers in the X space). A suitable empirical rule is to declare the i-th observation as a high leverage point if

$$h_{ii} \geq ck/n, i = 1, 2, ..., n. \tag{4.23}$$

where c is a constant such as 2, 2.5, or 3 (Hoaglin and Welsch, 1978; Huber, 1981; Vellman and Welsch, 1981).

To introduce with the group deleted version of residuals and leverage values, we put here the following measures for identifying multiple outliers and high leverage points (for better understanding, see Hadi, 1992; Imon, 2005). The group deleted residual (Imon, 2005) is defined as

$$
r^*_{i(R)} = \begin{cases} \dfrac{e_{i(R)}}{\hat{\sigma}_{(R)}\sqrt{1-h_{ii(R)}}}, & i \in R \\[3mm] \dfrac{e_{i(R)}}{\hat{\sigma}_{(R)}\sqrt{1+h_{ii(R)}}}, & i \notin R \end{cases} \tag{4.24}
$$

where

$$
e_{i(R)} = y_i - y_{i(R)} = y_i - x_i^T \hat{\beta}_{(R)} \tag{4.25}
$$

where $\hat{\beta}_{(R)} = (X_{(R)}^T X_{(R)})^{-1} X_{(R)}^T Y_{(R)}$; $X_{(R)}$ and $Y_{(R)}$ are the X and Y matrices after deleting the suspect group of outliers. The i-th diagonal element of the group deleted leverage matrix is

$$
h_{ii(R)} = x_i^T (X_{(R)}^T X_{(R)})^{-1} x_i, i = 1, 2, ... n \tag{4.26}
$$

The group deleted version of leverage values (Imon, 2005) are

$$
h^*_{i(R)} = \begin{cases} \dfrac{h_{ii(R)}}{1-h_{ii(R)}}, & i \in R \\[3mm] \dfrac{h_{ii(R)}}{1+h_{ii(R)}}, & i \notin R \end{cases} \tag{4.27}
$$

The i-th observation would be treated as an outlier if

$$
r^*_{i(R)} \geq median(r^*_{i(R)}) \pm 3 \times MAD(r^*_{i(R)}), i = 1, 2, ..., n \tag{4.28}
$$

and the i-th observation would be considered as a high leverage point if

$$
h^*_{ii(R)} \geq median(h^*_{ii(R)}) \pm 3 \times MAD(h^*_{ii(R)}), i = 1, 2, ..., n \tag{4.29}
$$

Besides the above leverage measures, different distance and cluster measures (see for example, Mahalanobis, 1936; Maronna and Zamar, 2002; Pena and Prieto, 2001; Rousseeuw and van Zomeren, 1990) are introduced for identifying high leverage points. It is to be noted that an outlier or a leverage point is not necessarily an influential observation and the converse is also true, that is an influential observation may not be an outlier or a leverage point. A multitude of influence measures is available in the literature; see, for example, Atkinson and Riani (2000), Belsley et al. (1980), Cook (1977, 1979, 1986), Cook and Weisberg (1982), Chatterjee and Hadi (1986, 1988, 2006), Hadi (1992), Nurunnabi et al. (2011). Cooks distance (Cook 1977) is one of the most popular influence measures defined as

$$
C_i^2 = \frac{(\hat{\beta} - \hat{\beta}_{(-i)})^T (X^T X)(\hat{\beta} - \hat{\beta}_{(-i)})}{k\hat{\sigma}^2}, i = 1, 2, ..., n \tag{4.30}
$$

where $\hat{\beta}_{(-i)}$ is the estimated parameter vector without the i−th observation, $\hat{\sigma}^2$ is the estimated error variance. Cooks distance in Eq. 4.30 can be expressed by standardized Pearsons residuals and leverage values as

$$C_i^2 = \frac{r^2 h_{ii}}{k(1 - h_{ii})}, i = 1, 2, ..., n \tag{4.31}$$

Cook (1977) suggests that observations with

$$C_i^2 \geq F_{k,n-k}^{0.5} \tag{4.32}$$

are declared influential observations, where $F_{k,n-k}^{0.5}$ is point of the F distribution with k and n-k degrees of freedom. From our experience, which is also supported by the example in subsection 5.1, this cut-off value, in particular, is not appropriate because they are inconsistent with the pattern of points in the corresponding graphs. We are with the views of Hadi (1992), according to him, Cut-off points should be used with caution. Diagnostic methods are not designed to be (and should not be used as) formal tests of hypotheses. They are designed to detect observations which influence regression results more than other observations in a data set. Thus the values of a given diagnostic measure should be compared to each other. This can best be done using graphical displays ... What matters here is the pattern of points in a plot and the relative value of the measure. Welsch and Kuh (1977) suggested an influence measure

$$WK_i = \frac{|x_i^T (\hat{\beta} - \hat{\beta}_{(-i)})|}{\hat{\sigma}_{(-i)} \sqrt{h_{ii}}} = |r_i^*| \sqrt{\frac{h_{ii}}{1 - h_{ii}}} \tag{4.33}$$

Points with

$$WK_i \geq \sqrt{k/(n-k)}, i = 1, 2, ..., n \tag{4.34}$$

are declared as influential observations (Belsley et al., 1980). We believe that a more appropriate cut-off point for the WK_i is obtained by substituting Eqs. (22) and (23) in Eq. [?] and it is

$$WK_i \geq t_{n-k-1}^{\alpha/2} \sqrt{ck/(n-ck)}, i = 1, 2, ..., n \tag{4.35}$$

Belsley et al. (1980) called Welsch-Kuhs distance as difference of fits (DFFITS), because it can be expressed as a scaled difference between $\hat{y}$ and $\hat{y}_{(-i)}$. These two above influence measures are based on single case deletion. It is well-evident that single case deletion measures are affected by masking and swamping. But the reality is that hardly ever datasets contain just a single observation (see Atkinson, 1986). To circumvent the problem of masking and swamping there are a number of robust regression methods and group deletion measures are in regression diagnostics. Most of them are computationally intensive, hence not suitable especially for large datasets. We make a brief description of a most recent group deletion influence measure here. Nurunnabi et al. (2011) proposed a two-step group deletion measure. First, they supposed to identify a subset of observations which are suspect of being outliers, high leverage, and/or influential observations. This subset can be obtained in various ways. For example, they can be supplied by the data analyst or we can view the data as a multivariate and apply any reasonably efficient multivariate outlier detection method to identify outliers in the multivariate data. For convenience, the authors preferred the BACON approach (Billor et al., 2000), although they also advised others methods for the identification of multivariate outliers. Nurunnabi et al. (2011) algorithm is in brief as follows.

d observations among a set of n observations are suspected as influential observations, a set of cases remaining in the analysis is R and a set of cases deleted is D. Hence without loss of generality, assume that these observations are the last d rows of X and Y so that

$$X = \begin{bmatrix} X_R \\ X_D \end{bmatrix} Y = \begin{bmatrix} Y_R \\ Y_D \end{bmatrix}, .$$ After formation of the deletion set indexed by D, compute the fitted values $\hat{Y}^{(-D)}$. Let $\hat{\beta}^{(-D)}$ be the corresponding vector of estimated coefficients when a group of observations indexed by D is omitted. We define the vector of difference between $\hat{y}_j^{(-D)}$ and $\hat{y}_{j(i)}^{(-D)}$ as

$$t_{(i)}^{(-D)} = (\hat{y}_1^{(-D)} - \hat{y}_{1(i)}^{(-D)}, ..., (\hat{y}_n^{(-D)} - \hat{y}_{n(i)}^{(-D)})^T \tag{4.36}$$

$$= (t_{1(i)}^{(-D)}, ..., t_{n(i)}^{(-D)})^T \tag{4.37}$$

and

$$t_{j(i)}^{(-D)} = \hat{y}_j^{(-D)} - \hat{y}_{j(i)}^{(-D)} = \frac{h_{ji} e_i^{(-D)}}{1 - h_{ii}}, \qquad j = 1, 2, ..., n. \tag{4.38}$$

where $h_{ji} = x_j^T (X^T X)^{-1} x_i$ and $e_i^{(-D)} = y_i - \hat{y}_i^{(-D)}$.

Finally, authors introduced the measure as squared standardized norm,

$$M_i = \frac{t_{(i)}^{(-D)^T} t_{(i)}^{(-D)}}{k V(\hat{y}_i^{(-D)})}, \qquad i = 1, 2, ..., n. \tag{4.39}$$

where $V(\hat{y}_i^{(-D)}) = s^2 h_{ii}$ and $s^2 = \frac{e^{(-D)^T} e^{(-D)}}{n-k}$.

Using Eqs. [?] to ([?]), finally the measure was defined as

$$M_i = \frac{1}{k s^2 h_{ii}} \sum_{i=1}^n h_{ji}^2 \frac{e_i^{(-D)^2}}{(1 - h_{ii})^2}. \tag{4.40}$$

The statistic considers the i-th observation to be an influential if it satisfies the rule

$$|M_i| \geq median(M_i) + 4.5 MAD(M_i), \qquad i = 1, 2, ..., n. \tag{4.41}$$

4.5.1 Examples

To see the performance of the diagnostics measures, we consider two well-known datasets from the regression literature.

Index	$\lvert r_i^* \rvert$ (2.015)	$r_{i(R)}^*$ (-0.444, 0.490)	h_{ii} (0.085)	$h_{ii(R)}$ (0.191)	Index	$\lvert r_i^* \rvert$ (2.015)	$r_{i(R)}^*$ (-0.444, 0.490)	h_{ii} (0.085)	$h_{ii(R)}$ (0.191)
1	0.431	0.135	0.022	0.028	25	0.065	0.054	0.023	0.027
2	1.522	0.118	0.037	0.078	26	-0.546	-0.109	0.024	0.025
3	-0.182	0.148	0.022	0.077	27	-0.641	0.023	0.021	0.058
4	1.522	0.118	0.037	0.078	28	-0.147	0.013	0.023	0.027
5	0.308	0.195	0.021	0.052	29	-1.187	0.002	0.023	0.111
6	0.914	0.122	0.027	0.031	30	1.389	0.768	0.198	0.650
7	-1.027	0.358	0.078	0.416	31	-1.009	-0.150	0.023	0.027
8	0.656	-0.056	0.039	0.086	32	0.342	-0.104	0.037	0.078
9	0.961	0.371	0.022	0.077	33	0.473	0.051	0.026	0.029
10	0.235	0.098	0.022	0.028	34	1.906	0.816	0.194	0.645
11	0.744	0.704	0.194	0.645	35	-1.272	-0.026	0.023	0.102
12	0.872	0.149	0.025	0.026	36	1.347	0.015	0.046	0.135
13	0.857	0.088	0.029	0.036	37	0.319	-0.072	0.034	0.059
14	-2.035	0.084	0.044	0.266	38	0.473	0.051	0.026	0.029
15	-1.375	-0.115	0.021	0.058	39	0.462	-0.045	0.034	0.059
16	-0.689	-0.136	0.024	0.025	40	1.092	0.190	0.025	0.026
17	-2.049	-0.167	0.023	0.102	41	-0.646	-0.082	0.023	0.027
18	-1.427	-0.272	0.024	0.025	42	0.188	-0.004	0.026	0.029
19	-1.576	-0.083	0.023	0.102	43	0.727	0.041	0.031	0.044
20	1.065	0.736	0.194	0.645	44	0.688	0.091	0.026	0.029
21	-1.151	-0.074	0.021	0.058	45	1.135	0.059	0.036	0.071
22	-1.450	-0.129	0.021	0.058	46	0.046	-0.031	0.026	0.029
23	-0.980	-0.191	0.024	0.025	47	-0.834	-0.163	0.024	0.025
24	-0.156	-0.116	0.030	0.040					

Table 4.3: Diagnostic measures (outliers and leverage points) for the Hertzsprung-Russel Diagram data. Measures exceeding their cutoff values (below the measure) are boldfaced.

4.5.1.1 Hertzsprung-Russel Diagram Data

The Hertzsprung-Rusell Diagram (HRD) data is a well-referred dataset, which is taken from Rousseeuw and Leroy (2003). The dataset consists observations about 47 stars and 2 variables (Temperature: logarithm of the effective temperature at the surface of the star and Light: the logarithm of light intensity of the star). On the scatter plot of light intensity versus temperature, shown in Figure 5 (a), four stars (11, 20, 30, and 34), which are known as the giants, are clear outliers and 3 other stars (7,

Index	CD_i (0.704)	WK_i (0.615)	M_i (0.234)	Index	CD_i (0.704)	WK_i (0.615)	M_i (0.234)
1	0.002	0.065	0.056	25	0.000	0.010	0.009
2	0.044	0.300	0.043	26	0.004	0.086	0.037
3	0.000	0.027	0.065	27	0.005	0.095	0.001
4	0.044	0.300	0.043	28	0.000	0.022	0.000
5	0.001	0.045	0.115	29	0.017	0.184	0.000
6	0.012	0.152	0.046	30	0.234	**0.691**	**8.044**
7	0.045	0.299	**0.793**	31	0.012	0.153	0.070
8	0.009	0.131	0.009	32	0.002	0.067	0.033
9	0.010	0.144	**0.409**	33	0.003	0.078	0.008
10	0.001	0.035	0.029	34	0.413	**0.935**	**8.846**
11	0.067	0.365	**6.586**	35	0.019	0.195	0.002
12	0.010	0.140	0.069	36	0.043	0.296	0.000
13	0.011	0.147	0.024	37	0.002	0.060	0.016
14	0.090	0.439	0.032	38	0.003	0.078	0.008
15	0.020	0.203	0.040	39	0.004	0.086	0.006
16	0.006	0.109	0.058	40	0.015	0.175	0.113
17	0.046	0.314	0.081	41	0.005	0.098	0.021
18	0.025	0.226	0.232	42	0.000	0.031	0.000
19	0.028	0.241	0.019	43	0.008	0.129	0.005
20	0.136	0.523	**7.198**	44	0.006	0.113	0.026
21	0.014	0.170	0.016	45	0.024	0.220	0.010
22	0.022	0.214	0.050	46	0.000	0.008	0.003
23	0.012	0.155	0.114	47	0.009	0.132	0.084
24	0.000	0.027	0.042				

Table 4.4: Influence measures for the Hertzsprung-Russel Diagram data. Measures exceeding their cutoff values (below the measure) are boldfaced.

9 and 14) are borderline outliers. The effect of these stars on the least squares line is dramatic. It shows that the light and temperature are negatively correlated! On the contrary, a robust regression (LMS) line has a positive slope. Various influence measures for the HRD data are shown in Table 3. We see externally Studentized residuals (r_i^*) identify only two observations (14 and 17), whereas $r_{i(R)}^*$ identifies four cases (11, 20, 30, and 34) as outliers and masks the two. The leverage values, h_{ii} identify four cases (11, 20, 30, and 34) as high leverage points, whereas $h_{ii(R)}$ identifies six cases (7, 11, 14, 20, 30 and 34) as high leverage points. Table 4 shows that Cooks distance fails to identify any of the influential cases. WKi identifies only two cases (30 and 34). When the BACON algorithm is employed to this data, six observations (7, 11, 14, 20, 30, and 34) are flagged as influential observations. We keep computing for multiple influence measure Mi for the entire data set considering the six (7, 11, 14, 20, 30 and 34) as suspect cases. Finally, we see from Table 4 and Figure 5 that only the group deleted influence measure M_i successfully identifies all six observations as influential.

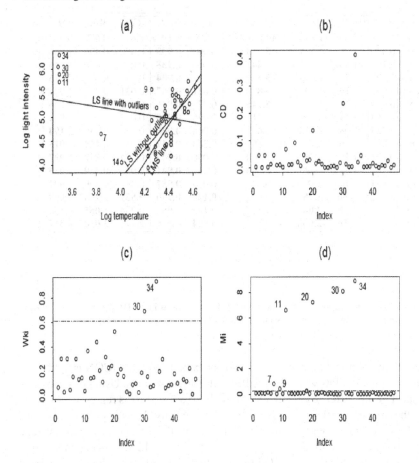

Fig. 4.5: Hertzsprung-Russel Diagram data; (a) Scatter plot with LS lines (with and without outliers) and LMS (robust) line (b) Index plot of Cooks distance (CD) (c) Index plot of WKi (d) Index plot of Mi

4.5.1.2 Hawkins, Bradu and Kass Data

Hawkins et al. (1984) construct a dataset designed to have masking and swamping problems. The dataset consists of 75 observations with 4 variables, one is a response variable and the other three are explanatory variables. It is well-evident that the first 10 observations are high leverage and outliers. The next 4 cases are so-called good leverage points because they are outliers in the space of the explanatory variables but their response values are consistent with the regression model suggested by the remaining 61 (1575) observations. As it can be seen from Table 5, the externally Studentized residual, r_i^*, fails to identify 9 of the 10 regression outliers and, instead, it erroneously identifies four cases (1114) as regression outliers. Consequently, the

Index	$\hat{y}_i$	$|Stdres|$	$|r_i^*|$	$r_{i(R)}^*$	h_{ji}	$h_{ji(R)}$	CD_i	WK_i	M_i
		(2.50)	(1.994)	(-4.144,-4.858)	(0.107)	(0.192)	(0.847)	(0.689)	(0.024)
1	6.320	1.55	1.568	**5.353**	0.063	**0.935**	0.040	0.406	**1.806**
2	6.105	1.83	1.863	**5.442**	0.060	**0.938**	0.053	0.470	**1.945**
3	7.297	1.40	1.405	**5.319**	0.086	**0.944**	0.046	0.430	**2.176**
4	6.939	1.19	1.190	**4.889**	0.081	**0.947**	0.031	0.352	**1.924**
5	6.939	1.41	1.423	**5.145**	0.073	**0.946**	0.039	0.399	**2.026**
6	6.564	1.59	1.606	**5.314**	0.076	**0.940**	0.052	0.459	**1.964**
7	6.287	2.08	**2.128**	**5.647**	0.068	**0.940**	0.079	0.575	**2.194**
8	6.463	1.76	1.789	**5.589**	0.063	**0.937**	0.052	0.464	**2.015**
9	6.891	1.26	1.260	**5.040**	0.080	**0.945**	0.034	0.372	**1.937**
10	6.861	1.41	1.423	**5.308**	0.087	**0.941**	0.048	0.439	**2.053**
11	7.631	**-3.66**	**-4.030**	0.946	0.094	**0.957**	0.348	**1.300**	0.091
12	8.972	**-4.50**	**-5.287**	0.902	**0.144**	**0.960**	**0.851**	**2.168**	0.099
13	6.818	**-2.88**	**-3.044**	1.197	**0.109**	**0.958**	0.254	**1.065**	0.153
14	3.902	**-2.56**	**-2.666**	0.872	**0.564**	**0.966**	**2.114**	**3.030**	**0.417**

Table 4.5: Diagnostic Measures for the most unusual observations in the Hawkins, Bradu and Kass data. Measures exceeding their cutoff values (below the measure) are boldfaced.

9 cases are masked and the next 4 cases are swamped. When BACON is applied to this dataset, all 14 points were declared as multivariate outliers. Using this subset as the suspect group, ri(R)* correctly identifies observations 110 as regression outliers. Albeit the single case leverage measure identifies only 3 cases (12, 13 and 14), the multiple leverage measure, hii(R), identifies all the 14 cases as high leverage points. Cooks distance identifies only two observations (12 and 14) as influential. WKi identifies four observations (1114) as influential. Whereas, the group deleted multiple influence measure Mi identifies all 14 cases as influential. Figure 6 shows that only group deletion influence measure is successful for proper identification of multiple influential cases.

Regression diagnostic methods also have some limitations as like robust methods. Most of the popular diagnostic methods are based on single case deletion approach. We see single diagnostic measures are failed to detect a group of unusual observations and they are affected by masking and/or swamping phenomena. In case of group deletion diagnostics, it is cumbersome and sometimes impossible to identify suspect group of unusual observations because of the sample size. Diagnostic techniques that do not consider robustness can make nonrobust decision. It is hard to derive exact/asymptotic distribution of estimates obtained after classical diagnostic methods and existence of several regression diagnostic techniques with little guidance available as to which is appropriate.

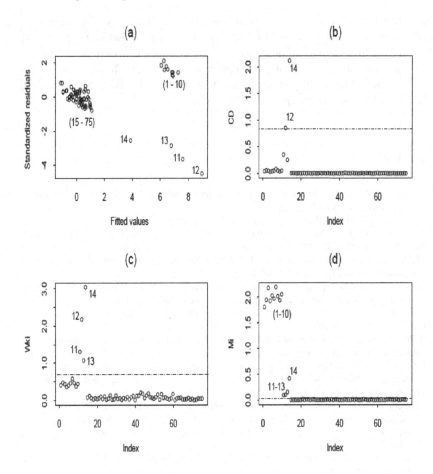

Fig. 4.6: Hawkins, Bradu and Kass data; (a) Scatter plot of standardized residuals versus fitted values (b) Index plot of Cooks distance (c) Index plot of WKi (d) Index plot of Mi

4.6 Concluding Remarks and Future Research Issues

Using robust and diagnostic regression is an important task before performing regression analysis and making decision. Without identifying influential observations OLS method is totally erroneous and misleading. Good diagnostics suggest both problems and possible solution for an effective analysis. Regression diagnostics with robust methods is more reliable than individual one. Outliers and influential observations should not routinely be deleted or automatically down-weighted because they are not necessarily bad observations. On the contrary, if they are correct, they might be the most informative cases in the data and have some thing more exploratory opportunity. Most of the existing methods are not efficient for large and high-dimensional data sets. There is no single universally applicable or generic outlier detection technique. Additional research is also needed to find easily compatible and robust approach for large and high dimensional datasets that is to be efficient in data mining and similar applications. Literature shows that only statistical approaches are not sufficient for outlier detection in real datasets. To fulfill the necessity, it is obvious that a full gamut of statistical (parametric and non parametric), machine learning and data mining effort is needed.

References

1. Atkinson, A.C. (1981), Two graphical displays for outlying and influential observations in regression. Biometrika, 68, 13 20.
2. Atkinson, A. C. (1986), Masking unmasked. Biometrika, 73, 533541.
3. Atkinson, A. C., Riani, M. (2000), Robust Diagnostic Regression Analysis. London, Springer.
4. Barnett, V., Lewis, T. B. (1995), Outliers in Statistical Data. NY, Wiley.
5. lBelsley, D. A., Kuh, E., Welsch, R. E. (1980), Regression Diagnostics: Identifying Influential Data and Sources of Collinearity. NY, Wiley.
6. Berka, P. (1997), Recognizing reliability of discovered knowledge, Principles of knowledge discovery and data mining, Lecture notes in computer science, Vol. 1263/1997, 307 − 314.
7. Berry, M. J. A., Linoff, G. (1997), Data Mining Techniques for Marketing, Sales and Customer Support, NY, Wiley.
8. Billor, N., Hadi A. S., Velleman, F. (2000), BACON: Blocked adaptive computationally efficient outlier nominator. Computational Statistics and Data Analysis, 34, 279298.
9. Box, G. E. P. (1953), Non-normality and tests on variance. Biometrika, 40, 318335.
10. Chatterjee, S., Hadi, A. S. (1986), Influential observations, high leverage points, and outliers in regression. Statistical Sciences, 1, 379416.
11. Chatterjee, S., Hadi, A. S. (1988), Sensitivity Analysis in Linear Regression. NY, Wiley.
12. Chatterjee, S., Hadi, A. S. (2006), Regression Analysis by Examples. NY, Wiley.
13. Cook, R. D. (1977), Detection of influential observations in linear regression. Technometrics, 19, 1518.
14. Cook, R. D. (1979), Influential observations in regression. Journal of the American Statistical Association, 74, 169174.
15. Cook, R. D. (1986), Assessment of local influence. Journal of Royal Statistical Society, B, 48(2), 133169.
16. Cook, R. D., Weisberg, S. (1982), Residuals and Influence in Regression. London, Chapman and Hall.
17. Cookley, C. W., Hettmansperger, T. P. (1993), A bounded influence, high breakdown, efficient regression estimator, Journal of the American Statistical Association, 88, 872880.
18. Dai, H., Liu, J. and Liu, H. (2006), 1st International Workshop on Reliability Issues in Knowledge Discovery (RIKD 06), http://doi.ieeecomputersociety.org/10.1109/ICDMW.2008.6, access 10-8-10.
19. Dai, H, Liu, J. (2008), 2nd International Workshop on Reliability Issues in Knowledge Discovery (RIKD 08). newsgroups.derkeiler.com/Archive/Comp/comp.../msg00009.html, access 10 − 8 − 10.
20. Dai, H., Liu, J., Smirnovi, E. (2010), 3rd International Workshop on Reliability Issues in Knowledge Discovery (RIKD 10), http://www.ourglocal.com/event/?eventid=4342, access 10 − 8 − 10.
21. Daniel, C., Wood, F. S. (1971), Fitting Equations to Data, NY, Wiley.
22. Efron, B., Tibshirani, R. J. (1993), An Introduction to the Bootstrap. NY, Wiley.
23. Elder, J. F. and Pregibon, D. (1995), A statistical perspective on KDD, in Proceedings of KDD-95, 87 − 93.

24. Ellenberg, J. H. (1976), Testing for a single outlier from a general regression. Biometrics, 32, 637645.
25. Fayyad, U., Piatetsky-Shapiro, G., Smyth, P. (1996), The KDD process for extracting useful knowledge from volumes of data, Communications of the ACM, 39 (10), 27 − 34.
26. Feng, Y., Wu, Z. (2006), Enhancing reliability throughout knowledge discovery process, in Proceedings of 1st International Workshop on Reliability Issues in Knowledge Discovery, Hong Kong, China.
27. Fox, J. (1993), Regression diagnostics. In M. S. L. Beck (Ed.), Regression analysis (245334). London, Sage Publications.
28. Gnanadesikan, R., Wilk, M. B. (1968), Probability plotting methods for the analysis of data, Biometrika, 55(1), 117.
29. Hadi, A. S. (1992), A new measure of overall potential influence in linear regression. Computational Statistics and Data Analysis, 14, 127.
30. Hadi, A. S., Simonoff, J. S. (1993), Procedures for the identification of outliers. Journal of the American Statistical Association, 88, 12641272.
31. Hampel, F. R. (1968), Contribution to the theory of robust estimation. Ph. D. Thesis, University of California, Berkley.
32. Hampel, F. R. (1975). Beyond location parameters: robust concepts and methods. Bulletin of the International Statistics Institute, 46, 375382.
33. Hampel, F. R., Ronchetti, E. M., Rousseeuw, P. J., Stahel, W. A. (1986), Robust Statistics: The Approach Based on Influence Function. NY, Wiley.
34. Hawkins, D. M. (1980), Identification of Outliers. London, Chapman and Hall.
35. Hawkins, D. M., Bradu, D., Kass, G. V. (1984), Location of several outliers in multiple regression data using elemental sets. Technometrics, 26, 197208.
36. Hoaglin, D. C., Welsch, R. E. (1978), The hat matrix in regression and ANOVA. American Statistician, 32, 1722.
37. Hossjer, O. (1994), Rank-based estimates in the linear model with high breakdown point. Journal of the American Statistical Association, 89, 149158.
38. Huber, P. J. (1964), Robust estimation of a location parameter. Annals of Mathematical Statistics, 35, 73101.
39. Huber, P. J. (1973), Robust regression: asymptotics, conjectures and Monte Carlo. Annals of Statistics, 1, 799821.
40. Huber, P. J. (1981), Robust Statistics. NY, Wiley.
41. Huber, P. J. (1991), Between robustness and diagnostics. In Stahel, W. and Weisberg, S. (Eds.), Direction in Robust Statistics and Diagnostics. 121130, NY, Springer-Verlag.
42. Imon, A.H.M.R. (2005), Identifying multiple influential observations in linear regression. Journal of Applied Statistics, 32(9), 929946.
43. Knorr, M. E., Ng, T. R., Tucakov, V. (2000), Distance-based outlier: algorithms and applications. VLDB Journal, 8, 327253.
44. Mahalanobis, P. C. (1936), On the generalized distance in statistics. Proceedings of the National Institute of Science of India, 12, 4955.
45. Mannila, H. (1996), Data mining: machine learning, statistics, and databases. http:reference.kfupm.edu.sa/contentda/data_mining_machine_learning_statistic_50921.pdf; access 6 − 8 − 10.
46. Mallow, C. P. (1975), On some topics in robustness, Unpublished memorandum, Bell telephone laboratories, Murray Hill, NJ.
47. Maronna, R. A., Zamar, R. H. (2002), Robust estimates of location and dispersion for high-dimensional data sets, Technometrics, 44, 307313.
48. Maronna, R. A., Martin, R. D., Yohai, V. J. (2006), Robust Statistics: Theory and Methods. NY, Wiley.
49. Nurunnabi, A. A. M. (2008), Robust diagnostic deletion techniques in linear and logistic regression, M. Phil. Thesis, Unpublished, Rajshahi University, Bangladesh.
50. Nurunnabi, A. A. M., Imon, A. H. M. R., Nasser, M. (2011), A diagnostic measure for influential observations in linear regression. Communication in Statistics-Theory and Methods, 40 (7), 11691183.

51. Pea, D., Prieto, F. J. (2001), Multivariate outlier detection and robust covariance estimation, Technometrics, 43, 286310.
52. Rousseeuw, P. J. (1984), Least median of squares regression. Journal of the American Statistical Association, 79, 871880.
53. Rousseeuw, P. J., Leroy, A. M. (2003), Robust Regression and Outlier Detection. NY, Wiley.
54. Rousseeuw, P. J., van Driessen, K. (1999), A fast algorithm for the minimum covariance determinant estimator. Technometrics, 41, 212223.
55. Rousseeuw, P. J., van Zomeren, B. C. (1990), Unmasking multivariate outliers and leverage points. Journal of the American Statistical Association, 85, 633639.
56. Simpson, D. G., Ruppert, D., Carroll, R. J. (1992), On one-step GM-estimates and stability of inference in linear regression, Journal of the American Statistical Association, 87, 439450.
57. Tukey, J. W. (1960), A survey of sampling from contaminated distributions: contributions to probability and statistics. Olkin, I. Ed., Stanford University Press, Stanford, California.
58. Tukey, J. W. (1962), The future of data analysis. Annals of Mathematical Statistics, 33, 167.
59. Velleman, P. F., Welsch, R. E. (1981), Efficient computing in regression diagnostics. American Statistician, 35, 234242.
60. Welsch, R. E., Kuh, E. (1977), Linear regression diagnostics, Sloan School of Management Working Paper, 923977, MIT, Cambridge: Massachusetts.
61. Willems, G., Aelst, S. V. (2004), Fast and robust bootstrap for LTS. Elsevier Science.
62. Yohai, V. J. (1987), High breakdown point and high efficiency robust estimates for regression. The Annals of Statistics, 15, 642656.

Chapter 5
Reliable Graph Discovery

Honghua Dai

Abstract A critical question in data mining is that can we always trust what discovered by a data mining system unconditionally? The answer is obviously not. If not, when can we trust the discovery then? What are the factors that affect the reliability of the discovery? How do they affect the reliability of the discovery? These are some interesting questions to be investigated. In this chapter we will firstly provide a definition and the measurements of reliability, and analyse the factors that affect the reliability. We then examine the impact of model complexity, weak links, varying sample sizes and the ability of different learners to the reliability of graphical model discovery. The experimental results reveal that (1) the larger sample size for the discovery, the higher reliability we will get; (2) the stronger a graph link is, the easier the discovery will be and thus the higher the reliability it can achieve; (3) the complexity of a graph also plays an important role in the discovery. The higher the complexity of a graph is, the more difficult to induce the graph and the lower reliability it would be. We also examined the performance difference of different discovery algorithms. This reveals the impact of discovery process. The experimental results show the superior reliability and robustness of MML method to standard significance tests in the recovery of graph links with small samples and weak links.

5.1 Introduction

With the rapid development in the area of data mining, more and more knowledge has been discovered from various types of data in a range of domain. A critical question is that can we always trust what discovered by a data mining system unconditionally? The answer is obviously not. If not, when can we trust them? What are the factors that affect the reliability of the discovery process? How do they affect the

Honghua Dai

Deakin University, 221 Burwood Highway, Burwood, Melbourne, VIC 3125, Australia, e-mail: honghua.dai@deakin.edu.au reliability of the discovery? Under which conditions the discovery is reliable. These are some interesting questions to be investigated.

In conventional view, reliability[1] is defined in terms of stability, equivalence and consistency. In knowledge discovery, it seems that we could adopt the conventional view and consider a discovery is reliable if it meets the stability, equivalence and consistency conditions. But the thing is not so simple. As the reliabilty of knowledge discovery can be affected by a number of factors. This makes it difficult to give a general definition to the reliability of data mining. There are huge number of issues need to be taken into consideration. In the following, we try to provide an explanation of stability, equivalence and consistency in terms of knowledge discovery reliability.

- **Stability.** The stability of data mining processes can be measured by repeating test over the same population. It is also referred as test-retest technique, i.e., the same form of a test on two or more separate occasions to the same group of examinees. However, some previous research revealed that this approach is not practical due to repeated measurements are likely to change the examinees. For example, the examinees could adapt the test format and thus tend to score higher in later tests.
- **Equivalence** assesses the outcome of a mining process out of two or more different patterns discovered, based on the same content, on one occasion to the same examinees. A data mining process is considered reliable in terms of equivalence if the outcomes of these two or more different discovered patters are equivalent.
- **Consistency.** Consistancy can be assessed with the test scores obtained from a single test at different occassions. If the discovery on multiple data sets draw from the same population derives the consistent results, the discovery is then be considered reliable, otherwise it is not. For instance, if at one occassion, a discovery algorithm derived a rule *if x > a then C*; and at another occassion, it discovered another rule **if x < a then C**, in such case, we say the discovery is inconsistent and thus unreliable. Another example is that let's say we are trying to discover customers attitude towards Window XP from certain data. One discovery reveals that " People feel very negative about Window XP in general." Another discovery shows "People enjoy using Window XP." People who strongly agree with the first statement should be strongly disagree with the second statement, and vice versa. If the rating of both statements is high or low among several discoveries, the discoveries are said to be inconsistent and patternless. The same principle can be applied to a test. When no pattern is found in the discovery process, i.e., the discovery response, probably the discovery is too difficult and the discovery system may just guess the answers randomly, or due to some other reasons.

In this chapter, we will examine the automating graph discovery which aims at developing methods of reliable recovering the structure (and parameters) of graphical models from sample data. Given such a method, several factors will affect the correctness of the discovered model, including the quality of the available data, the size of the sample obtained and the strength of the links to be discovered.

Having developed methods which for given large samples, discover graph models that are generally more reliable by one method than those discovered by another method [29], we report in this chapter the initial results on the reliability of the two methods when using small samples and in discovering weak links.

In Section 2, we discuss the reliability issues in graph discovery, in patrticular, we address the sample size and weak link discovery problems. In Section 3, we give a brief analysis of the relationship between sample size, link strength and the discovery of links. Section 4 presents the test strategies. Section 5 provides the experimental results of the graph model discovery algorithms across a range of sample sizes and with various small path coefficients. In particular we compare the results of the MML induction system MML-CI (the MML Causal Inducer) [29] with that of TETRAD II [9, 25, 26].

5.2 Reliability of Graph Discovery

Let $V = \{v_i : 1 \leq i \leq n\}$ (corresponding to random variables) be a set of nodes and $E \subset V \times V$ be a set of links, a graphical model M is a directed acyclic graph (DAG) $< V, E >$ together with numerical parameters reporting the strength of the connections, where $< x_i, x_j > \in E$ means that x_i is a direct cause of x_j relative to V. Such directed acyclic graphs that can be used for a range of applications. A typical application is to use the graph to represent causal theories are variously called causal models, causal graphs, causal networks and belief networks [6] and [19]. A causal network gives a concise specification of the joint probability distribution [17]. Each node in the causal network has a conditional probability table that quantifies the effects that the parents have on the node; linear causal networks (e.g., [30]) provide the same information under the assumption that each effect variable is a linear function of its parents, allowing the numerical parameters to be attached to causal links independently.

In recent decade, graph models have been widely employed for the representation of the knowledge with uncertainty, including use in expert systems [24]. In consequence, interest has grown in the learning of graph models as well. Various learning strategies have been developed. These methods include Clark Glymour et al.'s TETRAD systems based upon significance tests for partial correlations, Pearl and Verma's approach [17] and [18] using conditional independencies, Heckerman's Bayesian approach [10] and [11]. In 1995, Madigan and York introduced Markov Chain Monte Carlo Model Composition (MC^3) [13] for approximate Bayesian model averaging (BMA) and recently further developed the *Gibbs* MC^3 and the *Augmented* MC^3 algorithms [13] for the selection of Bayesian models. More recently Wallace *et al* developed the MML-CI [29] based on MML induction, a Bayesian minimum encoding technique and Suzuki proposed a MDL (Minimum Description Length) principle based Bayesian Network learning algorithm using the branch and bound technique [27]. However, there is no one work that specifically examined the reliablity issues in the discovery. There is almost no research has been in investigating the reliability issues of graph discovery. In this paper, we examine the problem of the reliability of the graph discovery algorithms which have been developed for inducing linear causal models, namely the MML based approach and the constraint based approach. In particular, we compare the models these algorithms produce when presented with varying sample sizes and samples generated from original causal structures with varying strengths of causal relationship. The reliability of the discovery technique in dealing with small samples is an important issue for machine learning, since autonomous, resource-constrained agents must be prepared to learn interactively with environments that will not tolerate unbounded sampling. We need to estimate the reliability of a derived model. Although in this chapter we do not report on reliability issues of large graph models, we would expect that problems with robustness with small samples for small models will manifest themselves also with large samples for large models, suggesting difficulty in scaling up a learning algorithm to cope with realistic examples of graph discovery. In this chapter, the large model refers to the model with large number of nodes and links.

To assure the reliability of discovered knowledge, it is essential to find out how reliability be affected. In the following section, we will examine the factors that affect reliability of graph discovery.

5.3 Factors That Affect Reliability of Graph Discovery

Our previous research reveals that a reliability problem could be caused by three major categories of factors: (1) data-oriented factors, (2) knowledge-oriented factors, and (3) algorithm-oriented factors.

1. *Data-oriented factors.*
   From the data point of view, the reliability problem can be caused by the following factors:

   - **Low Quality Data**. Algorithms are misled by low quality data which results in brittle rules being derived is a major cause of reliability problem. In this case the training data set $D_{Training}$ is not truly representative of the regularity to be learnt.
   - **Small sample size**. The sample size is not large enough to cover all the possible cases for learning. In the other words, the instances in the $D_{Training}$ may not be the real and complete representatives of the rule to be learnt. In this case the reliability problem is caused by the fact that the cases in D_{Test} are beyond what the algorithm can learn from $D_{Training}$.
   - **Biased sample**. In this case the sample size may be very large but the sample is biased and does not represent the true and complete situation in the real world. In this case, the reliability problem would also be caused by incorrect representative data.

The small sample size problem and the biased sample problem normally can be overcome by increasing the number and the different kinds of observations.

2. *Algorithm-oriented factors.*

From the algorithm point of view, the reliability problem can be caused by the following factors:

- **Overfitting**. The term overfitting (over-specialization) is used to describe the problem in which the rule learnt by the algorithm A is too specific to the training data set $D_{Training}$ to be useful on new unseen cases.
- **Algorithm's Own Defects**. The reliability problem could be caused by the defects of a learning algorithm itself, such as the incompleteness of inductive learning, i.e, the contradiction of the requirement of unlimited induction and the limited number of available observations. Such a cause is also related to the bias of the sample and the number of possible instances in the training data set $D_{Training}$.
- **Algorithm's Design Problem**. The reliability problem could also be caused by a learning algorithm's design scheme. Most inductive learning algorithms derive rules by looking at each individual attribute value of all available instances in $D_{Training}$ and trying to find a cut-off point for classification. Such kinds of algorithms can be easily affected by a noisy or erroneous data item and cause a false rule to be derived and thus cause reliability problem.

3. *Knowledge-oriented factors.*

The knowledge-oriented factors that could affect reliability of the discovered knowledge include the following:

- improper use of certain knowledge representation method.
- Knowledge is incorrectly structured.

5.4 The Impact of Sample Size and Link Strength

In general, any learning technique which converges on the underlying probability distribution in a prediction task, the reliability of the discovered graph will be sensitive to sample size, model complexity and the strength of the correlation between measured variables and this impact the discovery obviously. In general, the reliability of a recovered graph will be a function of sample size, quality of the data and the ability of the learner [7]. In the discovery of graphical models verisimilitude of the model discovered relative to the original model (and the probability distribution implied) will also be affected by sample size, model complexity and the strength of causal association between measured variables. For practical purposes, starting from similar prior domain information, better learning ability will reveal itself in *faster* convergence upon the underlying model, or, to put it the other way around, in the robustness of discovery given smaller sample sizes. Here we examine such reliability in MML based graph discovery approach and in the constraint based approach.

The probability of discovering from sample data the existence of a particular graph link depends, in part, upon the strength of that graph link. In the case of a single graph path between two nodes being a single, direct link (in standardized models) the path coefficient is identical to the correlation between the two nodes, making the relation between sample size and detectability of the link plain. The constraint based approach is sensitive to the strength of the graphical relation quite directly: it determines whether a link is present or not by applying significance tests potentially to all orders of partial correlation, removing the effects of all subsets of V excluding the nodes under consideration. In consequence, ordinary concerns about the robustness of significance testing apply to the constraint based approach — and for each link these concerns will apply not to a single significance test, but to a battery of significance tests. This is true even though the constraint based approach takes steps to reduce the number of significance tests required per pair of nodes, in its "PC algorithm" [25]. Things are worse than ordinary for TETRAD II, however: because a high-order partial correlation estimate depends upon estimates of the marginal correlations for each pair of variables involved, the uncertainties associated with each estimate will accumulate, which results in high standard errors (variance) for high-order partial correlation estimates and in the need for very large samples to get significant results. The reliance on significance tests for high-order partial correlations suggests that TETRAD II will be unlikely recover the structure of a larger model without quite large samples available. In other words, the larger the order of such a significance test, the greater the sample size must be for an effect of constant strength to be detected. As a result, as the authors admit [25], TETRAD II has a tendency to omit arcs for larger models even with fairly large sample sizes.

MML-CI does not depend upon a test as rigid as significance tests at a fixed level: it reports an arc whenever the presence of such an arc leads to a reduction in the message length for a joint encoding of the graph model and the sample data [29].

In MML-CI's discovery the relation between sample size and the strength of causal links remains, of course; but the possibility of MML-CI finding weaker links sooner seems intuitively more likely, because such links will be reported as soon as the improvement they afford in encoding the data overcomes the increased cost of reporting a somewhat more complex model.

5.5 Testing Strategy

To examine the influence of sample size on the reliability of the discovery of graph-ical models experimentally we chose six models varying in complexity: models 1 through 6 in Figure 5.1. We used these models to generate sets of sample data of various sizes stochastically, which in turn were given as input to MML-CI and TETRAD II to determine what graphical models would be discovered. In the case of TETRAD II default values were employed exclusively; No prior information about the temporal order of variables was provided to either algorithm.

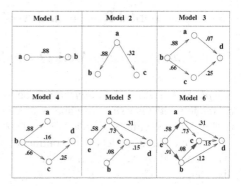

Fig. 5.1 Six test models

The first model is simplest, having only one link and two variables. In this case, the path coefficient is exactly equal to the correlation between the two variables. This makes the existence of the causal link extremely easy to find (although not its direction). Model six is the most complex model, having five variables and seven arcs. Three of the models contain weak links with coefficients less than 0.1, namely models 3, 5 and 6. These six artificial models were manually designed for the following testing purposes: (1) The learning difficulties associated with model complexity in terms of the number of variables; (2) The learning difficulties associated with model complexity in terms of the number of arcs; (3) The learning difficulties associated with the strength of the links. In each case we generated data sets with 10, 50, 100, 200, 500, 1000, 2000 and 5000 instances. Then we ran both MML-CI and TETRAD II using all eight data sets for each of the six models.

In a second experiment we looked at the effect of link strength on the recovered model. In this case we used model 6 (above) with the strength of the causal arc $b \rightarrow c$ varied between 0.08 and 0.16, in each case generating the same range of sample sizes as above.

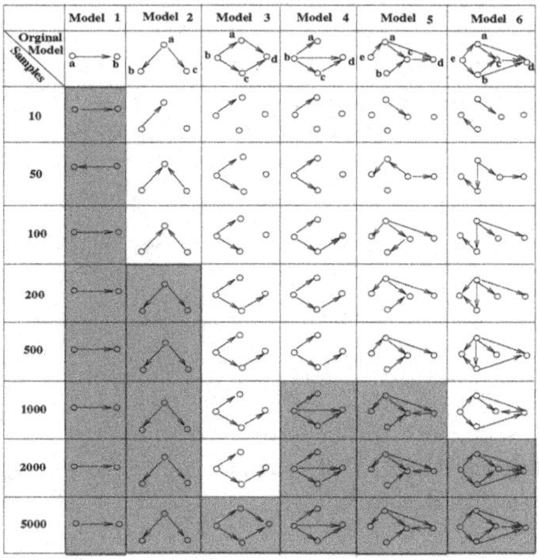

Fig. 5.2 MML-CI Sample
Size Test Results

5.6 Experimental Results and Analysis

5.6.1 Sample Size and Model Complexity

Sample Size and Graph Complexity In our experiments, we focus on linear graphical models with Gaussian error and assume no hidden variables. We use TETRAD II default settings with a significant level of 0.05. The PC algorithm is the one applied on fully measured models with continuous variables. Figure 5.2 reports the models discovered by MML-CI from the 48 data sets. while Figure 5.3 reports those discovered by TETRAD II. The shading indicates for each model at what point the algorithm discovered the original model or a model statistically equivalent to the original. *Statistically equivalent* causal models are those which can be used to specify the same class of probability distributions over the variables (perhaps using distinct parameterizations). [28] report a simple graphical criterion of equivalence which can be used to identify the statistically equivalent models in our figures: two causal models are statistically equivalent if and only if they have the same skeleton (undirected graph) and they have the same *v-structures* (nodes that are the children of two parents which are themselves non-adjacent). Such models cannot be distinguished on the basis of sample data alone [5], so the discovery of one is as good as the discovery of another in this experiment.

For TETRAD II, in Figure 5.3, undirected arcs reflect the fact that TETRAD was unable to determine an arc orientation; for these arcs, either orientation is allowed by TETRAD, so long as the resulting graph is acyclic and so long as no new v-structures are introduced by selecting such an orientation. We counted the resulting TETRAD graph as satisfactory (and so appears shaded) if no such selection of arc orientations results in a causal model that is not statistically equivalent to the original model.

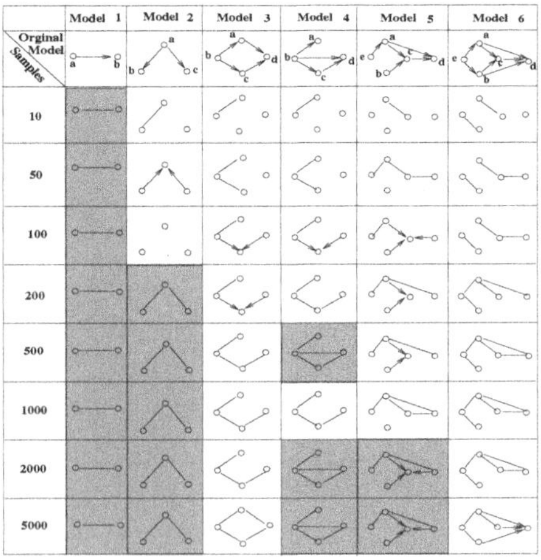

Fig. 5.3 TETRAD II Sample Size Test Results

	Comparison of Edges Omitted in MML-CI							
Models	**10**	**50**	**100**	**200**	**500**	**1K**	**2K**	**5K**
Model 4	75%	49%	29%	29%	29%	0	0	0
Model 5	79%	40%	20%	20%	20%	0	0	0
model 6	70%	55%	55%	40%	30%	15%	0	0
	Comparison of Edges Omitted in TETRAD							
Models	**10**	**50**	**100**	**200**	**500**	**1K**	**2K**	**5K**
Model 4	75%	49%	29%	29%	0	29%	0	0
Model 5	79%	40%	20%	20%	20%	20%	0	0
model 6	70%	55%	55%	40%	30%	30%	30%	20%

Table 5.1: Comparison of Edges Ommited

	Comparison of Arrows Omitted in MML-CI							
Models	**10**	**50**	**100**	**200**	**500**	**1K**	**2K**	**5K**
Model 4	80%	49%	29%	29%	29%	0	0	0
Model 5	79%	39%	20%	20%	0	0	0	0
model 6	70%	55%	55%	40%	30%	15%	0	0
	Comparison of Arrows Omitted in TETRAD							
Models	**10**	**50**	**100**	**200**	**500**	**1K**	**2K**	**5K**
Model 4	75%	48%	29%	29%	0	29%	0	0
Model 5	80%	40%	40%	20%	20%	20%	0	0
model 6	70%	55%	55%	40%	30%	30%	30%	20%

Table 5.2: Comparison of Arrows Ommited

Although in this study we have not performed significance tests on the results (i.e., by generating large numbers of samples of each model for each sample size), the trend is fairly clear. For all of the models showing any complexity (i.e., for model 3 and above)

Figure 5.2 shows that for less complicated graph, MML-CI has found the correct model at smaller sample sizes. than has TETRAD II. In the case of model 6 TETRAD II was unable to recover the weakest link even when supplied 5000 samples, while for model 3 TETRAD II found all the links but failed to discover the v-structure at node d. Figure 5.4 shows that the weaker the link is, the larger sample size is needed to recover the original graph. Tabel 5.1 shows that the larger the sample size is, the less edges be ommited in the discovered graph.

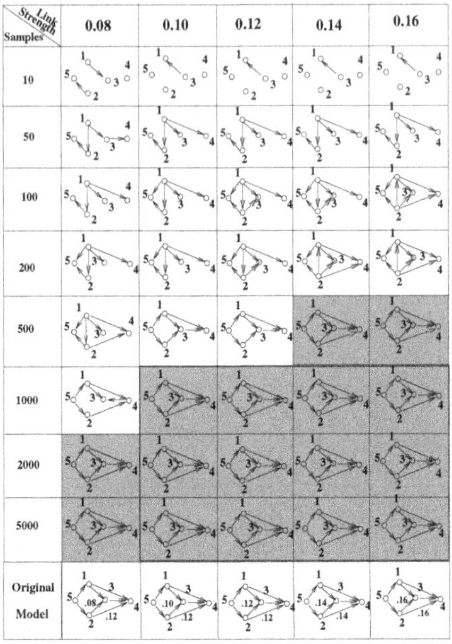

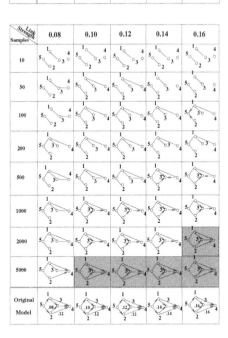

Fig. 5.4 MML-CI Weak Link Discovery Results

Fig. 5.5 TETRAD II Weak Link Discovery Results

Testing Models	No. of Nodes	No. of Edges	Discover ≥ 0.1 links Samples needed	Discover ≥ 0.01 links Samples needed
Model 1	2	1	10	*
Model 2	3	2	200	*
Model 3	4	4	200	500
Model 4	4	5	200	*
Model 5	5	5	1000	1000
Model 6	5	7	2000	2000

Table 5.3: Experimental Results of Samples Needed to Discover the Models

Table 5.4, and 5.2 compare MML-CI with TETRAD II in the manner used by Spirtes, et al. [25]. Figure 5.1 graphs the percentage of edges of the original model which MML-CI and TETRAD II have failed to recover, by sample size. Figure 5.2 graphs the percentage of arc orientations missed by each program (but not counting cases where a graph with an incorrect arc orientation is statistically equivalent to the original model). Of course, both algorithms display the expected convergence towards zero errors — expected because TETRAD II is, in effect, a classical estimation technique whereas MML-CI is, in effect, a Bayesian estimation technique, and so both fall under the general convergence results established for the respective classes of statistical inference procedures. It remains of interest, however, that in all of these measures MML-CI tends to display a more rapid convergence towards the true model — which is to say it appears to be more robust when dealing with smaller sample sizes.

Link Streng	Edges Omitted With Small Path Coefficients							
	10	50	100	200	500	1K	2K	5K
0.08	5	4	4	3	2	1	0	0
0.12	6	4	2	2	2	0	0	0
0.16	6	4	1	1	0	0	0	0

Table 5.4: Comparison of Edges Ommited in MML-CI

Sample Size and Weak Link Discovery Sample Size and Weak Link Discovery Figure 5.4 illustrates the experimental results for MML-CI on model 6 when the causal link from b to c takes varying degrees of strength, in particular coefficients ranging from 0.08 to 0.16. Unsurprisingly, the results clearly reveal the fact that the weaker the association the larger the sample required to discover it. With the weakest coefficient of 0.08 in Figure 5.4, MML-CI does not discover the link until provided with 2000 samples. Whereas with a weakest link of 0.10 and 0.14, the

Link	Edges Omitted With Small Path Coefficients							
Strength	10	50	100	200	500	1K	2K	5K
0.08	5	4	4	3	2	2	2	1
0.12	5	4	3	3	2	1	1	0
0.16	5	5	3	3	1	1	0	0

Table 5.5: Comparison of Edges Ommited in TETRAD

system discovered the link once provided with a data set with the sample size of 500 and 100 respectively.

Link	Arrows Omitted With Small Path Coefficient							
Streng	10	50	100	200	500	1K	2K	5K
0.08	5	4	4	3	2	1	0	0
0.12	6	4	2	2	1	0	0	0
0.16	6	4	1	1	0	0	0	0

Table 5.6: Comparison of Arrows Ommited in MML-CI

Link	Arrows Omitted With Small Path Coefficients							
Strength	10	50	100	200	500	1K	2K	5K
0.08	5	4	4	3	2	2	2	1
0.12	5	4	3	3	2	1	1	0
0.16	5	5	5	3	3	1	0	0

Table 5.7: Comparison of Arrows Ommited in TETRAD

Figure 5.5 illustrates like experimental results for TETRAD II. These results again show the inverse relationship between strength of causal relationship and the sample size required to discover it. Given coefficients above our original 0.8 TETRAD II was able to discover the link between b and c that it had missed before. It remains clear in all of the test cases that MML-CI recovers the original causal model with fewer samples than TETRAD II. Table 5.4 and 5.5; Table 5.6 and Table 5.7 report similar stories for the measures of arc omission and arrow omission. Finally, table 5.3 illustrates the sample sizes needed by MML-CI to discover weak links in all six models (the parentheses indicating which link was set to a low coefficient in each case).

5.7 Conclusions

The following conclusions appear to be supported by our experimental results. The relibility of knowledge discovery can be affected by data-oriented factors; kowledge oriented factors and algorithm oriented factors. In this paper, we examine the impact of model complexity, weak links, varying sample sizes and the ability of different learners to the reliability of graphical model discovery. The experimental results reveal that (1) the larger sample sizes for the discovery, the higher reliability we will get; (2) the stronger the graph links, the easier the discovery will be and thus the higher the reliability it can achieve; (3) the complexity of the graph also plays an important role in the discovery. The higher complexity of a graph, the more difficult to induce the graph and the lower reliability it would be. We also examined the performance difference of different discovery algorithms. The experimental results show the superior reliability and robustness of MML method to standard significance tests in the recovery of graph links with small samples and weak links.

Our experimental results also show theimpact of reliability of discovered knowledge by different learning algorithm. The following is the summary of the algorithm-oriented factors that affect reliability. (1) The theoretical difficulties of significance testing with robustness appear to be manifested in TETRAD II's inferior robustness with respect to sample size. This shows up, for example, in TETRAD II's inability to recover the weaker links (with coefficients below 0.1) with smaller samples. (2) The problem of arc omission given small samples is particularly acute for TETRAD II (in comparison with MML-CI) as model complexity increases, as predicted by our analysis in §3. From the experimental results we also find that MML-CI shows promise not just in finding causal models that are as good as those discovered by TETRAD II in general, but given the constraints imposed by small samples or by weak causal links the models discovered appear to be characteristically superior to those discovered using the significance testing methods of TETRAD. This is likely to be an especially important feature of causal discovery when causal models become large, for TETRAD's method of examining partial correlations of all orders in such cases is both computationally expensive and lacking robustness.

References

1. American Educational Research Association, American Psychological Association, and National Council on Measurement in Education. *Stardards for educational and psychological testing.* American Educational Research Association, iWashington DC:Authors, 1985.
2. Hussein Almuallim and Thomas G. Dietterich. Learning with many irrelevant features. *Proceedings of AAAI'91*, pages 547–552, 1991.
3. David Aha and Dennis Kibler. Noise-tolerance-based learning algorithms. In *Proceedings of 11th International Joint Conference on Artificial intelligence*, pages 794–799, Detroit, Michigan, 20–25 August, 1989.
4. Paul R. Cohen and Edward A. Feigenbaum. *The Handbook of Artificial Intelligence.* William Kaufmann, Stanford, California, 1982.

5. David M. Chickering. A transformational characterization of equivalent Bayesian network structures. In *Proc. of the 11th Conference on Uncertainty in Artificial Intelligence*, pages 87–98, 1995.
6. G. F. Cooper and E. Herskovits, A Bayesian Method for Constructing Bayesian Belief Networks from Databases, *Proc. of 7th Conference on Uncertainty in AI*, In: B.D. D'Ambrosio and P. Smets and P. P. Bonissone, Morgan Kaufmann,pages 86-94, 1991.
7. Honghua Dai. Learning of forecasting rules from large noisy meteorological data. *PhD. Dissertation, Department of Computer Science, RMIT*, 1994.
8. Douglas H. Fisher. Noise-tolerant conceptual clustering. *Proceedings of 11th International Joint Conference on Artificial intelligence*, pages 825–830, 20–25 August, 1989.
9. Clark Glymour and Richard Scheines and Peter Spirtes and Kevin Kelly, Discovering Causal Structure: Artificial Intelligence, Philosophy of Science, and Statistical Modeling, Academic Press, San Diego, 1987.
10. David Heckerman, A Bayesian Approach to Learning Causal Networks, *Proceedings of 11th Conference on Uncertainty in Artificial Intelligence*, PAGES 285-295, 1995.
11. David Heckerman and R. Shachter, A decision-based view of causality, *Proceedings of Tenth Conference on Uncertainty in Artificial Intelligence*, PAGES 302-310, Morgan Kaufmann, Seattle, WA, 1994.
12. Kenji Kira and Larry A. Rendell. The feature selection problem: Traditional methods and a new algorithm. *Proceedings of AAAI'92*, pages 129–134, 1992.
13. David Madigan and Steen A. Andersson and Michael D. Perlman and Chris T. Volinsky, NIPS 95 Workshop on Learning in Bayesian Networks and Other Graphical Models, Bayesian Model Averaging and Model Selection for Markov Equivalence Classes of Acyclic Digraphs, 1995.
14. Maciej Modrzejewski. Feature selection using rough sets theory. *In: Pavel B. Brazdil(Ed.), Machine Learning: ECML–3, Proceedings of European Conference on Machine Learning*, pages 213–226, April 5-7, 1993.
15. Steven W. Norton and Haym Hirsh. Classifier learning from noisy data as probabilistic evidence combination. *AAAI-92: Proceedings of the tenth National Conference on Artificial Intelligence*, pages 141—146, 1992.
16. Tim Niblett. Constructing decision trees in noisy domains. *, 1988.
17. Judea Pearl, Probabilistic Reasoning in Intelligent Systems, Morgan Kaufmann, San Mateo, California, 1988,
18. Judea Pearl and T. S. Verma, A Theory of Inferred Causation, *Principles of Knowledge Representation and Reasoning: Proceedings of the Second International Conference*, Ed: J. A. Allen and R. Fikes and E. Sandewall, pages 441-452, Morgan Kaufmann Publishers, San Mateo, California, April 22-25, 1991.
19. Stuart Russell and Peter Norvig, Artificial Intelligence: A Mordern Approach, pages 932, Prentice Hall, Englewood Cliffs, New Jersey 07632,1995.
20. Ross Quinlan. *C4.5: Programms for Machine Learning*. Morgan Kaufmann Publishers, San Mateo, California, USA, 1993.
21. Cullen Schaffer. When does overfitting decrease prediction accuracy in induced decision trees and rule sets? *In Y. Kodratoff(Ed.), Machine Learning, EWSL-91*, 1991.
22. Cullen Schaffer. Sparse data and the effect of overfitting avoidance in decision tree induction. *Proceedings of the Tenth National Conference on Artificial Intelligence*, pages 147–152, 1992.
23. Cullen Schaffer. Overfitting avoidance as bias. *Machine Learning*, 1993.
24. Glen Shafer. *Probabilistic Expert Systems*. SIAM Press, 1996.
25. R. Scheines, P. Spirtes, C. Glymour, and C. Meek. *TETRAD II: tools for causal modeling*. Lawrence Erlbaum Associates, Inc., Publishers, 365 Broadway, Hillsdale, New Jersey 07642, 1994.
26. Peter Spirtes and Clark Glymour and Richard Scheines, Causation, Prediction, and Search, Springer-Verlag, New York, Berlin, Heideberg, 1993.
27. Joe Suzuki, Learning Bayesian Belif Networks Based on the Minimum Description Length Principle: An Efficient Algorithm Using the B & B Techniques, pages 462-470, Ed: Lorenza Saitta, *Proceedings of the 13th International Conference on Machine Learning*, Morgan Kaufmann, 340 Pine St., 6th Floor, San Francisco, July, 1996.

28. T. Verma and J. Pearl. Equivalence and synthesis of causal models. In *Proceedings of the 6th Conference on Uncertainty in Artificial Intelligence*, pages 220–227, Boston, MA, 1990. Morgan Kaufmann.

29. Chris Wallace, Kevin Korb, and Honghua Dai. Causal discovery via MML. In *Proceedings of the 13th International Conference on Machine Learning* (**ICML'96**), pages 516–524, 1996.

30. Sewall Wright, The method of path coefficients, *Annals of Mathematical Statistics*, PAGES 161–215, VOl 5, 1934.

Chapter 6
Combining Version Spaces and Support Vector Machines for Reliable Classification

Evgueni Smirnov, Georgi Nalbantov, and Ida Sprinkhuizen-Kuyper

Abstract In this chapter we argue to use version spaces as an approach to reliable classification. [1] The key idea is to extend version spaces to contain the target hypothesis h_t or hypotheses similar to h_t. In this way, the unanimous-voting classification rule of version spaces is not capable of misclassifying new instances; i.e., instance classifications become reliable.

We propose to implement version spaces using support vector machines. The resulting combination is called version space support vector machines (VSSVMs). Experiments show that VSSVMs are able to outperform the existing approaches to reliable classification.

6.1 Introduction

Classifiers applied in critical-domain applications need to determine whether classifications they assign to individual instances are indeed reliable [13]. The two most prominent approaches to reliable classification are the Bayesian framework [12] and the typicalness framework [10, 13] (see section 6.8). The Bayesian framework is a natural approach to reliable classification but it can be misleading if prior probabil-

Evgueni N. Smirnov
Department of Knowledge Engineering, Maastricht University, P.O.BOX 616, 6200 MD Maastricht, The Netherlands. e-mail: smirnov@maastrichtuniversity.nl

Georgi Nalbantov
Faculty of Health, Medicine and Life Sciences, Maastricht University, P.O.BOX 616, 6200 MD Maastricht, The Netherlands. e-mail: g.nalbantov@maastrichtuniversity.nl

Ida Sprinkhuizen-Kuyper
Radboud University Nijmegen, Donders Institute for Brain, Cognition and Behaviour, 6525 HR Nijmegen, The Netherlands. e-mail: i.kuyper@donders.ru.nl

[1] This paper is an extension of [11].

ities cannot be plausibly estimated [13]. The typicalness framework overcomes this problem but it depends heavily on the classifier used.

In this chapter we argue to use version spaces [7, 8, 9] as an alternative approach to reliable classification that does not suffer from the problems presented above. The key idea is to construct version spaces containing the target hypothesis h_t or hypotheses similar to h_t. In this way the unanimous-voting rule of version spaces does not misclassify instances; i.e., instance classifications become reliable.

We analyze the instance classification of version spaces for the case when data is non-noisy and hypothesis space is expressive as well as for the opposite three cases. For the latter instance classification can be unreliable (incorrect) and we propose a volume-extension approach. The approach is to grow the volumes of version spaces so that instance misclassifications are blocked.

We propose implementing version spaces for reliable classification using support vector machines (SVMs) [12]. Their combination is called version space support vector machines (VSSVMs). We apply the volume-extension approach on VSSVMs. Our experiments show that VSSVMs are able to outperform the existing approaches to reliable-classification (mentioned above).

This chapter is organized as follows. The task of reliable classification is defined in Section 6.2. Section 6.3 considers version spaces for reliable classification and the volume-extension approach. SVMs are described in Section 6.4. Section 6.5 introduces VSSVMs. The volume-extension approach for VSSVMs is presented in Section 6.6. Section 6.7 and 6.8 provide experiments and a comparison. Section 6.9 concludes the chapter.

6.2 Task of Reliable Classification

The task of reliable classification is a sub-class of the classification task. We consider the task for two classes only. Let X be the instance space and Y be the class set $\{-1, +1\}$. The training data $\langle I^+, I^- \rangle$ are generated by an unknown probability distribution $P(X, Y)$ where $I^+ \subseteq X$ is the set of training instances of class $+1$ and $I^- \subseteq X$ is the set of training instances of class -1. Given a space H of hypotheses h ($h : X \to Y$), the task of reliable classification is to find a non-empty set of hypotheses $h \in H$ that correctly classify future, unseen instances. When correct classification is not possible, the classification process outputs 0.

6.3 Version Spaces

This section considers version spaces in the context of the task of reliable classification. Subsection 6.3.1 provides the definition and classification rule of version spaces. An analysis of the version-space classification is given in Subsection 6.3.2.

Subsection 6.3.3 introduces our new volume-extension approach that allows converting version spaces to an approach to reliable classification.

6.3.1 Definition and Classification Rule

Version spaces were introduced for two-class classification tasks only in [7, 8, 9]. Given a hypothesis space H, they are defined as sets of hypotheses $h \in$ that are consistent with the training data.

Definition 6.1. Given a hypothesis space H and training data $\langle I^+, I^- \rangle$, a hypothesis $h \in H$ is said to be consistent with $\langle I^+, I^- \rangle$, denoted by $cons(h, \langle I^+, I^- \rangle)$, if and only if $(\forall x_i \in I^+ \cup I^-) y_i = h(x_i)$.

Definition 6.2. Given a hypothesis space H and training data $\langle I^+, I^- \rangle$, the version space $VS(I^+, I^-)$ is defined as follows:

$$\{h \in H | cons(h, \langle I^+, I^- \rangle)\}.$$

The version-space classification rule is the unanimous-voting rule. An instance $x \in X$ receives classification $y \in Y$ if the version space $VS(I^+, I^-)$ is non-empty and all the hypotheses $h \in VS(I^+, I^-)$ assign the same class y to x. Otherwise, the instance x is not classified indicated by value 0.

Definition 6.3. Given a version space $VS(I^+, I^-)$, an instance $x \in X$ receives a classification $VS(I^+, I^-)(x) \in Y \cup \{0\}$ defined as follows:

$$VS(I^+, I^-)(x) = \begin{cases} +1 & VS(I^+, I^-) \neq \emptyset \wedge (\forall h \in VS(I^+, I^-)) h(x) = +1, \\ -1 & VS(I^+, I^-) \neq \emptyset \wedge (\forall h \in VS(I^+, I^-)) h(x) = -1, \\ 0 & \text{otherwise.} \end{cases}$$

An instance $x \in X$ is left unclassified if it receives a classification equal to 0. Hence, any version space $VS(I^+, I^-)$ separates the instance space X into two sets: the set of instances $x \in X$ that can be classified by $VS(I^+, I^-)$ and the set of instances $x \in X$ that cannot be classified by $VS(I^+, I^-)$. To specify the latter we introduce the notion of the volume of version spaces given below.

Definition 6.4. The volume $V(VS(I^+, I^-))$ of a version space $VS(I^+, I^-)$ is defined as the set of instances $x \in X$ that cannot be classified by $VS(I^+, I^-)$; i.e.,

$$\{x \in X | VS(I^+, I^-)(x) = 0\}.$$

The unanimous-voting rule can be implemented if and only if version spaces can be tested for collapse [5]. By Theorem 6.1 all the hypotheses $h \in VS(I^+, I^-)$ assign class $+1$ to instance $x \in X$ if and only if the version space $VS(I^+, I^- \cup \{x\})$ is empty. Analogously, all hypotheses $h \in VS(I^+, I^-)$ assign class -1 to instance $x \in X$ if and only if the version space $VS(I^+ \cup \{x\}, I^-)$ is empty.

Theorem 6.1. *For any instance $x \in X$:*

$$(\forall h \in VS(I^+, I^-))h(x) = +1 \leftrightarrow VS(I^+, I^- \cup \{x\}) = \emptyset,$$
$$(\forall h \in VS(I^+, I^-))h(x) = -1 \leftrightarrow VS(I^+ \cup \{x\}, I^-) = \emptyset.$$

The problem to test version spaces for collapse is equivalent to the consistency problem [5]. The consistency problem is to determine the existence of a hypothesis $h \in H$ consistent with data. Hence, the unanimous-voting rule of version spaces can be implemented by any algorithm for the consistency problem. *An algorithm for the consistency problem is called a consistency algorithm.*

6.3.2 Analysis of Version-Space Classification

Version spaces are sensitive with respect to the class noise in the training data and the expressiveness of the hypothesis space H [7, 8, 9]. The class noise indicates that the class labels of some of the training instances are incorrect. The expressiveness of the hypothesis space H indicates if the target hypothesis h_t is in H. Below we analyze the correctness of version-space classification with respect to class noise and the expressiveness of the hypothesis space.

Case 1: Non-noisy Training Data and Expressive Hypothesis Spaces. Since the hypothesis space H is expressive, the target hypothesis h_t belongs to H. Since the training data $\langle I^+, I^- \rangle$ are non-noisy, h_t is consistent with $\langle I^+, I^- \rangle$. Thus, by definition 6.2 the hypothesis h_t belongs to the version space $VS(I^+, I^-)$. In this way, if an instance $x \in X$ is classified by the version space $VS(I^+, I^-)$, x is classified by the target hypothesis h_t. This implies that x is classified correctly. Thus, version spaces output only correct classifications in this case.

Case 2: Noisy Training Data. Since the hypothesis space H is expressive, the target hypothesis h_t belongs to H. Since the training data $\langle I^+, I^- \rangle$ are noisy, h_t is inconsistent with $\langle I^+, I^- \rangle$. Thus, by definition 6.2 h_t does not belong to the version space $VS(I^+, I^-)$. In this way, any instance $x \in X$ can be misclassified by $VS(I^+, I^-)$, if $VS(I^+, I^-)$ does not contain any hypothesis classifying x as h_t. Thus, version spaces may err for some instance classifications in this case.

Case 3: Inexpressive Hypothesis Spaces. If the hypothesis space H is inexpressive, then the target hypothesis h_t does not belong to H. Thus, by definition 6.2 h_t does not belong to the version space $VS(I^+, I^-)$. In this way, any instance $x \in X$ can be misclassified by $VS(I^+, I^-)$, if $VS(I^+, I^-)$ does not contain any hypothesis classifying x as h_t. Thus, version spaces may err for some instance classifications in this case.

6.3.3 Volume-Extension Approach

The volume-extension approach is a new approach to overcome the problem with noisy training data and the problem of inexpressive hypothesis spaces (cases 2 and 3 given above). Given a hypothesis space H, if a version space $VS(I^+, I^-) \subseteq H$ misclassifies instances, the approach is to find a new hypothesis space H' so that the volume of the version space $VS'(I^+, I^-) \subseteq H'$ grows and blocks instance misclassifications. By Theorem 6.2 given below to find H' with such a property it is sufficient to guarantee that for ay data $\langle I^+, I^- \rangle$ if there does exist a consistent hypothesis $h \in H$, then there does exist a consistent hypothesis $h' \in H'$.

Theorem 6.2. *Consider hypothesis spaces H and H' so that for any data $\langle I^+, I^- \rangle$ if there does exist a hypothesis $h \in H$ consistent with $\langle I^+, I^- \rangle$, then there does exist a hypothesis $h' \in H'$ consistent with $\langle I^+, I^- \rangle$. Then, for any data $\langle I^+, I^- \rangle$ if $VS(I^+, I^-) \neq \emptyset$, then $V(VS(I^+, I^-)) \subseteq V(VS'(I^+, I^-))$.*

Proof. Consider arbitrary $\langle I^+, I^- \rangle$ such that $VS(I^+, I^-) \neq \emptyset$. Let x be an instance in X such that $x \in V(VS(I^+, I^-))$. By Definition 6.4 $VS(I^+, I^-)(x) = 0$. Since $VS(I^+, I^-) \neq \emptyset$, $VS(I^+, I^-)(x) = 0$ implies by definition 6.3:

$$(\exists h \in VS(I^+, I^-))h(x) \neq +1, \tag{6.1}$$
$$(\exists h \in VS(I^+, I^-))h(x) \neq -1. \tag{6.2}$$

By Theorem 6.1 formula (6.1) implies:

$$VS(I^+, I^- \cup \{x\}) \neq \emptyset \tag{6.3}$$

and formula (6.2) implies:

$$VS(I^+ \cup \{x\}, I^-) \neq \emptyset. \tag{6.4}$$

By Definition 6.2 $VS(I^+, I^-) \neq \emptyset$ implies that there exists a hypothesis $h \in H$ consistent with $\langle I^+, I^- \rangle$. This implies according to the theorem conditional part that there exists a hypothesis $h' \in H'$ consistent with $\langle I^+, I^- \rangle$. Thus, by Definition 6.2 we have:

$$VS'(I^+, I^-) \neq \emptyset. \tag{6.5}$$

Analogously, we can prove from formulas (6.3) and (6.4) that:

$$VS'(I^+, I^- \cup \{x\}) \neq \emptyset, \tag{6.6}$$
$$VS'(I^+ \cup \{x\}, I^-) \neq \emptyset. \tag{6.7}$$

By Theorem 6.1 formulas (6.5), (6.6), and (6.7) imply by Definition 6.3 that $VS'(I^+,I^-)(x) = 0$. Thus, by Definition 6.4 we conclude that $x \in V(VS'(I^+,I^-))$. $\square$

To realize how the volume-extension approach overcomes the problems with noisy training data and inexpressive hypothesis spaces we note that the common obstacles for both problems is that instances $x \in X$ are misclassified when:

- the version space $VS(I^+,I^-)$ does not contain the target hypothesis h_t, and
- the version space $VS(I^+,I^-)$ does not contain any hypothesis that classifies the instances x as h_t.

The volume-extension approach does not overcome the first obstacle, but it may overcome the second one. By extending the hypothesis space H' up to the point when it includes at least one hypothesis that classifies the instance x as the target hypothesis h_t we guarantee that the instance x receives the label 0 by Definition 6.3; i.e., it is not classified. This means that the the volume of the version space is extended to include the instance x. From this we may conclude that the volume-extension approach overcomes the problem with noisy training data and the problem of inexpressive hypothesis spaces by extending the volume of version spaces to include regions with misclassified instances. This result implies contrary to the traditional view in machine learning [8, 9] that *version spaces can be viewed as an approach to reliable classification.*

6.4 Support Vector Machines

Support Vector Machines (SVMs) were proposed for classification tasks [12]. SVM constructs a hyperplane used as a decision boundary for classification. The parameters of the SVM hyperplane are derived from the solution of the following optimization problem:

$$\max_\alpha \; \sum_{i=1}^l \alpha_i - \tfrac{1}{2} \sum_{i,j=1}^l \alpha_i \alpha_j y_i y_j k(x_i,x_j) \qquad (6.8)$$
$$\text{subject to } 0 \le \alpha_i \le C, \; i = 1,2,\cdots,l, \text{ and } \sum_{i=1}^l y_i \alpha_i = 0,$$

where $k(x_i,x_j) = \phi(x_i)'\phi(x_j)$ is a kernel function that calculates inner products of instances x_i and x_j in a higher dimensional feature space $\mathbb{F}$ and ϕ is a mapping from X to $\mathbb{F}$. Maximizing the term $-\sum_{i,j=1}^l \alpha_i \alpha_j y_i y_j k(x_i,x_j)$ corresponds to maximizing the margin between the two classes. The parameter C determines the trade-off between the margin and the amount of training errors. The alphas are the weights associated with the training instances. All instances with nonzero weights are "support vectors". They determine the SVM hyperplane consisting of all points x which satisfy $\sum_{i=1}^l y_i \alpha_i k(x_i,x) + b = 0$. The parameter b is found from the KKT conditions associated with (6.8).

The hypothesis space of SVMs is the set of all oriented hyperplanes in X or in a higher dimensional feature space $\mathbb{F}$. *The hypothesis space of SVMs is denoted by $H(p)$* where p is a kernel parameter. For the RBF kernel p is gamma and for the polynomial kernel p is the exponent. *The SVM hyperplane is denoted by $h(p,C,\langle I^+,I^-\rangle)$.*

We consider the asymptotic behaviors of SVMs for the parameter C [6]. When C increases, the weight of training errors increases, while other things stay equal. Consequently, the SVM algorithm will try to find a new balance between the margin width and amount of training errors. In particular, the margin will decrease and the amount of classification errors will generally go down. Therefore, for any data $\langle I^+,I^-\rangle$ the probability that $h(p,C,\langle I^+,I^-\rangle)$ is consistent with $\langle I^+,I^-\rangle$ increases with the parameter C.

6.5 Version Space Support Vector Machines

This section introduces our main contribution: version space support vector machines (VSSVMs). VSSVMs are defined as version spaces that can be implemented by SVMs. The hypothesis space for VSSVMs is specified in Subsection 6.5.1. Subsection 6.5.2 provides the VSSVM definition. The classification algorithm of VSSVMs is described in Subsection 6.5.3.

6.5.1 Hypothesis Space

The version-space classification rule can be implemented by any consistency algorithm [5]. The key idea of VSSVMs is to use a SVM as a consistency algorithm. By Theorem 6.1 to classify an instance $x \in X$ we need a consistency algorithm only for data $\langle I^+ \cup \{x\}, I^-\rangle$ and $\langle I^+, I^- \cup \{x\}\rangle$. Since a SVM is not a consistency algorithm in the hypothesis space $H(p)$ of the oriented hyperplanes [12], below we define a hypothesis sub-space $H(p,C,\langle I^+,I^-\rangle) \subseteq H(p)$ for which SVM is a consistency algorithm with respect to data sets $\langle I^+ \cup \{x\}, I^-\rangle$ and $\langle I^+, I^- \cup \{x\}\rangle$ for any instance $x \in X$.

The hypothesis space $H(p,C,\langle I^+,I^-\rangle)$ is defined with respect to the SVM parameters p and C as well as the training data $\langle I^+,I^-\rangle$. It is non-empty if the SVM hyperplane $h(p,C,\langle I^+,I^-\rangle)$ is consistent with data set $\langle I^+,I^-\rangle$. The hypothesis space $H(p,C,\langle I^+,I^-\rangle)$ consists of those hyperplanes that can be constructed by SVM with respect to data and that are consistent with those data. More precisely, it includes the hyperplane $h(p,C,\langle I^+,I^-\rangle)$ and the SVM hyperplanes $h(p,C,\langle I^+ \cup \{x\},I^-\rangle)$ and $h(p,C,\langle I^+,I^- \cup \{x\}\rangle)$ for any instance $x \in X$ that are consistent with $\langle I^+ \cup \{x\},I^-\rangle$ and $\langle I^+,I^- \cup \{x\}\rangle$, respectively.

Definition 6.5. Consider the SVM parameters p and C, and data set $\langle I^+, I^- \rangle$. If the SVM hyperplane $h(p,C,\langle I^+, I^- \rangle)$ is consistent with $\langle I^+, I^- \rangle$, then the hypothesis space $H(p,C,\langle I^+, I^- \rangle)$ equals:

$$\{h \in H(p) | h = h(p,C,\langle I^+, I^- \rangle) \vee$$
$$(\exists x \in X)(h = h(p,C,\langle I^+ \cup \{x\}, I^- \rangle) \wedge cons(h, \langle I^+ \cup \{x\}, I^- \rangle)) \vee$$
$$(\exists x \in X)(h = h(p,C,\langle I^+, I^- \cup \{x\} \rangle) \wedge cons(h, \langle I^+, I^- \cup \{x\} \rangle))\}.$$

Otherwise, the hypothesis space $H(p,C,\langle I^+, I^- \rangle)$ equals $\emptyset$.

SVMs have an efficient consistency test for the hypothesis space $H(p,C,\langle I^+, I^- \rangle)$ with respect to the data sets $\langle I^+ \cup \{x\}, I^- \rangle$ and $\langle I^+, I^- \cup \{x\} \rangle$ for any instance $x \in X$. The test involves the SVM hyperplanes $h(p,C,\langle I^+, I^- \rangle)$, $h(p,C,\langle I^+ \cup \{x\}, I^- \rangle)$, and $h(p,C,\langle I^+, I^- \cup \{x\} \rangle)$ only. It assumes that the instance-consistency property holds.

Definition 6.6. SVM has the instance-consistency property for data set $\langle I^+, I^- \rangle$ if and only if for any instance $x \in X$:

- if the hyperplane $h(p,C,\langle I^+ \cup \{x\}, I^- \rangle)$ is inconsistent with data set $\langle I^+ \cup \{x\}, I^- \rangle$, then for any instance $x' \in X$ the hyperplanes $h(p,C,\langle I^+ \cup \{x'\}, I^- \rangle)$ and $h(p,C,\langle I^+, I^- \cup \{x'\} \rangle)$ are inconsistent with the data $\langle I^+ \cup \{x\}, I^- \rangle$;
- if the hyperplane $h(p,C,\langle I^+, I^- \cup \{x\} \rangle)$ is inconsistent with data set $\langle I^+, I^- \cup \{x\} \rangle$, then for any instance $x' \in X$ the hyperplanes $h(p,C,\langle I^+ \cup \{x'\}, I^- \rangle)$ and $h(p,C,\langle I^+, I^- \cup \{x'\} \rangle)$ are inconsistent with the data $\langle I^+, I^- \cup \{x\} \rangle$.

We describe the SVM consistency test to decide if there does exist any hyperplane h in the hypothesis space $H(p,C,\langle I^+, I^- \rangle)$ that is consistent with data $\langle I^+ \cup \{x\}, I^- \rangle$ for some instance $x \in X$. For the test we first construct the hyperplane $h(p,C,\langle I^+, I^- \rangle)$. If the hyperplane $h(p,C,\langle I^+, I^- \rangle)$ is consistent with the data $\langle I^+ \cup \{x\}, I^- \rangle$, then there exists a hyperplane $h \in H(p,C,\langle I^+, I^- \rangle)$ that is consistent with the data $\langle I^+ \cup \{x\}, I^- \rangle$. If not, we check whether there exist other hyperplanes in $H(p,C,\langle I^+, I^- \rangle)$ that are consistent with the data $\langle I^+ \cup \{x\}, I^- \rangle$. We construct the hyperplane $h(p,C,\langle I^+ \cup \{x\}, I^- \rangle)$. If the hyperplane $h(p,C,\langle I^+ \cup \{x\}, I^- \rangle)$ is consistent with the data $\langle I^+ \cup \{x\}, I^- \rangle$, then there does exist a hyperplane $h \in H(p,C,\langle I^+, I^- \rangle)$ that is consistent with the data $\langle I^+ \cup \{x\}, I^- \rangle$. If not, by the instance-consistency property we conclude that there does not exist any hyperplane h in the hypothesis space $H(p,C,\langle I^+, I^- \rangle)$ that is consistent with data $\langle I^+ \cup \{x\}, I^- \rangle$.

The consistency test for hyperplanes in the hypothesis space $H(p,C,\langle I^+, I^- \rangle)$ with respect to $\langle I^+, I^- \cup \{x\} \rangle$ for any instance $x \in X$ is analogous. Thus, *SVM is a consistency algorithm in the hypothesis space* $H(p,C,\langle I^+, I^- \rangle)$ *with respect to* $\langle I^+ \cup \{x\}, I^- \rangle$ *and* $\langle I^+, I^- \cup \{x\} \rangle$ *for any instance* $x \in X$. Below in Theorems 6.3 and 6.4 we formalize the SVM consistency test for data $\langle I^+ \cup \{x\}, I^- \rangle$ and $\langle I^+, I^- \cup \{x\} \rangle$ for any instance $x \in X$.

Theorem 6.3. *If the instance-consistency property holds and $H(p,C,\langle I^+,I^-\rangle) \neq \emptyset$, then for any instance $x \in X$:*

$$(\exists h \in H(p,C,\langle I^+,I^-\rangle)) \; cons(h,\langle I^+ \cup \{x\},I^-\rangle) \leftrightarrow$$
$$[cons(h(p,C,\langle I^+,I^-\rangle),\langle I^+ \cup \{x\},I^-\rangle) \vee$$
$$cons(h(p,C,\langle I^+ \cup \{x\},I^-\rangle),\langle I^+ \cup \{x\},I^-\rangle)].$$

Proof. $(\rightarrow)$ Consider arbitrary instance $x \in X$ and hypothesis $h \in H(p,C,\langle I^+,I^-\rangle)$ so that $cons(h,\langle I^+ \cup \{x\},I^-\rangle)$. Since $h \in H(p,C,\langle I^+,I^-\rangle)$ we have:

$$cons(h(p,C,\langle I^+,I^-\rangle),\langle I^+ \cup \{x\},I^-\rangle) \text{ or} \tag{6.9}$$
$$(\exists x' \in X)[cons(h(p,C,\langle I^+ \cup \{x'\},I^-\rangle),\langle I^+ \cup \{x\},I^-\rangle) \vee$$
$$cons(h(p,C,\langle I^+,I^- \cup \{x'\}\rangle),\langle I^+ \cup \{x\},I^-\rangle)]. \tag{6.10}$$

Since the instance-consistency property holds, by definition 6.6 formula (6.10) implies:

$$cons(h(p,C,\langle I^+ \cup \{x\},I^-\rangle),\langle I^+ \cup \{x\},I^-\rangle). \tag{6.11}$$

From formulas (6.9) and (6.11) this part of the theorem is proven.

$(\leftarrow)$ This part of the proof follows immediately from definition 6.5. $\square$

Theorem 6.4. *If the instance-consistency property holds and $H(p,C,\langle I^+,I^-\rangle) \neq \emptyset$, then for any instance $x \in X$:*

$$(\exists h \in H(p,C,\langle I^+,I^-\rangle)) \; cons(h,\langle I^+,I^- \cup \{x\}\rangle) \leftrightarrow$$
$$[cons(h(p,C,\langle I^+,I^-\rangle),\langle I^+,I^- \cup \{x\}\rangle) \vee$$
$$cons(h(p,C,\langle I^+,I^- \cup \{x\}\rangle),\langle I^+,I^- \cup \{x\}\rangle)].$$

Proof. The proof is analogous to that of theorem 6.3. $\square$

By Theorem 6.3 to test if there exists a hyperplane $h \in H(p,C,\langle I^+,I^-\rangle)$ consistent with data $\langle I^+ \cup \{x\},I^-\rangle$ for any instance $x \in X$ we have to test if either the SVM hyperplanes $h(p,C,\langle I^+ \cup \{x\},I^-\rangle)$ is consistent with the data $\langle I^+ \cup \{x\},I^-\rangle$ or the hyperplane $h(p,C,\langle I^+ \cup \{x\},I^-\rangle)$ is consistent with the data $\langle I^+ \cup \{x\},I^-\rangle$. Testing if there exists a hyperplane $h \in H(p,C,\langle I^+,I^-\rangle)$ consistent with $\langle I^+,I^- \cup \{x\}\rangle$ for any instance $x \in X$ is analogous (see Theorem 6.4).

Input: An instance $x \in X$ to be classified;
      The parameters p and C of SVM;
      Training data $\langle I^+, I^- \rangle$.
Output: classification $y \in Y \cup \{0\}$ of the instance x.
      Construct the SVM hyperplane $h(p, C, \langle I^+, I^- \rangle)$;
      if $\neg cons(h(p, C, \langle I^+, I^- \rangle), \langle I^+, I^- \rangle)$
      then return 0;
      if $cons(h(p, C, \langle I^+, I^- \rangle), \langle I^+ \cup \{x\}, I^- \rangle)$ **then**
         Construct the SVM hyperplane $h(p, C, \langle I^+, I^- \cup \{x\} \rangle)$;
         if $\neg cons(h(p, C, \langle I^+, I^- \cup \{x\} \rangle), \langle I^+, I^- \cup \{x\} \rangle)$
         then return $+1$;
      if $cons(h(p, C, \langle I^+, I^- \rangle), \langle I^+, I^- \cup \{x\} \rangle)$ **then**
         Construct the SVM $h(p, C, \langle I^+ \cup \{x\}, I^- \rangle)$;
         if $\neg cons(h(p, C, \langle I^+ \cup \{x\}, I^- \rangle), \langle I^+ \cup \{x\}, I^- \rangle)$
         then return -1;
      return 0.

Fig. 6.1: The Classification Algorithm of VSSVMs.

6.5.2 Definition of Version Space Support Vector Machines

We define VSSVMs as version spaces in the hypothesis space $H(p, C, \langle I^+, I^- \rangle)$.

Definition 6.7. Consider a hypothesis space $H(p, C, \langle I^+, I^- \rangle)$ and training data sets $\langle I^{+\prime}, I^{-\prime} \rangle$ such that $I^{+\prime} \supseteq I^+$ and $I^{-\prime} \supseteq I^-$. Then, the version space support vector machine $VS_C^p(I^{+\prime}, I^{-\prime})$ is defined equal to:

$$\{h \in H(p, C, \langle I^+, I^- \rangle) | cons(h, \langle I^{+\prime}, I^{-\prime} \rangle)\}.$$

Since VSSVMs are version spaces, the inductive bias of VSSVMs is the restriction bias [9]. Since the SVM parameters p and C define the hypothesis space $H(p, C, \langle I^+, I^- \rangle)$, they control the inductive bias of VSSVMs.

6.5.3 Classification Algorithm

The classification algorithm of VSSVMs implements the unanimous-voting classification rule of version spaces and is based on Theorem 6.1. It assumes that the instance-consistency property holds. Thus, to test version spaces for collapse SVMs are employed according to Theorems 6.3 and 6.4.

The classification algorithm is given in Figure 6.1. Assume that an instance $x \in X$ is to be classified. Then, the SVM hyperplane $h(p, C, \langle I^+, I^- \rangle)$ is constructed. If $h(p, C, \langle I^+, I^- \rangle)$ is inconsistent with the training data $\langle I^+, I^- \rangle$, by Definition 6.5 the hypothesis space $H(p, C, \langle I^+, I^- \rangle)$ is empty. Thus, by Definition 6.7 the VSSVM $VS_C^p(I^+, I^-)$ is empty as well and by Definition 6.3 the algorithm returns 0; i.e., the classification of the instance x is unknown. If the hyperplane $h(p, C, \langle I^+, I^- \rangle)$

is consistent with the training data $\langle I^+, I^- \rangle$, by Definition 6.5 the hypothesis space $H(p, C, \langle I^+, I^- \rangle)$ is non-empty. Thus, by Definition 6.7 the VSSVM $VS_C^p(I^+, I^-)$ is non-empty as well. In this case the algorithm continues by testing whether the hyperplane $h(p, C, \langle I^+, I^- \rangle)$ is consistent with the data $\langle I^+ \cup \{x\}, I^- \rangle$. If so, then by Definition 6.7 the VSSVM $VS_C^p(I^+ \cup \{x\}, I^-)$ is non-empty and the algorithm constructs the SVM hyperplane $h(p, C, \langle I^+, I^- \cup \{x\} \rangle)$. If the hyperplane $h(p, C, \langle I^+, I^- \cup \{x\} \rangle)$ is inconsistent with the data $\langle I^+, I^- \cup \{x\} \rangle$, then by Theorem 6.4 we conclude that there does not exist any hyperplane $h \in H(p, C, \langle I^+, I^- \rangle)$ that is consistent with the data $\langle I^+, I^- \cup \{x\} \rangle$. Thus, by Definition 6.7 the VSSVM $VS_C^p(I^+, I^- \cup \{x\})$ is empty. Since $VS_C^p(I^+ \cup \{x\}, I^-)$ is non-empty and $VS_C^p(I^+, I^- \cup \{x\})$ is empty, by Theorem 6.1 the algorithm assigns class $+1$ to the instance x. If class $+1$ cannot be assigned, the algorithm checks analogously if it can assign class -1. If no classification from Y is assigned to the instance x, the indicator 0 is returned.

6.6 The Volume-Extension Approach for VSSVMs

To overcome the problems of noisy training data and inexpressive hypothesis spaces for VSSVMs we propose applying our volume-extension approach using the parameter C of SVMs. In Section 6.4 we showed that the probability that the SVM hyperplane $h(p, C, \langle I^+, I^- \rangle)$ is consistent with the data $\langle I^+, I^- \rangle$ increases with C. This implies in general that for any two values C_1 and C_2 of the parameter C such that $C_1 < C_2$ and arbitrary data $\langle I^+, I^- \rangle$ if the hyperplane $h(p, C_1, \langle I^+, I^- \rangle)$ is consistent with $\langle I^+, I^- \rangle$, then the hyperplane $h(p, C_2, \langle I^+, I^- \rangle)$ is consistent with $\langle I^+, I^- \rangle$ as well. Thus, given data $\langle I^+, I^- \rangle$, and hypothesis spaces $H(p, C_1, \langle I^+, I^- \rangle)$ and $H(p, C_2, \langle I^+, I^- \rangle)$, for any sets $I^{+\prime} \supseteq I^+$ and $I^{-\prime} \supseteq I^-$ if there exists a hyperplane in $H(p, C_1, \langle I^+, I^- \rangle)$ consistent with $\langle I^{+\prime}, I^{-\prime} \rangle$, then there exists a hyperplane in $H(p, C_2, \langle I^+, I^- \rangle)$ consistent with $\langle I^{+\prime}, I^{-\prime} \rangle$. This implies by Theorem 6.2 that the volume of the VSSVM $VS_{C_1}^p(I^+, I^-)$ is a subset of or equal to the volume of the VSSVM $VS_{C_2}^p(I^+, I^-)$. Thus, we conclude that the volume of VSSVMs increases with the parameter C.

From the above we propose to realize the volume-extension approach for our VSSVMs by increasing the parameter C of SVMs. The approach is demonstrated in Figure 6.2 for values of 30 and 1000 of the parameter C.

6.7 Experiments

VSSVMs were implemented for the Weka machine-learning environment [14]. We experimented with VSSVMs using the polynomial and RBF kernels. The evaluation method was the leave-one-out method. We evaluated four statistics of the classification performance of VSSVMs:

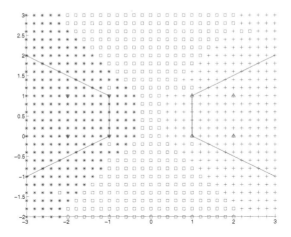

Fig. 6.2: The volume of VSSVMs in $\mathbb{R}^2$ for $C = 30$ and $C = 1000$. Instances in I^+ are marked by $\triangle$, instances in I^- are marked by $\triangledown$. The volume of the VSSVM for $C = 30$ is presented by $\square$ boxes. The volume of the VSSVM for $C = 1000$ is bounded by the lines.

- positive rejection rate *PRr* defined as the proportion of positive instances *unclassified* by VSSVMs;
- negative rejection rate *NRr* defined as the proportion negative instances *unclassified* by VSSVMs;
- true positive and true negative rates *TPr* and *TNr* [3] on instances *classified* by VSSVMs.

The (TPr, PRr) and (TNr, NRr) graphs of VSSVMs are shown in the first columns of Figure 6.3 and Figure 6.4 for 7 binary UCI datasets [4]. One point in the graphs represents a VSSVM for some values of the SVM parameters p and C. Subsequent points represent VSSVMs for the same value of the parameter p and increased values of the parameter C. Hence, the graphs show the potential of VSSVMs for reliable classification with respect to the parameter C.

The initial value p_0 of the kernel parameter p used in VSSVMs was chosen using sequential search so that p_0 is minimized and all $VS_C^{p_0}(I^+ \setminus \{x\}, I^-)$ and $VS_C^{p_0}(I^+, I^- \setminus \{x\})$ [2] are nonempty for some value of the parameter C. The initial value C_0 of C was chosen using binary search given p_0 so that C_0 is minimized and all $VS_{C_0}^{p_0}(I^+ \setminus \{x\}, I^-)$ and $VS_{C_0}^{p_0}(I^+, I^- \setminus \{x\})$ are nonempty.

The values p_0 and C_0 define VSSVMs represented as the most left points of the graphs on Figures 6.3 and 6.4. The PRr_0 and NRr_0 of these VSSVMs are nonzero and the graphs are undefined in the intervals $[0, PRr_0)$ and $[0, NRr_0)$. [3] Most initial

---

[2] These are VSSVMs if an instance x is left out in the leave-one-out validation.

[3] This is due to the fact that for the values p_0 and C_0 in our experiments VSSVMs consist of more than one hyperplane.

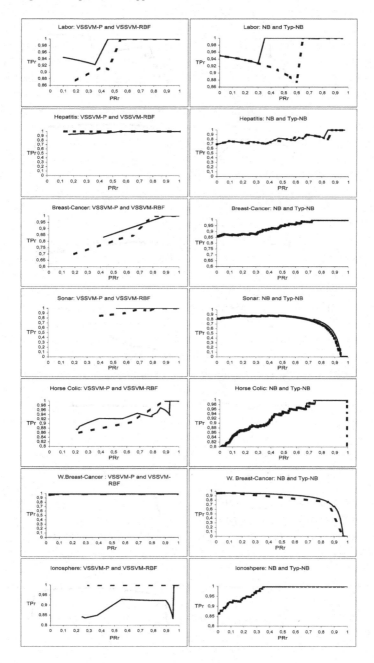

Fig. 6.3: The (TPr, PRr) graphs of VSSVM-RBF (——), VSSVM-P (– – –), NB (——), and Typ-NB (– – –).

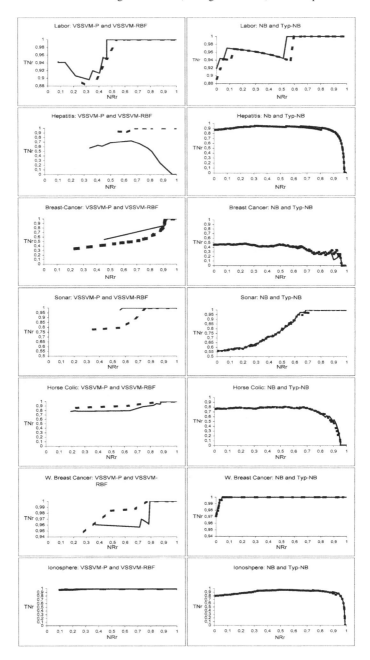

Fig. 6.4: The (TNr, NRr) graphs of VSSVM-RBF (——), VSSVM-P (– – –), NB (——), and Typ-NB (– – –).

VSSVMs have TPr_0 and TNr_0 lower than 1. This is due to noise in the datasets used in the experiments and/or inexpressive hypothesis spaces. To overcome these problems we applied our volume-extension approach by stepwise increasing the parameter C from C_0 to 10000. For each step we generated a VSSVM and plotted its (TPr, PRr) and (TNr, NRr) points on the graphs from Figures 6.3 and 6.4. The graphs show that VSSVMs reach TPr and TNr of 1. The only exception is the VSSVM with the RBF kernel for the hepatitis dataset. *Thus, we may conclude that the volume-extension approach is capable of solving the problems with noisy training data and inexpressive hypothesis spaces.*

We compare VSSVMs for the polynomial kernel (VSSVM-P) and for the RBF kernel (VSSVM-RBF) with respect to reliable classification using the graphs of Figures 6.3 and 6.4. For that purpose *we use the minimal rejection rates PRr_m and NRr_m* [4] *for which TPr and TNr are 1.* The PRr_m of VSSVM-P is lower than that of VSSVM-RBF for 5 out of 7 datasets. The NRr_m of VSSVM-P is lower than that of VSSVM-RBF for 2 out of 3 datasets. For the remaining 4 datasets NRr_m of VSSVM-P and VSSVM-RBF are equal. Thus, VSSVM-P is better for reliable classification than VSSVM-RBF in our experiments.

6.8 Comparison with Relevant Work

This section compares VSSVMs with relevant work. A comparison with the Bayesian framework is provided in Subsection 6.8.1, a comparison with typicalness framework in Subsection 6.8.2.

6.8.1 Bayesian Framework

The Bayesian framework [12] is the first approach used for reliable classification. This is due to the fact that the posterior class probabilities are natural estimates of the reliability of instance classifications. These probabilities are computed from prior probabilities. Since it is difficult to estimate plausibly the prior probabilities, the Bayesian framework can be misleading when used for reliable classification [13]. In this context we note that VSSVMs do not suffer from the aforementioned problem. This was confirmed by our experiments presented in Figures 6.3 and 6.4. In the second columns of Figures 6.3 and 6.4 we present (TPr, PRr) and (TNr, NRr) graphs of the Naive Bayes classifier (NB) (one of the most popular Bayesian classifiers). The graphs are constructed by stepwise increasing thresholds on the posterior probabilities of NB using the leave-one-out validation method. We compare VSSVMs and NB using the minimal rejection rates PRr_m and NRr_m. The comparison shows that:

---

[4] If a classifier has lower values of PRr_m and NRr_m, it can classify more instances.

- the PRr_m of VSSVM-P is lower than that of NB in 4 out of 7 datasets. The NRr_m of VSSVM-P is lower than NRr_m of NB in 5 out of 7 datasets. For the minority class the minimal rejection rates of VSSVM-P are lower than those of NB in 5 out of 7 datasets. For the majority class the minimal rejection rates of VSSVM-P are lower than those of NB in 4 out of 7 datasets.
- the PRr_m of VSSVM-RBF is lower than that of NB in 3 out of 7 datasets. The NRr_m of VSSVM-RBF is lower than that of NB in 4 out of 6 datasets. For the minority class the minimal rejection rates of VSSVM-RBF are lower than those of NB in 4 out of 7 datasets. For the majority class the minimal rejection rates of VSSVM-RBF are lower than those of NB in 3 out of 6 datasets. [5]

From the two points above we conclude that VSSVMs outperform NB for the task of reliable classification in our experiments.

6.8.2 Typicalness Framework

The typicalness framework is an approach to reliable classification that allows computing a p-value for each class a classifier can assign to an instance [10, 13]. The framework is valid if the data are drawn from the same unknown exchangeability distribution. Given instance space X, class set Y, training data D over $X \times Y$, and an instance $x \in X$ to be classified, the framework first computes for each class $y \in Y$ the strangeness scores of the instances in D and the labeled instance (x, y). The strangeness score estimates for an instance in $D \cup \{(x,y)\}$ how unusual this instance is relatively to the other instances in $D \cup \{(x,y)\}$. The p-value p_y of class y for the instance x is computed as the proportion of the instances in $D \cup \{(x,y)\}$ of which the strangeness scores are greater than or equal to that of the instance (x, y).

The main problem in applying the typicalness framework for a classifier is to design a strangeness function specific for that classifier. Thus, the typicalness framework depends heavily on the type of the classifier used. In this context we note that version spaces do not suffer from the aforementioned problem. In this paper we implemented version spaces using SVM classifiers. (We defined the hypothesis space from which SVMs are consistency algorithms and then used SVMs for implementing the version-space classification rule.) The same approach can be applied for any type of classifiers. Thus, we may conclude that version spaces are not dependent on the classifier employed.

To complete the comparison we consider a typicalness-based Naive Bayes classifier (Typ-NB) proposed in [13]. We compare empirically VSSVMs and Typ-NB with respect to reliable classification (see Figures 6.3 and 6.4) using the minimal rejection rates PRr_m and NRr_m. The comparison shows that:

- the PRr_m of VSSVM-P is lower than that of Typ-NB in 5 out of 7 datasets. The NRr_m of VSSVM-P is lower than NRr_m Typ-NB in 5 out of 7 datasets. For the

---

[5] The comparison is for 6 datasets for some cases since for the hepatitis data VSSVM-RBF, NB, and Typ-NB do not have NRr_m.

minority class the minimal rejection rates of VSSVM-P are lower than those of Typ-NB in 6 out of 7 datasets. For the majority class the minimal rejection rates of VSSVM-P are lower than those of Typ-NB in 4 out of 7 datasets.

- the PRr_m of VSSVM-RBF is lower than that of Typ-NB in 5 out of 7 datasets. The NRr_m of VSSVM-RBF is lower than that of Typ-NB in 5 out of 6 datasets. For the minority class the minimal rejection rates of VSSVM-RBF are lower than those of Typ-NB in 5 out of 7 datasets. For the majority class the minimal rejection rates of VSSVM-RBF are lower than those of Typ-NB in 3 out of 6 datasets (see footnote 5).

From the two points above we conclude that VSSVMs outperform Typ-NB for the task of reliable classification in our experiments.

6.9 Conclusion

In this paper we showed that if the volume-extension approach is employed, version spaces are capable of providing reliable classifications when training data are noisy and hypothesis spaces are inexpressive. Thus, contrary to the traditional view [7, 8, 9], the main conclusion is that version spaces do form an approach to reliable classification. To support this conclusion we implemented version spaces using SVMs. The resulting approach is called version space support vector machines (VSSVMs). The experiments show that VSSVMs are able to outperform the existing approaches to reliable classification. In this context we note that the scheme how we implemented version spaces using SVMs is applicable for any type of classifiers. Thus, we conclude that version spaces can be implemented for any type of classifiers.

We foresee three future research directions that extend the scope of applicability of version spaces and VSSVMs. The first one is to extend version spaces for non-binary classification tasks. The second direction is to extend version spaces for classification tasks for which no consistent hypotheses exist. The third direction is to speed up VSSVMs using incremental SVMs [1].

References

1. G. Cauwenberghs and T. Poggio. Incremental and decremental support vector machine learning. In *Advances in Neural Information Processing Systems 13, Papers from Neural Information Processing Systems (NIPS) 2000*, pages 409–415. MIT Press, 2001.
2. R. Duda, P. Hart, and D. Stork. *Pattern Classification*. Willey, second edition, 2000.
3. T. Fawcett. An introduction to ROC analysis. *Pattern Recognition Letters*, 27(8):861–874, 2006.
4. A. Frank and A. Asuncion. UCI machine learning repository, 2010.
5. H. Hirsh, N. Mishra, and L. Pitt. Version spaces and the consistency problem. *Artificial Intelligence*, 156(2):115–138, 2004.

6. S. Keerthi and C. Lin. Asymptotic behaviors of support vector machines with gaussian kernel. *Neural Computation*, 15:1667–1689, 2003.

7. T. Mitchell. *Version spaces: an approach to concept learning*. PhD thesis, Electrical Engineering Dept., Stanford University, Stanford, CA, 1978.

8. T. Mitchell. Generalization as search. *Artificial Intelligence*, 18(2):203–226, 1982.

9. T. Mitchell. *Machine learning*. McGraw-Hill, New York, NY, 1997.

10. G. Shafer and V. Vovk. A tutorial on conformal prediction. *Journal of Machine Learning Research*, 9:371–421, March 2008.

11. E. Smirnov, I. Sprinkhuizen-Kuyper, G. Nalbantov, and S. Vanderlooy. Version space support vector machines. In *Proceedings of the 17th European Conference on Artificial Intelligence (ECAI-2006)*, pages 809–810, 2006.

12. V. Vapnik. *Statistical Learning Theory*. John Wiley, NY, 1998.

13. V. Vovk, A. Gammerman, and G. Shafer. *Algorithmic Learning in a Random World*. Springer, New York, NY, 2005.

14. I. Witten, E. Frank. and M. Hall *Data Mining: Practical Machine Learning Tools and Techniques with Java Implementations*. Morgan Kaufmann, 2011.

Chapter 7
Reliable Ticket Routing in Expert Networks

Gengxin Miao, Louise E. Moser, Xifeng Yan, Shu Tao, Yi Chen, and Nikos Anerousis

Abstract Problem ticket resolution is an important aspect of the delivery of IT services. A large service provider needs to handle, on a daily basis, thousands of tickets that report various types of problems. Many of those tickets bounce among multiple expert groups before being transferred to the group with the expertise to solve the problem. Finding a methodology that can automatically make reliable ticket routing decisions and that reduces such bouncing and, hence, shortens ticket resolution time is a long-standing challenge. Reliable ticket routing forwards the ticket to an expert who either can solve the problem reported in the ticket, or can reach an expert who can resolve the ticket. In this chapter, we present a unified generative model, the Optimized Network Model (ONM), that characterizes the lifecycle of a ticket, using both the content and the routing sequence of the ticket. ONM uses maximum likelihood estimation to capture reliable ticket transfer profiles on each edge of an expert network. These transfer profiles reflect how the information contained in a ticket is used by human experts to make ticket routing decisions. Based on ONM, we develop a probabilistic algorithm to generate reliable ticket routing recommendations for new tickets in a network of expert groups. Our algorithm calculates all possible routes to potential resolvers and makes globally optimal recommendations, in contrast to existing classification methods that make static and locally optimal

Gengxin Miao
ECE Department, University of California, Santa Barbara, CA 93106, e-mail: miao@ece.ucsb.edu

Louise E. Moser
ECE Department, University of California, Santa Barbara, CA 93106, e-mail: moser@ece.ucsb.edu

Xifeng Yan
CS Department, University of California, Santa Barbara, CA 93106, e-mail: xyan@cs.ucsb.edu

Shu Tao
IBM T. J. Watson, 19 Skyline Drive, Hawthorne, NY 10532, e-mail: shutao@us.ibm.com

Yi Chen
CSE Department, Arizona State University, Tempe, AZ 95281, e-mail: yi@asu.edu

Nikos Anerousis
IBM T. J. Watson 19 Skyline Drive, Hawthorne, NY 10532, e-mail: nikos@us.ibm.com

recommendations. Experiments show that our method significantly outperforms existing solutions and, hence, yields better performance in real-world applications.

7.1 Introduction

Problem ticket resolution is critical to the IT services business. A service provider might need to handle, on a daily basis, thousands of tickets that report various types of problems from its customers. The service provider's ability to resolve the tickets in a timely manner determines, to a large extent, its competitive advantage. To manage ticket resolution effectively, human experts are often organized into expert groups, each of which has the expertise to solve certain types of problems. As IT systems become more complex, the types of reported problems become more diverse. Finding an expert group to solve the problem specified in a ticket is a long-standing challenge for IT service providers.

A typical ticket processing system works as follows. A ticket is initiated by a customer or by internal staff, and is subsequently routed through a network of expert groups for resolution. The ticket is closed when it reaches a *resolver group* that provides the solution to the problem reported in the ticket. Figure 7.1 shows an interaction network between groups with ticket routing examples. Ticket t_1 starts at group A and ends at group D, while ticket t_2 starts at group G and ends at group C. The sequences $A \to B \to C \to D$ and $G \to E \to C$ are called *ticket routing sequences*.

In a large network of expert groups, being able to route a new ticket to its resolver quickly is essential to reduce labor cost and to improve customer satisfaction. Today, ticket routing decisions are often made manually and, thus, can be quite subjective and error-prone. Misinterpretation of the problem, inexperience of human individuals, and lack of communication between groups can lead to routing unreliability and inefficiency. These difficulties call for computational models that can accurately represent the collaborative relationship between groups in solving different kinds of problems. Such models ought to provide fine-grain information not only to help experts reduce ticket routing errors, but also to help service enterprises better understand group interactions and identify potential performance bottlenecks.

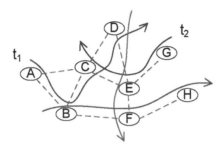

Fig. 7.1: Ticket Routing

In [23], Shao *et al.* proposed a Markov model-based approach to predict the resolver of a ticket, based on the expert groups that processed the ticket previously. In essence, their approach is a rule-based method, *i.e.*, if group A processed a ticket and did not have a solution, it calculates the likelihood that group B can resolve the problem. A drawback of that approach is that it is locally optimized and, thus, might not be able to find the best ticket routing sequence. Moreover, it does not consider the contents of the tickets. That is, it uses a "black-box" approach that can neither explain, nor fully leverage, the information related to why group A transfers a ticket to group B when it cannot solve the problem itself.

In this work, we address these issues by deriving a more comprehensive model that incorporates ticket content. Rather than simply calculating the transfer probability, *i.e.*, $P(B|A)$, between two groups A and B, we build a generative model that captures why tickets are transferred between two groups, *i.e.*, $P(w|A \rightarrow B)$, where w is a word in the ticket. In addition, we build a model that captures why a certain ticket can be resolved by a group B, *i.e.*, $P(w|B)$. Finally, we combine the local generative models into a global model, the Optimized Network Model (ONM), which represents the entire ticket resolution process in a network of expert groups.

The Optimized Network Model has at least three major applications. First, it can be trained using historical ticket data and then used as a recommendation engine to guide the routing of new tickets. Second, it provides a way to analyze the roles of expert groups, to assess their expertise levels, and to study the expertise awareness among groups. Third, it can be used to simulate the ticket routing process, and to help analyze the performance of an expert network under various ticket workloads. Due to space constraints, we focus on the first application and demonstrate the superiority of ONM over previous models for that application. We leave the other two applications for future work.

The technical contributions of this work are three-fold:

First, we propose a unified framework, the Optimized Network Model (ONM), to model ticket transfer and resolution in an expert network. We develop solutions to estimate the parameters of ONM, using maximum likelihood estimation. We use a gradient descent method to speed up the parameter learning process.

Second, we develop a novel ticket routing algorithm that analyzes all possible routes in the network, and determines the optimal route for a ticket to its resolver. As our experiments show, this algorithm significantly outperforms existing classification-based algorithms.

Third, we show that, unlike the sequence-only model [23], ONM can explain why tickets are transferred between groups and how intermediate transfer steps can be used in finding the resolver. Hence, it can be used to evaluate the roles and performance of expert groups in an expert network.

7.2 Related Work

We discuss below four categories of related work, namely, link prediction problem, information flow analysis, text classification problem, and expert finding problem.

Link prediction problem. Researchers have extensively studied the link prediction problem among social networks. The social network graph is represented using its adjacency matrix. When a random fraction of the edges in the graph is observed, the link prediction problem aims to predict the missing entries of the matrix. Candès and Recht [8] and Keshavan *et al.* [14] solved this problem using a low-rank estimation of the graph adjacency matrix. Backstrom *et. al.* [4] modified the random walk algorithm to allow the random walker to access the observed links more frequently. When only a block of the adjacency matrix is observed (*i.e.*, entire rows and columns of the matrix are missing) the low-rank estimation and the random walk approach no longer apply. Kim *et. al.* [15] developed an expectation maximization algorithm, assuming the number of missing nodes in the graph is known or can be estimated using other algorithms. However, all of the existing algorithm for link prediction focus on only the graph structure of the social network, neglecting the textual information on each edge. In the ticket routing problem, link prediction highly depends on the content of the tickets. Because the expertise of the expert groups differs significantly, the link structure in the social network differs largely due to the contents of the tickets.

Information flow analysis. Ticket routing aims to guide the information flow process at the top of a social network. Most of the research in this area uses email data to analyze information flow. Adamic *et al.* [2] studied the problem of finding the shortest paths between people using email connections, location information and organizational information. Ebel *et al.* [10] studied the static topology structure of an email network and exhibit a small world behavior despite the scale of the network. Wang *et al.* [25] analyzed the information spreading pattern using email to forward data collected from a large enterprize over two years. Again, the existing research on information flow analysis focus on the interaction patterns among the nodes in a social network, without considering the content very much. In our ticket resolution process, the ticket content is essential.

Text classification problem. Ticket routing can be considered an extension of the text classification problem, which has been extensively studied [6, 7, 13, 17, 21, 26, 27, 31]. For example, Calado *et al.* [7], Lu and Getoor [17], and Sen *et al.* [21] proposed methods to combine content and link information for document classification. Also relevant is the work of Yang and Liu [26], who studied the robustness of different text categorization methods.

Ticket routing is also related to the multi-class classification problem [20], but it has different characteristics. First, ticket routing involves multiple predictions if the current prediction is not correct, which leads to different evaluation criteria. Second, ticket routing takes place in a network of expert groups. Third, instead of relying on a single classifier, ticket routing requires leveraging the interactions between multiple local classifiers to find a globally optimized solution.

Belkin *et al.* [6] and Zhou *et al.* [31] introduced text classification using graph-based methods. Collective classification, such as stacked models [16], interactive classification [18], mean field relaxation labeling [28] and loopy belief propagation [29], are popular techniques for classifying nodes in a partially labeled graph. The problems studied in these methods are quite different from the ticket routing problem that is addressed in this article, which assumes the existence of a resolver in the network for a given ticket, and requires the classification to be applied repeatedly until the resolver is found.

Generative models and maximum likelihood estimation are standard approaches. Generative models seek the joint probability distribution over the observed data. Classification decisions are typically based on conditional probabilities formed using Bayesian rules. One example is the Naive Bayes classifier [12, 30], which assumes conditional independence between variables. Another example is the Gaussian Mixture Model [19], which estimates the probability distribution using a convex combination of several Gaussian distributions. Both of these models are good for analyzing sparse data. We chose the generative model because the transition probabilities in the ticket resolution sequences can be seamlessly embedded in the probabilistic framework.

Besides the generative models, discriminative models, such as the Support Vector Machine (SVM), have been shown to be effective for text classification [13]. One can potentially build a support vector classifier for each resolver and each transfer relationship. However, they are locally optimized for individual resolvers and transfer relationships; once trained, the SVM classifiers remain stationary. In our approach, the resolver predictions can be dynamically adjusted if previous predictions are incorrect.

Expert finding problem. The ticket routing problem is also related to the expert finding problem, *i.e.*, given a keyword query, find the most knowledgeable persons regarding that query. The expert finding algorithms proposed by Balog *et al.* [5] and Fang and Zhai [11] use a language model to calculate the probability of an expert candidate and generate the query terms. Serdyukov *et al.* [22] enhanced those models by allowing the candidates' expertise to be propagated within the network, *e.g.*, via email. Deng *et al.* [9] explored the links in documents such as those listed in DBLP [1]. Expert recommendation systems also use text categorization techniques [3, 24]. Because most expert finding algorithms are content-based, they share the same weakness of the Resolver Model (RM) given in Section 7.4.1.

Our study has demonstrated that better ticket routing performance can be achieved by combining ticket contents and routing sequences together. Nevertheless, considering existing sophisticated text classification methods and language models, it is an open research problem to investigate how to embed them in a collaborative network and learn their parameters in a holistic way for ticket processing.

7.3 Preliminaries

We use the following notation: $\mathcal{G} = \{g_1, g_2, ..., g_L\}$ is a set of expert groups in a collaborative network; $\mathcal{T} = \{t_1, t_2, ..., t_m\}$ is a set of tickets; and $\mathcal{W} = \{w_1, w_2, ..., w_n\}$ is a set of words that describe the problems in the tickets. A ticket consists of three components: (1) a problem category to which the ticket belongs, *e.g.*, a WINDOWS problem or a DB2 problem, that is identified when the ticket is generated, (2) the ticket contents, *i.e.*, a textual description of the problem symptoms, and (3) a routing sequence from the initial group to the final resolver group. Although some complex tickets can be associated with multiple problem categories or can involve multiple resolvers, most tickets are associated with one problem category and can be resolved by one expert group. Our model focuses on ticket routing in these common cases.

In the first step of routing, each ticket t is assigned to an initial expert group $g_{init}(t)$. If the initial group cannot solve the problem, it transfers the ticket to another group that it considers the right group to solve the problem. After one or more transfer steps, the ticket eventually reaches the resolver group $g_{res}(t)$. The route that the ticket takes is denoted $R(t)$. Table 7.1 shows a ticket example, which is first assigned to group HDBTOIGA, and is finally resolved by group NUS_N_DSCTS.

Table 7.1: A WINDOWS Ticket Example

ID	Description		Initial group
8805	User received an error R=12 when installing Hyperion. When tried to install again, got success msg, but unable to open the application in Excel		HDBTOIGA

ID	Time	Entry
8805	9/29/2006	... (multi transfer steps) ...
8805	10/2/2006	Ticket 8805 transferred to Group NUS_N_DSCTS
8805	10/2/2006	Resolution: enabled Essbase in Excel

To model the interactions between groups in an expert network, we need to understand how and why the tickets are transferred and resolved. Specifically, we aim to develop a modeling framework that consists of (1) a Resolution Model $M_g(t)$ that captures the probability that group g can resolve ticket t, and (2) a Transfer Model $M_{g_i \rightarrow g_j}(t)$ that captures the probability that group g_i transfers ticket t to group g_j, if g_i cannot resolve t. Our goal is to develop these two models, and then combine them into a unified network model, that represents the ticket lifecycle in the expert network, as shown in Figure 7.2.

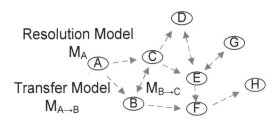

Fig. 7.2: Unified Network Model

7.4 Generative Models

The ticket contents and routing sequences of the historical tickets provide clues as to how tickets are routed by expert groups. In our expert network, each group has its own special expertise. Thus, if an expert group is capable of resolving one ticket, chances are it can also resolve other tickets with similar problem descriptions. Likewise, similar tickets typically have similar routing paths through the network. In this section, we characterize these properties using generative models.

7.4.1 Resolution Model (RM)

First, we build a generative model for each expert group using the textual descriptions of the problems the group has solved previously. Given a set $\mathcal{T}_i$ of tickets resolved by group g_i and $\mathcal{W}$ the set of words in the tickets in $\mathcal{T}_i$, we build a resolver profile P_{g_i} defined as the following column vector:

$$P_{g_i} = [P(w_1|g_i), P(w_2|g_i), ..., P(w_n|g_i)]^T \tag{7.1}$$

Equation (7.1) represents the word distribution among the tickets resolved by g_i. Here, $P(w_k|g_i)$ is the probability of choosing word w_k if we randomly draw a word from the descriptions of all tickets resolved by group g_i. Thus, $\sum_{k=1}^{n} P(w_k|g_i) = 1$.

Assuming that different words appear independently in the ticket content, the probability that g_i can resolve a ticket $t \in \mathcal{T}_i$ can be calculated from the resolver profile vector P_{g_i} as follows:

$$P(t|g_i) \propto \prod_{w_k \in t} P(w_k|g_i)^{f(w_k,t)} \tag{7.2}$$

where w_k is a word contained in the content of ticket t and $f(w_k, t)$ is the frequency of w_k in the content of t.

To find a set of most probable parameters $P(w_k|g_i)$, we use the maximum likelihood method. The likelihood that group g_i resolves all of the tickets in $\mathcal{T}_i$ is:

$$\mathcal{L}(\mathcal{T}_i, g_i) = \prod_{t \in \mathcal{T}_i} P(t|g_i) \tag{7.3}$$

We maximize the log likelihood:

$$P_{g_i} = \arg \max_{P(\mathcal{W}|g_i)} (\log(\mathcal{L}(\mathcal{T}_i, g_i)))$$

$$= \arg \max_{P(\mathcal{W}|g_i)} (\sum_{w_k} n(w_k, \mathcal{T}_i) \log(P(w_k|g_i)))$$

$$s.t. \quad \sum_{w_k \in \mathcal{W}} P(w_k|g_i) = 1$$

where $n(w_k, \mathcal{T}_i) = \sum_{t \in \mathcal{T}_i} f(w_k, t)$ is the total frequency of the word w_k in the ticket set $\mathcal{T}_i$. Thus, the maximum likelihood for the resolver profile vector P_{g_i} is given by:

$$P(w_k|g_i) = \frac{n(w_k, \mathcal{T}_i)}{\sum_{w_j \in \mathcal{W}} n(w_j, \mathcal{T}_i)} \tag{7.4}$$

The Resolution Model is a standard multi-class text classifier, which considers only ticket content. In the following discussion, we see that embedded in the ticket routing sequences are the transfer relations between groups, which can be used to improve the accuracy of our model.

7.4.2 Transfer Model (TM)

As Shao *et al.* [23] pointed out, not only the resolver group, but also the intermediate groups in the ticket routing sequences, contribute to the resolution of a ticket. The reason is that, even if an expert group cannot solve a problem directly, it might know which other group is capable of solving it. Thus, we use both the ticket content and the routing sequence to model the transfer between expert groups.

Considering an edge $e_{ij} = g_i \rightarrow g_j$ in the expert network, we let $\mathcal{T}_{ij}$ denote the set of tickets that are transferred along the edge e_{ij} and let $\mathcal{W}$ denote the set of words in the tickets in $\mathcal{T}_{ij}$. Using the same technique as described in Section 7.4.1, we build the transfer profile of an edge between two expert groups as the column vector:

$$P_{e_{ij}} = [P(w_1|e_{ij}), P(w_2|e_{ij}), ..., P(w_n|e_{ij})]^T \tag{7.5}$$

where $P_{e_{ij}}$ characterizes the word distribution among the tickets routed along edge e_{ij} and $P(w_k|e_{ij})$ is the probability of choosing word w_k if we randomly draw a word from the tickets transferred along edge e_{ij}. Similarly, we derive the maximum likelihood for the transfer profile of e_{ij} as follows:

$$P(w_k|e_{ij}) = \frac{n(w_k, \mathcal{T}_{ij})}{\sum_{w_\ell \in \mathcal{W}} n(w_\ell, \mathcal{T}_{ij})} \tag{7.6}$$

The Transfer Model for the edges can be combined with the Resolution Model for the nodes to form the network model shown in Figure 7.2. However, the parameters of these models are learned independently and, thus, might not achieve the best accuracy. To address this problem, we study how to optimize the network model by learning these parameters globally.

7.4.3 Optimized Network Model (ONM)

Both the Resolution Model and the Transfer Model are local models. They are not optimized for end-to-end ticket routing in the expert network. In this section, we present an optimized model that accounts for the profiles of the nodes and edges together Instead of considering only the tickets resolved by a certain expert group or transferred along a certain edge, this model learns its parameters based on the entire set of tickets, using both their contents and their routing sequences. As we will see, this global model outperforms the local models.

7.4.3.1 Routing Likelihood

When a set $\mathcal{T}_i$ of tickets is routed to a group g_i, some of the tickets will be resolved if g_i has the right expertise, while the rest of the tickets will be transferred to other groups. If g_i resolves a ticket, we assume that g_i transfers the ticket to itself. We let $\mathcal{T}_{ij}$ be the set of tickets that are transferred from group g_i to group g_j, where $\mathcal{T}_{ii}$ is the set of tickets resolved by group g_i itself. Thus, $\mathcal{T}_i = \bigcup_{j=1}^{L} \mathcal{T}_{ij}$, where L is the number of expert groups.

Given a ticket t and the expert group g_i that currently holds the ticket t, the probability that t is transferred from group g_i to group g_j is:

$$
\begin{aligned}
P(g_j|t,g_i) &= \frac{P(t|e_{ij})P(g_j|g_i)}{Z(t,g_i)} \\
&= \frac{(\prod_{w_k \in t} P(w_k|e_{ij})^{f(w_k,t)})P(g_j|g_i)}{Z(t,g_i)}
\end{aligned}
\tag{7.7}
$$

where $Z(t,g_i) = \sum_{g_j \in \mathcal{G}} P(t|e_{ij})P(g_j|g_i)$ and $P(g_j|g_i)$ is the prior probability that g_i transfers a ticket to g_j. $P(g_j|g_i)$ can be estimated by $|\mathcal{T}_{ij}|/|\mathcal{T}_i|$. To simplify the notation, we let $P(g_i|t,g_i)$ represent the probability that group g_i is able to resolve ticket t if t is routed to g_i. Hence, $P(w|e_{ii})$ is the resolution model of g_i. Because a ticket is often succinct with few redundant words, we assume $f(w_k,t) = 1$ if w_k occurs in t and $f(w_k,t) = 0$ otherwise. This assumption significantly simplifies the derivation of the model.

Each historical ticket t has a routing sequence $R(t)$. For example, $R(t) = g_1 \rightarrow g_2 \rightarrow g_3$, with initial group $g_{init}(t) = g_1$ and resolver group $g_{res}(t) = g_3$. We assume that an initial group g_1 is given for each ticket t, i.e., $P(g_1|t) = 1$ and that each expert group makes its transfer decisions independently. In this case, the probability that the routing sequence $g_1 \rightarrow g_2 \rightarrow g_3$ occurs is:

$$
\begin{aligned}
P(R(t)|t) &= P(g_1|t)P(g_2|t,g_1)P(g_3|t,g_2)P(g_3|t,g_3) \\
&= P(g_2|g_1)P(g_3|g_2)P(g_3|g_3) \times \frac{P(t|e_{1,2})P(t|e_{2,3})P(t|e_{3,3})}{Z(t,g_1)Z(t,g_2)Z(t,g_3)}
\end{aligned}
$$

We assume further that the tickets are independent of each other. Thus, the likelihood of observing the routing sequences in a ticket set $\mathcal{T}$ is:

$$
\mathcal{L} = \prod_{t \in \mathcal{T}} P(R(t)|t)
\tag{7.8}
$$

7.4.3.2 Parameter Optimization

To find a set of globally optimal parameters $P(w_k|e_{ij})$, we use maximum likelihood estimation to maximize the log likelihood:

$$\log \mathcal{L} = \sum_{t \in \mathcal{T}} \log P(R(t)|t) \tag{7.9}$$

$$= \sum_{t \in \mathcal{T}} \sum_{e_{ij} \in R(t)} \log \frac{P(t|e_{ij}) \times P(g_j|g_i)}{Z(t,g_i)}$$

$$= \sum_{e_{ij} \in \mathcal{E}} \sum_{t \in \mathcal{T}_{ij}} (\log(P(t|e_{ij})) + \log(P(g_j|g_i))) - \sum_{g_i \in \mathcal{G}} \sum_{t' \in \mathcal{T}_i} \log(Z(t',g_i))$$

where $\mathcal{E} = \{e_{ij}|1 \leq i,j \leq L\}$ and $P(t|e_{ij}) = \prod_{w_k \in t} P(w_k|e_{ij})$. The optimal transfer profile is given by the following constrained optimization problem:

$$P(\mathcal{W}|\mathcal{E})^* = \arg \max_{P(\mathcal{W}|\mathcal{E})} (\log \mathcal{L}) \tag{7.10}$$

$$\text{s.t.} \sum_{w_k \in \mathcal{W}} P(w_k|e_{ij}) = 1;$$

$$P(w_k|e_{ij}) \geq 0$$

where $\mathcal{W}$ is the set of words and $\mathcal{E}$ is the set of edges.

This optimization problem is not convex, and it involves many free dimensions (the degree of freedom is $(|\mathcal{W}| - 1) \times |\mathcal{G}|^2$). It cannot be solved efficiently with existing tools.

Thus, we seek a solution that is near-optimal but easier to calculate. Our approach is to update the parameters $P(w_k|e_{ij})$ iteratively to improve the likelihood. Specifically, we use the steepest descent method to maximize the lower bound of the log likelihood. By Jensen's inequality, we have

$$Z(t,g_i) \leq \prod_{w_k \in t} \sum_{g_\ell \in \mathcal{G}} P(g_\ell|g_i)P(w_k|e_{i\ell}) \tag{7.11}$$

Combining Equation (7.9) and Equation (7.11), we have:

$$\log \mathcal{L} \geq \lfloor \log \mathcal{L} \rfloor = \sum_{e_{ij}} \sum_{t \in \mathcal{T}_{ij}} (\log(P(t|e_{ij})) + \log(P(g_j|g_i)))$$

$$- \sum_{g_i \in \mathcal{G}} \sum_{t' \in \mathcal{T}_i} \sum_{w_k \in t'} \log(\sum_{g_\ell \in \mathcal{G}} (P(g_\ell|g_i) \times P(w_k|e_{i\ell})))$$

The gradient is given by:

$$\nabla \lfloor \log(\mathcal{L}) \rfloor = \frac{\partial \lfloor \log \mathcal{L} \rfloor}{\partial P(w_k|e_{ij})}$$

$$= \frac{\sum_{t \in \mathcal{T}_{ij}} n(w_k,t)}{P(w_k|e_{ij})} - \frac{P(g_j|g_i) \times \sum_{t' \in \mathcal{T}_i} n(w_k,t')}{\sum_{g_\ell \in \mathcal{G}} P(g_\ell|g_i) \times P(w_k|e_{i\ell})}$$

Using the values of $P(w_k|e_{ij})$ calculated in Equation (7.6) as the starting point, we iteratively improve the solution along the gradient. To satisfy the constraints, we calculate the projection of the gradient in the hyperplane defined by $\sum_{w_k \in \mathcal{W}} P(w_k|e_{ij}) = 1$ to ensure that the solution stays in the feasible region. The profiles of the edges in the network are updated one at a time, until they converge. Although the gradient-based method might produce a local optimum solution, it estimates the model parameters all together from a global perspective and provides a better estimation than the TM locally-optimized solution.

7.5 Ticket Routing

We now study the application of the generative models introduced in Section 7.4 to ticket routing. Given a new ticket t and its initial group $g_{init}(t)$, a routing algorithm uses a model $\mathcal{M}$ to predict the resolver group $g_{res}(t)$. If the predicted group is not the right resolver, the algorithm keeps on predicting, until the resolver group is found. The performance of a routing algorithm can be evaluated in terms of the number of expert groups that it tried until reaching the resolver. Specifically, we let the predicted routing sequence for ticket t_i be $R(t_i)$ and let $|R(t_i)|$ be the number of groups tried for ticket t_i. For a set of testing tickets $\mathcal{T} = \{t_1, t_2, \ldots, t_m\}$, we evaluate the performance of a routing algorithm using the Mean Number of Steps To Resolve (MSTR) [23] given by:

$$S = \frac{\sum_{i=1}^{m} |R(t_i)|}{m} \tag{7.12}$$

The ticket routing problem is related to the multi-class classification problem in that we are seeking a resolver (class label) for each ticket. It differs from a classification problem in that our goal is not to maximize the classification precision, but to minimize the expected number of steps before the right resolver is reached.

Nevertheless, we can adapt a multi-class classifier to fit our problem. We assume that a classifier C predicts group g as the resolver of ticket t, with probability $P(g|t)$. A simple approach is to rank the potential resolver groups in descending order of $P(g|t)$ and then transfer the ticket t to them one by one, until the right resolver is found. In this approach, the ranking of groups does not change, even if the current prediction is incorrect. We take the Resolution Model as the baseline method, for building a classifier. Then, we develop two dynamic ranking methods, using the Transfer Model and the Optimized Network Model, to achieve better performance.

7.5.1 Ranked Resolver

The Ranked Resolver algorithm is designed exclusively for the Resolution Model (RM). Expert groups are ranked based on the probability that they can resolve a ticket according to the ticket content.

Given a new ticket t, the probability that expert group g_i can resolve the ticket is:

$$P(g_i|t) = \frac{P(g_i)P(t|g_i)}{P(t)} \tag{7.13}$$

$$\propto P(g_i) \prod_{w_k \in t} P(w_k|g_i)^{f(w_k,t)}$$

Here, $P(g_i)$ is the prior probability of group g_i being a resolver group, which is estimated by $|\mathcal{T}_i|/|\mathcal{T}|$, where $\mathcal{T}_i$ is the set of tickets resolved by g_i and $\mathcal{T}$ is the ticket training set.

A routing algorithm for this model is to try different candidate resolver groups in descending order of $P(g_i|t)$. The algorithm works fine unless the new ticket t contains a word that does not appear in the training ticket set $\mathcal{T}$. In that case, $P(g_i|t)$ is zero for all i. To avoid this problem, we introduce a smoothing factor λ to calculate the probability, *i.e.*,

$$P(w|g_i)^* = \lambda \times P(w|g_i) + (1-\lambda)/|\mathcal{W}| \tag{7.14}$$

Using the smoothed value $P(w|g_i)^*$ guarantees a positive value of $P(g_i|t)$ for all i.

7.5.2 Greedy Transfer

The Greedy Transfer algorithm makes one step transfer predictions and selects the most probable resolver as the next step.

When a new ticket t first enters the expert network, it is assigned to an initial group g_{init}. Instead of calculating which group is likely to solve the problem, we determine the group to which to transfer the ticket, either the group that can solve the problem or the group that most likely knows which group can solve the problem. The probability that a ticket t is routed through the edge $e_{init,j} = g_{init} \rightarrow g_j$, where $g_j \in \mathcal{G} \setminus \{g_{init}\}$, is:

$$P(g_j|t,g_{init}) = \frac{P(g_j|g_{init})P(t|e_{init,j})}{\sum_{g_l \in \mathcal{G}} P(g_l|g_{init})P(t|e_{init,l})} \tag{7.15}$$

$$= \frac{P(g_j|g_{init}) \prod_{w_k \in t} P(w_k|e_{init,j})^{f(w_k,t)}}{\sum_{g_l \in \mathcal{G}} P(g_l|g_{init}) \prod_{w_k \in t} P(w_k|e_{init,l})^{f(w_k,t)}}$$

Note that smoothing is applied as described in Equation (7.14).

The expert group $g^* = \arg\max_{g_j \in \mathcal{G}} P(g_j|t,g_{init})$ is selected to be the next expert group to handle ticket t. If g^* is the resolver, the algorithm terminates. If not, the algorithm gathers the information of all previously visited expert groups to make the next step routing decision. If a ticket t has gone through the expert groups in $R(t)$ and has not yet been solved, the rank of the remaining expert groups in $\mathcal{G} \setminus R(t)$ is:

$$Rank(g_j) \propto \max_{g_i \in R(t)} P(g_j|t,g_i) \tag{7.16}$$

The ticket is then routed to the group with the highest rank. Note that the ranked order of the candidate resolvers might change during routing.

7.5.3 Holistic Routing

Th Holistic Routing algorithm recognizes the most probable resolver that can be reached within K transfer steps, and selects the next group from a global perspective. Instead of predicting only one step as do the Ranked Resolver and Greedy Transfer algorithms, the Holistic Routing algorithm calculates the probability that a candidate group can be reached and can solve the ticket in multiple steps.

For a new ticket t, the one step transition probability $P(g_j|t,g_i)$ between two expert groups g_i and g_j is calculated using Equation (7.15). Thus, we perform a breadth-first search to calculate the probability that a ticket t is transferred by g_i to g_j in exactly K steps. This probability can be estimated iteratively, using the following equations:

$$P(g_j, 1|t, g_i) = \begin{array}{ll} P(g_j|t, g_i) & \text{if } i \neq j \\ 0 & \text{otherwise} \end{array}$$

$$P(g_j, K|t, g_i) = \sum_{g_k \in \mathcal{G}; k \neq j} P(g_k, K-1|t, g_i) P(g_j|t, g_k) \quad \text{if } K > 1.$$

If $g_l = g_{init}$, the above equation can be written as:

$$P(g_j, K|t, g_l) = vM^K \tag{7.17}$$

where v is the unit vector whose lth component is 1 and other components are 0. The one step transfer probability matrix M is a $|\mathcal{G}| \times |\mathcal{G}|$ matrix, where $M(i, j)$ is the one step transition probability between the expert groups g_i and g_j given by:

$$M(i, j) = \begin{array}{ll} P(g_j|t, g_i) & \text{if } i \neq j \\ 0 & \text{otherwise} \end{array}$$

The probability that g_j can resolve the ticket t in K or fewer steps starting from the initial group g_{init} (which is used to rank the candidate resolver groups) is:

$$Rank(g_j|g_{init}) \equiv \sum_{k=1}^{K} P(g_j, k|t, g_{init}) \times P(g_j|t, g_j) \tag{7.18}$$

where $P(g_j|t, g_j)$ is the probability that g_j can resolve t if t reaches g_j, as in Equation (7.7). Starting with g_{init}, we route t to $g^* = \arg\max_{g_j \in \mathcal{G}; j \neq init} Rank(g_j|g_{init})$.

Theoretically, we can derive the rank in closed form for an infinite number of transfer steps. In practice, M^K decays quickly as K increases, due to the probability of solving the ticket at each step. Thus, a small value of K suffices to rank the expert groups. In our experiments, we set K equal to 3.

Given the predicted expert group g_k, if ticket t remains unresolved and needs to be transferred, the posterior probability of g_k being the resolver for t is zero and the one step transfer matrix M needs to be updated accordingly. Thus, if g_k is not the resolver, the elements in the kth row of M are updated by:

$$M(k,j) = \frac{P(g_j|t,g_k)}{\sum_{i,i \neq k} P(g_i|t,g_k)} \quad \text{for } j \neq k$$

Once M is updated, the algorithm re-ranks the groups according to Equation (7.18) for each visited group in $R(t)$. That is, $Rank(g_j) \propto max_{g_i \in R(t)} Rank(g_j|g_i)$. The group with the highest rank is selected as the next possible resolver.

For a given new ticket t, the Holistic Routing algorithm is equivalent to enumerating all of the possible routes from the initial group to any candidate group. For each route $r = \{g_1, g_2, \ldots, g_m\}$, we calculate the probability of the route given t as:

$$P(r|t) = P(g_m|t,g_m) \prod_{1 \leq j \leq m-1} P(g_{j+1}|t,g_j)$$

The probability that group g_j resolves ticket t is:

$$Rank(g_j) \equiv \sum_r P(r|t) \quad \text{for all } r \text{ ending at } g_j$$

Figure 7.3 shows an example where a ticket t enters the expert network at group A. We enumerate all of the routes that start at A and end at D to calculate how likely D resolves the ticket. Note that loops in the routes are allowed in the calculation in Equation (7.17). It is possible to calculate the resolution probability without loops. However, because the intermediate groups for each route must be remembered, the calculation might take a long time.

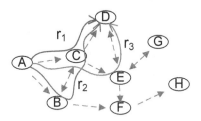

Fig. 7.3: Holistic Routing

7.6 Experimental Results

To validate the effectiveness of our models and the corresponding routing algorithms[1], we use real-world ticket data. The evaluation is based on tickets collected from IBM's problem ticketing system throughout 2006. When a ticket enters the system, the help desk assigns a category indicating a problem category for the ticket. For each problem category, a number of expert groups (ranging from 50 to 1,000) are involved in resolving the tickets.

For each problem category, we partition the data set into the training data set and the testing data set. Using the training data set, first we build the generative models introduced in Section 7.4. Then, we evaluate the effectiveness of the routing algorithms by calculating the number of routing steps (*i.e.*, MSTR) for the testing tickets. In particular, we compare our generative models with the Variable-Order Markov Model (VMS) proposed in [23]. Our experiments demonstrate:

- **Model Effectiveness:** The Optimized Network Model significantly outperforms the other models, in terms of precision accuracy and resolution rate.
- **Routing Effectiveness:** Among the Ranked Resolver, Greedy Transfer and Holistic Routing algorithms, Holistic Routing achieves the best performance, in terms of routing efficiency.
- **Robustness:** With respect to the size of the training data set, the time variability of the tickets, and the different problem categories, our solution that combines ONM and Holistic Routing consistently achieves good performance.

We obtained our experimental results using an Intel Core2 Duo 2.4GHz CPU with 4GB memory.

7.6.1 Data Sets

We present the results obtained from tickets in three major problem categories: AIX (operating system), WINDOWS (operating system), and ADSM (storage management), as shown in Table 7.2. Tickets in these three categories have quite different characteristics. The problem descriptions for WINDOWS and ADSM tickets tend to be more diverse and, hence, more challenging for our models. These three data sets involve approximately 300 to 850 expert groups. For a new ticket, finding a resolver group among so many candidates can be challenging.

Table 7.3 shows the distribution of resolution steps for tickets in the WINDOWS category. We are more interested in solving tickets with long resolution sequences, because these tickets received most of the complaints.

---

[1] The source code is available at http://www.uweb.ucsb.edu/ ~miao/resources.html.

Table 7.2: Ticket Resolution Data Sets

Category	# of tickets	# of words	# of groups
AIX	18,426	16,065	847
WINDOWS	16,441	8,521	638
ADSM	3,563	1,815	301

Table 7.3: Resolution Steps Distribution

Steps	Percentage
2	68%
3	25%
4	6%
5	1%

7.6.2 Model Effectiveness

First, we compare the effectiveness of the three generative models, Resolution Model (RM), Transfer Model (TM), and Optimized Network Model (ONM) developed in Section 7.4, against the Variable-Order Markov Model (VMS) introduced in [23]. VMS considers only ticket routing sequences in the training data.

Each of the above models has its corresponding routing algorithm. VMS uses the conditional transfer probability learned from routing sequences to predict the resolver group. For RM, we use the Ranked Resolver algorithm. For TM and ONM, we can use either the Greedy Transfer algorithm or the Holistic Routing algorithm. In these experiments, we use the Holistic Routing algorithm to evaluate both models. For comparison, we also include the results for ONM using the Greedy Transfer algorithm. More details for the comparison between the Greedy Transfer algorithm and the Holistic Routing algorithm are shown in Section 7.6.3.

Because a routing algorithm might generate an extremely long routing sequence to resolve one ticket (considering that we have more than 300 expert groups in each problem category), we apply a cut-off value of 10. That is, if an algorithm cannot resolve a ticket within 10 transfer steps, it is regarded as unresolvable. Using this cut-off value, we define the *resolution rate* of a ticket routing algorithm to be the proportion of tickets that are resolvable within 10 steps.

We randomly divide the tickets in each problem category into two subsets: the training data set and the testing data set. The former contains 75% of the tickets, and the latter contains 25% of the tickets. The four models are trained based on the training set, and the performance of the algorithms is compared.

Figure 7.4 compares the prediction accuracy of the four models. The x-axis represents the number of expert groups involved in the testing data set, where the routing decisions are made by a human. The y-axis represents the resulting MSTR when the testing tickets are routed automatically. Smaller MSTR means better prediction accuracy. As shown in the figure, TM and ONM (which combine the ticket contents and the routing sequences) result in better prediction accuracy than either the sequence-only VMS or the content-only RM. Moreover, ONM achieves better performance than TM, which indicates that the globally optimized model is more accurate in predicting a ticket resolver than the locally optimized model.

Combining together the ticket contents and the routing sequences not only boosts prediction accuracy, but also increases the resolution rate of the routing algorithm. Figure 7.5 shows that TM and ONM resolve more tickets than either VMS or RM.

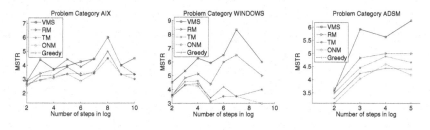

Fig. 7.4: Prediction Accuracy of Different Models

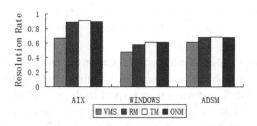

Fig. 7.5: Resolution Rate

For RM and TM, the training time is mainly spent on counting word frequencies on transfer edges and at resolvers. For all three data sets, the time is less than 5 minutes. For ONM, the transfer profiles are updated one at a time and the optimization process repeats for multiple rounds until the transfer profiles converge. The training process takes less than 3 hours for all three data sets.

7.6.3 Routing Effectiveness

Using the same experimental setup as in Section 7.6.2, we compare the routing effectiveness of the Greedy Transfer and Holistic Routing algorithms. Both of these algorithms can be executed on the TM and ONM generative models. We consider all four combinations: TM+Greedy, TM+Holistic, ONM+Greedy, and ONM+Holistic.

Figure 7.6 shows that, for each generative model, the Holistic Routing algorithm consistently outperforms the Greedy Transfer algorithm. These results validate our hypothesis that, even if an expert group is not the resolver for a problem ticket, it might have knowledge of which group can resolve the ticket. Therefore, besides the information about which groups resolve which tickets, the intermediate transfer groups can be instrumental in routing tickets to the right resolver, which is why the Holistic Routing algorithm has better performance.

The computational time for both routing algorithms to make a routing decision is less than 1 second, which is negligible compared to the time spent by the selected expert group to read and handle the ticket.

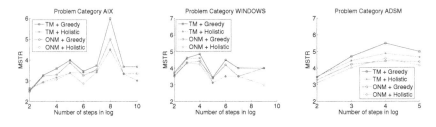

Fig. 7.6: Routing Efficiency: Greedy Transfer vs. Holistic Routing

7.6.4 Robustness

For our generative models and routing algorithms to be useful in practice, they must apply to a variety of problem categories and training samples. To confirm this, we divided the data in different ways with respect to the size of the training data set, the time variability of the tickets, and the different problem categories, as presented in Table 7.4. For each training set, we rebuilt the models and applied the routing algorithms to measure the resulting MSTR for the corresponding testing set. Given the previous results, we focus on ONM and Holistic Routing.

Table 7.4: Data Sets for Robustness

Training Set	Testing Set
Jan 1 - Mar 31, 2006	Apr 1 - Apr 30, 2006
Jan 1 - Apr 30, 2006	May 1 - May 31, 2006
Jan 1 - May 31, 2006	Jun 1 - Jun 30, 2006

As shown in Figure 7.7, with larger training data sets, the resulting MSTR tends to become smaller. Despite the variations in the size of the training set, our approach yields consistent performance. The problem descriptions in these ticket data sets are typically short and sparse. The results demonstrate that generative modeling is particularly effective for this type of data.

7.7 Conclusions and Future Work

We have presented generative models that characterize ticket routing in a network of expert groups, using both ticket contents and routing sequences. These models capture the capability of an expert group either to resolve a ticket or to transfer a ticket along a route to a resolver. The Resolution Model considers only ticket resolvers and builds a resolution profile for each expert group. The Transfer Model considers ticket routing sequences and establishes a locally optimized profile for each edge that represents possible ticket transfers between two groups. The Optimized Net-

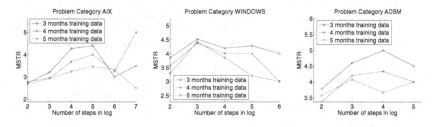

Fig. 7.7: Robustness of ONM and Holistic Routing with Various Training Data

work Model (ONM) considers the end-to-end ticket routing sequence and provides a globally optimized solution in the network. For ONM, we present a method to approximate the optimal solution which, in general, is difficult to compute.

Our generative models can be used to make routing predictions for a new ticket and minimize the number of transfer steps before the ticket reaches a resolver. For the generative models, we presented three routing algorithms to predict the next expert group to which to route a ticket, given its content and routing history. Experimental results show that the proposed algorithms can achieve better prediction accuracy, resolution rate, and routing efficiency than existing ticket resolution methods. Moreover, they are more robust in that they apply to a variety of problem categories and training samples.

Future work includes research on the use of generative models to analyze the roles of expert groups, to assess their expertise levels, and to study the expertise awareness among groups. It also includes investigation of the use of generative models to simulate the ticket routing process, in order to identify performance bottlenecks and optimize the allocation of human resources, and also to determine whether the routing performance is improved or degraded, if a group is removed from the expert network.

References

1. DBLP: http://www.informatik.uni-trier.de/~ley/db/.
2. L. A. Adamic and E. Adar. How to search a social network. Social Networks, 27:2005, 2005.
3. J. Anvik, L. Hiew, and G. C. Murphy. Who should fix this bug? In Proceedings of the 28th International Conference on Software Engineering, pages 361–370, May 2006.
4. L. Backstrom and J. Leskovec. Supervised random walks: Predicting and recommending links in social networks. In Proceedings of the 4th ACM International Conference on Web Search and Data Mining, pages 635–644, February 2011.
5. K. Balog, L. Azzopardi, and M. de Rijke. Formal models for expert finding in enterprise corpora. In Proceedings of the 29th Annual International ACMSIGIR Conference on Research and Development in Information Retrieval, pages 43–50, August 2006.
6. M. Belkin, P. Niyogi, and V. Sindhwani. Manifold regularization: A geometric framework for learning from labeled and unlabeled examples. Journal of Machine Learning Research, pages 2399–2434, 2006.

7. P. Calado, M. Cristo, E.Moura, N. Ziviani, B. Ribeiro-Neto, and M. A. Goncalves. Combining link-based and content-based methods for Web document classification. In Proceedings of the 12th ACM International Conference on Information and Knowledge Management, pages 394–401, November 2003.
8. E. J. Candes and B. Recht. Exact matrix completion via convex optimization. Foundations of Computational Mathematics, 9(6):717–772, 2009.
9. H. Deng, I. King, and M. R. Lyu. Formal models for expert finding on DBLP bibliography data. In Proceedings of the IEEE International Conference on Data Management, pages 163–172, December 2008.
10. H. Ebel, L. I. Mielsch, and S. Bornholdt. Scale-free topology of e-mail networks. Physical Review, E:035103, September 2002.
11. H. Fang and C. Zhai. Probabilistic models for expert finding. In Proceedings of the 29th European Conference on Information Retrieval, pages 418–430, April 2007.
12. A. Jamain and D. J. Hand. The naive Bayes mystery: A classification detective story. Pattern Recognition Letters, 26(11):1752–1760, 2005.
13. T. Joachims. Text categorization with suport vector machines: Learning with many relevant features. In Proceedings of the 10th European Conference on Machine Learning, pages 137–142, April 1998.
14. R. H. Keshavan, S. Oh, and A. Montanari. Matrix completion from a few entries. In Proceedings of the 2009 International Symposium on Information Theory, pages 324–328, June 2009.
15. M. Kim and J. Leskovec. The network completion problem: Inferring missing nodes and edges in networks. In Proceedings of the 2011 SIAM International Conference on Data Mining, April 2011.
16. Z. Kou and W. Cohen. Stacked graphical models for efficient inference in Markov random fields. In Proceedings of the 2007 SIAM International Conference on Data Mining, April 2007.
17. Q. Lu and L. Getoor. Link-based text classification. In Proceedings of the IJCAI Workshop on Text Mining and Link Analysis, August 2003.
18. J. Neville and D. Jensen. Iterative classification in relational data. In Proceedings of the AAAI Workshop on Statistical Relational Learning, pages 42–49, 2000.
19. H. H. Permuter, J.M. Francos, and I. Jermyn. A study of Gaussian mixturemodels of color and texture features for image classification and segmentation. Pattern Recognition, 39(4):695–706, 2006.
20. J. Platt, N. Cristianini, and J. Shawe-Taylor. Large margin DAGs for multiclass classification. In Proceedings of the Fourteenth Neural Information Processing Systems Conference, pages 547–553, December 2000.
21. P. Sen, G. Namata, M. Bilgic, L. Getoor, B. Gallagher, and T. Eliassi-Rad. Collective classification in network data. AI Magazine, 29(3), 2008.
22. P. Serdyukov, H. Rode, and D. Hiemstra. Modeling multi-step relevance propagation for expert finding. In Proceedings of the 17th ACM International Conference on Information and Knowledge Management, pages 1133–1142, October 2008.
23. Q. Shao, Y. Chen, S. Tao, X. Yan, and N. Anerousis. Efficient ticket routing by resolution sequence mining. In Proceedings of the 14th ACM SIGKDD International Conference on Knowledge Discovery and Data Mining, pages 605–613, August 2008.
24. X. Song, B. L. Tseng, C. Y. Lin, and M. T. Sun. ExpertiseNet: Relational and evolutionary expert modeling. In User Modeling, pages 99–108, 2005.
25. D. Wang, Z. Wen, H. Tong, C. Y. Lin, C. Song, and A. L. Barabasi. Information spreading in context. In Proceedings of the 20th International Conference on the World Wide Web, pages 735–744, March–April 2011.
26. Y. Yang and X. Liu. A re-examination of text categorization methods. In Proceedings of the 22nd Annual International ACM SIGIR Conference on Research and Development in Information Retrieval, pages 42–49, August 1999.

27. Y. Yang and J. O. Pedersen. A comparative study on feature selection in text categorization. In Proceedings of the Fourteenth International Conference on Machine Learning, pages 412–420, July 1997.
28. J. Yedidia, W. Freeman, and Y. Weiss. Constructing free-energy approximations and generalized belief propagation algorithms. IEEE Transactions on Information Theory, 51(7):2282–2312, 2005.
29. J. Yedidia, W. T. Freeman, and Y.Weiss. Generalized belief propagation. In Proceedings of the Fourteenth Neural Information Processing Systems Conference, pages 689–695, December 2000.
30. H. Zhang. The optimality of naive Bayes. In Proceedings of the 17th International FLAIRS Conference. AIII Press, May 2004.
31. D. Zhou, O. Bousquet, T. N. Lal, J. Weston, and B. S. Olkopf. Learning with local and global consistency. In Proceedings of the Eighteenth Neural Information Processing Systems Conference, pages 321–328, December 2004.

Chapter 8
Reliable Aggregation on Network Traffic for Web Based Knowledge Discovery

Shui Yu, Simon James, Yonghong Tian, and Wanchun Dou

Abstract The web is a rich resource for information discovery, as a result web mining is a hot topic. However, a reliable mining result depends on the reliability of the data set. For every single second, the web generate huge amount of data, such as web page requests, file transportation. The data reflect human behavior in the cyber space and therefore valuable for our analysis in various disciplines, e.g. social science, network security. How to deposit the data is a challenge. An usual strategy is to save the abstract of the data, such as using aggregation functions to preserve the features of the original data with much smaller space. A key problem, however is that such information can be distorted by the presence of illegitimate traffic, e.g. botnet recruitment scanning, DDoS attack traffic, etc. An important consideration in web related knowledge discovery then is the robustness of the aggregation method, which in turn may be affected by the reliability of network traffic data. In this chapter, we first present the methods of aggregation functions, and then we employe information distances to filter out anomaly data as a preparation for web data mining.

Shui Yu
School of Information Technology, Deakin University, Victoria, Australia, e-mail: syu@deakin.edu.au.

Simon James
School of Information Technology, Deakin University, Victoria, Australia, e-mail: sjames@deakin.edu.au.

Yonghong Tian
School of Electronic Engineering and Computer Science, Peking University, Beijing, China, e-mail: yhtian@pku.edu.cn.

Wanchun Dou
Department of Computer Science and Technology, Nanjing University, Nanjing, China, e-mail: douwc@nju.edu.cn

8.1 Introduction

Web based data mining is a very practical and promising field for knowledge discovery, and plenty work has been done in this area [13] [2] [9]. Moreover, reliability of web mining is also an important part for this field, which is evidenced by a number of international conferences and workshops [5] [4] [6]. Due to its size and complexity, the Internet is an invaluable resource when it comes to the study of networks, their underlying structure and features. More than just an information repository, understanding user interactions across the Internet can also provide insights into the behavior of social networks and ecological systems.

Faced with such massive amounts of information, it is helpful to aggregate network traffic data into a single value which represents a particular state of flow. In statistics, the most common way to aggregate information is to use the arithmetic mean, or in the case of skewed distributions or outliers, the median. There are many other aggregation functions, however which can provide a more reliable evaluation of the data. In particular, the ordered weighted averaging (OWA) function defined by Yager in [17] and its extensions (See [19] for a recent overview). The OWA generalizes both the median and arithmetic mean, and with an appropriate selection of parameters is able to aggregate an arbitrary number of "normal" arguments and discard outliers.

An important extension of the OWA function is the induced OWA, which orders its arguments using an auxiliary variable associated with the arguments rather than the arguments themselves. Distance-based aggregation or classification such as k-nearest neighbors, time-series smoothing and group decision making taking expertise into account can all be framed in terms of an induced OWA. Of interest to us is the ability of the induced OWA to reliably aggregate network traffic information, even in the presence of abnormal or attack data. To do this however, the induced OWA relies on an evaluation of similarity or distance between inputs, which in the case of Internet traffic will often take the form of distributions.

One of the challenges for reliable aggregation can then be framed in terms of evaluating the similarity between the current flow of traffic and legitimate user activity. Some of the common measures of similarity used information theory were recently compared toward this end in [21]. Once we are able to determine the reliability of information, we can then summarize it - either using a function like the OWA or another function if we remove the misleading data first.

In Section 8.2 we briefly introduce the motivation for the use of similarity- and distance-based aggregation functions, namely the threat of DDoS attacks and how this creates problems when it comes to the use of Internet traffic information in data analysis. We then give a brief overview of aggregation functions with a particular focus on the OWA and its extensions in Section 8.3. Some common measures of similarity drawn from information theory will be presented in Section 8.4, which is followed by comparisons of the information distances in Section 8.5. The last section summarizes the chapter.

8.2 The Reliability of Network Traffic Information

The enormous benefit provided to users as a result of the Internet's scale, and the ease with which information can be accessed and distributed comes at a price. Users and information providers can be vulnerable to viruses, security threats, and increasingly over the last decade - attacks designed to disrupt service.

Internet attacks with the aim of crashing a server or website so that legitimate users cannot access the information are known as Denial of Service (DoS) attacks. Peng et al. conducted a survey of such attacks and defense methods [12] [14], noting that a key challenge for defense was to be able to better discriminate between legitimate and malicious information requests. They note the exponential growth of attacks, with less than 20,000 reported in 2000 going up to almost 140,000 in 2003. It is further noted that the potential threat posed by DoS attacks may not just be in monetary terms but also to human life, as more and more emergency services come to rely on the Internet.

While some DoS attacks aim to crash systems by exploiting vulnerabilities in software code or protocols, the more prevalent form in recent years have been those which attempt to overload the resources of the server computer with fake or useless requests in huge volumes. These attacks can be more difficult to guard against since the vulnerability lies in physical bandwidth resources rather than an operating flaw, and the requests generated by the attacker may effectively mimic that of real users. A common strategy for delivering such attacks is for the attacker to take control of other computers, compromising their systems and distributing the attacks from up to 100s of 1000s of sources. These attacks are known as Distributed Denial of Service (DDoS) attacks [16] [11] [7].

In the case of DDoS attacks, distinguishing between legitimate and false requests at the packet level is impossible. One approach is to to distinguish attacks based on the flow of traffic at any point in time. The ability to do this has obvious benefits for defense against such attacks, however we can also see the benefit to assessments of the reliability of network traffic information. Since traffic flow can tell us so much about the Internet and other networks, we want to ensure that we have an accurate picture of user behavior and the relationship between nodes, and that this picture is not distorted by the presence of illegitimate data packets.

In the following sections, we investigate the problem of evaluating the reliability of network traffic information. We look to identify legitimate data based on the similarity of its distribution with the distribution patterns present in the case of usual traffic.

8.3 Aggregation Functions

The need to aggregation information into a single numerical descriptor arises naturally in various fields. In statistics, the most commonly employed aggregation functions are the arithmetic mean and the median. Recent books concerning aggregation functions include [1, 8, 15]. The following definitions will be useful.

Definition 8.1. A function $f : [0,1]^n \rightarrow [0,1]$ is called an aggregation function if it is monotone non-decreasing in each variable and satisfies $f(0,0,\ldots,0) = 0$, $f(1,1,\ldots,1) = 1$.

An aggregation function is referred to as *averaging* if the output is bounded by the maximum and minimum input. The arithmetic mean and median are examples of this type of aggregation. In their standard form, both these functions treat each input with equal importance. Weights, usually denoted w_i can be associated with each input, and where the weights are non-negative and satisfy $\sum_{i=1}^{n} w_i = 1$, the functions will remain averaging.

The weighted arithmetic mean is then the function

$$M_{\mathbf{w}}(\mathbf{x}) = w_1 x_1 + w_2 x_2 + \ldots + w_n x_n = \sum_{i=1}^{n} w_i x_i. \tag{8.1}$$

Rather than basing the importance on the source of the input, the ordered weighted averaging function assigns its weights based on their relative magnitude. It is given by

$$OWA_{\mathbf{w}}(x_1,\ldots,x_n) = \sum_{i=1}^{n} w_i x_{(i)}, \tag{8.2}$$

where the $(.)$ notation denotes the components of $\mathbf{x}$ being arranged in non-increasing order $x_{(1)} \geq x_{(2)} \geq \ldots \geq x_{(n)}$. The OWA is capable of expressing a number of order statistics such as the maximum function where $\mathbf{w} = (1,0,\ldots,0)$ and the minimum for $\mathbf{w} = (0,\ldots,0,1)$. It is also convenient for expressing the median $w_k = 1$, for $n = 2k+1$ (n is odd) or $w_k = w_{k+1} = 0.5$ for $n = 2k$ (n is even) and $w_i = 0$ otherwise.

The OWA was used in [19] to replace the sum of least squares in regression problems. Reliable linear models were hence fit to the data which did not consider abnormal or extreme values in the determination of the weights. Similar goals could be sought in web-knowledge discovery, where we want to understand and interpret the data, however we do not want these findings to be distorted by the presence of attack traffic. Sometimes however, we will be looking to aggregate information which may not be extreme itself, but may be generated by illegitimate traffic. With the reordering step, the OWA's behavior differs on different parts of the domain. The induced OWA provides a more general framework for this reordering process. An inducing variable can be defined, over either numerical or ordinal spaces, which then dictates the order by which the arguments are arranged.

The induced OWA as stated by Yager and Filev in [18] is given by

$$IOWA_{\mathbf{w}}(\langle x_1, z_1 \rangle, \ldots, \langle x_n, z_n \rangle) = \sum_{i=1}^{n} w_i x_{(i)}, \tag{8.3}$$

where the $(.)$ notation now denotes the inputs $\langle x_i, z_i \rangle$ reordered such that $z_{(1)} \geq z_{(2)} \geq \ldots \geq z_{(n)}$ and the convention that if q of the $z_{(i)}$ are tied, i.e. $z_{(i)} = z_{(i+1)} = \ldots = z_{(i+q-1)}$,

$$x_{\eta(i)} = \frac{1}{q} \sum_{j=\eta(i)}^{\eta(i+q-1)} x_j,$$

Where x_i provides information to be aggregated, z_i provides some information about x_i, e.g. the importance, distance from the source, time displacement of the reading etc. The input pairs $\langle x_i, z_i \rangle$ may be two independent features of the same input, or can be related by some function.

Example 8.1. For the weighting vector $\mathbf{w} = (0.6, 0.3, 0.1)$, and the input $\langle \mathbf{x}, \mathbf{z} \rangle = (\langle 0.2, 3 \rangle, \langle 0.7, 2 \rangle, \langle 0.05, 8 \rangle)$, the aggregated value for the induced OWA is

$$IOWA_{\mathbf{w}}(\langle x, z \rangle) = 0.6(0.05) + 0.3(0.2) + 0.1(0.7) = 0.16 \,.$$

In the following section, we have in mind the use of similarity between legitimate and attack traffic as our auxiliary variable. We can then allocate less or no weight to the traffic information which differs greatly to the usual flow patterns.

8.4 Information Theoretical Notions of Distance

To evaluate the reliability of web traffic data, we need to determine whether or not the current flow is consistent with legitimate activity. In other words, we are interested in how similar the current traffic pattern is to the normal state. Evaluating this similarity can be problematic in the case of DDoS attacks, since the aim of the attack is to overwhelm the victim with the sheer number of data packets and hence their content need not differ at all to legitimate requests. One approach is to consider the characteristics of the traffic's distribution and use these to form the basis of similarity assessments. The dominating characteristic of a DDoS attack is clearly the abnormally high volume of traffic, however this feature alone makes attacks difficult to distinguish from flash crowds, which are generated by legitimate users [20]. A key problem in assessing the reliability of data concerning network behavior is then the ability to discern between authentic packet flows, which may vary and include periods of high congestion as well as base low-level volumes, and traffic rates due to malicious attacks or other noise which could affect methods of knowledge discovery.

Mathematical notions of similarity differ depending on the application. In classification and statistical analysis, similarity between multi-variate objects is often defined in terms of Pearson's correlation coefficient or the cosine of the angle between their vectors. Similarity is also often interpreted in terms of distance, which once again can be measured in a number of different ways, usually using some metric. A metric is a function of two objects $d(\mathbf{x}, \mathbf{y})$ (which may be single- or multi-variate), which is non-negative and satisfies the following conditions:

1) $d(\mathbf{x}, \mathbf{y}) = 0 \Longleftrightarrow \mathbf{x} = \mathbf{y}$;

2) $d(\mathbf{x}, \mathbf{y}) = d(\mathbf{y}, \mathbf{x})$;

3) $d(\mathbf{x}, \mathbf{y}) + d(\mathbf{y}, \mathbf{z}) \geq d(\mathbf{x}, \mathbf{z})$.

Condition 2 ensures that the metric is symmetric, i.e. the distance between two objects is not dependent on the direction we take the distance in, while Condition 3 is referred to as the triangular inequality. In some situations, it might still be useful to measure distance using a function which does not satisfy one or more of these conditions, however we would not refer to these as metric functions.

In the case of random variables and distributions, information theoretical distance notions are applied. Some of these are related to metrics, while others attempt to measure mutual or discriminatory information, or the extent to which one distribution can be used to infer about another. The foundation of information distance is entropy [3], which is defined as

$$H(X) = -\sum_{x \in \chi} \Pr[X = x] \log \Pr[X = x]. \tag{8.4}$$

Where X is a discrete random variable, χ is the sample space of X. The logarithm is taken in base 2 (and can be used from here on), so we consider the entropy of a random variable X to be a measure of uncertainty in bits.

For two given flows with distributions $p(x)$ and $q(x)$, the relative entropy or Kullback-Leibler distance (KL distance) [3] is defined as follows.

$$D(p, q) = \sum_{x \in \chi} p(x) \log \frac{p(x)}{q(x)} \tag{8.5}$$

where χ is the sample space of X.

It is straightforward to see from Eq. (8.5) that KL distance satisfies the first condition of a metric function, i.e. that $D(p, q) = 0 \Longleftrightarrow p = q$ and fails the second since it is not symmetric. It can be shown (e.g. see [3]) that $D(p, q)$ is non-negative where p and q are distributions and we further note that it does not satisfy the triangular inequality.

There have been a few semi-metrics based on KL distance which correct for the problem of asymmetry, however still do not satisfy the triangular inequality. These include the Jeffrey distance and the Sibson distance.

The Jeffrey distance is given by,

$$D_J(p, q) = \frac{1}{2} [D(p, q) + D(q, p)]. \tag{8.6}$$

Rather than take the average of both directions, the Sibson distance averages the KL distance from $p(x)$ and $q(x)$ to their average over each x, i.e.

$$D_S(p,q) = \frac{1}{2} \left[D\left(p, \frac{1}{2}(p+q) \right) + D\left(q, \frac{1}{2}(p+q) \right) \right] \qquad (8.7)$$

The Hellinger distance is closer to more traditional notions of distance, equivalent to the Euclidean metric with a root transformation of the variables [10]. It satisfies all the properties of a metric, and is defined as,

$$D_H(p,q) = \left[\sum_{x \in \chi} \left(\sqrt{p(x)} - \sqrt{q(x)} \right)^2 \right]^{\frac{1}{2}}. \qquad (8.8)$$

We can see that each of these distances will evaluate differences between distributions on a different scale. For instance, since $D_S(p,q)$ measures uses the relative entropy between each of the distributions and their average, we could expect it to consistently produce smaller values than D_J. For purposes of reliability analysis, what is more important is the ability to effectively discern between distinct types of distributions. We require the functions to be sensitive enough to identify key events, which could be flash crowds or attacks (and preferably be able to distinguish between them), but not so sensitive that fluctuations in line with normal flow patterns result in relatively large difference measures. Research has been conducted on the aforementioned similarity functions, comparing them in terms of such sensitivity assessments [21].

8.5 Performance Comparison for Information Distances

We can illustrate the differences between D_J, D_S and D_H in discerning between legitimate and attack traffic with the following numerical experiments. We consider Poisson and Normal distributions respectively, since Internet traffic is generally assumed to conform to these flow patterns. A combination of Normal distributions with varying parameters can be used to represent any type of data distribution, so the results here should give a reasonable indication of how each of the distance-type measures perform. In particular we are interested in 1) the sensitivity of each of the distances when comparing random distributions generated from the same parameters - i.e. the sensitivity to fluctuations that would occur naturally in the case of legitimate user behavior, and 2) the ability to detect and distinguish between distributions characteristic of abnormal events - i.e. malicious attacks and flash crowds.

First of all, two Normal flows ($\mu = 10, \delta = 1$) are arranged, and the three functions are used to measure the information distance. The simulation is conducted 100 times, and the results are shown in Figure 8.1.

We perform a similar evaluation using two generated Poisson flows with the value of $\lambda = 10$. The results are shown in Figure 8.2.

For two flows sharing the same distribution and parameter(s), the distance between them should ideally be close to 0. We note in Figure 8.1 and Figure 8.2, that

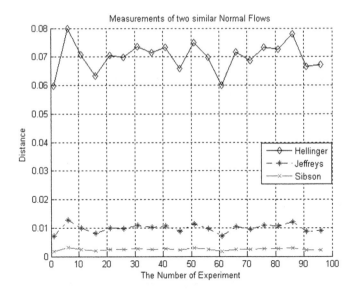

Fig. 8.1: Information distance for two Normal flows ($\mu = 10, \delta = 1$)under the different metrics.

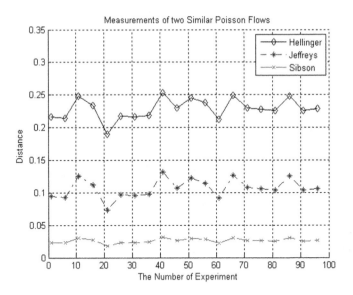

Fig. 8.2: Information distance for two Poisson flows $\lambda = 10$ under the different metrics.

Sibson's distance measure gives outputs on a scale much smaller than the Jeffrey and Hellinger distance.

Sensitivity to small changes in flow is another important factor in evaluating each measure's performance in monitoring base-rate traffic flows. We now investigate the behavior of each distance as the standard deviation of the Normal flow is adjusted from 0.1 to 3, i.e. 1% to 30% of the mean (keeping the value of $\mu = 10$). The results are shown in Figure 8.3.

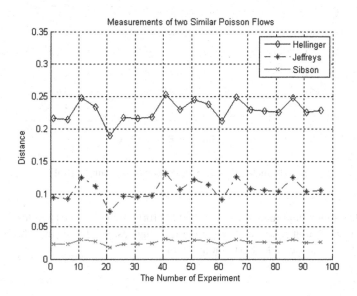

Fig. 8.3: The metric sensitivity of Normal flows ($\mu = 5$) against standard variations.

For the Poisson flows, we examine the sensitivity against arrival rate, which varies from 5 to 12. The results are shown in Figure 8.4.

Based on Figure 8.3 and 8.4, it is shown again that the Sibson's information distance remains quite low in terms of its output scale. The simulations demonstrated that it is quite stable where the parameters are gradually altered for both Normal and Poisson flows.

8.6 Summary

In this Chapter, we pointed out that a solid result of web data mining comes from a reliable data set, therefore, the data set for web data mining is critical for knowledge discovery. As the volume of web traffic is extraordinarily huge, we introduce the aggregation functions to deposit the traffic patterns with much smaller storage space while preserving the features of the original data. In order to filter out anomaly data,

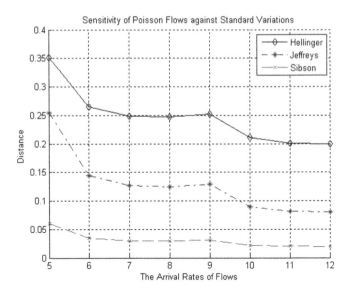

Fig. 8.4: The metric sensitivity of Poisson flows against arrival rate.

e.g. DDoS attack or botnet recruitment data, information distances are hired to carry out the task. Among the three information distances, we found that the Sibson's information distance is the best among them.

References

1. Beliakov, G., A. Pradera, & T. Calvo 2007. Aggregation Functions: A Guide for Practitioners. Springer, Heidelberg, Berlin, New York.
2. Cooley, Robert Walker 2000. Web Usage Mining: Discovery and Application of Interestin Patterns from Web Data.
3. Cover, Thomas M., & Joy A. Thomas 2006. Elements of Information Theory. John Wiley & Sons.
4. Dai, Honghua, & James Liu 2008. Proceedings of the IEEE International Workshop on Reliability Issues of Knowledge discovery. IEEE Computer Society.
5. Dai, Honghua, James Liu, & Huan Liu 2006. Proceedings of the IEEE International Workshop on Reliability Issues of Knowledge discovery. IEEE Computer Society.
6. Dai, Honghua, James Liu, & Evgueni Smirnov 2010. Proceedings of the IEEE International Workshop on Reliability Issues of Knowledge discovery. IEEE Computer Society.
7. El-Atawy, Adel, Ehab Al-Shaer, Tung Tran, & Raouf Boutaba 2009. Adaptive Early Packet Filtering for Protecting Firewalls against DoS Attacks. In Proceedings of the INFOCOM.
8. Grabisch, M., J.-L. Marichal, R. Mesiar, & E. Pap 2009. Aggregation Functions. Cambridge University Press, Cambridge.
9. Manavoglu, Eren, Dmitry Pavlov, & C. Lee Giles 2003. Probabilistic User Behavior Models. Data Mining, IEEE International Conference on, 0:203.
10. McLachlan, G J 1992. Discriminant analysis and statistical pattern recognition. Wiley-Interscience.

11. Moore, David, Colleen Shannon, Douglas J. Brown, Geoffrey M. Voelker, & Stefan Savage 2006. Inferring Internet denial-of-service activity. ACM Transactions on Computer Systems, 24(2):115–139.
12. Peng, Tao, Christopher Leckie, & Kotagiri Ramamohanarao 2007. Survey of network-based defense mechanisms countering the DoS and DDoS problems. ACM Computing Survey, 39(1).
13. Srivastava, Jaideep, Robert Cooley, Mukund Deshpande, & Pang-Ning Tan 2000. Web usage mining: discovery and applications of usage patterns from Web data. SIGKDD Explor. Newsl., 1:12–23.
14. Thing, Vrizlynn L. L., Morris Sloman, & Naranker Dulay 2007. A Survey of Bots Used for Distributed Denial of Service Attacks. In SEC, pages 229–240.
15. Torra, V., & Y. Narukawa 2007. Modeling Decisions. Information Fusion and Aggregation Operators. Springer, Berlin, Heidelberg.
16. Wang, Haining, Cheng Jin, & Kang G. Shin 2007. Defense against spoofed IP traffic using hop-count filtering. IEEE/ACM Transactions on Networking, 15(1):40–53.
17. Yager, R.R. 1988. On ordered weighted averaging aggregation operators in multicriteria decision making. IEEE Transactions on Systems, Man and Cybernetics, 18:183–190.
18. Yager, R.R., & D. P. Filev 1999. Induced ordered weighted averaging operators. IEEE Transactions on Systems, Man, and Cybernetics – Part B: Cybernetics, 20(2):141–150.
19. Yager, R. R., & G. Beliakov 2010. OWA operators in regression problems. IEEE Transactions on Fuzzy Systems, 18(1):106–113.
20. Yu, Shui, Robin Doss, & Wanlei Zhou 2008. Information Theory Based Detection Against Network Behavior Mimicking DDoS Attacks. IEEE Communications Letters, 12(4):319–321.
21. Yu, Shui, Theerasak Thapngam, Jianwen Liu, Su Wei, & Wanlei Zhou 2009. Discriminating DDoS Flows from Flash Crowds Using Information Distance. In Proceedings of the 3rd International Conference on Network and System Security, pages 351–356.

Chapter 9
Sensitivity and Generalization of SVM with Weighted and Reduced Features

Yan-xing Hu, James N.K.Liu, and Li-wei Jia

Abstract Support Vector Machine, as a modern statistical learning method based on the principle of structure risk minimization rather than the empirical risk minimization, has been widely applied to the small-sample, non-linear and high-dimensional problems. Many new versions of SVM have been proposed to improve the performance SVM. Some of the new versions focus on processing the features of SVM. For example, give the features weight values or reduce some unnecessary features. A new feature weighted SVM and a feature reduced SVM are proposed in this chapter. The two versions of SVM are applied to the regression works to predict the price of a certain stock, and the outputs are compared with classical SVM. The results showed that the proposed feature weighted SVM can improve the accuracy of the regression, and the proposed featured reduced SVM is sensitive to the data sample for testing.

9.1 Introduction

Support Vector Machine (SVM), based on Statistical Learning Theory, was first developed by Vapnik in 1995 [29]. When applied on the small sample set of non-linear and high-dimensional pattern recognition problems, it showed many special advantages. For example, it can avoid the curse of dimensionality and is easy to compute

Yan-xing Hu
Department of Computing, The Hong Kong Polytechnic University, Hong Kong, China
e-mail: csyhu@comp.polyu.edu.hk

James N.K.Liu
Department of Computing, The Hong Kong Polytechnic University, Hong Kong, China
e-mail: csnkliu@comp.polyu.edu.hk

Li-wei Jia
Software Engineering School of Xi'an Jiaotong University, Xi'an, China
e-mail: levijia@hotmail.com

[27]. Till now, SVM has become a hot topic of intensive study due to its successful application in classification and regression tasks. Most machine-learning methods can perform an empirical risk minimization (ERM) induction principle [28], which is effective when samples are enough. However, in most cases of the real world, the size of the sample collection is small. Accordingly, it is difficult to apply the expected risk minimization directly to the objective problems. Most expected risk minimization problems are converted to minimize the empirical risk. Unfortunately empirical risk minimization is not always equivalent to the expected risk minimization [24]. It implies that ERM cannot lead to a good generalization capability. The statistical learning theory, introduced by Vapnik, has shown a clear relationship between expected risk and empirical risk. By giving the principle of structural risk minimization, statistical learning theory (SLT) tried to improve the generalization capability to the largest extent. Support vector machines (SVMs) give rise a modern machine-learning technique based on SLT. Due to its extraordinary generalization capability, SVM has been a powerful tool for solving classification and regression problems, for example, it can work well in face detection [13] and complex classification problems such as cancer classification [2]. A classical SVM algorithm first maps the original input space into a high-dimensional feature space through some predefined nonlinear mapping and then constructs an optimal separating hyper-plane maximizing the margin between two classes in the feature space. Based on SLT, we know that, the bigger the margin scale takes, the better the generalization capability of SVMs will have. Accompany with the wide application of SVM, a lot of research has been conducted to improve the efficiency and accuracy of SVM. Many new versions of SVM are introduced to obtain a better performance for different real problems. For example, Weighted SVM [8], introduced by Yiming Huang, gives different weighted values to different samples to improve the precision of classification to the small sized samples; Fuzzy SVM [10], which was introduced by Chun-Fu Lin and Sheng-De Wang, gives the corresponding fuzzy similarity according the contribution of each training sample; and Large margin SVM [33], introduced by Daniel S. Yeung, has the focus to deal with the sensitivity of distribution of the sample points. It utilizes the Mahalanobis distance among the sample points instead of the Euclid distance so that the probability relationship among different points can be taken into consideration. The listed methods above all focus on the sample points distributed in the Euclid Space where the SVM is employed. However, some other studies have revealed interesting result when changes are made to the feature dimensions of the Euclid space.

Currently, there are mainly three orientations for the studies of feature dimensions in SVM. Firstly, some scientists focus on the feature selection of SVM in order to find the appropriate features for the structure of SVM e.g. [5, 20]. Secondly, some other researchers tried to improve the performance of SVM by giving each feature a different weight value. In the year of 2004, Xizhao Wang and Qiang He proved that given different weights to the features can improve the accuracy of SVM classifier [30]. In 2007, Linxiao Jin cited a case to illustrate that if we consider the difference of the correlative degrees of each feature in SVM, and then use SVM based on the weighted features to do the regression task, a better result will be obtained than using pure classical SVM [11]. The third one is the feature reduction. By identifying some important features and removing some unnecessary features, researchers hope not only to improve the performance of SVM but also to reduce the computation cost when SVM is employed. Rough set theory (RST) plays an important role in the research of the feature reduction of SVM. Many experiments proved that using RST to reduce some feature of SVM can improve the accuracy of SVM in classification works (e.g. [3, 14]). On the other hand, there are few studies talking about the condition when RST is applied to do the feature reduction for SVM in regression works. Some experiments by Yiqiang Tang and Junjun Mao have shown that by applying RST to perform the feature reduction for SVM in regression works, the accuracy of SVM regression can be improved [26]. It is noted that in their experiments, the number of training samples where the reduct results are derived is much larger than that of the testing samples in the regression work (the ratio is about 5:1). The results, however, are not persuasive enough.

The motivation of this chapter focuses on the study of processing the features of SVM in regression, mainly on the FW-SVM regression and applying RST to do the feature reduction for SVM regression. We will investigate whether applying RST to removing some features can improve the accuracy of SVM regression result. What is more, we will also introduce a grey correlation degree based FW-SVM and investigate whether the result is sensitive to the size of training sample set and testing set.

The remainder of this chapter is organized as follows. In section 2, we briefly introduce the theory of SVMs in the regression estimation and the conception of grey correlation degree. The method of FW-SVR based on grey correlation degree is also described in this section. Some main fundamental of RST and the algorithm that applying RST to do the feature reduction to SVM regression are also contained in section 2. Section 3 introduces the experiments and gives the experimental results, followed by the conclusion in section 4.

9.2 Background

9.2.1 The Classical SVM Regression Problem

The support vector machine (SVM) method was proposed by Vapnik. Based on the structure risk minimization principle, SVM method seeks to minimize an upper bound of generalization error instead of the empirical error as in other neural networks. Additionally, the SVM models generate the regression function by applying a set of high-dimensional linear functions [4, 22].

The SVM regression function is formulated as follows:

$$y = w\phi(x) + b \tag{9.1}$$

where $\phi(x)$ is called the feature, which is nonlinear and mapped from the input space $\Re^n$. The coefficients w and b are estimated by minimizing:

$$R(C) = C\frac{1}{n}\sum_{i=1}^{n} L_{\varepsilon}(d_i, y_i) + \frac{1}{2}\|w\|^2 \tag{9.2}$$

$$L_{\varepsilon}(d,y) = \begin{cases} |d-y|-\varepsilon, & |d-y| \geq \varepsilon, \\ 0 & \text{others}, \end{cases} \tag{9.3}$$

where both C and ε are prescribed parameters. $L_{\varepsilon}(d,y)$ is called the ε-intensive loss function which indicates that errors not larger than the parameter ε will not be penalized. The d_i is the actual value of the ith feature. The term $C\frac{1}{n}\sum_{i=1}^{n} L_{\varepsilon}(d_i, y_i)$ is the empirical error while the term $\frac{1}{2}\|w\|^2$ measures the flatness of the function. The constant $C>0$ determines the trade-off between the flatness of the function and the amount up to which deviations larger than ε are tolerated.

Then the slack variables ζ and ζ^* which represent the distance from the actual values to the corresponding boundary values of ε-tube are introduced. By introducing the slack variables, Eq. (3) can be transformed to the following constrained formation:

Minimize:

$$R(w, \zeta, \zeta^*) = \frac{1}{2}ww^T + C^*(\sum_{i=1}^{n}(\zeta + \zeta^*)) \tag{9.4}$$

Subject to:

$$w\phi(x_i) + b_i - d_i \leq \varepsilon + \zeta_i^*, \tag{9.5}$$

$$d_i - w\phi(x_i) - b_i \leq \varepsilon + \zeta_i, \tag{9.6}$$

$$\zeta_i, \zeta_i^* \geq 0, i = 1, 2, \cdots, n. \tag{9.7}$$

Finally, by introducing the Lagrangian multipliers and maximizing the dual function of Eq. (4), Eq. (4) can be changed to the following form:

$$R(\alpha_i - \alpha_i^*) = \sum_{i=1}^{n} d_i(\alpha_i - \alpha_i^*) - \varepsilon \sum_{i=1}^{n}(\alpha_i - \alpha_i^*) - \frac{1}{2}\sum_{i=1}^{n}\sum_{j=1}^{n}(\alpha_i - \alpha_i^*) \times (\alpha_j - \alpha_j^*)(\Phi(x_i) \cdot \Phi(x_k)) \tag{9.8}$$

with the constraints

$$\sum_{j=1}^{n}(\alpha_i - \alpha_i^*) = 0, 0 \leq \alpha_i \leq C, 0 \leq \alpha_i^* \leq C, i = 1, 2, \cdots, n \tag{9.9}$$

In Eq. (8), α_i and α_i^* are called Lagrangian multipliers and they satisfy the equalities:

$$\alpha_i \times \alpha_i^* = 0$$

$$f(x, \alpha_i, \alpha_i^*) = \sum_{i=1}^{l}(\alpha_i \times \alpha_i^*)K(x, x_i) + b. \tag{9.10}$$

In this equation, $K(x_i \cdot x)$ is called the kernel function. Kernel function is a symmetric function $K(x_i \cdot x) = (\Phi(x_i) \cdot \Phi(x))$ satisfying Mercer's conditions, when the given sample sets are not linear separable in the primal space, we may map the sample points with mapping into a high-dimensional feature space where linear ε-tube can be performed. Linear, Polynomial, Radial Basis Function (RBF) and sigmoid are four main Kernel functions in use. The RBF function:

$$K(x_i, x_j) = \exp(-\|x_i - x_j\|^2 / (2\sigma^2)) \tag{9.11}$$

is specified in this study. The SVMs employed this kernel function to estimate the nonlinear behavior of the forecasting data set because RBF kernels tend to give good performance under general smoothness assumptions [19].

9.2.2 Rough Set SVM Regression

9.2.2.1 Rough set under a decision table

Rough set theory was introduced by Zdzislaw Pawlak in 1982 as a new mathematical tool providing an approach to analyze decision tables for solving the imprecise or vague problems [21]. Using the concepts of lower and upper approximations in Rough set theory, the knowledge hidden in decision tables may be discovered and expressed. The following are some basic conceptions in RST.

A decision table is characterized by a 4-tuple $S = (U, A = C \cup D, V, F)$, where $U = \{x_1, x_2, \ldots x_n\}$ denotes a nonempty finite set called the universe, A denotes a nonempty finite set of attributes which contains condition attribute set $C = \{c_1, c_2, \cdots c_k\}$ and decision attribute set $D = \{d_1, d_2, \cdots d_h\}$, where $C \cap D = \emptyset$. V is the range of the information function F, $F = \{f_i | i \leq m\}$, $f_i : U \times A \to V$ is the information function.

Given an arbitrary non-empty subset $B \subseteq A$, an indiscernibility relation is given as follows:

$$IND(B) = \{(x_i, x_j) \in U \times U \,|\, \forall a \in B, a(x_i) = a(x_j)\} \tag{9.12}$$

Based on the indiscernibility relation, the definition of equivalence class can also be given as follows:

$$[x]_B = \{y \in U \,|\, (y, x) \in IND(B)\} \tag{9.13}$$

Then for a decision table, we can define the equivalence class with respect to C and D as follows:

$$\{C_i, i = 1, 2, \cdots, m\} = \{[x]_C | x \in U\}, C_i \neq C_j(i, j \in [1, m], i \neq j) \tag{9.14}$$

$$\{D_j, i = 1, 2, \cdots, n\} = \{[x]_D | x \in U\}, D_i \neq D_j(i, j \in [1, n], i \neq j \tag{9.15}$$

Especially, D_j is called the decision class. For the condition attribute set C, the lower and upper approximations of D_j can be respectively defined as follows:

$$\underline{C}(D_j) = \{x \mid [x]_C \subseteq D_j\} \tag{9.16}$$

$$\overline{C}(D_j) = \{x \mid [x]_C \cap D_j \neq \emptyset\} \tag{9.17}$$

We call the pair $(\underline{C}(D_j), \overline{C}(D_j))$ rough set (RS) of D_j, what is more, we define $BND_C(D_j) = \overline{C}(D_j) - \underline{C}(D_j)$ as the boundary region of D_j. Consequently, we can say that elements in $\underline{C}(D_j)$ are definitely included in D_j and those outside the boundary region are elements definitely not included in D_j. Thus, for the condition attribute set C, the positive region and negative region of D_j can also be given:

$$POS_C(D_j) = \underline{C}(D_j) \tag{9.18}$$

$$NEG_C(D_j) = U - \overline{C}(D_j) \tag{9.19}$$

An important measure in RST is the classification quality. We define the classification quality of approximation as:

$$\sigma_C(D_j) = \frac{|\underline{C}(D_j)|}{|D_j|} \tag{9.20}$$

where $|D_j|$ and $|\underline{C}(D_j)|$ denote the cardinality of D_j and $\underline{C}(D_j)$ respectively. For all the decision classes in Eq. (14), the classification quality is

$$\sigma_c(D) = \frac{\left|\sum_{i=1}^{n} \underline{C}(D_j)\right|}{|U|} \tag{9.21}$$

The following is the definition of the reduct for a decision table in RST.

For a certain decision table $S = (U, A = C \cup D, V, F)$, B is a reduct of C with respect to D, if $B \subseteq C$, and for all the decision classes $\{D_j, i = 1, 2, \cdots, n\}$,

$$POS_B(D_j) = POS_C(D_j). \tag{9.22}$$

In the meanwhile, for $\forall a_i \in B$,

$$POS_{B-\{a_i\}}(D_j) \neq POS_C(D_j) \tag{9.23}$$

In classical rough set model, Eq. (22) is equal to:

$$\sigma_B(D_j) = \sigma_C(D_j) \tag{9.24}$$

Finally, among all the reducts of a decision table, the one that contains the least of attributes is called the minimal reduct.

9.2.2.2 Rough set SVM regression

In a rough set SVM regression (RS-SVR), before the regression, the sample points are applied to form a decision table. The features of the points form the decision attributes of the decision table and the target value is considered as the decision attribute. When the decision table is formed, reduct algorithm in RST can be applied to get the reduct of the decision table [18, 23]. By the result of the reduct, unnecessary attribution can be removed, in another words, the number of the dimensions of the Euclid space is reduced. The SVM regression will be employed in the less-dimension Euclid space then.

The following is the algorithm to construct a RS-SVR problem:

Step 1: Collect a set of samples S containing a group of samples $e_1, e_2, \ldots, e_m$ as training set, samples in S can be described as $e_k = \{X_k, d_k\}, (1 \leq k \leq m)$, where $X_k \in \mathfrak{R}^n$, $X = \{\alpha_{k1}, \alpha_{k2}, \cdots, \alpha_{kn}\}$, $\alpha_{k1}, \alpha_{k2}, \cdots, \alpha_{kn}$ are the values of the n corresponding features and d_{kn} is the value of the target problem of the kth element.

Step 2: Using the samples in the training set to form a decision table, each sample $e_k = \{X_k, d_k\}$ can take up a row in the decision table. In the nth row, the values of constitute the values of $\alpha_{k1}, \alpha_{k2}, \cdots, \alpha_{kn}$ condition attributes and d_{kn} is seen as the decision attribute.

Step 3: If the decision attributes are continuous variables, before we calculate the reduct of this decision table, we have to do discretization to the values of the decision table.

Step 4: Find the reduct of the decision table, remove the features not belonging to the derived reduct.

Step 5: Employ SVM on the remained features to train the SVM regression function.

Step 6: For the samples in testing set, remove the features not belonging to the reduct.

Step 7: Use SVM regression to estimate the target value of the testing set.

9.2.3 Grey Correlation Based Feature Weighted SVM Regression

9.2.3.1 Grey correlational degree

Grey system theory was first given by Julong Deng in 1982. Grey correlation analysis is an important part of grey system theory [6]. The main idea of this method is to evaluate the relational degree between data sequences of the feature according to the similarity of the geometric shape of sequence curves. The higher of the similarity between the curves, the higher of the value we give to the correlation degree of the corresponding data sequences. The following is an example [9]:

There are six samples, a_0, a_1, a_2, a_3 are the four features of them, and the value sequences of the four features are shown in the following:

$a_0 = (18.5, 19.3, 20, 35, 37.9, 43.2)$, $a_1 = (7.8, 9.5, 12.5, 17.4, 24, 30.2)$,

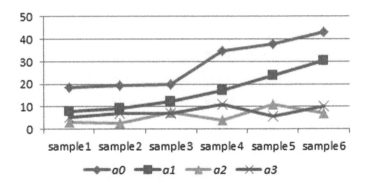

Fig. 9.1: The curves of the data sequences of the features

a_2= (3.2, 2.9, 7.6, 4, 11.2, 7.3), a_3= (5.5, 7.1, 7.1, 11.2, 5.7, 10).

Fig. 1 shows the curves of each sequence.

From the shape of the curves shown in Fig. 1, we can obviously find that the curve of a_1 is most similar with the curve of a_0, and the curves of other two are less similar with a_0. So we can say that a1 has the highest grey relational analysis with a_0. If we set a_0 as the target problem, and a_1, a_2, a_3 are the features, when we use these three features to do regression tasks for predicting a0 with SVM, we may give higher weight value to a1 since it has higher grey relation degree value than the other two features, a_2 and a_3.

The following gives the definition and detailed algorithm of calculating the grey correlation degree. If feature data sequences of a system are:

$$\begin{cases} X_0 = (x_0(1), x_0(2), \cdots, x_0(n)) \\ X_1 = (x_1(1), x_1(2), \cdots, x_1(n)) \\ \cdots \\ X_i = (x_i(1), x_i(2), \cdots, x_i(n)) \\ \cdots \\ X_m = (x_m(1), x_m(2), \cdots, x_m(n)) \end{cases} \quad (9.25)$$

Let

$$\gamma(x_0(k), x_i(k)) = \frac{\min\limits_{i} \min\limits_{k} |x_0(k) - x_i(k)| + \xi \max\limits_{i} \max\limits_{k} |x_0(k) - x_i(k)|}{|x_0(k) - x_i(k)| + \xi \max\limits_{i} \max\limits_{k} |x_0(k) - x_i(k)|}, \quad (9.26)$$

and

$$\gamma(X_0, X_i) = \frac{1}{n} \sum_{k=1}^{n} \gamma(x_0(k), x_i(k)) \quad (9.27)$$

where $\xi \in (0,1)$ is the discernibly coefficient normally given the value of 0.5; $\gamma(X_0,X_i)$ is the grey relation degree of X_0 and X_i, $\gamma(x_0(k),x_i(k))$ is the grey relation degree of X_0 and X_i at point k.

The following gives the steps of calculating the grey relational degree between value sequences:

Step1: Use the initial value method to do the variables transformation to the sequence. Let $X'_i = X_i/x_i(1) = (x'(1),x'(s),\cdots,x'(n)), i = 0,1,2,\cdots,m$.

Step2: Calculate the absolute difference between sequences and get the difference: denote $\Delta_i(k) = |x'_0(k) - x'_i(k)|$, where $i = 1,2,\cdots,m, k = 1,2,\cdots,n$.

Step3: Calculate the minimal difference value and maximal difference value: denote $M = \max_i \max_k \Delta_i(k)$, and $m = \min_i \min_k \Delta_i(k)$.

Step4: Calculate the relation coefficient $\gamma(x_0(k),x_i(k)):$, where $\xi \in (0,1), i = 1,2,\cdots,m, k = 1,2,\cdots,n$.

Step5: Calculate the grey relational degree: $\gamma(X_0,X_i) = \frac{1}{n} \sum_{k=1}^{n} \gamma(x_0(k),x_i(k))$.

9.2.3.2 The feature weighted SVM regression based on grey correlational degree

In Euclid space, for two sample points $X_i = (x_{i1},x_{i2},,x_{in})$, $X_j = (x_{j1},x_{j2},,x_{jn})$, the Euclid distance between these two sample points is $d(X_i,X_j) = \sqrt{\sum_{k=1}^{n} |x_{ik} - x_{jk}|^2}$, where x_{ik}, x_{jk} are the values of the kth ($k = 1, 2,,n$) feature dimension of the two points respectively, and $|x_{ik} - x_{jk}|$ is the distance between the two points in the kth feature dimension. Suppose that for a certain type of problem, different features supply different contributions to the target problem. Based on this assumption, we can give different weight values to different features in order to structure a feature weighted SVM to improve the performance of SVM. For the kth feature of the sample points, if a weight value w_k is given, where $w_{ik} \in [0,1]$, the distance between two points X_i, X_j in the kth feature dimension will be changed as $w_k|x_{ik} - x_{jk}|$, and in the meanwhile, the Euclid distance between these two points will be $d^w(X_i,X_j) = \sqrt{\sum_{k=1}^{n} w_k |x_{ik} - x_{jk}|^2}$, ($k = 1, 2,,n$). From the formula, we can see that feature-weighted transformation changes the positional relation of the sample points. For a feature dimension which is given a heavy weight, the distance between two points in this corresponding dimension turns relatively longer than the distances between the two points in other feature dimensions which are given light weight value. Accordingly, the change of the position relation of the sample points actually changes the shape of the feature Euclid space. This change thus offers a possibility to find an optimized hyperplane for SVM [30].

If the weight value given to each feature is $w = \{w_1,w_2,\cdots,w_k\}$, we set $W = \text{diag}(w_1,w_2,\cdots,w_k)$, and then the Eq. (8) can be converted to:

$$R(\alpha_i - \alpha_i^*) = \sum_{i=1}^{n} d_i(\alpha_i - \alpha_i^*) - \varepsilon \sum_{i=1}^{n} (\alpha_i - \alpha_i^*) -$$
$$\frac{1}{2} \sum_{i=1}^{n} \sum_{j=1}^{n} (\alpha_i - \alpha_i^*) \times (\alpha_j - \alpha_j^*)(\Phi(Wx_i), \Phi(Wx_j)) \qquad (9.28)$$

However, we still have to consider the non-linearly separable function, since that the main kernel functions we used are based on the inner product of the vectors, we can get $K(Wx_i \cdot Wx) = (\Phi(Wx_i) \cdot \Phi(Wx))$, then the final regression estimation function can be transformed to the following form:

$$\alpha_i \times \alpha_i^* = 0$$
$$f(x, \alpha_i, \alpha_i^*) = \sum_{i=1}^{l} (\alpha_i \times \alpha_i^*)K(Wx, Wx_i) + b. \qquad (9.29)$$

In this study, the grey correlation degree is used to structure the weight diagonal matrix. Firstly, we calculate the grey correlation degree using the data sequences of each feature and the objective problem from the training set. After the grey correlation degrees of the features are calculated, we can give the weight value to different features according to the grey correlation degree. A feature given a higher grey correlation degree with the objective problem represents that this feature has closer relation with the objective problem. In the process of SVM regression, it may give more contribution to the finding of the most optimized hyperplane to attain the right result. So, a higher weight value will be given to this feature; conversely, a smaller weight value will be given to the feature that has a lower grey correlation degree.

The reason why we use the grey correlation degree as the weight value is that based on the grey system theory, it has good generalization capability, which is one of the advantages of grey correlation degree. What is more, compared with other correlation analysis methods, the grey correlation analysis method needs less information and is easy to compute, it can discover the relationships of the whole group of features without any special requirements such as the independence and distributions of the features [15].

Then we can structure a grey correlational degree based FS-SVM regression problem with the following steps:

Step 1: Collect a set of samples S containing a group of samples $e_1, e_2, \ldots, e_m$ as training set, samples in S can be described as $e_k = \{X_k, d_k\}, (1 \le k \le m)$, where $X_k \in \mathfrak{R}^n$, $X = \{\alpha_{k1}, \alpha_{k2}, \cdots, \alpha_{kn}\}$, $\alpha_{k1}, \alpha_{k2}, \cdots, \alpha_{kn}$ are the values of the n corresponding features and d_{kn} is the value of the target problem of the kth element.

Step 2: Calculate the grey relational degree $\gamma(d, \alpha_i)(1 \le i \le n)$ by using the sequences of the values of d and $_i$ in the training set and structure the weight vector $V = (\gamma_{d1}, \gamma_{d2}, \cdots, \gamma_{dn})$. according to the grey correlation degree.

Step 3: Normalize the weight vector:

$$V' = (\gamma_{d1}/|V|, \gamma_{d2}/|V|, \cdots, \gamma_{dn}/|V|) = (\gamma'_{d1}, \gamma'_{d2}, \cdots, \gamma'_{dn}). \qquad (9.30)$$

Step 4: For every sample in the training set, let each feature multiply to the corresponding weight value, get the feature weighted training set.

$$X_k' = (\alpha_{k1}', \alpha_{k2}', \cdots, a_{kn}') = (\alpha_{k1}, \alpha_{k2}, \cdots, a_{kn}) \times (\gamma_{d1}', \gamma_{d2}', \cdots, \gamma_{dn}'). \quad (9.31)$$

Step 5: Use the new training set to train the SVM regression function

Step 6: For the samples in testing set, let each feature of the samples multiply to the corresponding weight value calculated in step 3 as we did in step 4.

Step 7: Use SVM regression to estimate the target value of the testing set.

In step 3, we give different values of weight to the feature attribution according to its grey relational degree. The feature which has closer relation with the objective problem will get a higher weight value. In other words, it has priority over other features, and provides greater contribution to the SVM regression output.

9.3 Experimental Results and Analysis

A series of experiments are designed to study the feature weighted SVR and RS-SVR introduced in this chapter. The data of stock prices of a single stock in China Shenzhen A-share market are applied as the dataset to conduct our experiments. As we know, the stock market is a complex, evolutionary, and non-linear dynamical system. Stock forecasting is characterized by data intensity, noise, non-stationary, high uncertainty, and hidden relationships [12]. So, the prediction of stock price movement has been a difficult problem for many years. However, the financial experts and scientists believe that the movements of stock price are not random but behaving in a highly non-linear and dynamic manner [1]. Established on the principle of structural risk minimization to estimate a function by minimizing an upper bound of generalization error, SVM regression method, as a non-linear regression method with the introduction of -insensitive loss function and kernel function, was applied to stock price forecast by researchers and has been shown to exhibit an excellent performance (e.g. [16, 25, 32]).

The objectives of these experiments are to attest the performance of proposed FW-SVR based on grey correlation degree and the RS-SVR, what is more, we will also study that whether the accuracies of FW-SVR and RS-SVR are sensitive to the size of the training set and testing set, in another words, the generalization ability of the FW-SVR and RS-SVR.

9.3.1 Data Collection

The stock 000063 of China's Shenzhen A-share market was chosen for the experiment. Under the assumption that the daily close price has some relationship with the daily condition of the stock, seven features were fixed to construct regression model [31], they are a_1, the daily close price of the last day, a_2, the daily lowest price, a_3, the daily highest price, a_4, the daily Trading Volume, a_5, AMO, a_6, Turnover Rate, and a_7, SSE 100 INDEX.

785 samples that contain historical data of the stock 000063 were collected for the experiment. The period range is from the 15th, September 2006 to the 31st, December, 2009. The reason why we chose this period is that the China's stock market experienced a high growth rate because of the hot domestic economic condition during the period and it soon suffered from the impact of the international financial crises. The tremendous fluctuation, from the historical peak point to the bottom, provides good sample sets to test the learning capability of the SVM regression algorithm.

9.3.2 Data Pre-processing

9.3.2.1 Shift windows

In this experiment, to test the learning capability of SVM regression and to follow and forecast the trend of the stock price movement, a shift window was designed. There were 30 samples in one window, which are about 5% of the total samples, and the first 25 of these samples were used as training data and the last 5 samples as testing data. Then we shifted forward this window by the shift step of 5 days. For example, the first shift window contains 30(trading) days of data from 15th, September, 2006 to 9th, November, 2006, in this shift window, the first 25 samples, which began on 15th, September and finished on 2nd, November, were used as training set, and the data of the following five days, from 3rd, November to 9th November, were used as testing data, we predict the stock price of these five days, and compared with the actual price of these five days. Then we shift the window forward and the training set started from 21st, September till 9th, November. The actual stock prices of these 25 samples were used as training set to predict the following 5 day's stock price. Analogically, we can predict all the stock price of our set by shifting the windows. In every window, the ratio of training samples and testing samples is 5:1.

9.3.2.2 Scaling the data set

Before each time of training and prediction, the data set is scaled to avoid features which have greater numeric value ranges from dominating the features which have smaller numeric ranges in the process of training and regression. In this experiment, the formula we applied to scale the data is:

$$v' = 2 \times \frac{v - \min_\alpha}{\max_\alpha - \min_\alpha} - 1 \tag{9.32}$$

where v' is the scaled value and v is the original value. After the scaling, all the values of the features were scaled within the range of [0, 1].

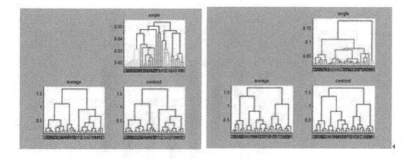

Fig. 9.2: Samples of clustering trees for the data of the first shift window

9.3.2.3 Structure the decision table and get the attribute reduct

One of the objectives of our experiments is to study the generalization ability of RS-SVR. There are 785 samples in this experiment, it is very complex to build such a large size decision table and calculate the reduct. Accordingly, we choose the data from the first shift window to structure the decision table and put the result on the whole data set. We first use dynamic hierarchical clustering method to discretize the data. In Fig. 2, we can see the samples of clustering trees.

Then we can have a decision table to calculate the reduction. After the calculation, the remained features in the reduct are $\{a_2, a_3, a_6\}$.

9.3.2.4 Calculate the weight values based on the grey correlation degree

The next step is to calculate the weight value for each feature. The data sequences of the features of the 30 samples in the first window were used. For each feature, from a_1 to a_7, there is a data sequence containing 30 values as well as the data sequence of the daily close price which is the target problem that we want to give a prediction. The grey correlation degree between each feature and the value of close price was calculated and then we normalized the result to structure the weight vector. For all the 7 features from a_1 to a_7, the weight vector is $V = (0.4386, 0.4519, 0.4481, 0.2682, 0.2807, 0.2683, 0.4242)$. Fig. 3 shows the weight distribution.

9.3.3 Kernel Function Selection and Parameter Selection

The kernel function that we chose in these experiments is RBF Kernel function. Many previous experiments for comparison have proved that RBF kernel function often has a better performance than other kernel functions in stock market prediction [7].

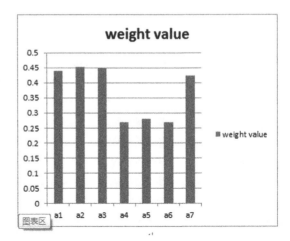

Fig. 9.3 The weight value
of each feature without the
reduction in the experiment

Fig. 9.4 The sample result of
finding the optimal parameters

Three parameters need to be fixed after we have chosen the kernel function: parameter c, which is the cost of C-SVM, parameter g, which is the value of γ in
RBF kernel function, and parameter p, which is the value of ε in the loss function.
The change of these parameters can obviously affect the performance of SVM in
regression tasks.

To find an optimal value of these parameters, we use the 30 samples in the first
window as training set to try the different combinations of the different values of
these parameters. The tool we used is LibSVM, phthon 3.1, and gnuplot 4.22, the
initial values of each parameter and step size were given, different combinations
were tried and the combination of values by which the training set can get the minimal MSE value were selected.

Fig. 4 gives a sample instance of parameter selection.

The prediction performance can be evaluated by the following statistical metrics
[17]: Normalized mean squared error (NMSE) measures the deviation between the
actual values and the predicted values. The smaller the values, the closer are the
predicted values to the actual values. The formula of NMSE is:

$$\text{NMSE} = 1/(\delta^2 n) \sum_{i=1}^{n} (a_i - p_i)^2, \text{where} \delta^2 = 1/(n-1) \sum_{i=1}^{n} (a_i - p_i)^2 \qquad (9.33)$$

Mean absolute error (MAE) measures the deviation between the actual values
and the predicted values. The smaller the values, the closer are the predicted values
to the actual values. The formula of MAE is:

$$\text{MAE} = 1/n \sum_{i=1}^{n} |a_i - p_i| \tag{9.34}$$

Directional symmetry (DS) indicates the correctness of the predicted direction of predicted value in terms of percentages. The formula of DS is:

$$\text{DS} = (100/n) \times \sum_{i=1}^{n} d_i, \text{where} d_i = \begin{cases} 1 \text{if}(a_i - a_{i-1})(p_i - p_{i-1}) \geq 0 \\ 0 \text{otherwise} \end{cases} \tag{9.35}$$

9.3.4 The Experiments

9.3.4.1 The comparison between Classical SVR and FW-SVR

In the first experiment, we focus on the comparison between the results of the classical SVR and FW-SVR.

Based on the Grey system theory, the grey correlation degree has a high generalization capability. In other words, the results derived from a small size data set can represent the condition of the whole sample set. In our experiment, more than 700 samples were collected to conduct the experiment. However, as discussed earlier, we only chose the first 30 samples which are about 5% of the total samples to calculate the grey correlation degree. So, to attest the generalization capability of the grey correlation degree, in the first step of the experiment, we firstly chose a sample set with a very shorter period containing 35 days of data. Then we extended the test set as large as possible. We used all the data collected as testing set in the second step of the experiment. In the first step, the ratio between samples used to get the weight value and the samples used to test is 1:1, and we extend the size of the testing set to extremely large in the second step, where the ratio between samples used to get the weight value and the samples used to test is 1:20.

Through the process of finding the optimal parameters, the parameters were set as $c = 16$, $g = 0.25$, $p = 0.0625$ for classical SVM regression (SVR), and we chose the same parameters for feature weighted SVM regression (FW-SVR) to test for possible improvement. The weight vector is $V = (0.4386, 0.4519, 0.4481, 0.2682, 0.2807, 0.2683, 0.4242)$ as given in above.

Table 1 and Table 2 present the comparison of prediction result of Classical SVR and FW-SVR for different size of samples. Fig. 5(a) shows the prediction results of classical SVR and Fig. 5(b) shows the prediction results of FW-SVR for the whole data set; and Fig. 6(a) shows the prediction results of classical SVR and Fig. 6(b) shows the prediction results of FW-SVR for the 35-day period data set.

The results shown in Fig. 5 and Fig. 6 demonstrate that both of these two methods, the classical SVR and the FW-SVR, can predict the main trend of the chosen stock. What is more, as demonstrated in Table.1, for both the 35-day period and the whole period regression, the new method shows a better performance than the classical SVM in the regression task: in the 35-day period regression, there are obvious

Table 9.1: The comparison of prediction result of Classical SVR and FW-SVR (35samples)

Samples: 35	NMSE	MAE	DS
Classical SVR	1.983	3.281	0.767
FW-SVR	1.327	3.226	0.755

Table 9.2: The comparison of prediction result of Classical SVR and FW-SVR (785samples)

Samples: 785	NMSE	MAE	DS
Classical SVR	1.591	3.931	0.670
FW-SVR	1.586	3.915	0.687

improvements for criteria NMSE and MAE, only the value of the criteria DS is off a little; in the whole period regression which contains 785 samples, the new method gets positive performance: the result shows improvements for all the three criteria NMSE, MAE and DS.

9.3.4.2 The comparison between Classical SVR and RS-SVR

In the second experiment, we mainly focus on the comparison between Classical SVR and RS-SVR. Similar to the FW-SVR, the results of the reduct used in RS-SVR are also derived from the first 30 samples which are about 5% of the total samples. Accordingly, in the second experiment, we also firstly chose a sample set with a very shorter period containing 35 days of data. Then, as we did in the first experiment, we extend the test set as large as possible. According to the result of the reduct, the features we used in this experiment are $\{a_2, a_3, a_6\}$.

Table 3 and Table 4 present the comparison of prediction result of Classical SVR and RS-SVR. In Fig. 7, the prediction results of RS-SVR for the whole data set is presented and Fig. 8 shows the prediction results of RS-SVR for the 35-day period data set. The results in Fig. 7 and Fig. 8 show that the RS-SVR can also describe the main trend of the chosen stock. However, we can notice that when there are only 35 samples, RS-SVR gains a lower NMSE value, a little higher MAE value, and the DS value is almost equal, which shows that the performance of RS-SVR is at least not worse than classical SVR, and even better. However, when it was applied to the whole data set, the performance of RS-SVR is poorer than the classical SVR.

Table 9.3: The comparison of prediction result of Classical SVR and RS-SVR(35samples)

Samples: 35	NMSE	MAE	DS
Classical SVR	1.983	3.281	0.767
RS-SVR	1.239	3.319	0.765

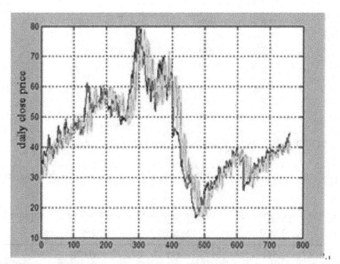

(a) The prediction results of classical SVR for the whole data set.

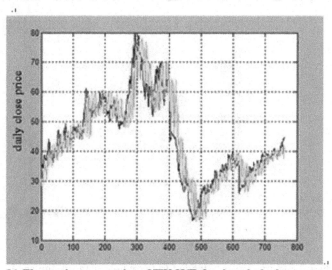

(b) The prediction results of FW-SVR for the whole data set.

Fig. 9.5: The prediction results of classical SVR and FW-SVR for the whole data set

9.3.4.3 The study about the generalization ability of FW-SVR and RS-SVR

From the results of the above two experiments, we can see that for the FW-SVR based on grey correlation degree, the regression accuracies are higher than classical SVR both on small testing site and large testing site; conversely, for the RS-SVR, in the condition of the testing set is small, the regression accuracy is higher than clas-

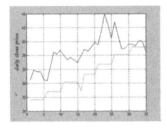

(a) Result of classical SVR for 35 days.

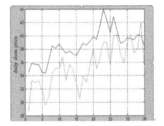

(b) Result of FW-SVR for 35 days.

Fig. 9.6: The prediction results of classical SVR and Fw-SVR for the 35-day period data set

Table 9.4: The comparison of prediction result of Classical SVR and RS-SVR (785samples)

Samples: 785	NMSE	MAE	DS
Classical SVR	1.591	3.931	0.670
RS-SVR	1.729	4.102	0.663

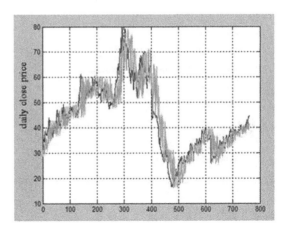

Fig. 9.7 The prediction results of RS-SVR for the whole data set

sical SVR, but when the testing set is extended to the whole data set, the accuracy of RS-SVR is lower than classical SVR.

Since the values of grey correlation degree which are used as the weight values in FW-SVR and the reduct for the RS-SVR are both derived from the data in the first shift window which is about 5% in quantity of the whole data set, we can naturally attribute the phenomenon mentioned in the last paragraph to the sensitiveness to the size of the testing set, in another words, the generalization ability. According to the grey system theory, the grey correlation degree has high generalization ability. People can find the hidden relation of the whole system from a small date set. So, the weight value we get from the first shift window can be used for the whole data set. On the contrary, the RST can find the hidden relationship of a system efficiently in

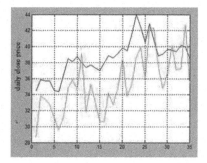

Fig. 9.8 The prediction results of RS-SVR for the
60-day period data set

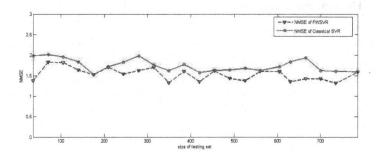

Fig. 9.9: The comparison of NMSE between FW-SVR and Classical SVR

order to help us to identify the necessary features and remove the redundant features
of SVR. However, the generalization ability are proved not good due to the strictly
requirement of classification in RST [34], and in the meanwhile, the stock market
is characterized by data intensity, noise, non-stationary, high uncertainty, and hidden relationships. Accordingly, when the testing set is small, the obtained reduct
can represent the main information of the stock price well in the shorter period,
accordingly, the result is positive as shown in our experiment; but accompanying
with increasing testing samples, the obtained reduct cannot represent the main information of the date set any more. This may be the reason why the accuracy of the
regression starts dropping.

To attest our assumption, a group of experiments are designed. We enlarge the
testing set from 35 samples to 785 samples step by step to do the regression. In
each step, 35 samples are added in the testing set and there are totally 22 steps for
the whole data set in the group of experiments. In each step, we use classical SVR,
RS-SVR, and FW-SVR to predict the target values; the NMSE of each regression
is noted; what is more, we also calculate the difference value of NMSE between
classical SVR and FWSVR and the difference value of NMSE between classical
SVR and RSSVR.

The results support our previous assumptions. Fig. 9 shows the comparison of
NMSE between FW-SVR and Classical SVR. Although there are some fluctuation,
for each size of testing set, the value of NMSE of FWSVR are always lower when

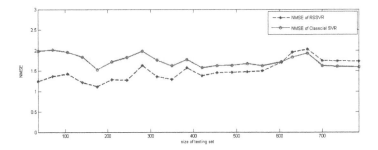

Fig. 9.10: The comparison of NMSE between RS-SVR and Classical SVR

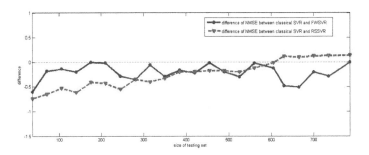

Fig. 9.11: The difference value of NMSE

compared with the value of NMSE of classical SVR. This phenomenon demonstrates that the FW-SVR based on the grey correlation degree has good generalization ability and not sensitive to the change of the size of the sample sets. The FW-SVR can improve the performance of classical SVR.

The result in Fig. 10 shows the comparison of NMSE between RS-SVR and Classical SVR. The value NMSE of RS-SVR is not always lower than that of classical SVR. In the initial stage, RS-SVR shows a better performance than classical SVR. Accompany with the extension of the training set, the performance of RS-SVR turns poorer, and the NMSE values become higher than those of the classical SVR. This phenomenon demonstrates that the RS-SVM can improve the accuracy of SVM just like Tang Yiqiang and Mao Junjun's experiment mentioned above when the size of testing set is small, but when the size of testing set turns bigger, the RS-SVM becomes sensitive to the size and its performance gets poorer.

Fig. 11 gives the difference value of NMSE between classical SVR and FW-SVR and difference value of NMSE between classical SVR and RS-SVR in each step. The fold line of difference value of NMSE between classical SVR and FW-SVR is stable at negative area showing that the NMSE values of FW-SVR are always lower than the NMSE values of classical SVR. The fold line of difference value of NMSE between classical SVR and RS-SVR shows an increasing trend and finally stay at positive area. Such a trend illustrates the lower generalization ability of RS-SVR. The RS-SVR is sensitive to the extension of the size of the testing set, and finally the performance becomes poorer than that of the classical SVR.

9.4 Conclusions and Future Works

In this chapter, we proposed two new versions of SVM for the regression study of processing the features of SVM. We give the weight value to each feature according to the correlation degree of them. This FW-SVR shows an improvement compared with classical SVR when dealing with the data set of a certain stock price. We also apply RST to the classical SVM, the RS-SVR is expected to reduce the computation cost and improve the accuracy in regression works. When the size of testing set is small, the result is positive. However, we find that the RS-SVR is sensitive to the size of testing set. Its performance becomes poorer than the classical SVR when the size of testing set turns bigger.

The study also proved the high generalization ability of grey correlation degree, conversely, the generalization ability of RST is relative poorer. As mentioned in grey system theory, even only a few data can reveal the relationship hidden in the system. On the other hand, when applied the RST to get the reduct of the features in SVR, we have to take more consideration on the ratio of the size of training set and size of testing set in order to give a tradeoff between the sensitiveness of RS-SVR and the reduction of the calculation cost.

There are mainly two problems which need to be addressed in our future research. One is that the data set used in our study is the price of a certain stock. More data sets need to be applied in our study to investigate the performance of the proposed FW-SVM. The other one is that when we use RST to get the reduct in a decision table, the discretization may lead some loss to the initial information. We will investigate the sensitivity of RS-SVM to the discretization in future.

Acknowledgements The authors are grateful for the partial support of GRF grant 5237/08E and CRG grant G-U756 of The Hong Kong Polytechnic University.

References

1. Bao, Y. K., Lu, Y. S., Zhang, J. L.: Forecasting stock price by SVMs regression artificial intelligence. Lecture Notes in Comput. Sci. **319**, 2295-303 (2004)
2. Cai, R. C., Hao, Z. F., Wen, W., Han, H.: Kernel based gene expression pattern discovery and its application on cancer classification. Neurocomputing. **73(13-15)**, 2562-2570 (2010)
3. Chen, P. J., Wang, G. Y., Yang, Y., Zhou, J.: Facial expression recognition based on rough set theory andsVM. Lecture Notes in Comput. Sci. **4062**, 772-777 (2006)
4. Cristianini, N., Taylor, J. S.: An introduction to support vector machines. Cambridge University Press. Cambridge, UK(2000)

5. Chen, Y. W., Lin, C. J.: Combining SVMs with various feature selection strategies. Stud. Fuzziness Soft Comput. **207**, 315-324 (2006)
6. Deng, J. L.: Introduction to Grey system theory. J. Gre. Syst. **1**(**1**), 103-104 (1989)
7. Dong, H., Fu, H. L., Leng, W. M.: Support vector machines for time series regression and prediction. J. Syst. Sim. **18** (**7**), 1784-1788 (2006)
8. Huang, Y. M., Du, S. X.: Weighted support vector machine for classification with uneven training class sizes. Mach. Learn. and. Cyb. **7**, 4365 - 4369 (2005)
9. Jian, L. R.: The Uncertain Decision Making Oriented Rough Set Method and The Application. Science publish hall, Beijing (2008)
10. Jiang, X. F., Zhang, Y., Lv, J.C.: Fuzzy SVM with a new fuzzy membership function, Neural. Comput. And. Appl. **15**, 268-276 (2006)
11. Research on support vector regression machine based on weighted feature. Comp. Eng. And. Appl. **43**(**6**), 42-44 (2007)
12. LeBaron, B.: Nonlinear dynamics and stock returns. J. Bus. **62**(**3**), 311-337 (1989)
13. Li, Y., Gong, S., Sherrah, J.: Support vector machine based multi-view face detection and recognition. Image Vis. Comput. **22**(**5**), 413-427 (2004)
14. Lingras, P., Butz, C.: Rough set based 1-v-1 and 1-v-r approaches to support vector machine multi-classification. Inf. Sci. **177**(**18**), 3782-3798 (2007)
15. Liu, S. F., Lin, Y.: Introduction to Grey Systems Theory. Unds. Comp. Sys. **68**, 1-18 (2011)
16. Lu, C. J., Lee, T. S.: Financial time series forecasting using independent component analysis and support vector regression. Decision. Supp. Syst. **47**(**2**), 115-125 (2009)
17. Makridakis, S., Winkler, R. L.: Sampling distribution of post sample forecasting errors. Appl.Stat. **38**,331-342 (1989)
18. Miao, D. Q.: Rough Set Theory Algorithms and Applications. Tinghua University publish, Beijng (2008)
19. Pai, P. F., Lin, C. S.: A hybrid ARIMA and support vector machines model in stock price forecasting. Omega. **33**(**6**) , 497-505 (2005)
20. Pal, M., Foody, G. M.: Feature Selection for classification of hyperspectral data by SVM. IEEE Trans. Geos. Rem. **48**(**5**), 2297 - 2307 (2010)
21. Pawlak, Z.: Rough sets, Int. J. Comput. And. Inf. Sci. **11**(**5**), 341-356 (1982)
22. Scholkopf, B., Smola, A. J.: Statistical Learning and Kernel Methods. MIT Press, Cambridge, MA (2000)
23. Slowron, A., Rauszer, C.: The discernibility matrices and function in information systems. In: SlowinskiR. (1st.) Handbook of Applications and Advance of Rough Sets Theory, pp. 331-362. Kluwer Academic Publishers, Dordrecht (1992)
24. Stitson, M. O., Weston, J. A. E., Gammerman, A., Vovk, V., Vapnik, V. N.: Theory of Support Vector Machines, Royal Holloway Technical Report, CSD-TR-96-17 (1996)
25. Tang, L. B., Huan, Y. S., Ling, X. T.: GARCH prediction using spline wavelet support vector machine machines. Neural. Comput. Appl. **18**(**8**), 913-917 (2009)
26. Tang, Y. Q., Mao, J. J.: China's power supply SVM regression forecast based on rough Set attribute reduction. Comput. Tec. And. Dev. **20**(**9**), 48-52 (2010)
27. Vapnik, V. N.: An overview of an overview of statistical learning theory. IEEE.Tran.Neur.Net, **10**(**5**), 988-999 (1999)
28. Vapnik, V. N.: Statistical Learning Theory. Wiley, NewYork (1998)
29. Vapnik, V. N.: The Nature of Statistical Learning Theory. Springer, NewYork (1995)
30. Wang, X. Z., He, Q.: Enhancing Generalization capability of SVM classifiers with feature weight adjustment. Lecture Notes in Comput. Sci. **3213**, 1037-1043 (2004)
31. Yang, H. Q., Chan, L. W., King, I.: Support vector machine regression for volatile stock market prediction. Lecture Notes in Comput. Sci. **2412**, 143-152 (2002)
32. Yeh, C. H.: A multiple-kernel support vector regression approach for stock market price forecasting. Exp. Syst. Appl. **38**(**3**), 2177-2186 (2011)
33. Yeung, Daniel S., Wang, D. F., Ng, W. Y., Tsang, Eric. C. C., Wang, X. Z.: Structured large margin machines: sensitive to data distributions. Mach.Learn. **68**(**2**), 171-200 (2007)
34. Ziarko, W.: Variable precision rough set model. J. Comput. Syst. Sci. **46**(**1**), 39-59 (1993)

Chapter 10
Reliable Gesture Recognition with Transductive Confidence Machines

Ida Sprinkhuizen-Kuyper, Louis Vuurpijl, and Youri van Pinxteren

Abstract The transductive confidence machines (TCMs) framework allows to extend classifiers such that their performance can be set by the user prior to classification. In this chapter we briefly survey different approaches of using the TCM framework. Most applications of TCM are constrained to relatively few data samples with a limited number of classes, due to the computational complexity of the TCM approach. A novel technique is presented for reducing the computational costs and memory consumption required for updating the non-conformity scores in the offline learning setting of TCMs. The improved TCM, using a k-nearest neighbor classifier, is evaluated by applying it to the NicIcon collection of iconic gestures, acquired in the critical domain of crisis management. For such domains, reliable classification is very important. The results show that TCMs outperform previous methods on this dataset, on both relatively easy data and on difficult test samples.

10.1 Introduction

Many applications of machine learning and pattern recognition demand robust and guaranteed performance with a given maximum error tolerance. Reliable classification is of paramount importance in critical-domain applications such as medical diagnosis, law enforcement, or crisis management, where mistakes made by intelli-

Ida Sprinkhuizen-Kuyper
Department of Artificial Intelligence, Radboud University Nijmegen, Nijmegen and
Radboud University Nijmegen, Donders Institute of Brain, Cognition and Behaviour, Nijmegen
e-mail: i.kuyper@donders.ru.nl

Louis Vuurpijl
Department of Artificial Intelligence, Radboud University Nijmegen, Nijmegen
e-mail: l.vuurpijl@donders.ru.nl

Youri van Pinxteren
Department of Artificial Intelligence, Radboud University Nijmegen

gent decision support systems can result in high costs. Designing a reliable classifier entails searching for a system which either classifies each new, unseen, instance with a confidence above a given threshold, or which rejects the instance if classification cannot be performed with sufficient confidence [16].

For reliable classification, we desire that the performance of a classifier can be set by the user prior to classification [19]. Preset performance and empirical performance are used to denote the user-specified performance and the performance of the classifier, respectively. Thus, empirical performance should be at least preset performance. We also desire that the classifier is efficient in the sense that the number of instances with a reliable and useful classification is high. A classifier is not efficient when it outputs many possible labels for most instances or when it refuses to classify most instances.

The most prominent methods for reliable classification are the version space framework [13], the Bayesian framework [9], the ROC isometrics approach [21], and the typicalness framework [15, 22]. The latter forms the basis for transductive confidence machines, which is the topic of this chapter. The version space framework has shown promising results, but is still limited to binary classification problems [13]. Although in an extensive empirical comparison, the ROC isometric approach is reported as competitive to the TCM framework, it is also limited to binary classification problems [21]. For reliable classification using the Bayesian framework, the credibility of the posterior class probabilities depends on the availability of robust priors, which in many real-world pattern recognition problems are difficult to attain [8].

Transductive confidence machines have been studied extensively by Vovk et al [4, 8, 15, 22]. They have been applied to a range of binary and multiple class problems, such as medical image analysis and diagnosis [2, 3, 7], offline digit recognition [14], and many other standard publicly available databases from the machine learning community [14, 21]. Transductive confidence machines allow to extend existing classifiers such that their error rate can be set by the user prior to classification. TCMs output predictions that are complemented with confidence values under the iid assumption [4, 22]. Virtually any classifier, like k-Nearest Neighbor (kNN) or Support Vector Machines (SVM), can be plugged into these approaches [14, 19, 21].

The main application of TCMs considered in this chapter pursues reliable and robust communication in crisis-management scenarios [1, 24], where pen input devices like a tabletPC or PDA are used to convey handwritten messages. It is generally acknowledged that handwriting recognition is a difficult problem [6, 13]. There is a huge variety of handwriting styles and handwritten shapes, even within handwriting produced by the same writer [18, 23]. The typical pen interactions that emerge in crisis management scenarios were explored in [25]. The categorization of the obtained pen gestures showed that next to route descriptions and markings of locations, the iconic sketchings of, e.g., cars, fires, casualties, accidents, or persons occurred quite frequently. In accordance with these observations, we designed and collected a suitable set of iconic gestures for specifying objects and events. The acquired database is called NicIcon [12] and is publicly available via http://www.unipen.org.

The number of applications of the TCM framework to handwritten text or gestures is limited In [14], one of the applications concerned scanned handwritten digit recognition, using TCMs. Recognition performance at the 1% significance level for the USPS dataset, containing 10 digit classes and 9298 data samples, was 97.9%. We will pursue handwritten gesture recognition on the NicIcon dataset, which contains 24441 data samples and 14 gesture classes. Given the critical-domain application of incident management, we are interested in exploring machine learning and pattern recognition techniques which reliably classify handwritten data. As we will assess in this chapter, transductive confidence machines seem a very appropriate framework for this goal.

The organization of this chapter is as follows. First, in Section 10.2, the TCM algorithm is explained and techniques will be presented for reducing the computational complexity and memory consumption of TCMs. In Section 10.3, four experiments are discussed. The first compares the original TCM method to our modified version by processing the well-known `pima` data set from the UCI benchmark repository [10]. The other three experiments concern the evaluation of our new TCM algorithm on the NicIcon dataset. The results show that TCMs outperform our previous methods on this dataset, on both relatively easy data and on difficult test samples.

10.2 Methods

10.2.1 Transductive Confidence Machines

Most classifiers assign a single label to an instance, but TCMs are allowed to assign multiple (or no) labels to each instance. Therefore, every instance has a so called prediction set. If there is uncertainty in the true label of the instance, a prediction set could contain multiple labels. To construct such a prediction set, TCMs operate in a transductive manner [19]. This means that TCMs reason from observed, specific (training) instances to specific (test) instances. Every possible label $y \in \mathcal{Y}$ is tried as a label for the unlabeled (test) instance x_{n+1}. In each try the example $z_{n+1} = (x_{n+1}, y)$ is formed and added to the training data $S = \{(x_1, y_1), \ldots, (x_n, y_n)\}$:

$$S^+ = \{(x_1, y_1), \ldots, (x_n, y_n), (x_{n+1}, y)\} = \{z_1, \ldots, z_{n+1}\} \ . \tag{10.1}$$

For every example in the extended set $z_1, \ldots, z_{n+1}$, a non-conformity measure is calculated. This measure tells us how non-conforming an example is in comparison to all other examples, so a relative high non-conformity score means that an example is probably labeled with the wrong label.

Virtually any classifier can be plugged into the TCM framework, because for every classifier a non-conformity measure can be calculated [19]. We used the k-

Nearest Neighbor classifier (kNN[1]) to calculate the non-conformity scores. In [15], Saunders et al. already formulated how a non-conformity score can be calculated for this classifier. This can be done as follows. Given example $z_i = (x_i, y_i)$, define an ascending ordered sequence $D_i^{y_i}$ with distances from x_i to its k nearest 'positive' neighbors with label y_i. Similarly, let $D_i^{-y_i}$ contain ordered distances from instance x_i to its k nearest 'negative' neighbors with a label different from y_i. Then, the non-conformity score is defined as:

$$\alpha_i = \frac{\sum_{j=1}^{k} D_{ij}^{y_i}}{\sum_{j=1}^{k} D_{ij}^{-y_i}} \, , \qquad (10.2)$$

with j as the j-th element in the distance sequence. This means that an example is non-conforming when it is far from its nearest neighbors with the same label and close to its nearest neighbors with a different label. See Figure 10.1 for clarification. We used different numbers of nearest neighbors (k) to find the best results for the used data set.

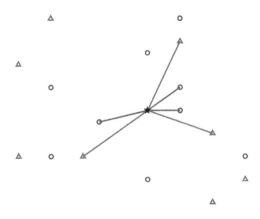

Fig. 10.1: Calculation of the non-conformity score α_i of the (black) star instance x_i. The (green) circles are its nearest neighbors of class y_i, while the (red) triangles are its nearest neighbors of other classes. In this example $k = 3$.

To determine the non-conformity of an example in the extended set, the non-conformity score must be compared to all other α_i's in the extended set S^+. The result is the p value of label y assigned to unlabeled instance x_{n+1} and is defined as follows:

$$p_y = \frac{|\{i = 1, \ldots, n+1 : \alpha_i \geq \alpha_{n+1}\}|}{n+1} \, . \qquad (10.3)$$

---

[1] We prefer the abbreviation kNN above NN to avoid conflicts with Neural Networks (NN)

Simply said, it calculates the fraction of examples that are more non-conforming than that particular example. If the p value is low this means that the example is very non-conforming, while a high p value means that the example is very conforming. So the p value indicates how likely it is that the tried label is actually the true label, it is the probability that the tried label is correct.

A TCM outputs the set of labels with p values above a predefined significance level ε. It checks for every unlabeled instance x_{n+1}, which p values are greater than the predefined significance level ε. The associated labels are then added to the prediction set:

$$\Gamma^{\varepsilon}(z_1,\ldots,z_n,x_{n+1}) = \{y \in \mathcal{Y} \mid p_y > \varepsilon\} \ , \tag{10.4}$$

with $\varepsilon \in [0,1]$. The output of a TCM is correct for an instance x_{n+1} when the prediction set contains the true label. So an empty prediction set or a prediction set not containing the true label is an error. The output of a TCM can be certain: the prediction set contains exactly one label, or uncertain when there are two or more labels in the prediction set. If $\varepsilon = 0$, all prediction sets will contain all possible labels and the number of errors will be zero. If $\varepsilon = 1$, almost all prediction sets will be empty and almost every prediction will then be an error.

Let Err_n^{ε} be the number of errors for a given ε after n classifications. The calibration property says:

$$\limsup_{n \to \infty} \frac{Err_n^{\varepsilon}}{n} = \varepsilon \ , \tag{10.5}$$

i.e. in the limit the error will be bounded by ε.

In the online learning setting, when the true label is provided after prediction for feedback, TCMs have been proven to satisfy this property [22, p. 20-22 & p. 193]. In this chapter we use the offline learning setting. In the offline learning setting, the classifier is learned on training data and subsequently used to classify instances one by one. In [19], Vanderlooy et al. have found strong empirical evidence that the calibration property also holds in the offline learning setting.

10.2.2 The TCM-kNN algorithm and its complexity

In this section we consider the TCM-kNN algorithm in more detail, i.e. the TCM algorithm implemented based on the kNN non-conformity measure as given in Eq. 10.2 (see [14, 20]). The pseudo code for the TCM is shown in Algorithm 1. The implementation supports incremental learning and decremental unlearning of a single example to keep time complexity low.

An efficient implementation of TCM-kNN first calculates non-conformity scores on training data, and updates these scores if needed for each new example [14]. Indeed, from the non-conformity score (Eq. 10.2) follows that the score of training example z_i only changes when the distance to the new unlabeled instance is: (1) smaller than the last (kth) element in sequence D_i^y, or (2) smaller than the last element in sequence D_i^{-y}, or both. Note that we will employ this observation in

input : $(x_1, y_1), \ldots, (x_n, y_n) \leftarrow$ sequence of training examples
$\quad\quad\quad x_{n+1} \leftarrow$ new unlabeled instance
$\quad\quad\quad \mathcal{Y} \leftarrow$ label space
output: $\{p_{y:y \in \mathcal{Y}}\} \leftarrow$ p-values

1   % Compute statistics of training data
2   **for** $i \leftarrow 1$ **to** n **do**
3 | Compute sequences $D_i^{y_i}$ and $D_i^{-y_i}$
4   **end**
5   **for** $i \leftarrow 1$ **to** n **do**
6 | $\alpha_i \leftarrow$ non-conformity score for (x_i, y_i)
7   **end**

8   % Compute distances from new unlabeled instance to training instances
9   **for** $i \leftarrow 1$ **to** n **do**
10 | $dist(i) \leftarrow d(x_i, x_{n+1})$
11 **end**

12 **for** *all* $y \in \mathcal{Y}$ **do**
13 | $idS \leftarrow$ indices of training examples with label y
14 | $idD \leftarrow$ indices of training examples with label different from y
15 | % Recalculate statistics to incorporate (x_{n+1}, y)
16 | **for** *all* $i \in idS$ **do**
17 | | **if** $D_{ik}^y > dist(i)$ **then**
18 | | | $\alpha_i \leftarrow$ new non-conformity score for (x_i, y_i)
19 | | **end**
20 | **end**
21 | **for** *all* $i \in idD$ **do**
22 | | **if** $D_{ik}^{-y} > dist(i)$ **then**
23 | | | $\alpha_i \leftarrow$ new non-conformity score for (x_i, y_i)
24 | | **end**
25 | **end**
26 | % Compute p-value
27 | $\alpha_{n+1} \leftarrow$ non-conformity score for (x_{n+1}, y)
28 | $p_y \leftarrow$ p-value for (x_{n+1}, y)
29 **end**

30 **return** $\{p_{y:y \in \mathcal{Y}}\}$

Algorithm 1: TCM-kNN

Section 10.2.4 to significantly reduce the complexity of the TCM-kNN conformity update mechanisms.

So, to re-calculate the non-conformity score of a training instance, we need the distance between that training instance and the added test instance. If that distance is very small, smaller than its largest (kth) nearest neighbor, the non-conformity score of the training instance will change and needs to be recalculated. For clarification of this discussion, see Figure 10.2.

Let the number of features be m and the number of training instances n. We want to compute prediction sets for l unlabeled/test instances. The number of classes is

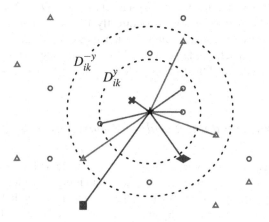

Fig. 10.2: Recalculation of the non-conformity score of the (black) star training instance. The (green) circles are again its nearest neighbors of class y_i, while the (red) triangles are its nearest neighbors of other classes. Here $k = 3$, so the three smallest distances are being summed. The (blue) cross, diamond and square are test instances. In case of the (blue) cross test instance, the non-conformity score of the training instance has to be recalculated and the corresponding D^y and D^{-y} have to be updated. In case of the (blue) diamond test instance, updates are only required if the test instance differs from class y_i. In case of the (blue) square test instance, the non-conformity score of the training instance does not have to be recalculated, regardless of its class.

$|\mathcal{Y}|$. Then the time complexity of Algorithm 1 is broken down as follows [20]: Lines 2-5 are only calculated once for training examples and we may assume $O(mn^2)$ as the dominating complexity. Lines 7-8 are specific for the unlabeled instance. From the remaining lines, the lines 13-18 are the most time intensive since they have time complexity $O(n)$.[2] These lines are nested in a loop at line 9, resulting in time complexity $O(|\mathcal{Y}|n)$. Thus, the overall complexity of TCM-kNN applied in the offline learning setting to compute l prediction sets is $O(mn^2) + O(mnl) + O(|\mathcal{Y}|nl)$.

When running experiments for a given training set of size n and a given test set of size l, the calculations of distances between all instances (training and test) and the training instances can be done once and the results can be stored. The problematic term in the complexity is $O(|\mathcal{Y}|nl)$ needed for recalculating the non-conformity scores of the training instances for each test instance, since it has to be repeated for each new value of k. Moreover, for large data sets the required memory for computing Eq. (10.2) becomes too high. To execute the innerloop for recalculating the non-conformity scores efficiently we need: (1) for each test instance and each possible label the distance to the k nearest training instances with that label ($lk|\mathcal{Y}|$ distances); (2) for each test instance the distance to each training instance (ln dis-

---

[2] The pseudo code may give the impression that the time complexity of these lines is $O(kn)$. However, by keeping track of the sum of elements in D_i^y and D_i^{-y}, we can update a single non-conformity score in constant time. Hence, a time complexity of $O(n)$ is obtained.

tances); (3) for each training instance z_i the sets D_i^y and D_i^{-y} ($2nk$ distances). I.e., we need $N_d = lk|\mathcal{Y}| + ln + 2nk$ distances directly available (in memory). Especially the ln distances between test and training instances are problematic in a setting were both training and test sets are huge. We will modify the algorithm to improve both on the memory needed and the time complexity (see Section 10.2.4).

10.2.3 The NicIcon dataset and DTW-based trajectory matching

The TCM framework was applied on the publicly available NicIcon database [12]. This is a collection of handwritten sketches containing so-called iconic gestures. These data were recently collected within the framework of the ICIS project (Interactive Collaborative Information Systems) [1]. A set of 14 icon classes which are important for this domain was designed such that gesture samples (i) have a visual resemblance to the objects they represent or resemble well known corresponding symbols (so that they are easy to learn by the users), and (ii) are distinguishable by the computer. The data were acquired from 32 different writers. Each writer had to draw 770 iconic gestures. After removal of bad samples, the data set contains a total of 24441 usable iconic gestures. Figure 10.3 shows an example of the different icon gestures and the 14 gesture classes.

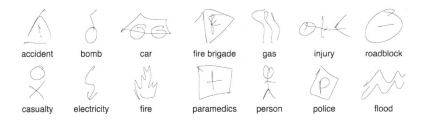

Fig. 10.3: Examples of the 14 gesture classes, as written by one of the participants to the data collection experiment. Data were collected on a pressure-sensitive pen tablet. Trajectories depicted in light grey represent parts where the writer lifts the pen from the tablet.

As explained in [12], two data subsets were constructed from the 24441 samples. Stratified random sampling was used, such that each subset contains the same relative number of samples per class. First, a writer dependent set (WD) was constructed, containing a training set of 60% and a test set of 40% of the available samples. Secondly, a writer independent (WI) set, where the train set contained all icons of 60% of the writers and the test set all icons of the other 40% of the writers. Writer independent classification is considered as more difficult in handwriting recognition, as the training set contains samples written by writers distinct from writers in the test set [18, 23].

Niels et al. [12] used three different classifiers to distinguish between the different icons: a multilayered perceptron, a linear multiclass SVM and Dynamic Time Warping (DTW) [11]. The latter algorithm was specifically designed for matching two gesture trajectories and yielded the best results of these three classifiers. The DTW distance between two data samples is computed as the averaged normalized Euclidean distance between all "matching" coordinates of a known prototypical data sample $\mathcal{A}$ and an unknown sample $\mathcal{B}$. Whether two coordinates $\mathcal{A}_i$ and $\mathcal{B}_j$ match is decided using three conditions: (i) the continuity condition, which is satisfied when index i is on the same relative position on $\mathcal{A}$ as index j is on $\mathcal{B}$ (the amount in which the relative positions are allowed to differ is controlled by a parameter c), (ii) the boundary condition, which is satisfied if both i and j are at the first, or at the last position of their sample, (iii) the penup/pendown condition, which is satisfied when both i and j are produced with the pen on the tablet, or when they are both produced with the pen above the tablet. The coordinates $\mathcal{A}_i$ and $\mathcal{B}_j$ match if either the boundary condition, or both other conditions are satisfied. Classification of a test sample is performed through nearest neighbour matching with the DTW distance function. The classification performance of the DTW classifier was respectively 98.06% on the WD set and 94.70% on the WI set. As we will show in Section 10.3, these performances can be improved considerably using our new technique.

The DTW distance δ^{DTW} can be used as an appropriate distance metric in our TCM-kNN framework. Note that for the data used in our experiments, we first computed a large distance matrix for further processing using the TCM method. For each data sample and for each class $y \in \mathcal{Y}$, the distance to the 50 closest other data samples with class y were sorted and stored for further processing. The number of 50 closest samples per class is chosen arbitrarily and provides the possibility to perform experiments on the TCM-kNN method with a varying number of k (from $1 \ldots 50$).

10.2.4 Modification

In Section 10.2.2 it was argued that for a computationally efficient implementation of the TCM-kNN algorithm, all required distances (N_d) should be available in memory. It is easy to see that this becomes practically impossible for large databases. For example, for our experiments on the the WD set, N_d would amount to about 2.4Gb of (double precision) distance information, with n, l, respectively, 14665 and 9776 and a limited $k = 3$. Although modern computing equipment is able to handle such an amount, we are still very much interested in reducing the significant time complexity of the TCM-kNN algorithm. Furthermore, for larger datasets, such as the UNIPEN database containing handwritten characters [5], much more memory is required. For example, for the UNIPEN-2 collection containing 123000 handwritten characters (with 26 classes), the required memory would amount to almost 60Gb, which requires dedicated hardware.

To reduce the required resources for computing the TCM-kNN algorithm, a limited number of distances between test and training instances is stored. Per training instance $z_i = (x_i, y_i)$, the distances of the 50 closest training instances of its own class y_i and distances of the 50 closest training instances of other classes are recorded. Per test instance, we store the 50 closest training instances of each class. The TCM-kNN algorithm is modified such that it only uses the $2nk$ distances needed to (re)calculate the non-conformity scores (α_i's) of each training instance, the $lk|\mathcal{Y}|$ distances to calculate the non-conformity scores of all test instances for all labels in $\mathcal{Y}$, and $lk'|\mathcal{Y}|$ ($k \leq k' \leq 50$) distances to (if needed) recalculate for each test instance the non-conformity scores of $2k'$ training instances. So instead of storing all nl distances between test and training instances, we store $50l|\mathcal{Y}|$ distances (and the indices of the 50 training instances) From these we use $lk'|\mathcal{Y}|$ distances for a given $k' \leq 50$. By this modification also the computational complexity per parameter setting (k, k') decreases from $O(ln|\mathcal{Y}|)$ to $O(lk'|\mathcal{Y}|)$.

Figure 10.4 shows that it is possible that a non-conformity score of a training instance is not recalculated, while it should be recalculated according to Algorithm 1. Note that this can only lead to a difference in the p value if the order of the non-conformity scores of the training instance and the test instance would change by the update. So, our intuition says that it can not have too large consequences, which is confirmed by the results from our experiments.

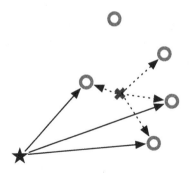

Fig. 10.4: Example of a situation where the non-conformity score of the (black) star training instance is not updated when the (blue) cross test instance has the same class. Note that for simplicity only instances of the same class are shown. The training instance uses $k = 3$ nearest neighbours and $k' = 4$ nearest training instances of this class are at most considered per test instance.

10.3 Experiments and Results

This section contains the results of our experiments. In Section 10.3.1, the validity of our modified TCM algorithm is assessed by comparing it to the original algorithm as used in [19], employing the same benchmark dataset. Subsequently, the results of our modified algorithm on respectively the NicIcon WD set (Section 10.3.2) and the WI set (Section 10.3.3) are described. Our final experiment explores whether our technique can improve on the performance of the DTW classifier for difficult samples, for which the test instances that were incorrectly classified in [12] are used. Our approach is evaluated by considering the performance of TCMs: (i) on a standard, medium-sized machine learning database; (ii) large-sized data with multiple classes for the relatively easy task of writer-dependent gesture recognition; (iii) the more difficult task of writer-independent gesture recognition; and (iv) the final experiment on highly ambiguous data samples.

10.3.1 Modified TCM algorithm

The modified TCM algorithm was described in Section 10.2.4. In order to assess whether our modifications have a significant impact on the performance of TCM, the well-known pima data set from the UCI benchmark repository [10] is used. The results of the original TCM algorithm on this dataset have been reported in [19] and all corresponding required data are available to one the authors of the current chapter. It should be noted that except for the modifications reported in Section 10.2.4, there is an additional difference between the method described in [19] and in the current chapter: a 10-fold cross validation for 5 random permutations of the training data was employed in [19]. Since we also compare our method to the DTW classifier described in [12] on two predefined datasets (WD and WI) for which random data set configurations could not be applied, we did not use 10-fold cross validation. In stead, we constructed one random train and test set, similar to the way the WD and WI sets were constructed.

The results of this assessment are depicted in Figure 10.5. To visualize performance of a TCM, we follow the convention as defined in [22]. Results are shown as graphs indicating four values for each significance level: (1) percentage of incorrect predictions, (2) percentage of uncertain predictions, (3) percentage of empty predictions, and (4) percentage of incorrect predictions that are allowed at the significance level. The first value represents the error rate as a percentage, while the second and third values represent efficiency. Note that the percentage of certain predictions is trivially derived from the reported percentages of the other types of prediction sets. Note that the percentage of empty predictions is at most the percentage of incorrect predictions. The line connecting the percentage of incorrect predictions allowed at each significance level is called the *error calibration line*.

Figures 10.5(a) and 10.5(b) illustrate the difference between using just one random permutation of the data and 5 different permutations. As can be observed, no difference is noticeable between both figures, so using multiple random permutations of the train and test set has only little impact. The results depicted in Figures 10.5(c) (original TCM on one random train/test set permutation of the pima data set) show a similar performance as in Figures 10.5(a) and 10.5(b). However,

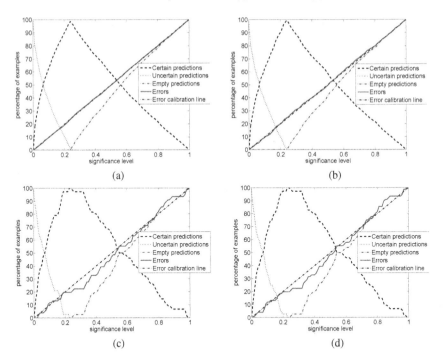

Fig. 10.5: Results on the pima data set with $k = 10$: (a) Original TCM algorithm with 10-fold cross validation and 5 random permutations, (b) Original TCM algorithm with 10-fold cross validation without random permutations, (c) Original TCM algorithm without cross validation and (d) Modified TCM algorithm.

the smoother plots of these figures display a smaller variance, which is due to the averaging of the results of 10-fold cross validation.

As explained in Section 10.2.4, our modified TCM algorithm stores the closest k' training instances for each test sample and uses these for updating the required non-conformity scores upon classifying any new extended test sample. For our experiments on the pima set, the performance of TCM-kNN was explored for different k with $k' = 10$, so $k \in \{1 \cdots 10\}$. Figure 10.5(d) depicts the results of our modified TCM algorithm for $k = 3$. The results are very similar to the results from Figure 10.5(c), where all distances between test and train instances are used. These tests indicate that our modified TCM algorithm yields approximately the same results as the original TCM algorithm, while requiring much lower computational and memory resources.

10.3.2 Writer Dependent Set

For the classification of the WD subset, it can be expected that a relatively small k is appropriate. Recall that the performance of the DTW classifier reported in [12] was 98.06% and that in the WD set, every writer that is in the test set is also present in the training set. Although a larger k is known to reduce noise in the data, we expect that for relatively easy data like the WD set, a larger k would only make the boundaries between the classes less distinct. In the case of TCM-kNN it is advantageous to have this kind of prediction, because it is very time-consuming to try a lot of different k's with this large data set. Therefore, experiments have focused on exploring $k \in \{1 \cdots 10\}$. As an example, please consider Figure 10.6, which depicts the results on the WD set for $k = 1$ and $k = 8$.

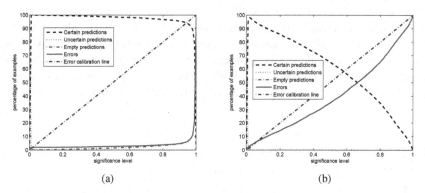

(a)   (b)

Fig. 10.6: Results on the WD set: (a) $k = 1$, (b) $k = 8$. Note that the error line and the empty predictions line run almost identical.

Compared to the results on the `pima` set depicted in Figure 10.5, the behaviour of the TCM-kNN for different significance levels ε for classifying the WD set is quite discrete. Almost all predictions are either certain or empty, across a wide range of significance levels. So for a small k the graph shows an error plot far below the error calibration line. A possible reason for this can be the combination of the high quality of the data set and the low value of k making the found p values quite discrete (either high or low). Furthermore, note that the number of empty predictions is much larger with a larger k resulting in an error curve closer to the error calibration line. This can be explained by the fact that for less distinct decision boundaries, there will be more confusion for conflicting test cases, such that the p-values will become lower (more spread), leading to more empty prediction sets. The same holds for explaining the low number of uncertain predictions. Only for very low significance levels, the number of uncertain predictions increases.

The maximum recognition performance (at the 1% significance level) we achieved was 98.62%, with $k = 4$, which slightly outperforms the results of DTW on the complete data set. However, this result could only be obtained by *forcing* the TCM-kNN to refuse empty predictions. To avoid empty predictions, TCMs can be modified to include the label with highest p-value into the prediction set, even though this p-value can be smaller than or equal to the significance level [3, 19]. When using this method to boost recognition results, the significance level still provides an upper bound on the error rate, although it cannot be established how tight this bound is [19].

10.3.3 Writer Independent Set

Recognition performance of the DTW classifier for the WI set is 94.7% [12], confirming that the task of writer independent classification is more difficult than writer dependent classification. Since this involves that a relatively high k may be required to get the best results on this set, we limited the number of test samples to 1000 to be able to explore a wide range of k values. Figure 10.7 shows the results on the WI set for $k = 2$ and $k = 27$. It is clear that a very small k still gives the best results. With $k = 27$, the percentage of incorrect predictions at each significance level lies approximately on the error calibration line. With smaller k's, the percentage of incorrect predictions at each significance level always stays (far) below the error calibration line.

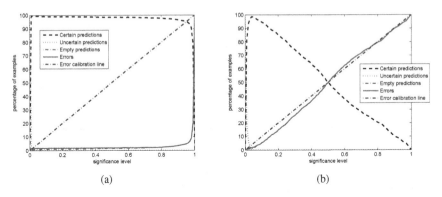

(a)   (b)

Fig. 10.7: Results on the WI set: (a) $k = 2$, (b) $k = 27$. Note that the error line and the empty predictions line run almost identical.

The recognition performance of the DTW method on the randomly selected subset of 1000 samples from the WI set appeared to be much higher (98.6%) than the performance on the complete set (94.7%). For writer independent recognition, reducing the number of writers results in a decrease of variance [18, 23], making the gestures selected for the smaller subest of 1000 samples easier to recognize. When classification results in case of empty prediction sets are not allowed (again, by including the label with the highest p-value into the prediction set), $k = 10$ yielded the best recognition performance. Note that this value of k is higher than with the WD set. The obtained performance was 99.6% at the 1% significance level, which is an improvement of 1.0% with regard to 98.6% achieved by DTW classifier on this subset.

10.3.4 Error Samples

In our final experiment the error samples, consisting of the test instances that were incorrectly classified by the DTW classifier, were processed by our TCM-kNN method. It is expected that a higher k is needed to get the best results, because these test samples are apparently difficult to classify. Therefore, we only consider the case where empty prediction sets are not allowed. If these were allowed, many predictions would be empty.

Classification with the DTW resulted in 190 incorrectly classified test samples from the WD set and 508 test samples from the WI set. Given the relatively small size of these sets, many different k could be explored. To establish the recognition performance for this experiment, we use the number of certain predictions minus the number of certain errors.

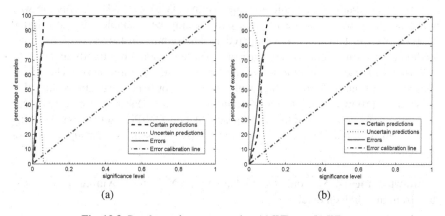

(a)   (b)

Fig. 10.8: Results on the error samples: (a) WD set, (b) WI set.

The results confirm that for difficult data, k should be high. The best results on the WD set were achieved for $k = 35$, with 99.47% certain predictions and 81.58% errors. This yields a certain improvement of 17.89%. On the WI set, the maximum of $k = 50$ nearest neighbors gave the best results. Here, 99.80% of the predictions is certain with 81.50% errors. This results in an improvement on the WI set of 18.30%. Both results are achieved at the significance level of 0.1. Below that value, the number of uncertain predictions (of which the correct class cannot be established) increases significantly (see Figure 10.8).

10.4 Conclusion and Discussion

In this chapter, we pursued reliable recognition of handwritten gestures using the TCM framework. Gesture recognition is a difficult multi-class pattern recognition problem with in many cases a large number of data samples. In order to reduce the computational and memory complexity of the TCM algorithm, we introduced a modification in the method for updating non-conformity scores in the case of offline learning of TCMs. The TCM-kNN approach was used, using the k-nearest neighbour classifier with as distance metric the DTW distance. Our new method was tested on the publicly available NicIcon database of iconic gestures, containing 14 gesture classes relevant to the domain of crisis management.

Several experiments have been performed. In the first experiment, the performance of our modified algorithm was evaluated by comparing it to the original TCM method. The `pima` database was used for this purpose. It was shown that both methods yield similar results. Three other experiments were performed on the NicIcon set. Results were compared to the results from the DTW classifier on the same data. For writer dependent recognition, we achieved a competitive performance of 98.62% at the 1% significane level. For writer independent recognition on a subset of the dataset, the performance was competitive at 99.6%. The final experiment, on the error test samples from the DTW classifier, showed that our TCM-kNN approach managed to correct almost 20% of the errors.

The key adaptation we applied to the original TCM method concerns the way non-conformity measures are updated upon testing new samples. In the original method, each test instance is compared to all training instances. Our modified method requires maximal $2k'$ comparisons, where k' should be slightly higher than the maximal k used for exploring different classification performances. The apparent speedup of our method and the results of our performance evaluations show that TCMs are a promising way to classify handwritten data. Our next efforts will focus on applying the new method to other datasets like the UNIPEN set and on exploring the suitability of our approach when using different classifiers, like support vector machines.

Acknowledgments. We would like to thank Ralph Niels for providing all necessary data from the NicIcon database.

References

1. Babuska, R., Groen, F. (eds.): Interactive Collaborative Information Systems, Studies in Computational Intelligence, vol. 281. Springer Verlag, Berlin (2010), iSBN=978-3-642-11687-2
2. Balasubramanian, V., Gouripeddi, R., Panchanathan, S., Vermillion, J.: Support vector machine based conformal predictors for risk of complications following a coronary drug eluting stent procedure. Computers in Cardiology 36, 5–8 (2009)

3. Bellotti, T., Luo, Z., Gammerman, A., Delft, F.W.V., Saha, V.: Qualified predictions for microarray and proteomics pattern diagnostics with confidence machines. International Journal of Neural Systems 15(4), 247258 (2005)
4. Gammerman, A., Vovk, V., Vapnik, V.: Learning by transduction. In: Cooper, G., Moral, S. (eds.) 14th Conference on Uncertainty in Artificial Intelligence (UAI-1998). pp. 148–155. Morgan Kaufmann (1998)
5. Guyon, I., Schomaker, L., Plamondon, R., Liberman, M., Janet, S.: UNIPEN project of on-line data exchange and recognizer benchmarks. In: Proc. 12th Int. Conf. on Pattern Recogn. pp. 29–33. Jerusalem, Israel (October 1994)
6. Jain, A., Duin, R., Mao, J.: Statistical pattern recognition: A review. IEEE Trans. on Pattern Analysis and Machine Intelligence 22(1), 4–37 (2000)
7. Lambrou, A., Papadopoulos, H., Gammerman, A.: Reliable confidence measures for medical diagnosis with evolutionary algorithms. IEEE Transactions on Information Technology in Biomedicine 15(1), 93–99 (2011)
8. Melluish, T., Saunders, C., Nouretdinov, I., Vovk, V.: Comparing the Bayes and typicalness frameworks. In: Raedt, L.D., Flach, P.A. (eds.) Proceedings of the 12th European Conference on Machine Learning (ECML-2001. pp. 360–371. LNCS, Springer (2001)
9. Mitchell, T.M.: Machine Learning. McGraw-Hill, New York (1997)
10. Newman, D.J., Hettich, S., Blake, C.L., Merz, C.J.: UCI repository of machine learning databases (1998)
11. Niels, R., Vuurpijl, L., Schomaker, L.: Automatic allograph matching in forensic writer identification. International Journal of Pattern Recognition and Artificial Intelligence (IJPRAI) 21, 61–82 (2007)
12. Niels, R., Willems, D., Vuurpijl, L.: The NicIcon database of handwritten icons. In: Proceedings of the 1st International Conference on Frontiers in Handwriting Recognition. pp. 296–301. Montreal, Canada (2008)
13. Plamondon, R., Srihari, S.: On-line and off-line handwriting recognition: A comprehensive survey. Trans. on Pattern Analysis and Machine Intelligence 22(1), 63–84 (January 2000)
14. Proedrou, K., Nouretdinov, I., Vovk, V., Gammerman, A.: Transductive confidence machines for pattern recognition. In: Raedt, L.D., Flach, P.A. (eds.) Proceedings of the 12th European Conference on Machine Learning (ECML-2001. pp. 381–390. LNCS, Springer (2001)
15. Saunders, C., Gammerman, A., Vovk, V.: Transduction with confidence and credibility. In: Dean, T. (ed.) Proceedings of the 16th international joint conference on Artificial intelligence. vol. 2, pp. 722–726. Morgan Kaufmann Publishers Inc., San Francisco, CA, USA (1999)
16. Smirnov, E., Nalbantov, G., Kaptein, A.: Meta-conformity approach to reliable classification. Intelligent Data Analysis pp. 901–915 (2009)
17. Smirnov, E., Sprinkhuizen-Kuyper, I., Nalbantov, G., Vanderlooy, S.: Version space support vector machines. In: Brewka, G., Coradeschi, S., Perini, A., Traverso, P. (eds.) Proceedings of the 17th European Conference on Artificial Intelligence (ECAI 2006). pp. 809–810. Riva del Garda, Italy (2006)
18. Srihari, S., Cha, S., Lee, S.: Establishing handwriting individuality using pattern recognition techniques. In: Proc. 6th Int. Conf. Document Analysis and Recogn. pp. 1195–1204. IEEE Computer Society, Seattle (2001)
19. Vanderlooy, S., van der Maaten, L., Sprinkhuizen-Kuyper, I.: Off-line learning with transductive confidence machines: An empirical evaluation. In: Perner, P. (ed.) Machine Learning and Data Mining in Pattern Recognition, LNCS, vol. 4571, pp. 310–323. Springer Berlin / Heidelberg (2007)
20. Vanderlooy, S., van der Maaten, L., Sprinkhuizen-Kuyper, I.: Off-line learning with transductive confidence machines: an empirical evaluation. Tech. Rep. MICC-IKAT 07-03, Universiteit Maastricht, Maastricht, The Netherlands (2007)
21. Vanderlooy, S., Sprinkhuizen-Kuyper, I.: A comparison of two approaches to classify with guaranteed performance. In: Kok, J.N., Koronacki, J., de Mántaras, R.L., Matwin, S., Mladenic, D., Skowron, A. (eds.) PKDD 2007: Proceedings of the 11th European conference on Principles and Practice of Knowledge Discovery in Databases. LNCS, vol. 4702, pp. 288–299. Springer, Berlin, Heidelberg (2007)

22. Vovk, V., Gammerman, A., Shafer, G.: Algorithmic Learning in a Random World. Springer, New York, NY, USA (2005)
23. Vuurpijl, L., Schomaker, L., van Erp, M.: Architectures for detecting and solving conflicts: two-stage classification and support vector classifiers. Int. J. of Doc. Analysis and Recogn. 5(4), 213–223 (July 2003)
24. Willems, D., Niels, R., Gerven, M.v., Vuurpijl, L.: Iconic and multi-stroke gesture recognition. Pattern Recognition 42(12), 3303–3312 (2009)
25. Willems, D., Vuurpijl, L.: Pen gestures in online map and photograph annotation tasks. In: Proc.of the tenth Int. Workshop on Frontiers in Handwriting Recognition (IWFHR06). pp. 297–402. La Baule, France (October 2006)

Part III
Reliability Analysis

Chapter 11
Reliability in A Feature-Selection Process for Intrusion Detection

Hai Thanh Nguyen, Katrin Franke, and Slobodan Petrović

Abstract Reliability of decision making performed by a real pattern-recognition system, such as intrusion-detection systems (IDSs), is a critical issue. Previous works have analyzed the reliability of a pattern classifier trained in the learning stage. However, the reliability in feature-selection stage was not studied so far. As we believe that reliability should be taken into account at the earliest possible stages, in this chapter we focus on the reliability of feature-selection. Firstly, we analyze the main factors that affect the reliability in the feature-selection process: **(i)** the choice of feature-selection methods and **(ii)** the search strategies for relevant features. Further on, we introduce a formal definition of a reliable feature-selection process. The definition provides formal measurements of reliability in feature-selection, i.e., the **steadiness** of a classifier's performance and the **consistency** in search for relevant features. Secondly, we propose new methods to address the main causes of unreliable feature-selection process. In particular, we introduce a new methodology of determining appropriate instances from a class of feature-selection methods. We call this class a generic-feature-selection (GeFS) measure. We also propose a new search approach that ensures the globally optimal feature subset by means of the GeFS measure. Finally, we validate our new proposed methods by applying the GeFS measure to intrusion detection systems.

Hai Thanh Nguyen
Norwegian Information Security Laboratory, P. O. Box 191, N-2802 Gjøvik, Norway
e-mail: hai.nguyen@hig.no

Katrin Franke
Norwegian Information Security Laboratory, P. O. Box 191, N-2802 Gjøvik, Norway
e-mail: katrin.franke@hig.no

Slobodan Petrović
Norwegian Information Security Laboratory, P. O. Box 191, N-2802 Gjøvik, Norway
e-mail: slobodan.petrovic@hig.no

11.1 Introduction

A critical question when utilizing pattern-recognition systems for decision making (e.g. intrusion detection) is whether we can trust the outcomes of a classifier. In other words, is the classification accuracy reliable? According to Fig.1, the total reliability of a pattern-recognition system is affected by the preprocessing reliability, the feature extraction/selection reliability and the classification reliability. The classification reliability has been studied in previous works (see for example [15,16]). However, the preprocessing reliability and feature-selection reliability were not analyzed so far. As we believe that reliability should be taken into account at the earliest possible stages, in this chapter we study the reliability in a feature-selection process.

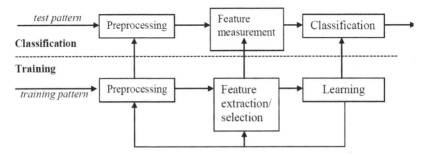

Fig. 11.1: The model for pattern recognition [19] formalizes the design of recognition systems. A recognition system consists of two phases: the training and the classification phases. Raw data represented as test and training patterns are normalized and cleaned from noise by the preprocessing modules. In the training phase, the feature extraction/selection module seeks representative patterns or features of the data. These features are then employed to train a classifier. This classifier, in turn, is applied to assign the test pattern to one of the classes in the classification phase.

A feature-selection process consists of a feature-selection method and a search strategy for relevant features, such as exhaustive search, best-first search or genetic search. There exists three categories of feature-selection methods: the filter, the wrapper and the embedded models [2,3]. The wrapper model utilizes a classifier's performance in assessing and selecting features, whereas the filter model considers statistical property of the data set without involving any learning algorithms. The embedded model integrates feature selection into learning process of a classifier.

We realize two main factors that affect the reliability in feature-selection process: (1) the choice of feature-selection methods and (2) the search strategies for relevant features.

Ad. 1 Each data set has its own statistical properties. Based on the estimation of these properties, a feature-selection method seeks representative patterns of the data. Thus, the wrong choice of feature-selection methods leads to non-representative patterns and the feature-selection results become unreliable. Further on, the classifier's performance might not be steady as the classifier has learnt on non-representative data set.

Ad. 2 The second factor is the search strategies employed in the feature-selection process. Even though we utilize appropriate feature-selection methods, the heuristic-search strategies might provide inconsistent results with different executions yielding different minima. Consequently, the feature-selection results are unreliable as well.

Based on our studies, in this chapter we first introduce a formal definition of a reliable feature-selection process. Our definition reflects the main factors that affect the reliability in a feature-selection process. Moreover, our definition establishes formal measurements of the feature-selection reliability, i.e., the **steadiness** of a classifier's performance and the **consistency** in search for relevant features.

We then propose new methods in order to address the main causes of the unreliable feature-selection process: (3) the inappropriate choice of feature-selection methods and (4) the heuristic search strategies.

Ad. 3 We introduce a new methodology for determining appropriate instances of a class including several feature-selection methods of the filter model, e.g. the correlation-feature-selection (CFS) measure [12] and the minimal-redundancy-maximal-relevance (mRMR) measure [13]. We call this class a generic-feature-selection (GeFS) measure. Following our new proposed methodology, we first analyze the statistical property of a data set. We then choose the CFS measure if the data set has many features that are linearly correlated to the class label and to each other. Otherwise, the mRMR measure is selected.

Ad. 4 We propose a new search approach that ensures the globally optimal feature subset by means of the GeFS measure. The new approach is based on solving a mixed 0-1 linear programming problem (M01LP) by using the branch-and-bound search algorithm. In this M01LP problem, the number of constraints and variables is linear in the number of full set features. In addition, the new proposed search method allows us to easily integrate expert knowledge in feature-selection process. That significantly increases the reliability of the feature relevance estimation.

In this chapter, we finally validate the capacity of our new proposed approaches in addressing the reliability issue in feature-selection. (5) The aim is to show that in order to yield the steadiness of a classifier's performance, analyzing the statistical property of a data set before determining appropriate instances of the GeFS measure is necessary. (6) We also show that our new proposed search approach is consistent in search for relevant features, thus provides more reliable feature-selection results than heuristic search strategies do.

Ad. 5 In order to do that, we choose the design of intrusion detection systems (IDSs) as a possible application. In particular, we apply the GeFS measure for selecting features from HTTP-traffic in Web application firewalls (WAFs). We conduct experiments on the publicly available ECML/PKDD-2007 data set [8]. Since this data set does not target any real Web application, we additionally generate our new CSIC-2010 data set [5]. We analyze the statistical properties of both data sets to provide more insights into their nature and quality. Subsequently, we determine appropriate instances of the GeFS measure for feature selection.

Ad. 6 The new proposed search approach is employed to obtain the globally optimal feature subset. We compare our new global search method with heuristic search strategies in term of reliability. In order to do that, we utilize the genetic search and the Peng's method [13] to select features from the data sets.

In addition, we apply four different classifiers (C4.5, CART, RandomTree and RandomForest [1]) to test the detection accuracies. The experiments show that our new proposed methods provide reliable feature-selection results and outperform the heuristic search approaches in term of reliability. In fact, by applying our new proposed methods we obtain 100% consistency in search for relevant features and 99.87 % steadiness of the WAF's detection accuracy; whereas, by utilizing the Peng's method we yield only 27% consistency and 92.14% steadiness of the WAF's detection accuracy.

The remainder of this chapter is organized as follows. Section 2 provides the formal definition of reliability in the feature-selection process. Section 3 describes the generic feature selection (GeFS) measure and its instances in more detail. Section 4 discusses our experiments in intrusion detection based on the ECML/PKDD 2007 data set and the CSIC 2010 data set. The last section concludes and summarizes our findings.

11.2 Definition of Reliability in Feature-Selection Process

In this section, we introduce a formal definition of a reliable feature-selection process. As we discuss in the introduction, the reliability of a feature-selection process is affected by the choice of feature-selection methods and the search strategy for relevant features. Thus, we measure the reliability of a feature-selection process via the **steadiness** of a classifier's performance and the **consistency** in search for relevant features as given below. We first provide several important notations.

Given a data set D, a classifier C and a feature-selection method FS. Suppose that we run the FS algorithm M-times to select features from the data set D . With different executions of a search strategy utilized in the feature-selection process, the feature-selection results might be different. Let $X_i, (i = \overline{1,M})$ be the selected feature subset in the ith run. $Acc_i, (i = \overline{1,M})$ is the classification accuracy of the classifier C performed on X_i. Acc_F is the classification accuracy of the C performed on full set of features.

Definition 1 (Consistency): A search strategy utilized in feature-selection process is consistent, with level of approximation α or $\alpha_{consistent}$, if, for a given M,

$$\frac{|X_1 \cap X_2 \cap ... \cap X_M|}{|X_1 \cup X_2 \cup ... \cup X_M|} = \alpha. \tag{11.1}$$

The greater the α is, the more consistent the search strategy is. When $\alpha = 1$ for every M, we say that the search strategy is truly consistent.

Definition 2 (Steadiness): A feature-selection method generates $\beta_{steadiness}$ of the classifier C, if, for a given M:

$$\beta = \frac{Acc_F - \frac{1}{M}\sum_{i=1}^{M}|Acc_F - Acc_i|}{Acc_F}. \tag{11.2}$$

The greater the β is, the better the classifier's steadiness is safeguarded by the feature-selection method is. Thus, the wrong choice of feature-selection methods might affect the steadiness of a classifier's performance.

Definition 3 (Reliability): A feature-selection method is called $(\alpha, \beta)_{reliable}$, if, for a given M, the search strategy utilized in the feature-selection process is $\alpha_{consistent}$ and the feature-selection method generates $\beta_{steadiness}$ of the classifier C.

In conventional view, the reliability [14] is defined in terms of stability, consistency and equivalence. However, in our case the equivalence condition contradicts our defined consistency condition. The reason is that in term of equivalence condition determined by Dai [17] a feature-selection process would be considered reliable if different selected feature subsets lead to the same performance of a classifier; whereas, the consistency condition allows only one feature subset to be selected by the search strategy. Thus, in feature selection we do not take the equivalence measurement into account.

In the next section, we introduce a generic-feature-selection (GeFS) measure. The new methodology for determining appropriate instances of the GeFS measure and the new search method for relevant features by means of the GeFS measure will be described subsequently.

11.3 Generic Feature Selection Measure

11.3.1 Definitions

In this subsection, we give an overview of the generic feature selection (*GeFS*) measure together with two instances: the correlation-feature-selection (CFS) measure [4,12] and the minimal-redundancy-maximal-relevance (mRMR) measure [4,13].

Definition 4: A generic feature-selection measure utilized in the filter model is a function $GeFS(x)$, which has the following form with $x = (x_1, \ldots, x_n)$:

$$GeFS(x) = \frac{a_0 + \sum_{i=1}^{n} A_i(x)x_i}{b_0 + \sum_{i=1}^{n} B_i(x)x_i}, x \in \{0,1\}^n \tag{11.3}$$

In this definition, binary values of the variable x_i indicate the appearance ($x_i = 1$) or the absence ($x_i = 0$) of the feature f_i; a_0, b_0 are constants; $A_i(x), B_i(x)$ are linear functions of variables $x_1, \ldots, x_n$; n is number of features.

Definition 5: The feature selection problem is to find $x \in \{0,1\}^n$ that maximizes the function $GeFS(x)$.

$$\max_{x \in \{0,1\}^n} GeFS(x) = \frac{a_0 + \sum_{i=1}^{n} A_i(x)x_i}{b_0 + \sum_{i=1}^{n} B_i(x)x_i} \tag{11.4}$$

There are several feature selection measures, which can be represented by the form (3), such as the correlation-feature-selection (CFS) measure, the minimal-redundancy-maximal-relevance (mRMR) measure and the Mahalanobis distance.

The mRMR Feature Selection Measure: In 2005, Peng et. al. [13] proposed a feature-selection method, which is based on mutual information. In this method, relevant features and redundant features are considered simultaneously. In terms of mutual information, the relevance of a feature set S for the class c is defined by the average value of all mutual information values between the individual feature f_i and the class c as follows: $D(S,c) = \frac{1}{|S|}\sum_{f_i \in S} I(f_i;c)$. The redundancy of all features in the set S is the average value of all mutual information values between the feature f_i and the feature f_j: $R(S) = \frac{1}{|S|^2}\sum_{f_i,f_j \in S} I(f_i;f_j)$. The mRMR criterion is a combination of two measures given above and is defined as follows:

$$\max_S \left[\frac{1}{|S|} \sum_{f_i \in S} I(f_i;c) - \frac{1}{|S|^2} \sum_{f_i,f_j \in S} I(f_i;f_j) \right] \tag{11.5}$$

Suppose that there are n full-set features. We use binary values of the variable x_i in order to indicate the appearance ($x_i = 1$) or the absence ($x_i = 0$) of the feature f_i in the globally optimal feature set. We denote the mutual information values $I(f_i;c)$, $I(f_i;f_j)$ by constants c_i, a_{ij}, respectively. Therefore, the problem (5) can be described as an optimization problem as follows:

$$\max_{x \in \{0,1\}^n} \left[\frac{\sum_{i=1}^n c_i x_i}{\sum_{i=1}^n x_i} - \frac{\sum_{i,j=1}^n a_{ij} x_i x_j}{(\sum_{i=1}^n x_i)^2} \right] \tag{11.6}$$

It is obvious that the mRMR measure is an instance of the GeFS measure that we denote by $GeFS_{mRMR}$.

Correlation Feature Selection Measure: The Correlation Feature Selection (CFS) measure evaluates subsets of features on the basis of the following hypothesis: *"Good feature subsets contain features highly correlated with the classification, yet uncorrelated to each other"* [12]. The following equation gives the merit of a feature subset S consisting of k features:

$$Merit_{S_k} = \frac{k\overline{r_{cf}}}{\sqrt{k + k(k-1)\overline{r_{ff}}}}$$

Here, $\overline{r_{cf}}$ is the average value of all feature-classification correlations, and $\overline{r_{ff}}$ is the average value of all feature-feature correlations. The CFS criterion is defined as follows:

$$\max_{S_k} \left[\frac{r_{cf_1} + r_{cf_2} + \dots + r_{cf_k}}{\sqrt{k + 2(r_{f_1 f_2} + \dots + r_{f_i f_j} + \dots + r_{f_k f_1})}} \right] \tag{11.7}$$

By using binary values of the variable x_i as in the case of the mRMR measure to indicate the appearance or the absence of the feature f_i, we can also rewrite the problem (7) as an optimization problem as follows:

$$\max_{x \in \{0,1\}^n} \left[\frac{(\sum_{i=1}^n a_i x_i)^2}{\sum_{i=1}^n x_i + \sum_{i \neq j} 2b_{ij} x_i x_j} \right] \qquad (11.8)$$

It is obvious that the CFS measure is an instance of the GeFS measure. We denote this measure by $GeFS_{CFS}$.

In the next subsection, we consider the optimization problem (4) as a polynomial mixed 0-1 fractional programming (P01FP) problem and show how to solve it.

11.3.2 Polynomial Mixed 0-1 Fractional Programming

A general polynomial mixed $0-1$ fractional programming ($PM01FP$) problem [6,7] is represented as follows, where $s.t.$ denotes the set of constraints:

$$\min \sum_{i=1}^m \left(\frac{a_i + \sum_{j=1}^n a_{ij} \prod_{k \in J} x_k}{b_i + \sum_{j=1}^n b_{ij} \prod_{k \in J} x_k} \right) \qquad (11.9)$$

$$s.t. \begin{cases} b_i + \sum_{j=1}^n b_{ij} \prod_{k \in J} x_k > 0, i = \overline{1, m}, \\ c_p + \sum_{j=1}^n c_{pj} \prod_{k \in J} x_k \leq 0, p = \overline{1, m}, \\ x_k \in \{0,1\}, k \in J; a_i, b_i, c_p, a_{ij}, b_{ij}, c_{pj} \in \Re. \end{cases}$$

By replacing the denominators in (9) by positive variables $y_i (i = \overline{1, m})$, the $PM01FP$ then leads to the following equivalent polynomial mixed $0-1$ programming problem:

$$\min \sum_{i=1}^m \left(a_i y_i + \sum_{j=1}^n a_{ij} \prod_{k \in J} x_k y_i \right) \qquad (11.10)$$

$$s.t. \begin{cases} b_i y_i + \sum_{j=1}^n b_{ij} \prod_{k \in J} x_k y_i = 1; y_i > 0, \\ c_p + \sum_{j=1}^n c_{pj} \prod_{k \in J} x_k \leq 0, p = \overline{1, m}, \\ x_k \in \{0,1\}; a_i, b_i, c_p, a_{ij}, b_{ij}, c_{pj} \in \Re. \end{cases} \qquad (11.11)$$

In order to solve this problem, Chang [6,7] proposed a linearization technique to transfer the terms $\prod_{k \in J} x_k y_i$ into a set of mixed $0-1$ linear inequalities. Based on this technique, the $PM01FP$ becomes then a mixed $0-1$ linear programming ($M01LP$), which can be solved by means of the branch-and-bound method to obtain the global solution.

Proposition 1: A polynomial mixed $0-1$ term $\prod_{k \in J} x_k y_i$ from (10) can be represented by the following program [6,7], where C is a large positive value:

$$\min z_i$$

$$s.t. \begin{cases} z_i \geq 0, \\ z_i \geq C(\sum_{k \in J} x_k - |J|) + y_i \end{cases} \qquad (11.12)$$

Proposition 2: A polynomial mixed $0-1$ term $\prod_{k \in J} x_k y_i$ from (11) can be represented by a continuous variable v_i, subject to the following linear inequalities [6,7], where C is a large positive value:

$$\begin{cases} v_i \geq C(\sum_{k \in J} x_k - |J|) + y_i, \\ v_i \leq C(|J| - \sum_{k \in J} x_k) + y_i, \\ 0 \leq v_i \leq C x_k, k \in J. \end{cases} \quad (11.13)$$

We now formulate the feature selection problem (4) as a polynomial mixed $0-1$ fractional programming ($PM01FP$) problem.

Proposition 3: The feature selection problem (4) is a polynomial mixed $0-1$ fractional programming ($PM01FP$) problem.

Remark: By applying Chang's method [6,7], we can transform this $PM01FP$ problem into an $M01LP$ problem. The number of variables and constraints is quadratic in the number n of full set features. This is because the number of terms $x_i x_j$ in (4), which are replaced by the new variables, is $n(n+1)/2$. The branch-and-bound algorithm can then be utilized to solve this $M01LP$ problem. But the efficiency of the method depends strongly on the number of variables and constraints. The larger the number of variables and constraints an $M01LP$ problem has, the more complicated the branch-and-bound algorithm is.

In the next section, we present an improvement of the Chang's method to get an $M01LP$ problem in which the number of variables and constraints is linear in the number n of full set features.

11.3.3 Optimization of the GeFS Measure

By introducing an additional positive variable, denoted by y, we now consider the following problem equivalent to (4):

$$\min_{x \in \{0,1\}^n} (-GeFS(x)) = -a_0 y - \sum_{i=1}^n A_i(x) x_i y \quad (11.14)$$

$$s.t. \left\{ b_0 y + \sum_{i=1}^n B_i(x) x_i y = 1; y > 0. \right. \quad (11.15)$$

This problem is transformed into a mixed 0-1 linear programming problem as follows:

Proposition 4: A term $A_i(x) x_i y$ from (14) can be represented by the following program, where C is a large positive value:

$$\min z_i$$

$$s.t. \begin{cases} z_i \geq 0, \\ z_i \geq C(x_i - 1) + A_i(x) y, \end{cases} \quad (11.16)$$

Proposition 5: A term $B_i(x)x_iy$ from (15) can be represented by a continuous variable v_i, subject to the following linear inequality constraints, where C is a large positive value:

$$\begin{cases} v_i \geq C(x_i - 1) + B_i(x)y, \\ v_i \leq C(1 - x_i) + B_i(x)y, \\ 0 \leq v_i \leq Cx_i \end{cases} \quad (11.17)$$

We substitute each term x_iy that will appear in (16), (17) by new variables t_i satisfying constraints from Proposition 2. The total number of variables for the $M01LP$ problem will be $4n + 1$, as they are x_i, y, t_i, z_i and $v_i(i = \overline{1,n})$. Therefore, the number of constraints on these variables will also be a linear function of n. As we mentioned above, with Chang's method [6,7] the number of variables and constraints depends on the square of n. Thus our new method actually improves Chang's method by reducing the complexity of the branch and bound algorithm.

We now present a new methodology for determining appropriate instances of the GeFS measure as well as a new search strategy for obtaining subsets of relevant features by means of this measure.

The search strategy for obtaining subsets of relevant features by means of the GeFS measure:

-*Step 1*: Analyze the statistical properties of the given dataset in order to choose the appropriate feature selection instance ($GeFS_{CFS}$ or $GeFS_{mRMR}$) from the generic feature selection measure GeFS. We choose the $GeFS_{CFS}$ measure if the dataset has many features that are linearly correlated to the class label and to each other. Otherwise, the $GeFS_{mRMR}$ measure is selected.

-*Step 2*: According to the choice of feature selection instance from *Step 1*, we construct the optimization problem (4) for the $GeFS_{CFS}$ measure or for the $GeFS_{mRMR}$ measure. In this step, we can use expert knowledge by assigning the value 1 to the variable if the feature is relevant and the value 0 otherwise.

-*Step 3*: Transform the optimization problem of the GeFS measure to a mixed 0-1 linear programming (M01LP) problem, which is to be solved by means of the branch-and-bound algorithm. A non-zero integer value of x_i from the optimal solution x indicates the relevance of the feature f_i regarding the GeFS measure.

11.4 Experiment

In this section, we validate our new proposed methods in addressing the reliability issue in feature-selection process. The aim is to show that in order to yield the steadiness of a classifier's performance, analyzing the statistical property of a data set before determining appropriate instances of the GeFS measure is necessary. We also show that our new proposed search approach is consistent in search for relevant features, thus provides more reliable feature-selection results than heuristic search strategies do. In order to do that, we apply the generic feature selection (GeFS) measure to Web attack detection. We first describe two data sets, on which the experiments were conducted: the ECML/PKDD 2007 data set [8] and our new CSIC 2010 data set [5]. We then analyze the statistical properties of these data sets for determining appropriate instances of the GeFS measure. The new proposed search approach is employed to obtain the globally optimal feature subset. We compare our new global search method with heuristic search strategies in term of reliability. In order to do that, we utilize the genetic search and the Peng's method [13] to select features from the data sets. Since there is no standard Web application firewall (WAF), we apply four different machine learning algorithms to evaluate the detection accuracy on data sets containing the selected features.

11.4.1 Data Sets

We conducted experiments on the ECML/PKDD 2007 data set, which was generated for the ECML/PKDD 2007 Discovery Challenge [8]. In fact, we utilized the training set, which is composed of 50,000 samples including 20% of attacks (i.e. 10,000 attacks and 40,000 normal requests). The requests are labeled with specifications of attack classes or normal traffic. The classes of attacks in this data set are: Cross-Site Scripting, SQL Injection, LDAP Injection, XPATH Injection, Path traversal, Command Execution and SSI attacks. However, the attack requests of this data set were constructed blindly and did not target any real Web application. Therefore, we additionally generated our new CSIC 2010 data set for experiments.

The CSIC 2010 data set contains the generated traffic targeted to an e-commerce Web application developed at our department. In this web application, users can buy items using a shopping cart and register by providing some personal information. The data set was generated automatically and contains 36,000 normal requests and more than 25,000 anomalous requests. In this data set the requests are labeled as normal or anomalous. We included attacks such as SQL injection, buffer overflow, information gathering, files disclosure, CRLF injection, XSS, server side include, parameter tampering and so on. In order to generate the traffic, we collected thousands of normal and anomalous values for the parameters of the web application. Then, we generated requests for every web-page and the values of the parameters, if any, were filled with the values collected (the normal values for the normal traffic and the anomalous ones for the anomalous traffic). Further details can be found in [5].

Table 11.1: Names of 30 features that are considered relevant for the detection of Web attacks [18]. $\star$ refers to features selected by the $GeFS_{CFS}$ from the CSIC-2010 data set; $\dagger$ refers to features selected by the $GeFS_{mRMR}$ from the CSIC 2010 data set; $\bullet$ refers to features selected by the $GeFS_{CFS}$ from the ECML/PKDD 2007 data set; and $\diamond$ refers to features selected by the $GeFS_{mRMR}$ from the ECML/PKDD 2007 data set.

Feature Name	Feature Name
Length of the request $\star$ $\diamond$	Length of the path $\star$
Length of the arguments $\star$ $\diamond$	Length of the header "Accept" $\dagger$
Length of the header "Accept-Encoding" $\dagger$	Length of the header "Accept-Charset" $\dagger$
Length of the header "Accept-Language" $\dagger$	Length of the header "Cookie" $\dagger$
Length of the header "Content-Length" $\dagger$	Length of the header "Content-Type"
Length of the Host $\dagger$	Length of the header "Referer" $\dagger$
Length of the header "User-Agent" $\dagger$	Method identifier
Number of arguments $\star$	Number of letters in the arguments $\star$
Number of digits in the arguments $\star$	Number of 'special' char in the arguments $\star$ $\dagger$ $\bullet$ $\diamond$
Number of other char in the arguments $\bullet$ $\diamond$	Number of letters char in the path $\star$
Number of digits in the path $\star$ $\dagger$	Number of 'special' char in the path $\star$
Number of other char in path $\dagger$	Number of cookies $\dagger$
Minimum byte value in the request $\diamond$	Maximum byte value in the request $\star$ $\dagger$
Number of distinct bytes	Entropy $\diamond$
Number of keywords in the path	Number of keywords in the arguments

11.4.2 Experimental Settings

By utilizing our expert knowledge about Web attacks, we listed 30 features that we considered relevant for the detection process (see Table 1). Some features refer to the length of the request, the length of the path or the headers, as length is important for detecting buffer-overflow attacks. We also observed that the non-alphanumeric characters were present in many injection attacks. Therefore, we took four types of characters into account: letters, digits, non-alphanumeric characters and other characters. As the non-alphanumeric characters have a special meaning in a set of programming languages, thus in Table 1 we refer to them as 'special' char. We analyzed the appearance of the characters in the path and in the argument's values. We also studied the entropy of the bytes in the request. Additionally, we collected the keywords of several programming languages that were often utilized in the injection attacks and counted the number of their appearances in different parts of the request as a feature.

We analyzed statistical properties of the data sets to see whether they had linear or non-linear relations between features. From this analysis, the appropriate feature selection instance from the GeFS measure was chosen for each data set according to the Step 1 of the proposed search method described above. In order to do that, we first visualized the whole data sets in the two-dimensional space to get a plot matrix. In this plot matrix, each element was the distribution of data points depending on the values of a feature and the class label or the values of two features. Fig. 2 and Fig. 3 show the sample distributions of data points of the CSIC 2010 data

Fig. 11.2: Nine samples of distributions of data points from the CSIC 2010 dataset. In a sample, the horizontal axis represents for a feature and the vertical axis represents for another feature.

set and the ECML/PKDD 2007 data set, respectively. We then calculated the correlation coefficients between the features. From these, we observed that the CSIC 2010 data set has many features that are linearly correlated to each other, whereas in the ECML/PKDD 2007 data set the non-linear relations between features are more representative. In fact, in the CSIC 2010 data set, more than 63 % of the correlation coefficients are greater than 0.5, whereas in the ECML/PKDD 2007 data set more than 83% of the correlation coefficients are less than 0.09. Therefore, we chose the $GeFS_{CFS}$ measure for selecting features from the CSIC 2010 data set, and the $GeFS_{mRMR}$ measure for selecting features from the ECML/PKDD 2007 data set. Moreover, the $GeFS_{CFS}$ and the $GeFS_{mRMR}$ measures were also applied to the ECML/PKDD 2007 and to the CSIC 2010 data sets, respectively, to see how the wrong choices of feature selection methods would negatively affect the detection performance.

We applied the new proposed search method to find globally optimal feature subsets by means of the $GeFS_{CFS}$ and the $GeFS_{mRMR}$ measures. We compare our new global search method with heuristic search strategies in term of reliability. In order to do that, we utilize the genetic search and the Peng's method [13] to select features from the data sets. Four classifiers with 10-fold cross validation were utilized to evaluate detection performances before and after feature selection: C4.5, CART, RandomTree and RandomForest [1]. All the obtained results are listed in the Tables 2, 3 and 4.

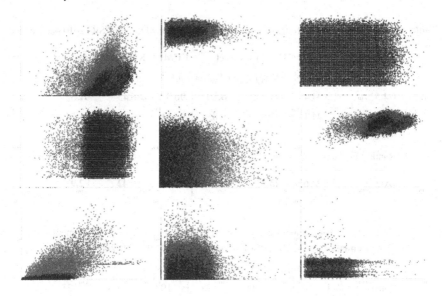

Fig. 11.3: Nine samples of distributions of data points from the ECML/PKDD 2007 data set. In a sample, the horizontal axis represents for a feature and the vertical axis represents for another feature.

11.4.3 Experimental Results

Table 2 shows the number of full-set features and the number of features selected by the $GeFS_{CFS}$ measure and the $GeFS_{mRMR}$ measure (Table 1 shows which features were selected). Table 3 summarizes the detection rates of four different classifiers performed on the CSIC 2010 data set and the ECML/PKDD 2007 data set. Table 4 indicates the consistency and steadiness values of four different feature-selection methods, i.e., the $GeFS_{CFS}$, the $GeFS_{mRMR}$, the GA_{CFS} (genetic search with the CFS measure) and the mRMR (Peng's method).

Table 11.2: Full-set features and the number of selected features.

Data Set	Full-set	$GeFS_{CFS}$	$GeFS_{mRMR}$
CSIC 2010	30	11	14
ECML/PKDD 2007	30	2	6

Table 11.3: Detection rates of four different classifiers performed on the CSIC 2010 data set and the ECML/PKDD 2007 data set.

Classifiers	CSIC 2011 data set			ECML/PKDD 20007 data set		
	Full-set	*GeFS$_{CFS}$*	*GeFS$_{mRMR}$*	*Full-set*	*GeFS$_{CFS}$*	*GeFS$_{mRMR}$*
C4.5	94.49	94.06	79.80	96.37	86.45	91.62
CART	94.12	93.71	79.85	96.11	86.45	91.54
RandomTree	92.30	92.70	71.36	96.89	86.39	93.41
RandomForest	93.71	93.68	71.70	98.80	86.39	95.18
Average	**93.65**	**93.53**	**75.67**	**97.04**	**86.42**	**92.93**

Table 11.4: Consistency and steadiness values of different feature-selection methods.

Measurements	CSIC 2011 data set			ECML/PKDD 20007 data set		
	GeFS$_{CFS}$	*GeFS$_{mRMR}$*	*GA$_{CFS}$*	*GeFS$_{CFS}$*	*GeFS$_{mRMR}$*	*mRMR*
Consistency(%)	100	100	25	100	100	27
Steadiness(%)	99.87	80.80	97.33	89.05	95.76	92.14

It can be observed from Table 3 that following our new proposed methodology the choice of appropriate instances of the GeFS measure leads to steady performance of classifiers. In fact, the $GeFS_{CFS}$ measure performed well on the CSIC 2010 data set and provided better results than the $GeFS_{mRMR}$ measure. In more detail, with the $GeFS_{CFS}$ measure we almost keeps the detection accuracies with only 0.12% of difference, whereas with the $GeFS_{mRMR}$ measure we reduce 17.89% of detection rates. On the ECML/PKDD 20007 data set, the $GeFS_{mRMR}$ measure provides better results than the $GeFS_{CFS}$ measure.

Following the definitions 1 and 2, we calculated the consistency and steadiness values of the feature-selection methods. These values are shown in Table 4. We observed that our new proposed search method for relevant features is consistent with 100% consistency. The heuristic search strategies provided un-consistent feature-selection results with only 25% consistency. At the same time, the steadiness values generated by the heuristic search strategies are less than the ones obtained by utilizing our globally search approach.

Therefore, based on all these experiments we can conclude that our new proposed methods provide reliable feature-selection results and outperform the heuristic approaches in term of reliability.

11.5 Conclusions

Reliability in a feature-selection process is a critical issue of real pattern-recognition system, e.g. intrusion detection systems. In the present chapter, we have introduced a formal definition of a reliable feature-selection process. Our definition provides formal measurements of the feature-selection reliability, i.e., the **steadiness** of a classifier's performance and the **consistency** in search for relevant features. In order to tackle the main causes of the unreliable feature-selection process, we have proposed new methods. In particular, we have introduced a new methodology for determining appropriate instances of a class of feature-selection methods. This class is called a generic-feature-selection (GeFS) measure. We have also proposed a new search approach that ensures the globally optimal feature subset by means of the GeFS measure. Finally, we have validated the capacity of our new proposed approaches in addressing the reliability issue in feature-selection by applying the GeFS measure to intrusion detection. The experiments show that our new proposed methods provide reliable feature-selection results and outperform the heuristic approaches in term of reliability.

Acknowledgements We would like to thank Gjøvik University College, Norwegian Information Security Laboratory. We would also like to thank Carmen Torrano-Gimenez and Gonzalo Alvarez from Instituto de Física Aplicada, Consejo Superior de Investigaciones Científicas, Spain for their supports in conducting experiments.

References

1. Duda, R. O., Hart, P. E., and Stork, D. G.: Pattern Classification. John Wiley& Sons, USA, (2001).
2. Guyon, I., Gunn, S., Nikravesh, M. and Zadeh, L. A.: Feature Extraction: Foundations and Applications. Series Studies in Fuzziness and Soft Computing, Springer, (2005).
3. Liu, H., Motoda, H.: Computational Methods of Feature Selection. Chapman & Hall/CRC, (2008).
4. Nguyen, H. T., Franke, K., and Petrovic, S.: Towards a Generic Feature-Selection Measure for Intrusion Detection. In 20th International Conference on Pattern Recognition, pp. 1529-1532, (2010).
5. Torrano-Gimenez, C., Perez-Villegas, A., and Alvarez, G.: A Self-Learning Anomaly-Based Web Application Firewall. In Proceedings of Computational Intelligence In Security For Information Systems (CISIS09), pp. 85-92, (2009).
6. Chang, C-T.: On the polynomial mixed 0-1 fractional programming problems, European Journal of Operational Research, vol. 131, issue 1, pages 224-227, (2001).
7. Chang, C-T.: An efficient linearization approach for mixed integer problems, European Journal of Operational Research, vol. 123, pages 652-659, (2000).
8. Rassi, C., Brissaud, J., Dray, G., Poncelet, P., Roche, M. and Teisseire, M.: Web Analyzing Traffic Challenge: Description and Results. In Proceedings of the Discovery Challenge ECML/PKDD'2007, pp. 47-52 (2007).
9. McHugh, J.: Testing Intrusion Detection Systems: A Critique of the 1998 and 1999 DARPA Intrusion Detection System Evaluations as Performed by Lincoln Laboratory. Proc. ACM Transactions on Information and System Security (TISSEC), 3(4), pp. 262-294, (2000).

10. Becher, M.: Web Application Firewalls. VDM Verlag Dr. Mueller e.K., February 1, (2007). ISBN-10: 383640446X, ISBN-13: 978-3836404464.
11. Lee, W.: A data mining framework for building intrusion detection models. In IEEE Symposium on Security and Privacy, pages 120-132, (1999).
12. Hall, M.: Correlation Based Feature Selection for Machine Learning. Doctoral Dissertation, University of Waikato, Department of Computer Science, (1999).
13. Peng, H., Long, F., and Ding, C.: Feature selection based on mutual information: criteria of max-dependency, max-relevance, and min-redundancy. IEEE Transactions on Pattern Analysis and Machine Intelligence, Vol. 27, No. 8, pp.1226-1238, (2005).
14. American Educational Research Association, American Psychological Association, and National Council on Measurement in Education. Stardards for educational and psychological testing. American Educational Research Association, iWashington DC:Authors, (1985).
15. Dai, H.: A Case Study on Classification Reliability. In Proceeding of the Data Mining Workshops, pp.69 - 73, (2008).
16. Fumera, G., Roli, F., and Giacinto, G.: Multiple Reject Thresholds for Improving Classification Reliability. Joint IAPR Int. Workshops on Syntactical and Structural Pattern Recognition and Statistical Pattern Recognition (S+SSPR 2000), vol. 1876, pp. 863-871, (2000).
17. Dai, H.: A Study on Reliability in Graph Mining, In: Proceedings of IEEE ICDM Workshops 2006, pp775-779, (2006).
18. H.T. Nguyen, C. Torrano, G. Alvarez, S. Petrovic, K. Franke, "Application of the Generic Feature Selection Measure in Detection of Web Attacks", in 4th International Conference on Computational Intelligence in Security for Information Systems (CISIS 2011), vol. 6694 of LNCS, 25-32, Springer-Verlag, Mlaga, Spain, June, 2011.
19. Jain, A. K., Duin, R. P. W., and Mao, J.: Statistical Pattern Recognition: A Review. IEEE Transactions on Pattern Analysis and Machine Intelligence In Pattern Analysis and Machine Intelligence, IEEE Transactions on, Vol. 22, No. 1, pp. 4-37, (2000).

Chapter 12
The Impact of Sample Size and Data Quality to Classification Reliability

Honghua Dai

Abstract The reliability of an induced classifier can be affected by several factors including the data oriented factors and the algorithm oriented factors [3]. In some cases, the reliability could also be affected by knowledge oriented factors. In this chapter, we analyze three special cases to examine the reliability of the discovered knowledge. Our case study results show that (1) in the cases of mining from low quality data, rough classification approach is more reliable than exact approach which in general tolerate to low quality data; (2) Without sufficient large size of the data, the reliability of the discovered knowledge will be decreased accordingly; (3) The reliability of point learning approach could easily be misled by noisy data. It will in most cases generate an unreliable interval and thus affect the reliability of the discovered knowledge. It is also reveals that the inexact field is a good learning strategy that could model the potentials and to improve the discovery reliability.

12.1 Introduction

With the rapid development of data mining, many classification rule induction methods have been created. Most of these methods are found very useful in solving real world application problems. These include decision tree algorithms, Nave Bayesian methods, etc. These developed approaches have strongly pushed the area to transfer the developed technology into real world applications. However when we apply the discovered knowledge in solving real world problems, it is essential to insure that the discovered knowledge is reliable. To examine this reliability issue, in this chapter we will conduct three case studies. We will provide an original data set and then introduce errors in the data. Wee will use different learning algorithm to examine the impact of algorithms to the reliability of the discovered knowledge. We then used

Honghua Dai
Deakin University, 221 Burwood Highway, Burwood, Melbourne, VIC 3125, Australia, e-mail: honghua.dai@deakin.edu.au

run the decision tree induction algorithm in Weka on the training data sets to derive decision trees and test the derived decision trees using the original data set and the data sets with introduced errors. In the second sets of our experiments, we run the inexact field learning algorithm, the Fish_net algorithm using the same data sets to examine the reliability of the discovered knowledge.

In general, classification can be divided into two major categories: the traditional classification and rough classification or inexact classification. In some cases, traditional classification is also called exact classification and the rough classification is also called inexact classification.

12.2 The original data sets and the data set with introduced errors

To examine the reliability of the classifier derived by a learning algorithm, we manually selected the data set as shown in Table 12.1.

Assume that the true values of each attributes in all the observations should be as shown in Table 12.1.

Instances	x	y	z	γ
Instance 1	2.6	-2	1	1
Instance 2	0.8	4	3.3	1
Instance 3	-5	0	6.9	0
Instance 4	5.5	1.5	4.8	1
Instance 5	0.7	-4	0	0
Instance 6	-10	-1	-2	0

Table 12.1: Theoretical Data Set

In real application, observation or measurement error appears frequently. We assume that the error is less than 0.3. To examine the impact of low quality data to the reliability of discovered knowledge, we introduce such errors in the original data set to create another set of data with errors as shown in Table 12.2.

Instances	x	y	z	γ
Instance 1	2.6	-2	1	1
Instance 2	.8-.3	4	3.3	1
Instance 3	-5	0	6.9	0
Instance 4	5.5	1.5	4.8	1
Instance 5	0.7+0.3	-4	0	0
Instance 6	-10	-1	-2	0

Table 12.2: Actual Data Set

Note that we have introduced errors to the values of the attribute x in instance I2 and Instance I5.

12.3 The examination of the impact of Low Quality Data to the reliability of discovered knowledge

In [3], it is pointed out that the reliability could be affected by low quality data. However it does not show how the reliability be affected in detail. The following designed experiment reveals the fact.

Case Study 1. The examination of the impact of low quality data to the reliability of derived classifier.

For the data sets in Table 12.1 and 12.2, we run J48 in Weka [10]. Figure 17.1 shows the derived J48 pruned tree from the original data as shown in Table 12.1.

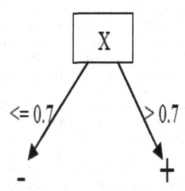

Fig. 12.1 Decision tree derived from original data

You can easily find that this classifier fits the original data as shown in Table 12.1 perfectly which gives 100

We also run J48 on the data set with introduced errors as shown in Table 12.2, the derived J48 pruned tree this time is as follows:

We can see the difference of the derived decision trees caused due to the introduced error. Figure 17.2 shows the decision tree derived from the data set shown in Table 12.2 with introduced error 0.3 to the values of the attribute x as in the instances 2 and 5. The classification that distinguished by the value of attribute x in the interval (-5, 0.7] has been changed from negative to positive. We call this interval

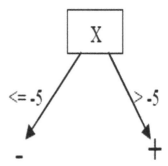

Fig. 12.2 Decision tree derived from the data with introduced errors

the unreliable interval. The smaller the unreliable interval is, the more reliable the discovered knowledge be and the better the learner.

In practical data mining applications, we actually do not know the unreliable interval. What we know are the data sets as shown in Table 2 and we apply a data mining algorithm, such as J48 as we used to the data set in Table12.1. After we discovered the knowledge using a learning algorithm, it is naturally to ask that shall we trust the discovered knowledge. In general, the answer is not simple. As we can see from this case study, the error is as small as only 0.3. However this caused unreliable interval (-5, 0.7] is quite big. In this learning, all the new cases with attribute value falls in the unreliable interval will be classified incorrectly. In real application, the data we can have is the data as shown in Table 2. As a consequence, the knowledge we can obtain is the knowledge as shown in Figure 17.2. If we use this derived knowledge in classification, for any value of X belongs to (-5, 0.7], the object will be classified as class +. However the true classification should be the class as we can know from the decision tree as shown in Figure 17.1.

In summary, based on our study, we observed that this data-oriented reliability problem in classifications is caused mainly due to two reasons:

1. the quality of the data
2. the ability in dealing with low quality data of the learner.

12.4 Can we trust the knowledge discovered from a small data set?

In our previous research [4], we examined the effect of the sample size in knowledge discovery from databases. For any learning technique which converges on the underlying probability distribution in a prediction task, the reliability of the discovered knowledge will be sensitive to the sample size, the model complexity and the strength of the correlation between measured variables.

Case Study 2. The impact of data size to the reliability of the discovered knowledge.

In data mining, in some cases the data we needed to induce the knowledge may not be sufficient. Typically the data size is too small. This will cause reliability problem in general. To examine the impact of data size to the reliability of discovered knowledge, we use the same example as we used in the chapter 5. We choose 6 graphs [4] as shown in Figure 17.3, and for each one of the 6 graphs, we generate 8 data sets with a sample size of 10, 50, 100, 200, 500, 1000, 2000 and 5000 instances respectively. We then run our MML-CI algorithm on each one of these 8 data sets for each one of the 8 graphs. From the experimental results [4], we find that,

1. The results show the parallel relationship between model complexity and the sample size required to discover it. The more complex the model is, the larger sample is required to have a better reliable discovery.
2. Our experimental results also show that the reliability of the discovered model is also affected by the strength of the links. It shows the inverse relationship between strength of the link and the sample size required to discover the knowledge. The weaker the link is, the larger the sample is required to achieve a better reliable discovery. This reveals that if the knowledge to be discovered is a complex model, it is very unlikely that it can be discovered from a small data set.
3. In real application, the available data may not be in the right size that we need to conduct a reliable discovery. For example, if we are required to discover the model 3 from a given data set with 200 instances, it is clearly shown from our results in [4] that the discovered model is not the real reflection of the true model. Thus, the discovered knowledge is obviously unreliable.

12.5 A Comparison of a traditional classifier learner and an inexact classifier learner

Most traditional learning algorithms are exact learning algorithms which in general work well in good cases and on high quality data sets. However, many real situations are very often not crisp and deterministic and they cannot be described precisely at some level or under some conditions. In such cases, an inexact learning approach would be more appropriate.

Exact learning algorithms derive rules on the assumption that an exact rule can be found from a given data set and hope that the derived rule can make the classification correctly. However in many cases, particularly in real applications this is not always the case. Most of the data from real world applications are inexact. It seems

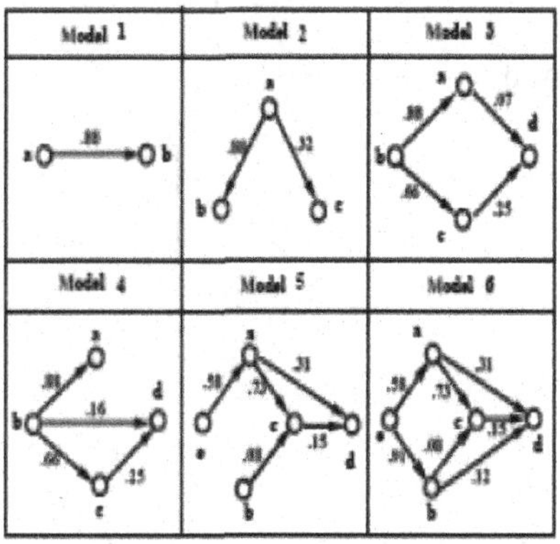

Fig. 12.3 Six selected test Graphic models

unrealistic to pursue an exact rule from such inexact information unless we are able to find some way to filter out the inexact factors. This is almost impossible, as in many cases, we actually do not know the location of the problem. In some applications it is not necessary to find exact laws/equations because in practice, complex exact formulas such as, a partial differential equations, need to be evaluated using numerical approximation anyway.

In many cases the quality of the data given to a learner is not so high, it contains high levels of noisy data, missing values, erroneous data and irrelevant features. In such cases it usually happens that the better the derived rules fit the training data the poorer the prediction accuracy. The reason is that if the derived rules fit the LQD (low quality data) training data perfectly, the rule was derived according to false representatives and applying the derived rules on new cases will cause the LPA (low prediction accuracy) problem. On the other hand, if instead of pursuing an exact fit of the LQD we consider inexact fitting of the data by tracing the main trends, this could be a possible way for overcoming the reliability problem. For this reason, in order to improve the reliability of the discovered knowledge, we use an alternative learning approach in contrast to traditional exact learning called inexact learning. Inexact learning does not pursue the exact fitting of the derived rule to the training data set, but pursues the achievement of a higher accuracy rate on new unseen cases and in almost all cases improves the reliability of the discovered knowledge.

The approach we used in the Case Study 1 is an exact approach which is also a point learning approach. Point learning is the learning approach that derives rules from data on the basis of looking at each individual values of each attribute in every instance.

Case Study 3. The impact of learning approaches to the reliability of the discovered knowledge.

To examine the impact of different learning algorithms to the reliability of the discovered knowledge, we now use another classifier learner to discover knowledge from the data sets we used in Case study 1. Instead of using the exact point learning approach J48, we now use an alternative approach, an inexact field learning approach [3] to the data set s shown in Table 12.1, we first derive the contribution functions as follows,

$$\mu_x = \begin{cases} 0 & x \leq -2.87 \\ 1 & x \geq 2.37 \\ (x+2.87)/5.24, & x \in [-2.87, 2.37] \end{cases} \tag{12.1}$$

And

$$\mu_y = \begin{cases} 0 & y \leq -8/3 \\ 1 & y \geq 4/3 \\ (y+8/3)/4, & y \in [-8/3, 4/3] \end{cases} \tag{12.2}$$

Based on the algorithm, we do not need to construct a contribution function for attribute z. We use these contribution functions to calculate the average contributions for each instance, and then work out the positive and negative contribution field. Based the positive and negative contribution field, we work out threshold = 0.63. Therefore the final inexact rule derived from the data in Table 12.1 is,

$$\mu_y = \begin{cases} If(\mu_x + \mu_y)/2 \geq T, THEN+; \\ ELSE-. \end{cases} \quad (12.3)$$

It is same as we found in Case Study 1, you can easily find that tested on the original training set as shown in Table 12.1, it fits the data perfectly and gives 100

Now we use the same inexact field learning approach again on the data as show in Table 12.2. As nothing changes to attribute y, so the contribution function will be exactly the same. So we only need to re-construct the contribution function for attribute x. Applying to data set in Table 12.2, the contribution function for attribute x is,

$$\mu_x^* = \begin{cases} 0 & x \leq -3 \\ 1 & x \geq 2.5 \\ (x+3)/5.5, & x \in [-3, 2.5] \end{cases} \quad (12.4)$$

We use the same way to find the threshold $\tau^* = 0.62$. So the final inexact rule derived from the data in Table 12.2 is,

$$\mu_y = \begin{cases} If(\mu_x^* + \mu_y)/2 \geq T, THEN+; \\ ELSE-. \end{cases} \quad (12.5)$$

Compare the rule (3) and (5), you can find two differences:

1. The threshold difference, i.e., = 0.63 and * = 0.62 is 0.01 which is very small.
2. The difference between x and μ_x^* generates two intervals [-3, -2.87] and [2.37, 2.5]. The beauty is that although we have two difference intervals, the classification will not be affected no matter we use x or μ_x^* in the two difference intervals because the contribution functions have already modeled the potential. To make it easier to be understood, lets look at:

$$\begin{aligned} \mu_x &: [-3, -2.87] = [0, 0] \\ \mu_x^* &: [-3, -2.87] = [0, 0.005] \\ \mu_x &: [2.37, 2.5] = [1, 1] \\ \mu_x^* &: [2.37, 2.5] = [0.98, 1] \end{aligned} \quad (12.6)$$

We can clearly see that both $\mu_x : [2.37, 2.5]$ and $\mu_x^* : [2.37, 2.5]$ support +, and both $\mu_x : [-3, -2.87]$ and $\mu_x^* : [-3, -2.87]$ still support negative. This shows that the rule (5) induced from the data set in Table 12.2 with introduced error can still achieves 100% accuracy rate tested on the original data set as shown in Table 12.1.

This demonstrates that the inexact field is error tolerant and more reliable especially when the algorithm is applied to mining from low quality data.

12.6 Conclusion and future work

To assure that the discovered knowledge is reliable is particularly important in applying data mining in solving real world application problems.

This chapter uses case studies to examine reliability to be affected by three major factors in induction of classification rules. The first case study shows that the reliability of the derived classifier being affected by the introduced errors. An unreliable interval is generated and the classification accuracy is decreased. The second case study shows that without sufficient large data set, it is unlike to be able to discover a reliable rule. The third case study shows that the reliability of the discovered knowledge is also related to the discovery algorithms. The rule discovered by one algorithm could be more reliable than another algorithm.

References

1. A Ailberschatz and A. Tuzhilin, What makes patters interesting in knowledge discovery systems, IEEE Transaction on Knowledge and data engineering, 8(6):970-974. 1996.
2. P. Berka, Recognizing reliability of Discovered knowledge, Lecture Notes in Computer Science, 1263:307-314. 1997.
    [3] Honghua Dai, A Study on Reliability in Graph Mining, In: Proceedings of IEEE ICDM Workshops 2006. pp775-779, 18 December 2006, Hong Kong, China.
    [4] Honghua Dai, Kevin B. Korb, Chris S. Wallace, Xindong Wu: A Study of Causal Discovery With Weak Links and Small Samples. In: Proceedings of the 15th International Joint Conferences on Artificial Intelligence (IJCAI 1997): 1304-1309. NAGOYA, Japan, August 23-29, 1997.
3. Honghua Dai, Learning of Inexact Forecasting Rules from very large noisy meteorological databases, PhD thesis, 1994, RMIT University.
4. Honghua Dai, Xiaoshu Hang, Gang Li: Inexact Field Learning: An Approach to Induce High Quality Rules from Low Quality Data. ICDM 2001: 586-588
5. E. Smirnov, S. Vanderlooy, and I. Sprinkhuizen-Kuyper, Meta-typicalness approach to reliable classification. In Proceedings of the 17th European Conference on Artificial Intelligence (ECAI 2006), pp810-811,2006.
6. S. Vanderlooy, I. Sprinkhuizen-Kuyper, and E. Smirnov, Reliable classification in ROC space. In Proceedings of the 15th Benelearn Machine Learning Conference, pp 27-36, 2006.
7. Yi Feng, Zhaohui Wu and Zhongmei Zhou, Enhancing Reliability throughout Knowledge Discovery Process, In Proceeding of the IEEE International Workshop on Reliability Issues of Knowledge Discovery (RIKD2006), pp 754-758, 2006.
8. Glenn Shafer, Vladimir Vovk, A Tutorial on Conformal Prediction, Journal of Machine Learning Research 9 (2008) 371-421.
9. Ian H. Witten and Eibe Frank, Data Mining: Practical machine learning tools and techniques, Morgan Kaufmann Publishers, 2005.

Chapter 13
A Comparative Analysis of Instance-based Penalization Techniques for Classification

Georgi Nalbantov, Patrick Groenen, and Evgueni Smirnov

Abstract Several instance-based large-margin classifiers have recently been put forward in the literature: Support Hyperplanes, Nearest Convex Hull classifier and Soft Nearest Neighbor. We examine those techniques from a common fit-versus-complexity framework and study the links between them. Finally, we compare the performance of these techniques vis-a-vis each other and other standard classification methods.

13.1 Introduction

Recently, three classification methods have been introduced in the literature: Support Hyperplanes (SH) [8], Nearest Convex Hull classifier [10] (NCH) and Soft Nearest Neighbor (SNN) [9]. All of them can be classified as instance-based large-margin penalization classifiers. In the following we argue why these three techniques should perform well based on their favorable generalization qualities. We specifically look at links between Support Vector Machines (SVM) [14], SH, NCH and SNN and approach them intuitively from a common generalization error-versus-complexity point of view. We argue that a pecking order of these techniques for the classification of a particular test observation may be followed, implying that in some cases one technique may be preferable over another. The instance-based nature of

Georgi Nalbantov
Faculty of Health, Medicine and Life Sciences, Maastricht University, P.O.BOX 616, 6200 MD Maastricht, The Netherlands. e-mail: g.nalbantov@maastrichtuniversity.nl

Patrick Groenen
Econometric Institute, Erasmus University Rotterdam, P.O. Box 1738, 3000 DR Rotterdam, The Netherlands. e-mail: groenen@few.eur.nl

Evgueni Smirnov
Department of Knowledge Engineering, Maastricht University, P.O.BOX 616, 6200 MD Maastricht, The Netherlands. e-mail: smirnov@maastrichtuniversity.nl

the SH, NCH, and SNN arises from the fact that these classifiers do not output an explicit formulation of a decision boundary between the classes.

The chapter is organized as follows. First, we revise quickly the role of penalization/capacity control for learners in general and argue that the error-versus-complexity paradigm could be applied to instance-based techniques. Second, we make an intuitive comparison between SVM, SH, NCH and SNN (in the so-called separable case). Finally, we present some empirical results and conclude.

13.2 Penalization in learning

The need for penalization in learning techniques has long been discussed in both the statistical and artificial intelligence/machines learning/data mining communities [5]. Examples of techniques that explicitly employ some kind of penalization are Ridge Regression, Lasso, Support Vector Machines, Support Vector Regression, etc. [5]. Penalization is referred to the practice of purposefully decreasing the ability of a given learner to cope with certain tasks. This ability is referred to as the learner's capacity. Arguably, a decreased learner's capacity is responsible for a better prediction performance by mitigating the problem of overfitting. Data overfitting occurs when a learner fits the training data too well, producing very low amount of errors. The amount of errors is referred to as the empirical risk, the empirical error, or the loss. The main idea behind penalization techniques is that the sum empirical error plus capacity control term should be minimized to achieve good prediction results on new data, or in other words, to achieve good generalization ability. In general, if the empirical error over the training data set is rather small, implying a possible overfitting of the training data, then the capacity of the learner is expected to be high. Thus, the generalization sum empirical error plus capacity would be relatively high. Hence the need to put up with some increased empirical error over the training data set, which is to be more than offset by a decrease in the learner's capacity. The latter decrease could come about by explicitly penalizing in some way the class of function to which a learner belongs.

Instance-based, or lazy classification techniques do not have an explicit rule or a decision boundary derived from the training data with which to classify all new observations, or instances [12]. Rather, a new rule for classifying a test instance is derived each time such an instance is given to the learner. A good example of a lazy technique is kNN.

At first sight, a direct application of the idea for penalization of on instance-based learners seems hard to materialize. This follows from the fact that penalization in general is applied to a given class of functions/learners. Out of this class, one optimal function should in the end be chosen to classify *any* test observation. This optimal learner produces minimal generalization sum. The idea for penalization can however also be applied to instance-based classifiers. In this case the function (taken from a given function class) that is used for the classification of a *particular* test instance should be penalized.

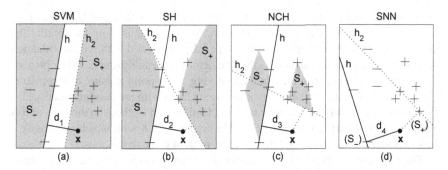

Fig. 13.1: Binary classification with SVM, SH, NCH and SNN in Panels (a), (b), (c) and (d), respectively. In all cases the classification of test point **x** is determined using hyperplane h, which is in general different for each method. Equivalently, **x** is labeled $+1$ (-1) if it is farther away from set S_- (S_+).

Below we give an intuitive account of three rather new instance-based classification techniques: Support Hyperplanes (SH) [8], Nearest Convex Hull classifier [10] (NCH) and Soft Nearest Neighbor (SNN) [9]. We approach them from a common generalization framework and discuss the links between them and Support Vector Machines (SVM) [14].

13.3 Three instance-based classification methods

Given a separable-by-a-hyperplane data set that consists of positive and negative observations, let us assume that we would like to classify a new observation **x** using a hyperplane, denoted as h. There are two types of hyperplanes – those which classify correctly all training data points (called for short consistent hyperplanes) and those which do not classify correctly all training data points (called for short inconsistent hyperplanes). For the sake of clarity, let us consider as consistent also any hyperplane that does not misclassify any training points.

There are two main factors to be considered in choosing the appropriate hyperplane h. First, h should not be too close to the observation **x**. Intuitively speaking, the farther h is from **x**, the bigger the self-confidence of h in the classification label it assigns to **x**. Second, h should not make too many mistakes when it classifies the training data. If one chooses h to be extremely far from **x**, then at one point h will misclassify either all positive or all negative observations. On the other hand, if h classifies correctly all training points, then h might be too close to **x**, in which case it assigns a label to **x** with rather little self-confidence. Thus, in general one cannot have both a big distance between h and **x**, and a big degree of consistency of h with respect to the training data. A balance between these two desirable properties has unavoidably to be sought. The strife to choose a hyperplane h that is highly consistent with the training data is referred to the strife to minimize the empirical risk, or empirical/training error. The idea to demand h to be as far away from $\mathbf{x}$ as possible can be thought of as a sort of regularization or penalization: the smaller the distance between h and $\mathbf{x}$, the greater the penalty associated with the classification of $\mathbf{x}$. The intuitive assertion here is that the degree of penalization could be proxied by a certain distance. In sum, when classifying a test point $\mathbf{x}$ using a hyperplane, given a separable binary training data set, one is faced with the familiar penalty plus error paradigm [5, 14]. Below we cast four classification methods in the light of this paradigm: SVM, SH, NCH and SNN. The hyperplane h with which to classify a new observation $\mathbf{x}$ is in general different for each of these techniques.

The h hyperplane in SVM classification (see Figure 1a) is defined as the farthest-away from $\mathbf{x}$ consistent hyperplane that is parallel to another consistent hyperplane, h_2, in such a way that the distance between these two hyperplanes (referred to as the "margin") is maximal. Since h is consistent with the training data, the empirical error it makes on the data is zero. The magnitude of the penalty associated with the classification of magnitude of the penalty can be considered to be positively related to the inverse of the distance between $\mathbf{x}$ and h ($1/d_1$ in terms of Figure 1a). The (theoretical) instance-based SVM classification algorithm can be stated as follows: first add $\mathbf{x}$ to the data set with -1 label and compute the distance d_1 to h (as defined above). Second, add $\mathbf{x}$ to the data set with $+1$ label and compute the distance d_1^* to h_2. Third, classify $\mathbf{x}$ using h (that is, as -1) if $d_1 > d_1^*$; classify $\mathbf{x}$ using h_2 (as $+1$) if $d_1 < d_1^*$; otherwise, if $d_1 = d_1^*$, the classification of $\mathbf{x}$ is undetermined.

The h hyperplane in Support-Hyperplanes classification (SH) [8](see Figure 1b) is defined as the farthest-away from $\mathbf{x}$ consistent hyperplane. Since h is consistent with the training data, the empirical error it makes on the data is zero. The magnitude of the penalty associated with the classification of $\mathbf{x}$ can be considered to be positively related to the inverse of the distance to h ($1/d_2$ in terms of Figure 1b). It can be shown that $d_2 \geq d_1$ always. Therefore, the sum empirical error plus penalty for SH is always smaller than the corresponding sum for SVM. Arguably, this suggests that SH possess better generalization ability than SVM. The SH classification algorithm can be stated as follows. First, add $\mathbf{x}$ to the training data set with -1 label and compute the distance d_2 to h. Note that h is consistent with both the original training data and with $\mathbf{x}$. That is, h assigns label -1 to $\mathbf{x}$. Second, add $\mathbf{x}$ to the original data set with $+1$ label and compute the distance d_2^* to h_2. In this case h_2 is defined as the farthest-away hyperplane from $\mathbf{x}$ that is consistent with both $\mathbf{x}$ and the original training data. Third, classify $\mathbf{x}$ using h (that is, as -1) if $d_2 > d_2^*$; classify $\mathbf{x}$ using h_2 (as $+1$) if $d_2 < d_2^*$; otherwise, if $d_2 = d_2^*$, the classification of $\mathbf{x}$ is undetermined.

The h hyperplane in Nearest Convex Hull classification (NCH) [10] (see Figure 1c) is defined as the farther of two hyperplanes. The first one is the farthest away from $\mathbf{x}$ hyperplane that is consistent with all positive observations and $\mathbf{x}$, where $\mathbf{x}$ has label -1. The second hyperplane is the farthest away from $\mathbf{x}$ hyperplane that is consistent with all the negative observations and $\mathbf{x}$, where $\mathbf{x}$ has label $+1$. Effectively, $\mathbf{x}$ is classified as $+1$ (-1) if it is closer to the convex hull of $+1$ (-1) points. The magnitude of the penalty associated with the classification of $\mathbf{x}$ is considered to be positively related to the inverse of the distance from $\mathbf{x}$ to h ($1/d_3$ in terms of Figure 1c). It can be shown that $d_3 \geq d_2 \geq d_1$ always. The empirical error on the training set is not however guaranteed to be equal to zero. This happens because h should be consistent with at least all positive or all negative observations, and not with both all negative and all positive observations. As can be seen from Figure 1c, the h hyperplane actually misclassifies two of the negative training data points. Thus, the generalization sum training error plus penalty is not guaranteed to be smaller for NCH than for SH or SVM. The NCH classification algorithm can be stated as follows. First, add $\mathbf{x}$ to the training data set with -1 label and compute the distance d_3 to h, the hyperplane that is consistent with all $+1$ points and $\mathbf{x}$. This distance is the distance between $\mathbf{x}$ and the convex hull of the positive points. Second, add $\mathbf{x}$ to the training data set with $+1$ label and compute the distance d_3^* to h_2, the hyperplane that is consistent with all -1 points and $\mathbf{x}$. Third, classify $\mathbf{x}$ using h (that is, as -1) if $d_3 > d_3^*$; classify $\mathbf{x}$ using h_2 (as $+1$) if $d_3 < d_3^*$; otherwise, if $d_3 = d_3^*$, the classification of $\mathbf{x}$ is undetermined.

The Soft Nearest Neighbor classification (SNN) [9] can also be presented along similar lines as SVM, SH and NCH. In the separable case SNN is equivalent to the classical 1NN classifier [12]. The h hyperplane in 1NN classification (see Figure 1d) is the farther of two hyperplanes. The first one is farthest away from $\mathbf{x}$ hyperplane that is consistent with the closest positive observation and $\mathbf{x}$, where $\mathbf{x}$ has label -1. The second hyperplane is the farthest away from $\mathbf{x}$ hyperplane that is consistent with the closest negative observation and $\mathbf{x}$, where $\mathbf{x}$ has label $+1$. Effectively, $\mathbf{x}$ is classified as $+1$ (-1) if its closest training point has label $+1$ (-1). The magnitude of the penalty associated with the classification of $\mathbf{x}$ is considered to be positively related to the inverse of the distance from $\mathbf{x}$ to h $(1/d_4$ in terms of Figure 1d). It can be shown that $d_4 \geq d_3 \geq d_2 \geq d_1$ always, suggesting (somewhat counterintuitively) that 1NN provides for the greatest penalization among the four techniques under consideration. However, the empirical error on the training data set is absolutely not guaranteed to be equal to zero. In fact, h is not even guaranteed to be consistent with either all positive or all negative points, as the case is in NCH classification (and SH and SVM classification as well, for that matter). Thus, the h hyperplane in 1NN is likely to commit the greatest amount of errors on the training data set as compared to SVM, SH and NCH. Consequently, the generalizability sum empirical error plus penalty may turn out to be the highest. Note however that it could also turn out to be the lowest for some $\mathbf{x}$, in which case 1NN exhibits the highest generalization ability. The 1NN classification algorithm can be (theoretically) stated as follows. First, add $\mathbf{x}$ to the training data set with label -1 and compute the distance d_4 to h, the hyperplane that is consistent with $\mathbf{x}$ and the closest positive point. Second, add $\mathbf{x}$ to the training data set with $+1$ label and compute the distance d_4^* to h_2, the hyperplane that is consistent with $\mathbf{x}$ and the closest negative point. Third, classify $\mathbf{x}$ using h (that is, as -1) if $d_4 > d_4^*$; classify $\mathbf{x}$ using h_2 (as $+1$) if $d_4 < d_4^*$; otherwise, if $d_4 = d_4^*$, the classification of $\mathbf{x}$ is undetermined.

13.4 Alternative specifications

There is an alternative, but equivalent, formulation of the SVM, SH, NCH and SNN techniques in terms of distances to sets as opposed to distances to hyperplanes. The corresponding sets for each technique are depicted in Figure 1 as shaded areas. A common classification rule for all methods can be defined as follows: a new point **x** should be classified as -1 if it is farther from set S_+ than from set S_-; **x** should be classified as $+1$ if it is farther from set S_- than from set S_+; otherwise, if the distance to both S_+ and S_- is the same, the class of **x** is undetermined. Sets S_+ and S_- are defined differently for each method.

For SVM, set S_+ is defined as the set of all points that are classified as $+1$ by all hyperplanes that lie inside the SVM margin. Set S_- is similarly defined as the set of all points that are classified as -1 by all hyperplanes that lie inside the SVM margin.

For SH, set S_+ is the set of all points classified as $+1$ by all hyperplanes that are consistent with the training data. The latter include all hyperplanes that lie inside the SVM margin plus all the rest of the consistent hyperplanes. Analogically, set S_- is defined as the set of all points that are classified as -1 by all consistent hyperplanes. The collection of all consistent hyperplanes is referred to in the literature as the version space of hyperplanes with respect to a given training data set. A conservative version-space classification rule is to classify a test point **x** only if all consistent hyperplanes assign one and the same classification label to it, or in other words if **x** belongs to either S_+ or S_- [13].

For the NCH classifier, set S_+ is the set of all points that are classified as $+1$ by all hyperplanes that are consistent with the positively-labeled data points. In other words, S_+ is the convex hull of the positive observations. Set S_- is defined as the set of all points that are classified as -1 by all hyperplanes that are consistent with the negatively-labeled data points. Thus, S_- is the convex hull of the negative points.

Lastly, for the 1NN classifier, which is the hard-margin version of the SNN classifier, the S_+ set consists of just one point: the closest to **x** positively-labeled point. Set S_- also consists of just one point: the closest to **x** negatively-labeled point.

13.5 Estimation

Here we review the estimation of SVM, SH, NCH and SNN for the sake of completeness. Further details can be found, e.g., in [2], [8], [9], [10] and [14]. We examine a common setup for the four techniques: a binary classification data set $\{\mathbf{x}_i, y_i\}_{i=1}^{l}$, where each $\mathbf{x}_i$ is an n-dimensional vector of values for the predictor variables and each y_i is either a $+1$ or a -1 observation label. The classification task is: given a test point **x**, output its predicted label. Each of the techniques solves an optimization problem to find an optimal hyperplane h, $\mathbf{w}^{*\prime}\mathbf{x} + b^* = 0$, with which to classify the test observation in the way presented in Section 13.3. Here **w** is a vector of hyperplane coefficients, b is the intercept, and the start sign * indicates optimal values.

13.5.1 Support Vector Machines

SVM solve the classification task by maximizing the so-called margin between the classes. In the separable case, the margin is equal to the distance between the convex hulls of the two classes at the optimal SVM solution. Formally, the margin is equal to the distance between hyperplanes $\mathbf{w}'\mathbf{x}+b = -1$ and $\mathbf{w}'\mathbf{x}+b = 1$, presented already as h and h_2 in Figure 1a. Thus, the margin equals $2/\|\mathbf{w}\|$. Maximizing the margin is equivalent to minimizing the term $0.5\|\mathbf{w}\|^2 = 0.5\mathbf{w}'\mathbf{w}$. Formally, to find the SVM hyperplane h, one solves the following optimization problem:

$$\min_{\mathbf{w},b} \quad \frac{1}{2}\mathbf{w}'\mathbf{w} \tag{13.1}$$
$$\text{s.t.} \quad y_i(\mathbf{w}'\mathbf{x}_i+b) \geq 1, \ i = 1,2,\ldots,l$$

If there is no hyperplane that is able to separate classes, so-called slack variables ξ_i are introduced. This case is referred to as the nonseparable case or the class-overlapping case. Then, problem (13.1) becomes:

$$\min_{\mathbf{w},b,\xi} \quad \frac{1}{2}\mathbf{w}'\mathbf{w}+C\sum_{i=1}^{l}\xi_i \tag{13.2}$$
$$\text{s.t.} \quad y_i(\mathbf{w}'\mathbf{x}_i+b) \geq 1-\xi_i, \ \xi_i \geq 0, \ i = 1,2,\ldots,l,$$

where $C > 0$ is a manually adjustable constant that regulates the trade-off between the penalty term $0.5\mathbf{w}'\mathbf{w}$ and the loss $\sum_{i=1}^{l}\xi_i$.

Optimization problem (13.2) can be dualized as:

$$\max_{\alpha} \quad \sum_{i=1}^{l}\alpha_i - \frac{1}{2}\sum_{i,j=1}^{l}\alpha_i\alpha_j y_i y_j(\mathbf{x}_i'\mathbf{x}_j) \tag{13.3}$$
$$\text{s.t.} \quad 0 \leq \alpha_i \leq C, \ i = 1,2,\ldots,l, \text{ and } \sum_{i=1}^{l}y_i\alpha_i = 0,$$

where the α's are the Lagrange multipliers associated with (13.2). The advantage of the dual is that different nonlinear mappings $\mathbf{x} \to \phi(\mathbf{x})$ of the data can easily handled. Thus, if one first transforms the data into a higher-dimensional space, where the coordinates of the data points are given by $\phi(\mathbf{x})$ instead of $\mathbf{x}$, then the dot product $\mathbf{x}_i'\mathbf{x}_j$ will appear as $\phi(\mathbf{x}_i)'\phi(\mathbf{x}_j)$ in dual optimization problem. It turns out than there exist so-called kernel functions $\kappa(\mathbf{x}_i,\mathbf{x}_j) \equiv \phi(\mathbf{x}_i)'\phi(\mathbf{x}_j)$ that can compute this dot product efficiently, without explicitly carrying the transformation mapping. Popular kernels are the linear, $\kappa(\mathbf{x}_i,\mathbf{x}_j) = \mathbf{x}_i'\mathbf{x}_j$, polynomial of degree d, $\kappa(\mathbf{x}_i,\mathbf{x}_j) = (\mathbf{x}_i'\mathbf{x}_j +$

$1)^d$ and the Radial Basis Function (RBF) kernel $\kappa(\mathbf{x}_i, \mathbf{x}_j) = \exp(-\gamma \| \mathbf{x}_i - \mathbf{x}_j \|^2)$. The mapping $\mathbf{x} \to \phi(\mathbf{x})$ when the RBF kernel is used corresponds to a mapping into an infinite-dimensional space. The manually-adjustable γ parameter of the RBF kernel determines the proximity of any two points in this infinite-dimensional space.

13.5.2 Support Hyperplanes

In the separable case, the h hyperplane in SH classification, with which to classify test point $\mathbf{x}$, can be found as the solution of the following optimization problem:

$$\min_{\mathbf{w}, b, y_{l+1}} \quad \frac{1}{2} \mathbf{w}' \mathbf{w} \tag{13.4}$$
$$\text{s.t.} \quad y_i(\mathbf{w}' \mathbf{x}_i + b) \geq 0, \ i = 1, 2, \ldots, l$$
$$y_{l+1}(\mathbf{w}' \mathbf{x} + b) = 1, y_{l+1} \in \{-1, 1\}.$$

This problem is partially combinatorial due to the constraint that the predicted label of $\mathbf{x}$, y_{l+1}, can take on only two values. Therefore, one usually solves two separate optimization subproblems. One time $y_{l+1} = -1$, and another time $y_{l+1} = -1$. The value of y_{l+1} that minimizes problem (13.4) is the predicted label of $\mathbf{x}$. Note that the distance between $\mathbf{x}$ and h is defined as $1/\sqrt{\mathbf{w}^{*\prime} \mathbf{w}^*}$ by the equality constraint $y_{l+1}(\mathbf{w}' \mathbf{x} + b) = 1$.

In the nonseparable case, SH introduce slack variables ξ_i, similarly to SVM. As a result, the nonseparable version of (13.4) becomes:

$$\min_{\mathbf{w}, b, y_{l+1}, \xi} \quad \frac{1}{2} \mathbf{w}' \mathbf{w} + C \sum_{i=1}^{l} \xi_i \tag{13.5}$$
$$\text{s.t.} \quad y_i(\mathbf{w}' \mathbf{x}_i + b) \geq 0 - \xi_i, \ \xi_i \geq 0, \ i = 1, 2, \ldots, l$$
$$y_{l+1}(\mathbf{w}' \mathbf{x}_{l+1} + b) = 1, y_{l+1} \in \{-1, 1\}.$$

As in (13.4), two separate optimization problems have to be solved to determine the optimal y_{l+1}. Each of these two subproblems can be dualized as:

$$\max_{\alpha} \quad \alpha_{l+1} - \frac{1}{2} \sum_{i,j=1}^{l+1} \alpha_i \alpha_j y_i y_j (\mathbf{x}_i' \mathbf{x}_j) \tag{13.6}$$
$$\text{s.t.} \quad 0 \leq \alpha_i \leq C, \ i = 1, 2, \ldots, l, \ \text{and} \ \sum_{i=1}^{l+1} y_i \alpha_i = 0.$$

Similarly to SVM, different kernels can be substituted for the dot product $\mathbf{x}_i' \mathbf{x}_j$.

13.5.3 Nearest Convex Hull classifier

The optimization problem for the NCH classifier is almost identical to the SH one. The only difference is that in each of the two optimization subproblems observations from only one class are considered. This property enables NCH to handle the multi-class classification case with ease, unlike SVM and SH. In the two-class problem at hand, let us denote with S_+ the set of observations that belong to the positive class and with S_- the set of observations that belong to the negative class. Next, two optimization problems are solved, one per each class k:

$$\min_{\mathbf{w}_k, b_k} \frac{1}{2} \mathbf{w}_k' \mathbf{w}_k \qquad (13.7)$$
$$\text{s.t.} \quad \mathbf{w}_k' \mathbf{x}_i + b_k \geq 0,\ i \in S_k$$
$$-(\mathbf{w}_k' \mathbf{x} + b_k) = 1.$$

The distance to each class is defined as $1/\sqrt{\mathbf{w}_k^{*'} \mathbf{w}_k^{*}}$ by the equality constraint in (13.7). The class associated with smallest such distance is assigned to the test point $\mathbf{x}$. Notice that this distance is inversely related to the objective function $0.5\mathbf{w}_k' \mathbf{w}_k$. Therefore, the class k that achieves the maximal value for this objective function should be assigned to $\mathbf{x}$.

In the nonseparable case each of the optimization subproblems is expressed as:

$$\min_{\mathbf{w}_k, b_k, \xi} \frac{1}{2} \mathbf{w}_k' \mathbf{w}_k + C \sum_{i \in S_k} \xi_i \qquad (13.8)$$
$$\text{s.t.} \quad \mathbf{w}_k' \mathbf{x}_i + b_k \geq 0 - \xi_i,\ \xi_i \geq 0,\ i \in S_k$$
$$-(\mathbf{w}_k' \mathbf{x} + b_k) = 1,$$

where the ξ's are slack variables. In dual form, (13.8) becomes:

$$\max_{\alpha} \quad \alpha_{l_k+1} - \frac{1}{2} \sum_{i,j=1}^{l_k+1} \alpha_i \alpha_j y_i y_j (\mathbf{x}_i' \mathbf{x}_j) \qquad (13.9)$$
$$\text{s.t.} \quad 0 \leq \alpha_i \leq C,\ i = 1, 2, \ldots, l_k,\ \text{and}\ \sum_{i=1}^{l_k+1} y_i \alpha_i = 0,$$

allowing for the employment of kernel functions, as in SVM and SH. Here $i = 1, 2, \ldots, l_k$ denotes the elements of class k.

13.5.4 Soft Nearest Neighbor

In the separable case, SNN is equivalent to the 1NN classifier. Instead of computing the distances between $\mathbf{x}$ and all data points to determine the nearest neighbor of $\mathbf{x}$ however, SNN take a different approach. Observe that the distance to the nearest neighboring point is equal the maximal radius of a (hyper)sphere with center $\mathbf{x}$ that does not contain any training data points. To find this radius $\mathbf{R}$, one solves the following optimization problem:

$$\max \quad \mathbf{R}^2 \tag{13.10}$$
$$\text{s.t.} \quad \mathbf{R}^2 \leq \| \mathbf{x}_i - \mathbf{x} \|^2, \ i = 1, 2, \ldots, l$$

In SNN classification, one first finds the distances between $\mathbf{x}$ and the closest point from each of the two (or, in general k) classes. Point $\mathbf{x}$ is then assigned to the class, which such point is closer/closest to $\mathbf{x}$. Denoting with S_+ and S_- the sets of positive and negative observations, respectively, SNN thus solve one optimization problem per each class k, of the form:

$$\max \quad \mathbf{R}^2 \tag{13.11}$$
$$\text{s.t.} \quad \mathbf{R}^2 \leq \| \mathbf{x}_i - \mathbf{x} \|^2, \ i \in S_k.$$

The class that produces the minimal value for the objective function $\mathbf{R}^2$ of (13.11) is then assigned to point $\mathbf{x}$. Similarly to the SVM, SH and NCH approaches, one can introduce slack variables ξ_i. In this case (13.11) becomes:

$$\max \quad \mathbf{R}^2 - C \sum_{i \in S_k} \xi_i \tag{13.12}$$
$$\text{s.t.} \quad \mathbf{R}^2 \leq \| \mathbf{x}_i - \mathbf{x} \|^2 + \xi_i, \ \xi_i \geq 0, \ i \in S_k.$$

The $C > 0$ parameter controls the trade-off between the length of the radius and amount of training errors. A training error occurs if a point lies inside the hypersphere. Each of the k quadratic optimization problems (13.12) can be expressed in dual form as:

$$\min_{\alpha} \quad \sum_{i \in S_k} \alpha_i (\mathbf{x}_i' \mathbf{x}_i - 2(\mathbf{x}_i' \mathbf{x}) + \mathbf{x}' \mathbf{x}) \tag{13.13}$$
$$\text{s.t.} \quad 0 \leq \alpha_i \leq C, \ i \in S_k, \text{ and } \sum_{i \in S_k} \alpha_i = 1.$$

This formulation allows for the employment of different kernels, which can replace the dot products $\mathbf{x}_i' \mathbf{x}_i$, $\mathbf{x}_i' \mathbf{x}$ and $\mathbf{x}' \mathbf{x}$. Notice that unlike (13.12), (13.13) is a linear programming problem.

Table 13.1: Leave-one-out accuracy rates (in %) of the Support Hyperplanes, Nearest Convex Hull and Soft Nearest Neighbor classifiers as well as some standard methods on several data sets. Rbf, 2p and lin stand for Radial Basis Function, second-degree polynomial and linear kernel, respectively.

	SH rbf	SH 2p	SH lin	NCH rbf	NCH 2p	NCH lin	SNN rbf	SNN 2p	SNN lin	SVM rbf	SVM 2p	SVM lin	kNN
Sonar	**91.35**	87.98	79.80	**91.35**	90.38	87.98	88.46	76.92	87.50	88.94	82.21	80.77	86.54
Voting	**96.77**	96.31	**96.77**	95.85	85.48	95.85	94.47	94.01	93.78	96.54	96.31	**96.77**	93.32
W.B.C.	**97.42**	96.85	97.00	**97.42**	97.14	97.28	**97.42**	97.28	97.28	97.00	96.85	96.85	97.00
Heart	**85.56**	81.90	**85.56**	**85.56**	82.59	84.07	85.19	80.74	**85.56**	**85.56**	81.11	85.56	84.44
A.C.A.	**87.39**	86.70	86.80	86.38	85.36	86.09	85.80	85.51	85.65	**87.39**	79.86	87.10	85.94
Hep.	**87.70**	86.45	86.45	85.16	84.52	84.52	87.10	85.16	85.16	**86.45**	86.45	86.45	85.81

13.6 Comparison results

The basic optimization algorithms for SH, NCH and SNN classification, (13.6), (13.9) and (13.13) respectively, are implemented via a modification of the freely available LIBSVM software [3]. We tested the performance of SH, NCH and SNN on several small- to middle-sized data sets that are freely available from the SlatLog and UCI repositories [4] and have been analyzed by many researchers and practitioners (e.g. [1], [6], [7], [11] and others): *Sonar, Voting, Wisconsin Breast Cancer* (W.B.C.), *Heart, Australian Credit Approval* (A.C.A.), and *Hepatitis* (Hep.). Detailed information on these data sets can be found on the web sites of the respective repositories. We stop short of carrying out an extensive experimental study, since this falls out of the main scope of the paper. Furthermore, large data sets are harder to handle due to the instance-based nature of the SH, NCH and SNN classifiers.

We compare the results of SH, NCH and SNN to Support Vector Machines (SVM) and k-Nearest Neighbor (kNN). We measure model performance by the leave-one-out (LOO) accuracy rate. For our purposes – comparison between the methods – LOO seems to be more suitable than the more general k-fold cross-validation (CV), because it always yields one and the same error rate estimate for a given model, unlike the CV method (which involves a random split of the data into several parts).

Table 1 presents performance results for all methods considered. We note that the method's parameters were tuned using grid search. Thus, we report only the highest LOO accuracy rate obtained.

Overall, the instance-based penalization classifiers SH, NCH and SNN perform quite well on all data sets. Most notably, SH achieve best accuracy rates on all the six data sets. NCH replicate this success three times. SVM also perform best on four data sets. The SNN classifier achieves best accuracy rate on just two data sets, but five times out of six performs better than its direct competitor, kNN.

13.7 Conclusion

We have studied from a common generalization perspective three classification methods recently introduced in the literature: Support Hyperplanes, Nearest Convex Hull classifier and Soft Nearest Neighbor. In addition, we have compared them to the popular Support Vector Machines. A common theme in SH, NCH and SNN is their instance-based nature. In addition, these methods strive to find a balance between learner's capacity and learner's fit over the training data. Last but not least, the techniques can be kernelized, which places them also in the realm of kernel methods. We have provided a rather intuitive treatment of these techniques and the generalization framework from which they are approached. Further research could concentrate on more detailed such treatment and on the derivation of theoretical test-error bounds. Extensive experiments with different loss functions, such as the quadratic one, have also to be carried out. Last but not least, ways to improve the computational speed can also be explored.

References

1. L. Breiman. Bagging predictors. *Machine Learning*, 24:123–140, 1996.
2. C. Burges. A tutorial on support vector machines for pattern recognition. *Data Mining and Knowledge Discovery*, 2:121–167, 1998.
3. C. Chang and C. Lin. LIBSVM: a library for support vector machines, 2006. Software available at http://www.csie.ntu.edu.tw/~cjlin/libsvm.
4. A. Frank and A. Asuncion. UCI machine learning repository, 2010.
5. T. Hastie, R. Tibshirani, and J. Friedman. *The Elements of Statistical Learning: Data Mining, Inference, and Prediction*. Springer-Verlag New York, Inc., 2009. 2nd edition.
6. R. King, C. Feng, and A. Sutherland. Statlog: comparison of classification algorithms on large real-world problems. *Applied Artificial Intelligence*, 9(3):289–334, 1995.
7. T. Lim, W. Loh, and Y. Shih. A comparison of prediction accuracy, complexity, and training time for thirtythree old and new classification algorithms. *Machine Learning*, 40:203–228, 1995.
8. G. Nalbantov, J. Bioch, and P. Groenen. Classification with support hyperplanes. In *Proceedings of 17th European Conference on Machine Learning, ECML 2006, Berlin, Germany*, pages 703–710. Springer Berlin / Heidelberg, 2006.
9. G. Nalbantov. *Essays on Some Recent Penalization Methods with Application in Finance and Marketing*. PhD thesis, Econometric Institute, Erasmus University Rottedam, 2008.
10. G. Nalbantov and E. Smirnov. Soft nearest convex hull classifier. In *Proceedings of 19th European Conference on Artificial Intelligence, ECAI 2010, Lisbon, Portugal, August 16-20, 2010*, pages 841–846. IOS Press, 2010.
11. C. Perlich, F. Provost, and J. Simonoff. Tree induction vs. logistic regression: A learning-curve analysis. *Journal of Machine Learning Research*, 4:211–255, 2003.
12. D. Stork R. Duda, and P. Hart. *Pattern Classification*. Willey, 2000. 2nd edition.
13. E. Smirnov, I. Sprinkhuizen-Kuyper, G. Nalbantov, and S. Vanderlooy. Version space support vector machines. In A. Perini G. Brewka, S. Coradeschi and P. Traverso, editors, *Proceedings of the 17th European Conference on Artificial Intelligence*, ECAI 2006, pages 809–810. IOS Press, Amsterdam, The Netherlands, 2006.
14. V. Vapnik. *The Nature of Statistical Learning Theory*. Springer-Verlag New York, Inc., 1995. 2nd edition, 2000.

Chapter 14
Subsequence Frequency Measurement and its Impact on Reliability of Knowledge Discovery in Single Sequences

Min Gan, and Honghua Dai

Abstract Subsequence frequency measurement is a basic and essential problem in knowledge discovery in single sequences. Frequency based knowledge discovery in single sequences tends to be unreliable since different resulting sets may be obtained from a same sequence when different frequency metrics are adopted. In this chapter, we investigate subsequence frequency measurement and its impact on the reliability of knowledge discovery in single sequences. We analyse seven previous frequency metrics, identify their inherent inaccuracies, and explore their impacts on two kinds of knowledge discovered from single sequences, frequent episodes and episode rules. We further give three suggestions for frequency metrics and introduce a new frequency metric in order to improve the reliability. Empirical evaluation reveals the inaccuracies and verifies our findings.

14.1 Introduction

Reliability is normally used to describe how reliable, stable, dependable or trustworthy a system is. In statistics, reliability refers to the consistency of a set of measurements or of a measuring instrument [23]. Reliability theory in statistics [3] has been well developed. In recently years, reliability issues in knowledge discovery (RIKD) have gained increasing attention in the community of information technology. RIKD investigates theory and techniques with the aim to ensure the reliability of discovered knowledge. Since RIKD was recognized [4], researchers have explored a number of reliability issues. For example, Feng et al. [10] examine the reliability from a process perspective. They pointed out eight factors contributing to the reliability in six phases of knowledge discovery, and provided ten suggestions to enhance the reliability. Dai [2] investigated the reliability of graph mining. In [3], Dai gained a

Min Gan and Honghua Dai
Deakin University, 221 Burwood Highway, Burwood, Melbourne, VIC 3125, Australia, e-mail: mg@deakin.edu.au, honghua.dai@deakin.edu.au

insight into classification reliability by examining special cases with considerations of data oriented and algorithm oriented impact factors. However, RIKD is far less well developed. In this chapter, we focus on the reliability of knowledge discovery in single sequences (KDISS).

Given a single sequence, such as a long DNA or a sequence of web logs, KDISS involves conventional mining tasks (classification, clustering and anomaly detection) and the discovery of different types of patterns like frequent episodes, episode rules, partial orders and significant episodes etc.. Many of these tasks are frequency-based KDISS (FBKDISS). This means occurrence frequencies of subsequences are used in the mining process. Therefore, frequency measurement is a key process. Subsequence frequency measurement in single transaction setting such as a single sequence is essentially different from the one in multi-transaction setting, i.e., a database of multiple transactions [12]. In a database, the frequency of any pattern is fixed as it is defined as the fraction of transactions that contain this pattern [1, 2]. In contrast, the frequency of a pattern in single transaction setting (e.g., a long sequence or a large graph) can be measured in different ways [17, 19]. Thus, for a same pattern, its frequency may be different when different frequency metrics are used.

A general framework of FBKDISS is shown in Fig. 1. The framework in Fig. 1 is an ideal and reliable knowledge discovery process. However, as shown in Fig. 2, the actual framework of FBKDISS is unreliable as different resulting sets (RSs) may be discovered from a same sequence under different frequency metrics. It is natural to raise a series of questions: which resulting sets are more reliable? which sets should be used? which frequency metric should be adopted? Can we find a standard and reliable frequency metric? Unfortunately, there have been seven typical metrics for measuring subsequences' frequencies in a single sequence [11] and different researchers/users may choose different metrics. Thus, different results may be obtained from the same input. In this chapter, we analyse seven previous frequency metrics, explore inherent inaccuracies and their impacts on the reliability, and attempt to give some suggestions and introduce a new frequency metric to improve the reliability. This chapter is based on our previous works in [11, 12]. Our main contributions are as follows.

1. We identify inaccuracies inherent in seven frequency metrics taking into account three properties: anti-monotonicity, maximum-frequency and window-width restriction.
2. We explore the impact of frequency metrics on two kinds of FBKDISS, frequent episode mining and episode rule discovery.
3. We provide some suggestions for choosing and defining frequency metrics and introduce a new frequency metric in order to improve the reliability.
4. The reliability of the previous metrics and the impact on discovered knowledge are evaluated empirically.

The rest of this chapter is organised as follows. Preliminaries are presented in Section 2. Section 3 reviews definitions and analyses properties of previous frequency metrics. In Section 4 we identify the inaccuracies inherent in previous metrics and explore their impacts on frequent episodes and episode rules. In Section 5, we provide suggestions for defining appropriate frequency metrics, and introduce a new frequency metric. Section 6 addresses experimental evaluation. The chapter is concluded in Section 7.

14.2 Preliminaries

Ordinarily terminologies in [15, 16, 18, 21, 22] are used in this chapter. Let I be an alphabet, where each letter denotes a distinct type of data element.

Definition 14.1. (Sequence) A sequence over I is defined as an ordered list of data elements, denoted as $S = \langle (e_1, t_1)(e_2, t_2)...(e_n, t_n) \rangle$, where each data element (e_i, t_i) is distinguished by both its type $e_i \in I$ and its occurrence time (timestamp) t_i, and t_i is before t_{i+1} for all $i = 1, 2, ..., n - 1$. The length of S, $|S|$, is n. For simplicity, let each t_i take a value from $\{1, 2, ...\}$, and $t_i = j$ means the i-th data element occurs at the j-th timestamp.

We assume that in this chapter any input sequences S is consecutive, i.e., $S = (e_1, 1)(e_2, 2)...(e_n, n)$, where (e_j, i) denotes the data element of type e_j that occurs at the j-th timestamp.

Definition 14.2. (Sliding Window) Given sequence $S = \langle (e_1, 1)(e_2, 2)...(e_n, n) \rangle$, a sliding window in S from starting time st to ending time et, denoted as $win(S, st, et)$, is defined as $(e_{st}, st)(e_{st+1}, st + 1)...(e_{et}, et)$, where $1 \leq st < et \leq n$. The width of the window is defined as $et - st$ [16].

Definition 14.3. (Episode, Sub-episode) A serial episode, i.e., subsequence α, over I is an ordered list of types of data elements, denoted as $\alpha = \langle a_1 a_2...a_m \rangle$, where $a_j \in I$ ($j = 1, 2, ..., m$). The length of α, $|\alpha|$, is m. Essentially episode α imposes a

Fig. 14.1: A reliable framework of FBKDISS

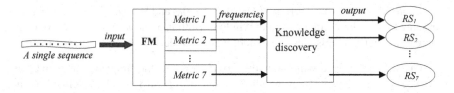

Fig. 14.2: The actual framework of FBKDISS

constraint on relative order of occurrences of a_j, i.e., a_j always occurs before a_{j+1} for all $j = 1, 2, ..., m-1$. An episode $\alpha = \langle a_1 a_2 ... a_m \rangle$ is a sub-episode of another episode $\beta = \langle b_1 b_2 ... b_n \rangle$, denoted as $\alpha \sqsubseteq \beta$, if there exist $1 \le i_1 < i_2 < ... < i_m \le n$, s.t. $a_j = b_{i_j}$ for all $j = 1, 2, ..., m$.

In this chapter, we use subsequences and serial episodes interchangeably. In the rest of the chapter, episodes are referred to as serial episodes, i.e., subsequences.

Definition 14.4. (Occurrence, Minimal Occurrence) Given $S = \langle (e_1, 1)(e_2, 2) ... (e_n, n) \rangle$ and episode $\alpha = \langle a_1 a_2 ... a_m \rangle$, if there exist $1 \le i_1 < i_2 < ... < i_m \le n$ s.t. $a_j = e_{i_j}$ for all $j = 1, 2, ..., m$, then we say α occurs in S, and $o = \langle (e_{i_1}, i_1)(e_{i_2}, i_2) ... (e_{i_m}, i_m) \rangle$ is an occurrence of α in S. For simplicity, we use $\langle i_1, i_2, ..., i_m \rangle$ to denote o and $o[j] = i_j$ ($j = 1, 2, ..., m$). Furthermore, if $st \le i_1 < i_m \le et$, then we say window $win(S, st, et)$ contains α. The width of occurrence $o = \langle i_1, i_2, ..., i_m \rangle$ is defined as $i_m - i_1$. An occurrence of α in S, $o = \langle i_1, i_2, ..., i_m \rangle$, is minimal if α has no other occurrence in S, $o' = \langle i'_1, i'_2, ..., i'_m \rangle$, s.t. $(i_1 < i'_1 \wedge i'_m \le i_m) \vee (i_1 \le i'_1 \wedge i'_m < i_m)$ (i.e., $[i'_1, i'_m] \subset [i_1, i_m]$). The set of all (minimal) occurrences of α in S is denoted as $O(S, \alpha)$ ($MO(S, \alpha)$).

For simplicity, in the rest of this chapter $S = \langle (e_1, 1)(e_2, 2) ... (e_n, n) \rangle$ is abbreviated as $S = \langle (e_1)_1 (e_2)_2 ... (e_n)_n \rangle$.

14.3 Previous Frequency Metrics and Their Properties

In subsection 3.1, definitions of seven previous frequency metrics are reviewed. Their properties are analysed in subsection 3.2.

14.3.1 Definitions of Seven Frequency Metrics

To date, seven typical frequency metrics have been proposed for episodes. The metrics are named *fixed-win-freq* [19], *mo-freq* [20, 21], *auto-win-growth-freq* [13], *maxgap-mo-freq* [22], *T-freq* [16], *non-overlapped-freq* [18] and *distinct-bound-st-freq* [15] respectively. In this following their definitions are listed in ascending order of the proposed year. Let $S = (e_1)_1 (e_2)_2 ... (e_n)_n$, $\alpha = \langle a_1 a_2 ... a_m \rangle$, $o = \langle i_1, i_2, ..., i_m \rangle$ and $o' = \langle i'_1, i'_2, ..., i'_m \rangle$. Example 1 is used to illustrate the definitions.

Example 14.1. Given $S = \langle (c)_1 (a)_2 (a)_3 (c)_4 (b)_5 (b)_6 \rangle$ and $S' = \langle (a)_2 (a)_3 (c)_4 (b)_5 (b)_6 \rangle$, assume the fixed/maximal bound of window width is 3 and $max\_gap = 2$. We compute frequencies of episodes $\langle ab \rangle$, $\langle acb \rangle$ and $\langle c \rangle$ under the seven frequency metrics.

Given S and a fixed window width $fixed\text{-}win = w$, the frequency of α over sequence S with fixed window width w, $fixed\text{-}win\text{-}freq(S, \alpha, w)$, is defined as the number of windows with width w that contain α [19]. In Example 1, $fixed\text{-}win\text{-}freq$ $(S, \langle c \rangle, 3) = 4$ because there are four windows with width 3 that contains $\langle c \rangle$, i.e.,

$win(S,1,4)$, $win(S,2,5)$, $win(S,3,6)$ and $win(S,4,6)$ (note that the window width is not required to be w when $|S| - st < w$), and $fixed\text{-}win\text{-}freq(S, \langle ac \rangle, 3) = 3$ because there are three windows with width 3 that contain $\langle ac \rangle$, i.e., $win(S,1,4)$, $win(S,2,5)$ and $win(S,3,6)$.

In [20, 21], $mo\text{-}freq(S, \alpha)$ is defined as the number of the minimal occurrences of α in S. In Example 1, $mo\text{-}freq(S, \langle ab \rangle) = 1$ since in the four occurrences, $\langle 2,5 \rangle$, $\langle 2,6 \rangle$, $\langle 3,5 \rangle$ and $\langle 3,6 \rangle$, only $\langle 3,5 \rangle$ is minimal.

In [13], given S and α, the restriction of window width for α is specified as $w = (m - 1) \times max\_gap$, where $m = |\alpha|$, max_gap is a user-specified maximum gap between any two consecutive elements in each episode. The frequency of α in S, $auto\text{-}win\text{-}growth\text{-}freq(S, \alpha, max\_gap)$, is defined as

$$\frac{|\{win|win \in W_m(S,w) \wedge win \text{ contains } \alpha\}|}{|W_m(S,w)|} \quad (14.1)$$

where $W_m(S,w)$ denotes the set of windows in S with width w, and $|W_m(S,w)| = |S| - 1 + w - 1$. In Example 1, for $\alpha = \langle ab \rangle$, $w = (2-1) \times 2 = 2$, $|W_m(S,w)| = (6 - 1 + 2 - 1) = 6$, $auto\text{-}win\text{-}growth\text{-}freq(S, \langle ab \rangle, 2) = 1/6$ since there is only one window with width 2 that contains $\langle ab \rangle$, i.e., $win(S,3,5)$. Similarly, for $\beta = \langle acb \rangle$, $w = (3-1) \times 2 = 4$, $|W_m(S,w)| = (6-1+4-1) = 8$, $auto\text{-}win\text{-}growth\text{-}freq(S, \langle acb \rangle, 2) = 2/8 = 1/4$ since in $W_m(S,w)$ there are two windows with width 4 that contain $\langle acb \rangle$, i.e., $win(S,2,6)$ and $win(S,3,6)$.

In [22], given S, window width w and max_gap, the frequency of α in S with width w and gap max_gap is defined as $maxgap\text{-}mo\text{-}freq(S, \alpha, w, max\_gap) = \sum_{0 \leq i < w} |mo(S, \alpha, i, max\_gap)|$, where $mo(S, \alpha, i, max\_gap)$ is the set of all minimal occurrences of α in S with width i, and the gap between any two consecutive timestamps in each occurrence is no more than max_gap. In Example 1, $maxgap\text{-}mo\text{-}freq(S, \langle ab \rangle, 4, 2) = 1$ because there is only one such minimal occurrence, $win(S,3,5)$.

In [16], given S, α and window width w, the head frequency of α in S with window width w is defined as $H\text{-}freq(S, \alpha, w) = |\{win[S, st, et]\}|$, where $win[S, st, et]$ satisfies (1) $et - st = w$ when $|S| - st \geq w$, and (2) there exists occurrence o of α in S, s.t. $w[S, st, et]$ contains o and $o[1] = st$. Then $T\text{-}freq$ is defined as $T\text{-}freq(S, \alpha, w) = \min_{\forall \beta \sqsubseteq \alpha}(H\text{-}freq(S, \beta, w))$. In Example 1, $H\text{-}freq(S, \langle a \rangle, 3) = 2$, $H\text{-}freq(S, \langle c \rangle, 3) = 2$ and $H\text{-}freq(S, \langle ac \rangle, 3) = 2$, so $T\text{-}freq(S, \langle ac \rangle, 3) = 2$. Similarly we obtain $T\text{-}freq(S', \langle ac \rangle, 3) = 1$.

In [18], $non\text{-}overlapped\text{-}freq(S, \alpha)$ is defined as the maximal cardinality of the sets of non-overlapped occurrences of α in S. Two occurrences of α in S, o and o', are said to be non-overlapped if $o[1] > o'[m]$ or $o'[1] > o[m]$, where $m = |\alpha|$. In Example 1, $non\text{-}overlapped\text{-}freq(S, \langle ab \rangle) = 1$.

In [15], given window width w, interval $[st, et]$ is called a matching bound of α in S with window width w, if $et - st = w$ when $|S| - st \geq w$, and there exists occurrence o of α in S, s.t. $o[1] = st$ and $win[S, st, et]$ contains o. The set of matching bounds of α in S with window width w is denoted as $boundlist(S, \alpha, w)$. Then $distinct\text{-}bound\text{-}st\text{-}freq(S, \alpha, w)$ is defined as the number of distinct starting timestamps in $boundlist(S, \alpha, w)$. In Example 1, $boundlist(S', \langle ac \rangle, 3) = \{[2,5],[3,6]\}$ and $boundlist(S', \langle c \rangle, 3) = \{[4,6]\}$, so we have $distinct\text{-}bound\text{-}st\text{-}freq(S', \langle ac \rangle, 3) = 2$ and $distinct\text{-}bound\text{-}st\text{-}freq(S', \langle c \rangle, 3) = 1$.

14.3.2 Properties

We consider three major properties of the frequency metrics, window-width restriction, anti-monotonicity and maximum-frequency.

The restriction of window width is intended for bounding the closeness of data elements in any occurrence of each episode [19]. In existing frequency metrics, the restriction of window width can be classified into three categories: fixed/maximal window width [15, 16, 19], unbounded window width [18, 20, 21], and variant window width [13, 22].

Definition 14.5. Anti-monotonicity Frequency metric $freq'$ is anti-monotonic if for any two episodes α and β and any sequence S, $freq'(S, \beta) \leq freq'(S, \alpha)$ when $\alpha \sqsubseteq \beta$, where $freq'(S, \alpha)$ represents the frequency of α in S under $freq'$.

Anti-monotonicity is a common principle that frequency metrics should obey in frequent pattern mining [1]. A pattern is frequent if its frequency is no less than a user specified minimal threshold min_freq [1]. The anti-monotonicity principle guarantees that a pattern can be pruned safely if any of its sub-patterns is infrequent, and any infrequent pattern need not be extended [1]. Anti-monotonicity avoids over-count of some duplicate occurrences. However, we identify that, in frequent episode discovery, an anti-monotonic frequency metric does not guarantee that no frequent patterns are missed. Therefore, we consider another property called maximum-frequency.

Definition 14.6. Maximum-Frequency. Given a restriction of window width w, an anti-monotonic metric, $freq'$, satisfies the maximum-frequency principle, if for $\forall \alpha$ and $\forall S$, $\neg \exists freq^*$, s.t. $freq^*$ has the same restriction of window width, $freq^*$ is anti-monotonic and $freq^*(S, \alpha, w) > freq'(S, \alpha, w)$.

The maximum-frequency property ensures that no proper occurrences are missed in the computation of frequency.

Three properties of the seven frequency metrics are summarised in Table 14.1. The abbreviations of frequency metrics are listed in Column 1. In columns 3 and 4, 'Y' ('N') means a metric has (not) the property. In Example 1, we can see that $auto\text{-}win\text{-}growth\text{-}freq$ is not anti-monotonic as $auto\text{-}win\text{-}growth\text{-}freq(S, \langle acb \rangle, 2) = 1/4 > auto\text{-}win\text{-}growth\text{-}freq(S, \langle ab \rangle, 2) = 1/6$, and $distinct\text{-}bound\text{-}st\text{-}freq$ is not anti-monotonic either, because $distinct\text{-}bound\text{-}st\text{-}freq(S', \langle ac \rangle, 3) = 2 > distinct\text{-}bound\text{-}st\text{-}freq(S', \langle c \rangle, 3) = 1$. Metrics $mo\text{-}freq$ and $maxgap\text{-}mo\text{-}freq$ do not satisfy the maximum-frequency principle since only minimal occurrences are counted. The $non\text{-}overlapped\text{-}freq$ does not satisfy the maximum-frequency principle since some overlapped occurrences are missed. The $T\text{-}freq$ does not satisfy the maximum-frequency principle since $fixed\text{-}win\text{-}freq(S, \alpha, w) \geq T\text{-}freq(S, \alpha, w)$.

Table 14.1: Three properties of the seven frequency metrics

freq	window	anti-monotonicity	max-freq
fixed-win-freq	fixed-win	N	
mo-freq	unbounded	Y	N
auto-win-growth	variant-win	N	
maxgap-mo-freq	variant-win	Y	N
T-freq	fixed-win	Y	N
non-overlapped	unbounded	Y	N
distinct-bound-st	max-win	N	

14.4 Inherent Inaccuracies and Their Impacts on Discovered Knowledge

We identify inaccuracies inherent in the previous frequency metrics and explore their impacts on frequent episode discovery and episode rule mining in subsections 4.1 and 4.2 respectively. Subsection 4.3 summarises our findings.

14.4.1 Frequent Episodes

An episode α is frequent in S if $freq(S, \alpha) \geq min\_freq$. The problem of frequent episode mining is to discover all frequent episodes from a given sequence [19]. Therefore, frequency metrics have direct impacts on frequent episode discovery.

First, the bound of window width restricts the width of occurrences. The occurrences with widths greater than the given bound are not counted in the computation of frequency. Although *mo-freq* and *non-overlapped-freq* use unbounded window width, the restriction of window width is inherent in their constraints on occurrences. For *mo-freq*, non-minimal occurrences are not counted. For *non-overlapped -freq*, overlapped occurrences are not counted. The greater the bound of window width is, the larger the resulting sets would be.

Now we examine the properties of anti-monotonicity and maximum-frequency, and investigate their impacts on the accuracy of obtained frequencies and discovered knowledge. In the analysis of the accuracy of frequencies, we consider whether each obtained frequency is accurate, i.e., whether it reflects the actual frequency. Two aspects are examined: (1) whether duplicate occurrences could be over-counted, and (2) whether proper occurrences could be missed.

Anti-monotonicity is a necessary condition for guaranteeing the correctness of discovered sets of frequent episodes. On the one hand, non-anti-monotonicity in-dicates over-count of duplicate occurrences, and thus obtained frequencies could be greater than actual frequencies. Therefore, infrequent episodes could be intro-duced into the result as frequent ones. On the other hand, under non-anti-monotonic frequency metrics, frequent episodes could be pruned when conducting the down-ward pruning strategy, i.e., an candidate episode is pruned if any of its sub-episodes is infrequent [1]. Thus, non-anti-monotonic metrics have the risk of obtaining incomplete resulting sets. Discovered sets under both *auto-win-growth-freq* and *distinct-bound-st-freq* are incomplete since they are not anti-monotonic. For example, in Example 1, when $auto\text{-}win\text{-}growth\text{-}freq(S, \langle ab \rangle, 2) = 1/6$ is obtained, all supper-episodes of $\langle ab \rangle$ are not considered since $\langle ab \rangle$ is infrequent (*min_freq* is assumed to be $1/4$). Thus the frequent episode $\langle acb \rangle$ is missed. In Example 1, $\langle c \rangle$ and $\langle ac \rangle$ in S' are in the similar situation.

However, in frequent episode mining, anti-monotonicity can not guarantee the correctness of discovered sets. In the following, examples are used to demonstrate the incorrectness of obtained frequencies under anti-monotonic metrics, such as *fixed-win-freq*, *mo-freq*, *maxgap-mo-freq*, *non-overlapped-freq* and *T-freq*.

The result discovered under *fixed-win-freq* could be incorrect since infrequent episodes could be included in the result due to over-count of duplicate occurrences. In Example 1, the actual frequency $freq(S, \langle c \rangle, 3)$ is 1, but the obtained $fixed\text{-}win\text{-}freq(S, \langle c \rangle, 3)$ is 4. If *min_sup* = 3, then infrequent episode $\langle c \rangle$ is included in the result.

Although *mo-freq* is anti-monotonic, the result discovered under *mo-freq* could be incomplete because some non-minimal frequent episodes could be missed. In Example 1, if *min_freq* = 2 and $w = 3$, $\langle ab \rangle$ should be in the result because $freq(\langle ab \rangle, 3) = 2$ with two occurrences $win[S, 2, 5]$ and $win[S, 3, 6]$. But under *mo-freq*, $\langle ab \rangle$ becomes infrequent because the obtained $mo\text{-}freq(S, \langle ab \rangle)$ is 1. Thus, frequent episode $\langle ab \rangle$ is missed. The *maxgap-mo-freq* has the same situation of *mo-freq*.

The *non-overlapped-freq* has the similar situation of *mo-freq*. The result discovered under metric *non-overlapped-freq* may be incomplete because some non-overlapped frequent episodes could be missed. In Example 1, if *min_freq* = 2 and $w = 3$, $\langle ab \rangle$ is missed under *non-overlapped-freq*, because the obtained $non\text{-}overlapped\text{-}freq(S, \langle ab \rangle) = 1 < min\_freq$.

The result obtained under *T-freq* could contain infrequent episodes. In Example 1, intuitively, $T\text{-}freq(S, \langle ac \rangle, 3)$ should be as same as $T\text{-}freq(S', \langle ac \rangle, 3)$ since S can be generated by inserting a c in front of S' and the inserted c does not affect the frequency of $\langle ac \rangle$ in S'. However, $T\text{-}freq(S, \langle ac \rangle, 3) = 2 \neq T\text{-}freq(S', \langle ac \rangle, 3) = 1$. It indicates that occurrences of $\langle ac \rangle$ in S are over-counted. That is to say infrequent (false) episodes could be introduced into the result.

From the above analysis, we see that the three factors/properties have impacts on the correctness of the discovered sets. Inaccuracies could be contained in the results obtained under seven previous frequency metrics. The above analysis demonstrates that anti-monotonicity is necessary but insufficient for guaranteeing the accuracy of frequencies and the correctness of discovered sets of frequent episodes. The maximum-frequency property also has impact on the accuracy of frequencies and the correctness of discovered sets. Frequent episodes could be missed under metrics that do not satisfy the maximum-frequency property, such as *mo-freq*, *maxgap-mo-freq* and *non-overlapped-freq*. Infrequent patterns could be included in the result under metrics that satisfy the maximum-frequency property, such as *fixed-win-freq*, or under metrics that do not satisfy the maximum-frequency property, such as T-*freq*.

14.4.2 Episode Rules

Episode rules are essentially associations among episodes. Two major types of episode rules have been proposed.

1. Type 1 (Association between two Subepisodes [22]): Given S and episode $\alpha = \langle a_1 a_2 ... a_m \rangle$ ($m > 1$), let $prefix(\alpha) = \langle a_1 a_2 ... a_{m-1} \rangle$ and $suffix(\alpha) = \langle a_m \rangle$. An episode rule r w.r.t. α is an association between the prefix and the suffix, i.e., r: $prefix(\alpha) \to suffix(\alpha)$.
2. Type 2 (Association between two Episodes within Maximal Lag [14]) Given S, a maximal bound of occurrence width, w, and a maximal bound of time lag, *max_lag*, an episode rule is represented as $\alpha \to_{lag \leq max\_lag} \beta$, which means if episode α occurs, then episode β is likely to occur within time *max_lag*.

Episode rule mining is to discover the episode rules whose frequencies and confidences are no less than user specified thresholds *min_freq* and *min_conf* respectively. For type 1, in [22], given S, α, *maxgap* and w, the frequency is defined as $freq(prefix(\alpha) \to suffix(\alpha)) = maxgap\text{-}mo\text{-}freq(S, \alpha, w, maxgap)$, and the confidence is defined as

$$conf(prefix(\alpha) \to suffix(\alpha)) = \frac{maxgap\text{-}mo\text{-}freq(S, \alpha, w, maxgap)}{maxgap\text{-}mo\text{-}freq(S, prefix(\alpha), w, maxgap)} \tag{14.2}$$

For type 2 in [14], given S, α, β, maximal width w and $max\_lag = L$, the frequency of $\alpha \to_{lag \leq L} \beta$, $freq(\alpha \to_{lag \leq L} \beta)$ is defined as

$$|\{o | o \in MO(S, \alpha, w) \land \exists o' \in MO(S, \beta, w), s.t.\ 0 < o'[1] - o[1] \leq L\}| \tag{14.3}$$

In above, $MO(S, \alpha, w)$ denotes the set of all minimal occurrences of α in S with maximal width w. The confidence of $\alpha \to_{lag \leq L} \beta$, $conf(\alpha \to_{lag \leq L} \beta)$ is defined as $freq(\alpha \to_{lag \leq L} \beta) / freq(\alpha)$, where $freq(\alpha) = |MO(S, \alpha, w)|$.

Metrics *maxgap-mo-freq* and *mo-freq* were adopted in [22] and [14] respectively. Theoretically, any of the seven frequency metrics can be used in the two types of episode rules. In the following, we investigate the impact of the seven frequency metrics on the frequency and confidence of an episode rule.

For episode rules of Type 1, the impact on the frequency of rule $prefix(\alpha) \to suffix(\alpha)$ (i.e., $freq(\alpha)$) is as same as the impact on $freq(\alpha)$. For Type 2 rule, $\alpha \to_{lag \leq max\_lag} \beta$, frequency metrics have impacts on frequencies of episodes α and β. The impacts on frequencies of episodes have been addressed in Section A. The impacts on confidences of type 1 rules and the impacts on frequencies and confidences of type 2 rules are illustrated by examples as follows.

If $fixed\text{-}win\text{-}freq$ is adopted, $freq(prefix(\alpha) \to suffix(\alpha))$ can be defined as $fixed\text{-}win\text{-}freq(S, \alpha, w)$, and $freq(\alpha \to_{lag \leq L} \beta)$ can be defined as $|\{win[S, st, et]|$ win $contains$ $\alpha, \exists win'[S, st', et'], s.t.$ win' $contains$ $\beta \wedge 0 < st' - st \leq L\}|$.

Example 14.2. Given $S = \langle (a)_1 (c)_2 (a)_3 (d)_4 \rangle$, $w = 2$ and $max\_lag = 2$, under metric $fixed\text{-}win\text{-}freq$, we compute $conf(\langle a \rangle \to \langle c \rangle)$ and $conf(\langle a \rangle \to_{lag \leq 2} \langle c \rangle)$.

For rule $\langle a \rangle \to \langle c \rangle$, we have $freq(\langle a \rangle \to \langle c \rangle) = fixed\text{-}win\text{-}freq$ $(S, \langle ac \rangle, 2) = 1$ and $fixed\text{-}win\text{-}freq(S, \langle a \rangle, 2) = 3$ since there are three windows with width 2 that contain $\langle a \rangle$, i.e., $win[S, 1, 3]$, $win[S, 2, 4]$ and $win[S, 3, 4]$. So the obtained $conf(\langle a \rangle \to \langle c \rangle)$ is 1/3. For rule $\langle a \rangle \to_{lag \leq 2} \langle c \rangle$, in the three windows containing $\langle a \rangle$, only $win[S, 1, 3]$ is followed by a window $win[S, 2, 4]$ that contains $\langle c \rangle$ and satisfies $2 - 1 \leq max\_lag$. Thus we obtain $conf(\langle a \rangle \to_{lag \leq 2} \langle c \rangle) = 1/3$. But in fact, the actual confidence of both $\langle a \rangle \to \langle c \rangle$ and $\langle a \rangle \to_{lag \leq 2} \langle c \rangle$ should be 1/2 because among the two occurrences of $\langle a \rangle$, only one is followed by the occurrence of $\langle c \rangle$ within the lag of 2. In this example, for both types of episode rules, the obtained confidence 1/3 is less than the actual confidence 1/2. If $min\_conf = 1/2$, then both $\langle a \rangle \to \langle c \rangle$ and $\langle a \rangle \to_{lag \leq 2} \langle c \rangle$ will be missed. Therefore, the completeness of discovered sets of both types of episode rules can not be guaranteed under $fixed\text{-}win\text{-}freq$.

Example 14.3. Given $S = \langle (a)_1 (a)_2 (b)_3 (c)_4 (b)_5 \rangle$ and $max\_lag = 3$, we compute the confidence of a few episode rules under metrics $mo\text{-}freq$, $maxgap\text{-}mo\text{-}freq$ and $non\text{-}overlapped\text{-}freq$.

Firstly, we compute intuitively accurate confidence $conf'$. We only constrain occurrence width by $max\_gap = 3$, i.e., the gap between any two consecutive time-samps in any occurrence is required to be no more than 3. Under the three frequency metrics, the frequency and confidence of episode rules can be defined similarly as [9],[17]. For rule $\langle a \rangle \to \langle b \rangle$, $freq(S, \langle a \rangle, 3) = 2$ and $freq(S, \langle ab \rangle, 3) = 2$. So we have $conf'(\langle a \rangle \to \langle b \rangle) = 1$. For rule $\langle ab \rangle \to_{lag \leq 3} \langle c \rangle$, $\langle ab \rangle$ has two occurrences $\langle 1, 3 \rangle$ and $\langle 2, 5 \rangle$, among which only $\langle 1, 3 \rangle$ has a corresponding occurrence of $\langle c \rangle$, $\langle 4 \rangle$, that satisfies $4 - 1 = 3 \leq max\_lag$. Therefore, we have $conf'(\langle ab \rangle \to_{lag \leq 3} \langle c \rangle) = 1/2$. In the following we compute the confidence under the three metrics.

Metric 1 ($mo\text{-}freq$). For rule $\langle a \rangle \to \langle b \rangle$, we have $mo\text{-}freq(S, \langle ab \rangle) = 1$ and $mo\text{-}freq(S, \langle a \rangle) = 2$. Therefore, the obtained confidence is $conf(\langle a \rangle \to \langle b \rangle) = 1/2$. For rule $\langle ab \rangle \to_{lag \leq 3} \langle c \rangle$, $\langle ab \rangle$ has only one minimal occurrence $\langle 2, 3 \rangle$. For $\langle 2, 3 \rangle$, there exists a minimal occurrence of $\langle c \rangle$, $\langle 4 \rangle$, that satisfies $4 - 2 = 2 \leq max\_lag$. So the obtained confidence is $conf(\langle ab \rangle \to_{lag \leq 3} \langle c \rangle) = 1$.

Metric 2 ($maxgap\text{-}mo\text{-}freq$). Similarly, we obtain that $conf(\langle a \rangle \to \langle b \rangle) = 1/2$ and $conf(\langle ab \rangle \to_{lag \leq 3} \langle c \rangle) = 1$.

Metric 3 ($non\text{-}overlapped\text{-}freq$). For rule $\langle a \rangle \to \langle b \rangle$, we have $freq(\langle a \rangle \to \langle b \rangle) = non\text{-}overlapped\text{-}freq(S, \langle ab \rangle) = 1$ and $non\text{-}overlapped\text{-}freq(S, \langle a \rangle) = 2$. Therefore, the obtained confidence is $conf(\langle a \rangle \to \langle b \rangle) = 1/2$. For rule $\langle ab \rangle \to_{lag \leq 3} \langle c \rangle$, $\langle ab \rangle$ has only one non-overlapped occurrence $\langle 2, 3 \rangle$. For $\langle 2, 3 \rangle$, there is one non-overlapped occurrence of $\langle c \rangle$, $\langle 4 \rangle$, that satisfies $4 - 2 = 2 \leq max\_lag$. So the obtained confidence is $conf(\langle ab \rangle \to_{lag \leq 3} \langle c \rangle) = 1$.

Comparing the obtained confidences with the intuitively accurate confidences, we find that under the three metrics, the obtained confidence for rules of type 1 could be less than the intuitively accurate confidence, and the obtained confidence for rules of type 2 could be greater than the intuitively accurate confidence. That is to say, rules could be missed for rules of type 1, and false rules could be included in the result for rules of type 2.

Example 14.4. Given $S = \langle (c)_1 (a)_2 (a)_3 (c)_4 \rangle$, $w = 2$ and *max_lag* $= 2$, we compute the confidence of episode rules under frequency metric $T\text{-}freq$.

According to the definition of $T\text{-}freq$, we have $T\text{-}freq(S, \langle ac \rangle, 2) = 2$ and $T\text{-}freq(S, \langle a \rangle, 2) = 2$. So $conf(\langle a \rangle \to \langle c \rangle) = 1$. However, intuitively $conf(\langle a \rangle \to \langle c \rangle) = 1/2$ is more reasonable if $\langle 4 \rangle$ is used only once as an occurrence of $\langle c \rangle$ after the occurrences of $\langle a \rangle$.

14.4.3 Findings

Upon the above analysis, our findings are summarised as follows.

1. The restriction of window width is necessary for any frequency metric to limit the closeness of an occurrence; variant window width w.r.t. episode length seems more reasonable than fixed/maximal window width.
2. Anti-monotonicity is necessary but insufficient for guaranteeing the accuracy of obtained frequencies.
3. Maximum-frequency has impact on the accuracy of obtained frequencies; No matter they satisfy maximum-frequency or not, anti-monotonic metrics could introduce inaccuracies into obtained frequencies.
4. The above three factors have impacts on the accuracy of obtained frequencies, and hence have impacts on the results in the discovery of frequent episodes and episode rules.
5. Each previous frequency metric has inherent inaccuracies, and thus has impact on the soundness and completeness of the results (the impacts are summarised in Table 14.2).

In Table 14.2, '$\{\alpha\}$' denotes the set of frequent episodes, '$\{r_1\}$' denotes the set of episode rules of Type 1, and '$\{r_2\}$' denotes the set of episode rules of Type 2. The 'F' represents 'false', and 'Y' in Column 'F' means that false patterns could be included in the result. The 'M' represents 'missed', and 'Y' in Column 'M' means that patterns could be missed under the metric. The soundness of the result can not be guaranteed if false patterns could be included. The completeness of the result can not be guaranteed if patterns could be missed. Note that the impact of the restriction of window width is not included in Table 14.2.

Table **14.2:** The impact of the seven metrics on results

freq	$\{\alpha\}$		$\{r_1\}$		$\{r_2\}$	
	F	M	F	M	F	M
fixed-win-freq	Y		Y	Y	Y	Y
mo-freq		Y		Y	Y	Y
auto-win-growth	Y	Y	Y	Y	Y	Y
maxgap-mo-freq		Y		Y	Y	Y
T-freq	Y		Y		Y	
non-overlapped		Y		Y	Y	Y
distinct-bound-st	Y	Y	Y	Y	Y	Y

14.5 Suggestions and A New Frequency Metric

This section provides three suggestions for frequency metrics of episodes. In Sub-section 5.3, we introduce a new frequency metric that satisfies the three suggested conditions, and develop a naive algorithm to compute the frequency.

14.5.1 Restriction of Window Width

In the three types of window width restrictions, we recommend to restrict occurrence width by *max_gap*.

Definition 14.7. Given $S = \langle (e_1)_1 (e_2)_2 ... e(e_n)_n \rangle$ and *max_gap*, for any episode $\alpha = \langle a_1 a_2 ... a_m \rangle$, $o = \langle i_1, i_2, ..., i_m \rangle$ is called an occurrence of α in S w.r.t. *max_gap* iff it satisfies (1) $e_{i_j} = a_j$ for $j = 1, 2, ..., m$, (2) $1 \leq i_1$ and $i_m \leq n$, and (3) $i_j - i_{j-1} \leq$ *max_gap* for $j = 2, 3, ... m$.

14.5.2 Strict Anti-Monotonicity

As shown in Section 3, anti-monotonicity is insufficient for guaranteeing accurate frequencies. We re-examine Example 1 in Section 3 to explore why inaccurate frequencies could be obtained for anti-monotonic metrics such as *fixed-win-freq*, *mo-freq*, *maxgap-mo-freq*, *T-freq* and *non-overlapped-freq*. The *fixed-win-freq* could be inaccurate since duplicate occurrences are counted. For example, in Example 1, $fixed\text{-}win\text{-}freq(S, \langle c \rangle, 3) = 4$ because occurrence $o = \langle 4 \rangle$ of $\langle c \rangle$ is counted four times. The inaccuracy in *T-freq* results from the count of redundant occurrences. For example, in Example 1 $T\text{-}freq(S, \langle ac \rangle, 3) = 2$ because two occurrences of $\langle ac \rangle$, $o = \langle 2, 4 \rangle$ and $o' = \langle 3, 4 \rangle$ are counted. We notice that one of o and o' is redundant since they share the same element at the same timestamp 4. To obtain accurate frequencies, we define non-redundant occurrences and only count non-redundant occurrences.

Definition 14.8. (Non-redundant Sets of Occurrences) Given S, α and max_gap, a set of occurrences of α in S with restriction of max_gap is non-redundant, if for any two occurrences, $o = \langle i_1, i_2, ..., i_m \rangle$ and $o' = \langle i'_1, i'_2, ..., i'_m \rangle$ $(o \neq o')$ in this set, $\neg \exists j \in \{1, 2, ..., m\}$, s.t. $e_{i_j} = e_{i'_j}$.

The set of all non-redundant sets of occurrences of α in S with max_gap is denoted as $nR\text{-}O(S, \alpha, max\_gap)$. In $nR\text{-}O(S, \alpha, max\_gap)$, the sets with the maximal cardinality are included in $MaxnR\text{-}O(S, \alpha, max\_gap)$.

In checking anti-monotonicity, we only consider non-redundant occurrences.

Definition 14.9. (Strict Anti-monotonicity) A frequency metric, $freq'$, is strictly anti-monotonic if (1) it is anti-monotonic, and (2) given any S, any α and $max\_gap = k$,

$$freq'(S, \alpha, k) \leq \min_{\forall \beta \sqsubseteq \alpha, \forall OS \in MaxnR\text{-}O(S, \beta, k)} (|OS|) \qquad (14.4)$$

Definition 14.10. (Strict Maximum-Frequency) Given $max\_gap = k$, an strict anti-monotonic metric, $freq'$, satisfies the strict maximum-frequency principle, if for $\forall \alpha$ and $\forall S$, $\neg \exists freq^*$, s.t. $freq^*$ has the same restriction of max_gap, $freq^*$ is strict anti-monotonic and $freq^*(S, \alpha, k) > freq'(S, \alpha, k)$.

We recommend that any frequency metric for episodes restrict occurrence width by *max-gap* and satisfy both the principles of strict anti-monotonicity and strict maximum-frequency.

14.5.3 A New Frequency Metric and Its Computation

Based on the maximal non-redundant set of occurrences, a naive maximal strictly anti-monotonic frequency metric with $max\_gap = k$ can be defined as

$$MaxnR\text{-}O\text{-}freq(S, \alpha, k) = \max_{\forall OS \in nR\text{-}O(S, \alpha, k)} (|OS|) \qquad (14.5)$$

This metric is similar to 'repetitive support' in [9]. However, $MaxnR\text{-}O\text{-}freq$ is different from repetitive support because repetitive support has no restriction on occurrence width and it is defined for sequential patterns in a database of sequences. Notice that it is time-expensive to compute $MaxnR\text{-}O\text{-}freq$ since all non-redundant sets of occurrences need to be considered. To achieve a more efficient computation, in $MaxnR\text{-}O(S, \alpha, max\_gap)$ we choose a special set called the leftmost maximal non-redundant set, denoted as $LMaxnR(S, \alpha, max\_gap)$. To define the set, the occurrences in any non-redundant set are ordered by the starting timestamp in ascending order, i.e. in any sorted set $\{o_1, o_2, ..., o_r\} \in nR\text{-}O(S, \alpha, k)$, $o_j[1] < o_{j+1}[1]$ holds for all $j = 1, 2, ..., r - 1$.

Definition 14.11. (*LMaxnR-O*) The leftmost maximal non-redundant set of occurrences of α in S with $max\_gap = k$, $LMaxnR\text{-}O(S, \alpha, k)$, is defined as the occurrence set, $OS = \{o_1, ..., o_r\}$, that satisfies (1) $OS \in MaxnR\text{-}O(S, \alpha, k)$ and (2) for

$\forall OS' = \{o'_1,...,o'_r\} \in MaxnR\text{-}O(S,\alpha,k), o_j[l] < o'_j[l]$ holds for all $j = 1,...,r$ and $l = 1,...,|\alpha|$.

Definition 14.12. (*LMaxnR-O-freq*) The metric based on *LMaxnR-O* is defined as $LMaxnR\text{-}O\text{-}freq(S,\alpha,max\_gap) = |LMaxnR\text{-}O(S,\alpha,max\_gap)|$.

Property 14.1. The *LMaxnR-O-freq* satisfies the three recommended properties, i.e., *max-gap* restriction, strict anti-monotonicity and strict maximum-frequency.

The essence of computing *LMaxnR-O-freq* is to construct *LMaxnR-O*. Given S, $\alpha = \langle a_1 a_2...a_m \rangle$ and $max\_gap = k$, $LMaxnR\text{-}O(S,\alpha,k)$ can be constructed recursively as follows. If $m = 1$, let $LMaxnR\text{-}O(S,\alpha,k) = O(S,\alpha,k)$. If $m > 1$, $LMaxnR\text{-}O(S,\alpha,k)=Join(LMaxnR\text{-}O(S,prefix(\alpha),k), LMaxnR\text{-}O(S,suffix(\alpha),k))$. As shown in Fig. 3, the basic idea of the *Join* operation is, for each occurrence o'_j in $LMaxnR\text{-}O(S,prefix(\alpha),k)$, to find the leftmost occurrence o^*_r in $LMaxnR\text{-}O(S,suffix(\alpha),k)$ that comes after the last timestamp of o'_j, and to insert $o_j = o'_j \circ o^*_r$ into $LMaxnR\text{-}O(S,\alpha,k)$. In Example 1, if $max\_gap = 3$, we have $LMaxnR\text{-}O(S,\langle a \rangle,3) = \{\langle 2 \rangle, \langle 3 \rangle\}$, $LMaxnR\text{-}O(S,\langle b \rangle,3) = \{\langle 5 \rangle, \langle 6 \rangle\}$, and $LMaxnR\text{-}O(S,\langle ab \rangle,3) = Join(LMaxnR\text{-}O(S,\langle a \rangle,3), LMaxnR\text{-}O(S,\langle b \rangle,3)) = \{\langle 2,5 \rangle, \langle 3,6 \rangle\}$.

14.6 Empirical Evaluation

We discover frequent episodes and episode rules under different frequency metrics, and compare the results with that obtained under *LMaxnR-O-freq*. All algorithms were implemented in Java, and were performed on a computer of an Intel processor at 1.86 Ghz and a RAM of 2 Gb, running Windows XP.

Five synthetic long sequences were generated with major parameters $|I| = 500$ and $|S| = 10000$. In the experiments, we specify $min\_sup = 10000 \times 5\% = 500$, $min\_conf = 0.35$, $w = 12$, $max\_gap = 3$ and $max\_lag = 5$. The seven discovered sets

---

Algorithm 1: Join

 Input : $LMaxnR\text{-}O(S,prefix(\alpha),k)$, $LMaxnR\text{-}O(S,suffix(\alpha),k)$
 Output : $LMaxnR\text{-}O(S,\alpha,k)$
1 $start \leftarrow 1$;
2 for $j=1$ to $|LMaxnR\text{-}O(S,prefix(\alpha),k)|$ **do**
3 **for** $r = start$ to $|LMaxnR\text{-}O(S,suffix(\alpha),k)|$ **do**
4   **if** $0 < o^*_r[1] - o'_j[m-1] \le k$ **then**
5 $o_j \leftarrow o'_j \circ o^*_r = \langle o'_j[1],...,o'_j[m-1],o^*_r[1]\rangle$;
6   Insert o_j into $LMaxnR\text{-}O(S,\alpha,k)$;
7 $start \leftarrow r + 1$;

8 Return $(LMaxnR\text{-}O(P,S))$;

Fig. 14.3: The Join operation

of patterns (frequent episodes or episode rules) under the seven frequency metrics are denoted as P_1 (*fixed-win-freq*), P_2 (*mo-freq*), P_3 (*auto-win-growth-freq*), P_4 (*max-gap-mo-freq*), P_5 (*T-freq*), P_6 (*non-overlapped-freq*) and P_7 (*distinct-bound -st-freq*) respectively, where the metric for P_k is attached in the brackets. We use P_0 to denote the discovered set under the proposed frequency metric, *LMaxnR-O-freq*. Taking P_0 as a standard resulting set, the difference between P_k ($k = 1, 2, ..., 7$) and P_0 is evaluated by three classes of patterns.

1. Missed (M) patterns — patterns missed by P_k, i.e., the patterns in P_0, but not in P_k.
2. False (F) patterns — patterns in P_k, but not in P_0.
3. Inaccurate (I) patterns — patterns in $P_k \cap P_0$ with different frequencies/confidences in P_k and P_0.

For the three classes of patterns, we define three corresponding ratios: $R_M^k = \frac{|P_0 \backslash P_k|}{|P_0|}$, $R_F^k = \frac{|P_k \backslash P_0|}{|P_0|}$ and

$$R_I^k = \frac{|\{p | p \in P_k \cap P_0, freq_k(p) \neq freq_0(p)\}|}{|P_0|}$$

$$or \quad \frac{|\{p | p \in P_k \cap P_0, conf_k(p) \neq conf_0(p)\}|}{|P_0|} \quad (14.6)$$

where $k = 1...7$, $freq_k(p)$ ($freq_0(p)$) represents the frequency of episode/rule p in P_k (P_0), and $conf_k(p)$ ($conf_0(p)$) represents the frequency of episode rule p in P_k (P_0). Let $TI = R_M^k + R_F^k + R_I^k$.

Table 14.3: A comparison between P_k and P_0 for frequent episodes

	R_M^k	R_F^k	R_I^k	TI^k
k=1	0.000	0.124	0.313	0.437
k=2	0.045	0.012	0.162	0.219
k=3	0.023	0.091	0.282	0.396
k=4	0.045	0.000	0.125	0.170
k=5	0.000	0.075	0.226	0.301
k=6	0.053	0.016	0.183	0.252
k=7	0.000	0.062	0.212	0.274

Table 14.4: A comparison between P_k and P_0 for episode rules (type 1)

	R_M^k	R_F^k	R_I^k	TI^k
k=1	0.000	0.142	0.281	0.423
k=2	0.051	0.008	0.143	0.202
k=3	0.019	0.083	0.242	0.344
k=4	0.050	0.000	0.137	0.142
k=5	0.000	0.063	0.201	0.264
k=6	0.067	0.012	0.152	0.231
k=7	0.000	0.074	0.252	0.326

Table 14.5: A comparison between P_k and P_0 for episode rules (type 2)

	R_M^k	R_F^k	R_I^k	TI^k
k=1	0.008	0.163	0.276	0.446
k=2	0.062	0.006	0.153	0.221
k=3	0.023	0.094	0.235	0.352
k=4	0.064	0.005	0.117	0.186
k=5	0.004	0.069	0.188	0.261
k=6	0.071	0.009	0.164	0.244
k=7	0.006	0.067	0.262	0.335

Table 14.3 shows the comparison between P_k and P_0 for frequent episodes. Each value is an average from five tests over five sequences. Tables 14.4 and 14.5 show the comparison between P_k and P_0 for episode rules of Type 1 and Type 2 respectively.

The results conform to the analysis in Section 4. It is important to note the difference between the result in Table 2 and that in Tables 3-5. The missed and false patterns due to the restriction of window width are not considered in Table 2. For example, when $k = 2$, no false episodes appear for *mo-freq* in Table 14.2, while $R_F^2 = 0.012$ in Table 3 since *mo-freq* has no restriction on window width.

14.7 Conclusion

Subsequence frequency measurement is a key issue in frequency based knowledge discovery in single sequences. The adoption of frequency metrics has direct impact on the discovered knowledge. This chapter investigated subsequence frequency measurement in single sequences and its impact on FBKDISS. We identified the inaccuracies inherent in seven previous frequency metrics and explored their impacts on the correctness of discovered sets of frequent episodes and episode rules. Based on the findings, we provided three suggestions for finding appropriate frequency metrics and introduced a new frequency metric, *LMaxR-O-freq*. Empirical evaluation revealed the inaccuracies and verified our findings. It is important to note that no standard metrics have been commonly accepted for subsequence frequency measurement in single sequences. However, the suggestions and the frequency metric proposed in this chapter are helpful for improving the reliability of knowledge discovery in single sequences.

References

1. Agrawal, R., Imielinski, T., Swami, A.: Mining association rules between sets of items in large databases. In: Proc. ACM-SIGMOD Int. Conf. Management of Data, pp. 207-216 (1993)
2. Agrawal, R., Srikant, R.: mining sequential patterns. In: Proceedings of International Conference on Data Engineering, pp. 3-14, (1995)

3. Barlow, R. E., Proschan, F.: Mathematical Theory of Reliability. J. Wiley and Sons. Reprinted (1996) SIAM, Philadelphia, PA. (1965)

4. Berka, P.: Recognizing reliability of discovered knowledge. Lecture Notes in Computer Science, 1263, pp. 307-314 (1997)

5. Bringmann, B., Nijssen, S.: What is frequent in a single graph? In: Proceedings of Pacific-Asia Conference on Knowledge Discovery and Data Mining, pp. 858-863 (2008)

6. Chen, Z., Ordonez, C., Zhao, K.: Comparing reliability of association rules and OLAP statistical tests. In: Proceedings of the 2st IEEE Internatioanl Workshop on Reliability Issues in Knowledge Discovery, pp. 8-17 (2008)

7. Dai Honghua: A study on reliability in graph discovery. In: Proceedings of the 1st IEEE Internatioanl Workshop on Reliability Issues in Knowledge Discovery, pp. 775-779 (2006)

8. Dai Honghua: A case study on classification reliability. In: Proceedings of 2nd IEEE Internatioanl Workshop on Reliability Issues in Knowledge Discovery, pp. 69-73 (2008)

9. Ding, B., Lo, D., Han, J., Khoo, S.C.: Efficient mining of closed repetitive gapped subsequences from a sequence database, In: Proceedings of International Conference on Data Engineering, pp. 1024-1035 (2009)

10. Feng, Y., Wu, Z., Zhou Z.: Enhancing reliability through knowledge discovery process. In: Proceedings of 1st IEEE Internatioanl Workshop on Reliability Issues in Knowledge Discovery, pp. 754-758 (2006)

11. Gan, M., Dai, H.: A study on the accuracy of frequency measures and its impact on knowledge discovery in single sequences. In: Proceedings of 3st IEEE Internatioanl Workshop on Reliability Issues in Knowledge Discovery, pp. 859-866 (2010)

12. Gan, M., Dai, H.: Obtaining accurate frequencies of sequential patterns over a single sequence. ICIC Express Letters, 5(4) (in press) (2011)

13. Gemma, C.G.: Discovering unbounded episodes in sequential data. In: Proceedings of the 7th European Conference on Principles and Practice of Knowledge Discovery in Databases, pp. 83-94 (2003)

14. Harms, S. K., Deogun, J. S.: Sequential association rule mining with time lags. Journal of Intelligent Information Systems, 22 (1), pp. 7-22 (2004)

15. Huang, K., Chang, C.: Efficient mining of frequent episodes from complex sequences, Information Systems, 33 (1), pp. 96-114 (2008)

16. Iwanuma, K., Ishihara, R., Takano, Y., Nabeshima, H.: Extracting frequent subsequences from a single long data sequence: a novel anti-monotonic measure and a simple on-line algorithm. In: Proceedings of the 3rd International Conference on Data Mining, pp.186-193 (2005)

17. Kuramochi, M., Karypis, G.: Finding frequent patterns in a large sparse graph. Data Mining and Knowledge Discovery, 11(3), pp. 243-271 (2005)

18. Laxman, S., Sastry, P., Unnikrishnan, K.: A fast algorithm for finding frequent episodes in event streams. In: Proceedings of the 13th ACM SIGKDD Conference on Knowledge Discovery and Data Mining, pp. 410-419 (2007)

19. Mannila, H., Toivonen, H., Verkamo, A.: Discovering frequent episodes in sequences. In: Proceedings of the 1st ACM SIGKDD Conference on Knowledge Discovery and Data Mining, pp. 210-215 (1995).

20. Mannila, H., Toivonen, H., Discovering generalized episodes using minimal occurrences. In: Proceedings of the 2nd ACM SIGKDD Conference on Knowledge Discovery and Data Mining, pp.146-151 (1996).

21. Mannila, H., Toivonen, H., Verkamo, A. I.: Discovery of frequent episodes in event sequences. Data Mining and Knowledge Discovery, 1(3), pp. 259-289 (1997).

22. Meger, N., Rigotti, C., Constraint-based mining of episode ruels and optimal window sizes. In: Proceedings of European Conference on Principles and Practice of Knowledge Discovery in Databases, pp. 313-324 (2004).

23. Wikipedia, The Free Encyclopedia, http://en.wikipedia.org/wiki/Reliability_(statistics)

Part IV
Reliability Improvement Methods

Chapter 15
Improving Reliability of Unbalanced Text Mining by Reducing Performance Bias

Ling Zhuang, Min Gan, and Honghua Dai

Abstract Class imbalance in textual data is one important factor that affects the reliability of text mining. For imbalanced textual data, conventional classifiers tend to have a strong performance bias, which results in high accuracy rate on the majority class but very low rate on the minorities. An extreme strategy for unbalanced learning is to discard the majority instances and apply one-class classification to the minority class. However, this could easily cause another type of bias, which increases the accuracy rate on minorities by sacrificing the majorities.

This chapter aims to investigate approaches that reduce these two types of performance bias and improve the reliability of discovered classification rules. Experimental results show that the inexact field learning method and parameter optimized one-class classifiers achieve more balanced performance than the standard approaches.

15.1 Introduction

Textual data are ubiquitous in reality. Nowadays textual databases are rapidly growing with more and more electronic documents being collected from various sources, such as research publications, electronic newspapers, digital libraries, e-mail and Web pages. Unlike conventional structured data, textual data are semistructrued. Consequently, most available approaches for mining structured data are not applicable to processing textual data. Thus, text mining has become an increasingly important research area in data mining and knowledge discovery [6].

In the real word, the class distribution in a substantial portion of textual data is often imbalanced [9]. A data set is said to be imbalanced when one class is represented by a large number of examples, while the other only by a few [7]. Class imbalance appears to be a commonly encountered problem in text classification. For

Ling Zhuang, Min Gan, Honghua Dai
School of Information Technology, Deakin University, Melbourne, VIC 3125, Australia e-mail: ling.zhuang@gmail.com, mg@deakin.edu.au, honghua.dai@deakin.edu.au

example, in a document filtering system, documents relevant to a preferred topic are generally far less than those irrelevant. On such a unevenly distributed data set, conventional classifiers tend to have a strong performance bias, which results in high accuracy rate on the majorities and very low rate on the minority class. An extreme solution to this problem is the one-class learning strategy. By discarding the distracting majorities, one-class learning sets the classification boundary by enclosing the minority instances. However, overfitting minorities is inevitable in this case. This is the performance bias on minority class.

These two types of performance bias cause the classification results unreliable in all circumstances. As indicated in [2, 3], the reliability of an induced classifier can be affected by several factors including the data oriented factors and the algorithm oriented factors. The uneven class distribution feature in the data set is one data oriented factor impacting the classifier reliability.

Although more and more researchers have realized this problem, especially in real applications, when most data set is unbalanced, studies in this area is relatively less developed. This chapter aims to investigate various novel strategies that reduce the performance bias and improve the reliability of discovered classification rules when data is unevenly distributed. We will study the above two types of performance bias respectively and present our solutions.

The rest of this chapter is organised as follows. Section 2 addresses how to reduce bias on majority class. Section 3 discusses the improvement of reliability by reducing bias on minority class. Section 4 presents experimental results. Section 5 concludes this chapter.

15.2 Reducing Bias On Majority Class

In text classification, along with instance-imbalance, feature-imbalance is inevitable in certain cases. Assume that the feature sets from the majority and minority class in a document collection are separated. Since the majority class has a larger number of documents than the minority, it is more likely to have a larger vocabulary(feature set) than the minority. When applying feature selection to reduce the learning complexity in such case, as discussed in [5], most existing methods fail to produce predictive features for a difficult minority class. The lack of target examples makes the normal feature scoring approaches have a bias towards attributes with more frequent occurrences in majorities. This is regarded as the dual imbalance problem when instance imbalance leads to feature imbalance.

15.2.1 Preliminaries

We use D, to denote a training document set; m, number of total documents; n, number of total terms. A head rope $h_j(1 \leq j \leq n)$ with respect to term j consists of the lower and upper bounds of a point set D_j, where D_j is the set of values of the term j occur in the instances in the given instance set [1]. Let D^+ be the positive document class and D^- be the negative one; h_j is the positive head rope if h_j is derived from D^+. Otherwise, it is the negative one. Positive and negative head ropes construct the PN head rope pair for an attribute.

15.2.2 Feature Selection Fish-Net

The feature selection Fish-Net is an extended version of the original Fish-Net [1]. The procedure is summarized as follows. Step 1 to 3 comprises the feature selection phase; Step 4 to 7 comprises the classification rule construction phase.

Algorithm: Feature Selection Fish-Net

Input: A pre-processed training document matrix with binary class labels {P,N}, the original feature set F.

Output: A selected feature subset Fs, a β-rule which is composed of contribution functions for each selected attribute, a threshold α and resultant head rope.

Procedures:

1. For each feature $f \in F$, calculate its average and variance in both positive and negative class:

$$Average' = \bar{x}' = \frac{Df}{N} \times \frac{Sum}{N} \tag{15.1}$$

$$Variance' = \varepsilon' = \frac{\frac{Df}{N} \cdot \Sigma(x_i - \bar{x})^2 + \frac{\overline{Df}}{N} \cdot \Sigma(x_i - \bar{x})^2}{N-1} \tag{15.2}$$

2. Work out the head rope pair for each feature $f \in F$:

$$h_j^+ = [h_{l_j}^+, h_{u_j}^+] = [\overline{x_j^+} - \varepsilon_j^+, \overline{x_j^+} + \varepsilon_j^+]$$

$$h_j^- = [h_{l_j}^-, h_{u_j}^-] = [\overline{x_j^-} - \varepsilon_j^-, \overline{x_j^-} + \varepsilon_j^-]$$

3. Select those features whose PN head rope pair satisfies $h_{u_j}^- < h_{l_j}^+$. These comprise the feature subset Fs.

4. For each selected feature $f \in Fs$, find out its fields regarding each class as follows:

$$h_j^+ = [h_{l_j}^+, h_{u_j}^+] = [min_{1 \leq i \leq m}\{d_{ij}(d_i \in D^+)\},$$

$$max_{1 \leq i \leq m}\{d_{ij}(d_i \in D^+)\}(d_{ij} \neq 0)]$$

The same technique applies to derive the negative head rope $h_j^- = [h_{l_j}^-, h_{u_j}^-]$.

5. For each selected feature $f \in Fs$, construct its contribution function using fields $[h_{l_j}^+, h_{u_j}^+]$ and $[h_{l_j}^-, h_{u_j}^-]$.

6. According to the contribution function, work out resultant head rope pair $\langle h^+, h^- \rangle$. For each instance in the training set, we compute the contribution as follows:

$$Contribution = \frac{Sum}{N} * \frac{N}{N_{total}} \tag{15.3}$$

where *Sum* is the sum of contribution values of all attributes in each instance; N is the number of non-zero values the instance has in Fs; N_{total} is the number of features(including non-selected ones) the instance has. The positive resultant head rope h^+ is constructed from all positive instances and h^- is constructed from all negative instances.

7. Determine the threshold α by examining the discovered head rope pair.

In the original Fish-Net, the embedded feature selection mechanism is to look at the head ropes of each attribute. To derive head ropes on text data, not only we need to consider the value of one feature, but also we should incorporate its distribution among documents. In equation (1)(2), Df is the number of documents contain a feature f in a single class and $\overline{Df}$ is the number of those does not. If f appears in every document, i.e., $Df = N$, then it turns out to be the normal average and variance. Apparently, Df/N reflects the popularity f is in that class and this value is a tradeoff between the feature distribution and its normal average value. The more frequent f is in the class, the higher weight Df/N will give to the normal average. The variance calculation is based on the following assumption: the instances are separated into those ones with the feature f and those without. The popularity rate Df/N and $\overline{Df}/N$ give weights on the two sections. If f appears in more than half of the instances, then the first part of variance will dominate the final result, otherwise the second part will.

The second phase is to construct the classification rule on the training data with the selected features. First of all, we need to set up the real head rope pair for each selected feature. We calculate the real fields by ignoring all 0 values and taking the minimum and maximum value as the lower and upper bound of the head rope. This is due to that among the selected features, there still exists different levels with respect to classification performance. Secondly, the contribution value for each instance is calculated. In the original Fish-Net, it is obtained by averaging the sum of all contribution values. However, this is not feasible in text data. The number of features a document includes varies and mostly depends on the document length. This easily causes the feature imbalance problem. If we average the sum of contribution values with the total number of features, we will find the longer documents have higher contribution values and this makes shorter documents difficult to classify.

N/N_{total} is the percentage of features selected for classification in an instance. This adds weight to the average contribution value. The reason for this is by considering this situation: in a feature subset, a longer document could possibly have the same amount of features selected as the short ones. However, for the longer document, it could also have a much larger vocabulary which are not selected and more supportive to the majority class. For the short document, the selected features could already be all the words it has.

15.3 Reducing Bias On Minority Class

Empirical results in [11] show that on heavily-unbalanced data, one-class classifier achieves much better performance than the conventional two-class ones. However, when only minorities are participating in the training, there is a high probability that the classifier will overfit the target class so that the performance on majorities deteriorates. This performance bias on the minorities decreases the reliability of one-class learning on unbalanced data, since it is sacrificing the accuracy on majority instances.

Parameter selection is an important issue for classifers sensitive to parameters. The optimization criteria should reflect the estimated classification performance on both target and outlier classes. Therefore, although the majorities are excluded in the training procedure to avoid their distractions on minorities, they could be employed when estimating the performance of constructed classifier.

We present the one-class classification framework to optimize the parameters and reduce the classification bias on minority class in imbalance learning. It is divided into three stages: 1)Learning Stage; 2)Evaluation Stage; 3)Optimization Stage. In the first stage, only minority instances are participating in the one-class learning procedure; however, in the second stage, both majority and minority examples are involved in estimating the generalization performance. We will discuss the details of of each stage in the following sections.

15.3.1 Learning Stage

This is the step where the one-class classifier is constructed using the minority class. One-Class Support Vector Machine(OC SVM) and Support Vector Data Description(SVDD) are employed in this chapter. One-class SVM [12] could be summarized to two steps: firstly, map the data into a feature space corresponding to an appropriate kernel function; secondly, separate the mapped vectors from origin with maximum margin. SVDD [4] is a data domain description method which aims to obtain a boundary around a target data set. It offers the ability to map the data into a high dimensional feature space and more flexible descriptions could be achieved by this mapping.

Parameters involved in the two learning schemes are strongly related. Firstly, for both one-class SVM and SVDD employing the Gaussian kernel ($k(x,y) = e^{-||x-y||^2/s}$), the width parameter s needs to be taken into account. In SVDD, when increasing s, the volume of the closed region is enlarged. While we aim to reduce the volume covered by the boundary and avoid the overfitting problem, s plays an important role to control the balance. Another parameter appears in both approaches is the rejection rate $v \in (0, 1]$. It determines the ratio of points considered to be "outliers" in the target class thus influences the size of region. The smaller value v has, the bigger size the estimated region will be. Hence, similar as the width parameter s,

v also determines the trade-off between the covered region and possible overfitting problem.

15.3.2 Evaluation Stage

Leave-one-out estimator is shown to be almost unbiased [8] among various generalization performance estimation approaches. However, it is very expensive to run, especially in cases with huge amount of training data. Hence, k-fold cross-validation is an alternative option. These two methods are applied to estimate the performance on minority class.

Note that majority instances are not involved in the training procedure. To estimate the performance of one-class classifier on majorities, we first construct the classifier on the entire minorities. The majority class then is regarded as the validation set. All the instances in this set are "outliers" for this classifier. Accordingly the accuracy rate on negative class could be calculated.

The overall performance is measured upon the accuracy of both positive and negative classes. In our experiment, we employed geometric means.

15.3.3 Optimization Stage

Parameter selection based on design of experiments(DOE) basically is to start with a very coarse grid covering the whole search space and iteratively refine both the grid resolution and search boundaries, keeping the number of samples at each iteration roughly constant [13].

A combination of three-level experiment design(or 3^k factorial design, which means that k factors are considered, each at 3 levels) with the two-level experiment design constitutes the sampling pattern in our experiment design search method. In a two parameter space, if each parameter is considered as one factor, this approach will produce thirteen solutions($3^2 + 2^2 = 13$). Please note that when we select the points, we first discretize each parameter space by dividing it into three or two equal-length sections. In this chapter, the middle point of each section is chosen as the representative for each level.

In each search iteration, the system evaluates the classifier performance at the sampled points, i.e., with the selected parameter settings. The one with the best performance will be chosen and the search space is refined around it. Currently in our experiment, we half the parameter range after each iteration. If the new search space could center around the best point without going outside the original boundary, that is the best choice. Otherwise, the new search range will start from or end to the closest original bound and then extend to the other half section. This process is repeated as many times desired or once the points in the refined search space could not improve the previous performance any more.

15.4 Experimental Results

15.4.1 Data Set

Table 15.1: Accuracy Comparison of Feature Selection Fish-Net, Naive Bayes MultiNomial and SVM

Dataset	FS FishNet			NB			SVM		
	P	N	G	P	N	G	P	N	G
earn	0.874	0.99	0.93	0.93	0.992	0.96	0.977	0.994	0.985
acq	0.866	0.968	0.916	0.757	0.997	0.869	0.922	0.992	0.956
money-fx	0.883	0.956	0.919	0.419	0.994	0.645	0.698	0.99	0.831
grain	0.899	0.947	0.922	0.57	0.997	0.754	0.879	0.999	0.937
crude	0.847	0.935	0.89	0.635	0.996	0.795	0.836	0.993	0.911
trade	0.863	0.898	0.88	0.331	1	0.575	0.735	0.994	0.855
interest	0.756	0.974	0.858	0.008	0.999	0.089	0.573	0.998	0.756
ship	0.708	0.992	0.838	0.382	0.998	0.617	0.629	0.998	0.792
wheat	0.873	0.967	0.919	0.085	1	0.292	0.789	0.998	0.887
corn	0.679	0.972	0.812	0.089	1	0.298	0.839	0.999	0.916
Average	*0.825*	0.96	*0.888*	0.421	*0.997*	0.589	0.788	0.996	0.883

Reuters-21578 "ModApte" Split contains 9603 documents in the training set and 3299 documents in the test set. We choose 10 most frequent topic categories in the experiments. Table 15.2 lists for each topic, the number of positive documents in the training set(#+Tr), the number of positive documents in the test set(#+T). The total number of terms extracted is 6362.

The geometric mean $g = \sqrt{acc_P * acc_N}$, where acc_P indicates the accuracy on the positive instances(TP/(TP + FN)) and acc_N is the accuracy on the negative instances(TN/(TN + FP)), is used more popular in evaluating classifiers on highly imbalanced datasets. It is high when both acc_P and acc_N are high and when the difference between acc_P and acc_N is small. By optimizing this measurement, it is ensured that the accuracy on each of the class is maximized while keeping them balanced.

15.4.2 Results on Inexact Field Learning

Classification accuracy of the Naive Bayes Multinomial(NB), Support Vector Machine(SVM) and Feature Selection FishNet(FS Fishnet) is reported in Table 15.1. We list the results in terms of three different performance measurements: accuracy on positive and negative minority class(P and N), geometric mean(G). The last row of Table 15.1 gives the average value of each classifier with regard to every measurement.

Table 15.2: Reuters-21578 ModApte Dataset Description

Data set	# +Tr	# +T
earn	2866	1083
acq	1632	715
money-fx	475	151
grain	371	127
crude	330	160
trade	369	117
interest	347	131
ship	197	89
wheat	212	71
corn	181	56

Table 15.3: Comparison With Standard One-class Classifiers

Dataset	OC	OS	NN	NB	NN2	P	P-OC	P-S
Money	0.514	0.563	*0.642*	0.493	0.468	0.484	0.550	0.585
Grain	0.585	0.523	0.473	0.382	0.333	0.402	*0.742*	0.48
Crude	0.544	0.474	0.534	0.457	0.392	0.398	*0.715*	0.7
Trade	0.597	0.423	0.569	0.483	0.441	0.557	0.634	*0.709*
Interest	0.485	0.465	0.487	0.394	0.295	0.454	*0.609*	0.592
Ship	*0.539*	0.402	0.361	0.288	0.389	0.370	0.427	0.445
Wheat	0.474	0.389	0.404	0.288	0.566	0.262	*0.647*	0.545
Corn	0.298	0.356	0.324	0.254	0.168	0.230	0.542	*0.571*
Average	0.505	0.449	0.474	0.380	0.380	0.395	*0.608*	0.578

In general, accuracy of all three learning algorithms on majority class is very high, reaching more than 95% in most cases. But on minorities, it hardly could achieve even 90%. For Naive Bayes MultiNomial, the recall on positive class decreases dramatically along with the reduced number of positive instances. On the majority class, SVM achieves nearly 100% accuracy rate for each topic and accuracy on minority instances are much better than Naive Bayes. However, it has the same problem as NB, especially on the last five topics, that the performance has an obvious drop down with the decreasing number of positive examples. Feature Selection Fish-net maintained much more balanced accuracy rates in most cases. With the increasing of imbalance ratio, it keeps a relatively constant accuracy result on minority class without loss of majority class performance. The average value shows that the FS Fishnet obtains the highest recall rate on positive class and geometric mean.

15.4.3 Results on One-class Classifiers

Table 15.3 shows the comparison results of the Parameter Optimized One-Class SVM(P-OC) and Parameter Optimized SVDD(P-S) with one-class SVM(OC), Outlier-SVM(OS), Neural Networks(NN), Naive Bayes(NB), Nearest Neighbour(NN2), Prototype Algorithm(P). The evaluation measurement is F_1 measure. The algorithms we compared with are under these settings: the standard One-class SVM(RBF kernel, binary document representation), Outlier-SVM(Linear kernel, binary document representation), Neural Networks, one-class Naive Bayes, one-class Nearest Neighbour(Hadamard document representation) and Prototype Algorithm(tf-idf document representation). The listed F_1 results are the best among various document representations and parameter settings [10].

In most cases, the parameter optimized approaches, either one-class SVM or SVDD, achieve much better results than the stand-alone one-class classifiers. The last row of Table 15.3 presents the average F_1 accuracy for each learning method. The parameter optimized one-class SVM beats all the other schemes. The optimized SVDD is slightly worse. The standard one-class SVM with the default settings performs the best compared with the other one-class learning approaches. However, by further optimizing its parameters, the average accuracy is increased about 10%. This further indicates the significance of parameter selection.

15.5 Conclusion

Results of unbalanced text classification tend to be unreliable as the skewed data affects the reliability of text classifiers with performance bias. In this chapter, we have considered two different types of performance bias in unbalanced text classification in order to improve the reliability. Firstly, it is the performance bias on majority class which conventional classifiers tend to have on unevenly distributed data set. In addition, we argued that along with instance imbalance, feature imbalance is inevitable, especially on high-dimensional data set. We regard this as the dual imbalance problem and a novel inexact field learning algorithm is presented as a solution. Secondly, when one-class classification strategy is applied to unbalanced data, the performance bias tends to turn towards minorities. This is due to that majority instances are discarded during one-class classification procedure. We propose a one-class classification framework to avoid the overfitting problem. Our approaches improve the reliability of discovered classification rules on imbalance learning. Experimental results show that our proposed approaches outperform the standard methodologies.

References

1. Dai, H., Ciesielski, V.: Learning of inexact rules by the fish-net algorithm from low quality data. In: Proceedings of the Eighth Australian Joint Artificial Intelligence Conference, pp. 108–115, (1994)
2. Dai, H.: A study on reliability in graph mining. In: Proceedings of IEEE ICDM workshops 2006, pp. 775–779, (2006)
3. Dai, H.: A case study on classification reliability. In: Proceedings of IEEE ICDM workshops 2006, pp. 69–73, (2008)
4. David, R. P. D., Tax, M.J.: Support vector domain description. Pattern Recognition Letters, 20, pp. 1191–1199, (1999)
5. Forman, F., A pitfall and solution in multi-class feature selection for text classification. In: Proceedings of the 21st International Conference on Machine Learning, (2004).
6. Han, J., Kamber, M.: Data Mining: Concepts and Techniques. Second Edition, Elsevier, (2006)
7. Japkowicz, N.: Learning from imbalanced data sets: a comparison of various strategies. In Proceedings of the AAAI Workshop on Learning from Imbalanced Data Sets, pp. 10–15, (2000)
8. Lunts, A., Brailovskiy, V.: Evaluation of attributes obtained in statistical decision rules. Engineering Cybernetics, pp. 98–109, (1967)
9. Liu, Y., Loh, H. T., Sun, A.: Imbalanced text classification: A term weight approach. Expert Systems with Applications, 36, pp. 690–701, (2009)
10. Manevitz, L. M., Yousef M.: One-class svms for document classification. Journal of Machine Learning Research, 2, pp. 139–154, (2001)
11. Raskutti, B., Kowalczyk, A.: Extreme re-balancing for svms: a case study. SIGKDD Explorations, 6, pp. 60–69, (2004)
12. Scholkopt, B., Platt, J. C., Shawe-Taylor, J., Smola, A. J., Williamson, R. C.: Estimating the support of a high-dimensional distribution. Neural Computation, 13, pp. 1443–1471, (2001)
13. Staelin, C.: Parameter selection for support vector machines. Technical Report HPL-2002-354R1, Hewlett-Packard Company, 2003.

Chapter 16
Formal Representation and Verification of Ontology Using State Controlled Coloured Petri Nets

James N.K.Liu, Ke Wang, Yu-Lin He, and Xi-Zhao Wang

Abstract Ontologies are widely used in many areas. Different automatic or semi-automatic extraction techniques have been proposed for building domain ontology in recent years. The correctness of the extracted ontology, however, has often been ignored or not verified formally. With increasingly complex and sophisticated real-world domains, the issue of correctness and verification of ontology is becoming more important. This chapter proposes a formal technique for ontology representation and its verification, based on State Controlled Coloured Petri Net (SCCPN), which is a high level net combining Coloured Petri Net and State Controlled Petri Net. It provides the capability of detection and identification of potential anomalies in ontology. We first describe the formal representation of ontology by SCCPN. The definition of SCCPN for modeling ontologies and the mapping between them are presented in detail. Moreover, the ontology inference in SCCPN is also formulated with specified inference mechanisms. After modeling ontology by SCCPN, the formal verification of potential anomalies (including redundancy, circularity and contradiction) is discussed. It is based on the reachable markings generated by transition firings in the Petri nets.

James N.K.Liu
Department of Computing, The Hong Kong Polytechnic University, Hong Kong, China
e-mail: csnkliu@comp.polyu.edu.hk

Ke Wang
School of Management, Shanghai University, Shanghai, China
e-mail: mr.wangkk@gmail.com

Yu-Lin He
College of Mathematics and Computer Science, Hebei University, Baoding, China
e-mail: fuchengrenyulin@126.com

Xi-Zhao Wang
College of Mathematics and Computer Science, Hebei University, Baoding, China
e-mail: xizhaowang@ieee.org

16.1 Introduction

An ontology is a means of representing semantic knowledge [9], which can facilitate capture and construction of domain knowledge and enable representation of skeletal knowledge to facilitate integration of knowledge bases irrespective of the heterogeneity of knowledge source [25]. It further enables advanced functionality in knowledge systems and forms the knowledge base for future innovations. In general, ontology can be a formal representation of concepts and their interrelationships [8]. It can take the simple form of a taxonomy (i.e. knowledge encoded in some hierarchical structure) or a vocabulary with standardized machine interpretable terminology supplemented with natural language definitions, and also can be used to describe a logical domain theory with very expressive, complex, and meaningful information [20]. As such, ontologies are useful in many areas, such as knowledge management, natural language processing, information retrieval, and especially the semantic web which is increasingly popular, but then the engineering of knowledge construct using relation tagging of concepts is very time consuming and expensive involving a large amount of human resources. This is despite the fact that several tools including Ontolingua [3], OilEd [1], Protg [21], and OntoEdit [27] are developed for the construction and management of ontologies. Recently, different automatic or semi-automatic extraction techniques have been proposed and implemented in several contexts for building domain ontology (e.g. [17, 2, 13]).

Along with the considerable progress has been made in developing extraction techniques, an essential and vital problem that how to evaluate, or verify and validate, the extracted ontologies emerges. It is becoming even more important, with increasingly complex and sophisticated real-world domains. However, no comprehensive and global approach to this problem has been proposed to date [4]. A deep core of preliminary ideas and guidelines for this issue is still missing [6], despite the fact that growing interest has been paid on it (e.g. [26, 29]) and some important developments have been obtained in recent years.

In literature, the term ontology evaluation has been used in a much broader way, and usually subsumes ontology verification and ontology validation. In general, it refers to a judgment of the ontology with respect to a set of predefined criteria, standards, requirements, etc. To evaluate a given ontology, the criteria may include consistency, completeness, conciseness, expandability, sensitiveness, etc [6]. In the area of expert system, there is a general consensus that validation refers to the process of building the right system, while verification refers to the process of building the system right [18]. From this perspective, it is relatively easy and reasonable to get that ontology verification referring to the process of building the ontology right (in other words, substantiating that the ontology correctly implements its specifications). The goal of ontology verification is to ensure the consistency and completeness of the ontology and to guarantee that the building of the ontology proceeds in a way that meets the requirements. In this chapter, the process of verification focuses on the checking of potential anomalies in ontology that may cause inconsistency and incompleteness.

To allow for the automation of ontology verification, i.e. automatic detection of anomalies in ontology, a more formal approach for ontology representation and verification is necessary. Fortunately, high level Petri nets, with impressive modeling and analysis power, provide us a promising way for this purpose. Petri nets, introduced by Petri [19], are known to be well-suited for modeling and analysis of parallel and asynchronous activity operating systems. High level Petri nets, which have extensively been used for many AI applications, particularly for modeling expert systems (e.g. [31, 23, 22]), are extended from the basic models of Petri nets with more compact representations and more powerful modeling capabilities, such as Coloured Petri nets [11]. The high level Petri net theory not only providing a formal representation of the knowledge structure and explicit control mechanism with coloured token for the knowledge inference, but also offers various means of checking the correctness, consistency and completeness of the knowledge base. Via mapping ontologies onto Petri nets, it is to be anticipated that further analysis on ontologies can be made by adopting high level net approaches, especially for verification, which has not been well addressed.

The main contribution of this chapter focuses on providing a the formal description technique for ontology representation and verification using a high level net approach. Firstly, ontologies are modeled by State Controlled Coloured Petri Net (SCCPN), which is a high level net combining Coloured Petri Net and State Controlled Petri Net. The concepts and their associated relationships in ontologies are represented by the structure of SCCPN. The high order coloured tokens in SCCPN provide richer modeling capability and differentiate the dynamic knowledge inference from the state of different concepts and transitions. After mapping ontology onto SCCPN, formal verification, which provides the capability of detection and identification of potential anomalies in ontology, is proposed. It is based on the reachable markings generated by transition firings in the Petri nets.

The rest of this chapter is organized as follows. Section 2 describes the approach for modeling ontology by SCCPN. The definition of SCCPN for modeling ontologies and the mapping between them are presented in detail. Next, Section 3 discusses the ontology inference in SCCPN. The inference is formulated with specified inference mechanisms. The formal verification of potential anomalies (including redundancy, circularity and contradiction) is discussed in Section 4. The analysis of the performance of the proposed SCCPN approach is presented in Section 5. Finally, Section 6 concludes this chapter with a summary and some discussions on future work.

16.2 Modeling Ontology by SCCPN

16.2.1 Formal Formulation of Ontology

Although ontologies have been widely used for knowledge sharing in various areas by diverse communities, there is no common formal definition of ontology. However, most approaches and ontology languages share the same core components, including [7]:

1. Classes (concepts): sets of individuals in a domain, are the main entities of an ontology. Classes in the ontology are usually organized in taxonomies through which inheritance mechanisms can be applied.
2. Individuals (instances): particular individuals (or the basic objects) in a domain, represent the instances of classes.
3. Relations: ways in which classes and individuals can be related to one another, are formally defined as subsets of the product of classes and individuals in the domain. Various kinds of relations can be defined in an ontology, among which the essential relations shared by most ontologies including:

   a. Specialization (subsumption): also called Is-A relation, is a reflexive, transitive, and anti-symmetric (a partial order) relation on the classes.
   b. Exclusion (disjointness): is a symmetric and irreflexive relation on the classes. The intersection of two classes with the relation of exclusion is empty.
   c. Instantiation (membership): is an anti-symmetric relation between class and individual, and represents the creation of a real individual or instance as a member of a class.

For the purpose of mapping ontology onto a Petri net, we adopt a definition of ontology that includes the core components as follows.

Definition 16.1. An ontology is a tuple $O := (C, I, R, \leq, \perp, \in)$, where
   C is a finite set of classes;
   I is a finite set of individuals;
   R is a finite set of relations;
   $\leq$ is a relation on $C \times C$ called specialization;
   $\perp$ is a relation on $C \times C$ called exclusion;
   $\in$ is a relation on $C \times I$ called instantiation.

16.2.2 SCCPN Notations and Interpretations

A State Controlled Coloured Petri Net, formerly proposed for the formal description and verification of hybrid rule/frame based expert systems [24], is a combination of Coloured Petri Net proposed by Jensen [11] and State Controlled Petri Net (SCPN) proposed by Liu and Dillon [15, 14, 12]. While modeling ontologies, the mapping

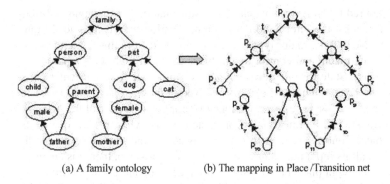

(a) A family ontology   (b) The mapping in Place /Transition net

Fig. 16.1: An ontology graph and its mapping in a Place/Transition net

between ontology and SCCPN is shown in Table 1. The components of ontology are represented separately in the SCCPN as follows.

Table 16.1: Mapping between ontology and SCCPN

Ontology	SCCPN
Classes	Class Places
Class	Colour Sets
Individuals	Instance Tokens
Specialization	Transitions
Exclusion	Transitions
Instantiation	Creation of Instance Token in Class Place
Further Relations	Transitions
Predicates	Predicate Places
Predicate States	State Tokens

For a concise ontology graph, classes are transformed as places, and their hierarchical relations are represented by transitions which are linked to the corresponding places. Individuals of a class are indicated by tokens in a place. Accordingly, the instantiation of a particular class is represented by creating an instance token in the corresponding place. With these mappings, a concise ontology graph can be easily transformed into a Place/Transition net, with the most primitive form of Petri net. An illustrative example is shown in Fig. 1. Fig. 1(a) represents a family ontology. All its classes and their hierarchical relations are mapped onto a Place/Transition net as shown in Fig. 1(b). In this net, the places, denoted by $p_i(1 \leq i \leq 11)$, represent the corresponding classes in the ontology graph. The transitions, denoted by $t_j(1 \leq j \leq 10)$, represent the hierarchical relations between two classes.

However, to represent more information contained in an ontology and enhance the constructed net's capability of inference, a more sophisticated net, i.e. the SCCPN, should be designed. Firstly, colour sets are employed to denote the class attributes. A coloured token records its class type information. To distinguish different kinds of relations, the information concerning relation type is also added into the colour sets. Next, three major types of tokens are defined in the net, namely instance token, state token, and control token. Instance token represents a particular instance of a class. State token records the state of inference for a particular class (i.e., via which type of relation the class is involved in the inference), and the state of predicates (i.e., true or false). Control token is employed to control the firing or executing of transitions. A transition becomes active, just when at least one of its input places has a control token. If a transition is active and the transition condition is met (i.e., all its input places have the correct state tokens), then it is enabled. Furthermore, each input place of a transition has a self-loop arc for maintaining the state of class or predicate while inferring, i.e., the state of input places will not be changed by the execution of their associated transition. Finally, to enable inverse inference along with the hierarchical relations in the transformed net, an additional relation inverse to specialization, i.e. generalization relation, is added into the Petri net. Namely, the specialization (Is-A) relation in an ontology is mapped onto two transitions linking the corresponding places with opposite directions, one of which represents the relation from subclass to its superclass, and the other from superclass to subclass.

It should be noted that in some ontology languages, such as OWL, the user defined properties should be distinguished into two cases while mapping them onto the SCCPN. If it describes a relation between two or among more classes, it is regarded as a further relation (it means not a standard relation shared for all approaches and tools, such as specialization and exclusion), and is to be mapped onto the SCCPN by a transition linking with the corresponding places. If it asserts a fact or property that a class holds, then it would be treated as a predicate, and is to be mapped onto the SCCPN by a place, which is linked by a transition to the class that holds this property.

The formal definition of SCCPN and the mechanism for inference will be formulated in the following sections. Here an illustrative example, with enhanced structure comparing to the example in Fig. 1, is shown in Fig. 2. Fig. 2(a) represents a segment of the family ontology, and its mapping in SCCPN is shown in Fig. 2(b). To distinguish different type of places and transitions, the notations of place and transition are both extended to 2-dimensional variables. $p_{ci}(1 \leq i \leq 4)$ denotes the class place, and it represents the class in the ontology, where p_{c1}, p_{c2}, p_{c3}, p_{c4} are the class of "mother", "parent", "female", and "male" respectively. $p_{pj}(j = 1)$ denotes the predicate place. $t_{k\bullet}(1 \leq k \leq 5)$ represents different kind of relations. $t_{1\bullet}$ is the relation of specialization from subclass to superclass, and $t_{2\bullet}$ is its inverse. The information in the rectangles of Fig. 2(a) are some properties adhered to the corresponding classes. "⊥male" means an exclusion relation of the class "female" with "male". It is represented by the transitions between p_{c3} and p_{c4}. Since exclusion is a symmetric relation, it is mapped onto two transitions with opposite directions (see t_{31} and t_{32}). "Predicate: lacks Y chromosome" is a fact that the class "female" holds. It is modeled by a predicate place (i.e. p_{p1}) linking to the corresponding class. t_{41} denotes the relation between the predicate and the class

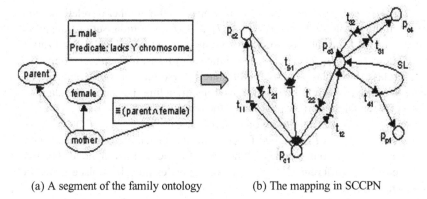

(a) A segment of the family ontology   (b) The mapping in SCCPN

Fig. 16.2: An ontology and its mapping in SCCPN

who holds it. "($\equiv$parent$\wedge$female)" formulates a necessary and sufficient relation between the classes "mother" and (parent$\wedge$female), i.e. mother$\Rightarrow$parent$\wedge$female, and parent$\wedge$female$\Rightarrow$mother. The former is represented by t_{11} and t_{12}, and the latter, a sufficient relation from (parent$\wedge$female) to "mother", is modeled by the transition t_{51}. In addition, the SL in Fig. 2(b) is a self-loop arc of the place p_{c3}. It maintains the state of p_{c3} while executing t_{41}. Each input place of a transition has a self-loop arc as SL shows, whereas, for the simplicity of representation, other self-loop arcs are not displayed in the figure.

16.2.3 Formal Definition of SCCPN

The formal definition of SCCPN is formulated as follows. It is adopted and extended from the SCCPN for modeling hybrid rule/frame based expert systems [24], the SCPN [15, 16] and Colored Petri Nets [30, 28] for representing knowledge (rule) base. It is also modified for the purpose of application in the area of ontology engineering. Since the rich information has been contained in ontologies and their many mechanisms for knowledge inference, the SCCPN model for ontology representation and inference is more complex than the above models for rule based or rule/frame based systems.

Definition 16.2. The SCCPN that models an ontology is a 9-tuple $O := (\Sigma, P, T, A, N, C, G, E, I)$, where

$\Sigma = \{w_1, w_2, \cdots, w_i\}$ is a finite set of non-empty types, called colour set;

$P = \{P_c, P_p\}$ is a finite set of places: $P_c = \{p_{c1}, p_{c2}, \cdots, p_{cj}\}$, a finite set of places that model the classes in the ontology, called class places, $j \geq 1$; $P_p = \{p_{p1}, p_{p2}, \cdots, p_{pk}\}$, a finite set of places that model the predicates asserted in the ontology, called predicate places, $k \geq 0$; $P_c \cap P_p = \emptyset$;

$T = \{T_1, T_2, \cdots, T_l\}$ is a finite set of transitions, l is the number of relation types contained in the ontology, $l \geq 2$: $T_1 = \{t_{11}, T_{12}, \cdots, T_{1m}\}$, a finite set of transitions that are connected from subclass to superclass, model the hierarchical specialization (Is-A) relation; $T_2 = \{t_{21}, T_{22}, \cdots, T_{2m}\}$, a finite set of transitions that are connected from superclass to subclass, i.e., $t_{1\bullet}$ and $t_{2\bullet}$ are inverse relations with opposite directions; Similarly, T_3 is a finite set of transitions modeling the exclusion relations, and $T_4, \cdots, T_l$ model the further relations in the ontology; $T_n \cap T_o = \emptyset$;

$A = \{a_1, a_2, \cdots, a_q\}$ is a finite set of arcs, $q \geq 1$, $P \cap T = P \cap A = T \cap A = \emptyset$;

$N : A \rightarrow P \times T \cup T \times P$ is a node function, it maps each arc onto a pair where the first element is the source node and the second is the destination node. The two nodes have to be of different kinds (i.e. one of the nodes must be a place while the other is a transition);

$C : P \rightarrow \Sigma$ is a colour function, it maps each place onto a colour set;

$G : T \rightarrow booleanvalue$ is a guard function, it is defined from T into expressions such that: $\forall t \in T, [Type(G(t)) = boolean\, value \wedge Type(Var(G(t))) \subseteq \Sigma]$;

$E : A \rightarrow expression$ is an arc expression function, it is defined from A into expressions such that: $\forall a \in A, [Type(E(a)) = C(p(a))_{MS} \wedge Type(Var(G(t))) \subseteq \Sigma]$;

$I : P \rightarrow expression$ is an initialization function, it is defined from P into closed expressions such that:$\forall p \in P, [Type(I(p)) = C(p)_{MS}]$.

Definition 16.3. The node functions $N : A \rightarrow P \times T \cup T \times P$ can be further classified into the following 4 different types:

$B_c : T \rightarrow P$ is an input control function, a mapping from transitions to the bags of places;

$O_c : T \rightarrow P$ is an output control function, a mapping from transitions to the bags of places;

$B_s : T \rightarrow P$ is an input state function, a mapping from transitions to the bags of places;

$O_s : T \rightarrow P$ is an output state function, a mapping from transitions to the bags of places.

And for each transition $t_i \in T$ in the SCCPN, $B_s(t_i) \cap O_s(t_i) \neq \emptyset$, $B_c(t_i) \cap O_c(t_i) = \emptyset$, such that: $p_j \in B_s(t_i) \Rightarrow p_j \in O_s(t_i)$, $p_j \in B_c(t_i) \Rightarrow p_j \notin O_c(t_i)$.

It should be noted that, for the simplicity of representation, the instance tokens are indicated by a colour defined in the colour set, i.e., the instance token is treated as a special case, with a particular colour, of the state tokens. It is reasonable since it also can be seen as indicating the instantiation relation, as discussed in the following section. Therefore, in the definition of node function, only input/output control and state function are represented. Similarly, in the following discussion of markings, only control marking and state marking are considered, and the instance tokens are represented in the state marking.

16.3 Ontology Inference in SCCPN

16.3.1 Markings for Representation of Inference

The states of the SCCPN can be formally represented by markings. The formally analysis of ontology inference is based on the reachable markings generated by transition firings in the net. In SCCPN, a marking M is composed of M_s that depicts the marking for the state tokens and M_c that depicts the marking for the control tokens. Formally, they are defined as follows.

Definition 16.4. A marking M of SCCPN is a function that $M = (M_s, M_c)$, where

M_s depicts the marking for the state places, i.e. the distribution of state tokens in the places. It is represented with the form of a space vector spanned by the number of places in the net. Each element M_{sp} (the subscript $p \in P$ indicates a particular place) is a multi-set over the colour set attached to the place, denoting the state marking of a corresponding place.

M_c depicts the marking for the control places, i.e. the distribution of control tokens in the places. It is a space vector spanned by the number of places in the net, mapping from places to non-negative integers, which indicates the amount of control tokens contained in the places.

The multi-set (or bag) is employed to allow multiple appearances of the tokens with identical colours. Unlike single-set that adding an element a into a set $\{a, b\}$ we still have the set $\{a, b\}$, for the multi-set, if adding the element a into a multi-set $\{a, b\}$ we get the multi-set $\{a, a, b\}$, which now has two appearances of the element a. The multi-set can be described by a formal sum of the elements with a corresponding coefficient saying how many times a typical element appears. Taking the multi-set $\{a, a, b\}$ for instance, it also can be described as $2'a + 1'b$.

Definition 16.5. A transition t_i is minimally active in a marking M, if $M_{ci} = 1$ for a place $p_{ci} \in B_c(t_i)$. In other words, a transition becomes minimally active, just when one of its input places has a control token.

Definition 16.6. A transition t_i is minimally enabled in a marking M, if t_i is minimally active and M_s satisfies such that $G(t_i)$ becomes true. In other words, if a transition is minimally active and the transition condition is met, then it is minimally enabled.

When a transition is enabled, it can be executed or fired. With the executing of a transition, the marking M changes to another marking M'. If M' is obtained from M by the execution of transition t_i, it is said that M' is directly reachable from M, denoted as $M[t_i > M'$.

Definition 16.7. A marking M^n is said to be reachable from a marking M^0 if and only if (iff) there exists a finite sequence of firings that transform M^0 to M^n, i.e. a sequence having M^0 as initial marking and M^n as end marking such that $M^0[t_1 >$

$M^1[t_2 > M^2 \cdots M^{n-1}[t_n > M^n$, where n is a Natural Number, denotes the length of the sequence. Denoting $\sigma = (t_1, t_2, \cdots, t_n)$, it is said that M^n is reachable from M^0 by σ, and being denoted as $M^n = \delta(M^0, \sigma)$. The set of markings which are reachable from M^0 is denoted by $[M^0 >$.

The guard functions and update of markings, i.e. the inference mechanisms, will be specified in the following sections.

16.3.2 Inference Mechanisms for Different Relation Types

Since different types of relations are contained in ontologies, and all are modeled by transitions linking to corresponding components in the SCCPN, it has to specify the inference mechanisms for different relation types by formulating the guard functions and arc expression functions.

For the simplicity of representation, we only consider one colour set, denoted by , which are used to indicate different relation types. Each output token created by a transition will be coloured with corresponding colour. It records that this token is created by which type of relation. As defined above, T_1 models the specialization (Is-A) relation, T_2 is the inverse relation of T_1 , T_3 models the exclusion relation, and $T_4, \cdots, T_l$ model the further relations, respectively. Correspondingly, $CR = 1, 2, 3, \cdots, l$ respectively indicates the specialization relation, generalization relation, exclusion relation, and other further relations. For the convenience of the following description, let $CR = 0$ denote an instance token. It also can be seen as indicating the instantiation relation. For the different relation type, its inference mechanism is specified as follows.

1. Specialization (Is-A) relation

$$G(t_{1\bullet}) = \begin{cases} True \ if\, CR(B_s(t_{1\bullet})) = 0\, or\, 1 \\ False \ if\, CR(B_s(t_{1\bullet})) \neq 0\, or\, 1 \end{cases}, \text{ where } CR(B_s(t_{1\bullet})) = 0\, or\, 1 \text{ denotes}$$

that the state token in the place $B_s(t_{1\bullet})$ has a colour $CR = 0\, or\, 1$. In other words, the transitions in T_1 can be enabled only if the colour CR of the token in its input place is 0 or 1.

$E : CR(O_s(t_{1\bullet}) - B_s(t_{1\bullet})) = 1$. It denotes that the new token created in the output place (except the input place), by executing the transitions in T_1, has the colour $CR = 1$. For the implication of inference, the colour $CR = 1$ can be explained as "true". For example, the class "parent" can be inferred by the class "mother" via the Is-A relation. The colour $CR = 1$ indicates this inference with the meaning "a mother definitely is a parent".

2. Generalization relation

$$G(t_{2\bullet}) = \begin{cases} True \ if\, CR(B_s(t_{2\bullet})) = 0\, or\, 2 \\ False \ if\, CR(B_s(t_{2\bullet})) \neq 0\, or\, 2 \end{cases}, E : CR(O_s(t_{2\bullet}) - B_s(t_{2\bullet})) = 2. \text{ Simi-}$$

larly, these two functions imply that the transitions in T_2 can be enabled only if the colour CR of the state token in its input place is 0 or 2, and the new token created in the output place (except the input place) has the colour $CR = 2$. For the implication of inference, the colour $CR = 2$ can be explained as "may be". For example, the class "mother" and "father" both can be inferred by the class "parent" via the generalization relation. The colour $CR = 2$ indicates this inference with the meaning "a parent may be a mother, or may be a father".

3. Exclusion relation

$$G(t_{3\bullet}) = \begin{cases} True & if\, CR(B_s(t_{3\bullet})) = 0\, or\, 1 \\ False & if\, CR(B_s(t_{3\bullet})) \neq 0\, or\, 1 \end{cases}, E : CR(O_s(t_{3\bullet}) - B_s(t_{3\bullet})) = 3.\text{ For the}$$

implication of inference, the colour $CR = 3$ can be explained as "false". For example, the class "male" can be inferred by the class "female" via the exclusion relation. The colour $CR = 3$ indicates this inference with the meaning "a female definitely is not a male". Moreover, the guard functions and colour functions for the transitions modeling further relations in ontology can be similarly specified.

16.3.3 An Illustrative Example

An illustrative example of ontology inference is shown in Fig. 3. The SCCPN in Fig. 3 is identical with Fig. 2(b), which models the segment of a family ontology as shown in Fig. 2(a). For the simplicity of representation, all self-loop arcs are not displayed in the figure.

Fig. 3(a) shows the initial state of inference, denoted by the marking M^0, in which the place p_{c1} contains a control token and an instance token $(CR = 0)$. With the control token presenting in the input place, t_{11} and t_{12} are both active. As defined above, the presence of this instance token makes the guard functions of transitions t_{11} and t_{12} become true, thus t_{11} and t_{12} are enabled.

By executing t_{11} in Fig. 3(a), a new state of the net, denoted by the marking M^1, can be obtained as shown in Fig. 3(b). A new state token with colour $CR = 1$ and a control token are created in the output place p_{c2}. Meanwhile, the control token in the input place is destroyed, and the instance token is returned to the input place via the self-loop arc. The inference result implies that an instance of the class "mother" is also a "parent". And then the state of SCCPN shown in Fig. 3(b) cannot be further inferred, since no transition is enabled.

If executing the transition t_{12} in Fig. 3(a), a new result of inference, denoted by the marking M^2, can also be obtained as shown in Fig. 3(c). Similarly, the result implies that an instance of the class "mother" is also a "female". With the presence of a state token with colour $CR = 1$ and a control token in the place p_{c3}, transitions t_{31} and t_{41} are both enabled. Thus Fig. 3(c) can be further inferred.

Via executing t_{31} and t_{41} in Fig. 3(c) separately, the results as shown in Fig. 3(d) (with marking M^3) and Fig. 3(e) (with marking M^4) are obtained correspondingly, and both of them cannot be inferred further. The result in Fig. 3(d) implies that an instance of the class "mother" cannot be a "male". And Fig. 3(e) means that the instance of the class "mother" lacks Y chromosome, as represented by the predicate place p_{p1}.

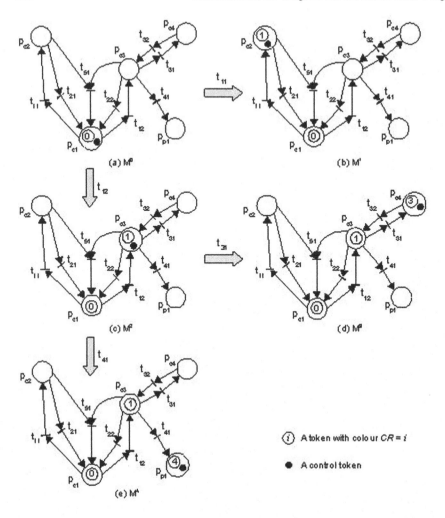

Fig. 16.3: An illustrative example of ontology inference

The reachable markings, representing the inference of the given example in Fig. 3, are shown in Fig. 4. For the simplicity of display, the markings are presented in the form of matrix, in which the first column denotes the marking of coloured state tokens (i.e. M_s) and the second column denotes the marking of control tokens (i.e. M_c). The elements in the column for representing M_s are multi-sets over the colour set, indicating the appearances of state tokens in a place; whereas those in the column for M_c are non-negative integers, indicating the number of control tokens contained in a place.

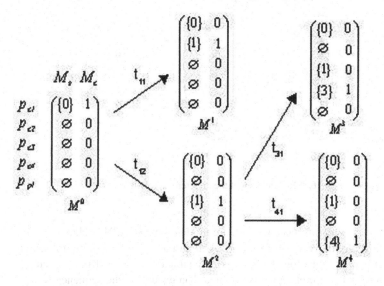

Fig. 16.4: The sequence of markings reachable from M^0

16.4 Potential Anomalies in Ontology and Formal Verification

Some possible errors can be made by ontologists when building taxonomic knowledge in an ontology, as presented in [6]. The ontologies built by automatic or semi-automatic extraction techniques may be also not free from errors and anomalies. In the discussion of this chapter, we focus on the following potential anomalies.

In the following discussion concerning anomalies detection and verification, for simplicity and to reduce the complexity of computing, the generalization relation is omitted in the SCCPN, since it is a reverse of the specialization relation being employed to enhance the inference capability of ontology, and the omission doesn't affect the ontology verification.

16.4.1 Redundancy

16.4.1.1 Redundancy of the hierarchical relations

It occurs between classes when there is more than one explicit definition of the hierarchical (Specialization) relations between them. An example and its mapping in SCCPN are shown in Fig. 5. As shown in Fig. 5(a), "mother" is defined as a subclass of "parent", and "parent" is a subclass of "person". It implies that "mother" is also a subclass of "person", thus, redundancy occurs while adding an explicit definition of Is-A relation between "mother" and "person".

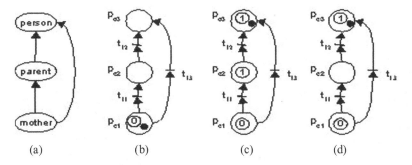

Fig. 16.5: Redundancy of the hierarchical relations

The example and its inference process are modeled by SCCPN as shown in Fig. 5(b), (c), and (d). Initially, as an instance token and a control token are presented in the place p_{c1}, both transitions t_{11} and t_{13} are enabled (see Fig. 5(b)). If executing t_{11}, transition t_{12} will be consequently enabled. Via executing the sequence t_{11}, t_{12}, a state token with colour $CR = 1$ is created in the place p_{c3}, and the state of the net after executing the sequence is shown in Fig. 5(c). Whereas, if executing t_{13}, a state token with colour $CR = 1$ will also be created in the place p_{c3}, as shown in Fig. 5(d). Comparing Fig. 5(c) and (d), it implies that the same result of inference can be obtained via different processes.

16.4.1.2 Identical properties asserted by classes with inheritance relation

For two classes with specialization relation, if the superclass has some properties, they are also held by the subclass due to the inheritance. Thus, it is redundant to define identical properties for both two classes, which have the inheritance relation (i.e. inherit via the specialization relation).

An example of this case and its mapping in SCCPN are shown in Fig. 6. Since the predicates asserted by "mother" and "female" are identical (see Fig. 6(a)), they are represented by the same predicate place p_{p1} in SCCPN. Similar with the example in Fig. 5, the same state of the place p_{p1} (i.e. contains a state token with colour $CR = 4$) can be inferred via different paths (i.e. sequence t_{11}, t_{41} as shown in Fig. 6(c), and t_{42} as shown in Fig. 6(d)) from the initial state (see Fig. 6(b)).

These two cases of redundancy can be detected by examining the alternative paths and markings generated from the initial marking. The formal verification is presented as follows.

Proposition 16.1. *For a given initial marking M^0, that minimally enables a nontrivial transition sequence σ_i, iff the ontology has redundancy as defined above, then $\exists \sigma_j, \exists p$ ($p \in P$, indicates a particular place), such that these sequences have the following properties:*

$(1)\, \sigma_i \cap \sigma_j = \emptyset;$

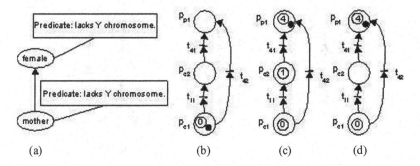

Fig. 16.6: Identical properties asserted by classes with inheritance relation

$(2)\ |\sigma_i| \neq |\sigma_j|;$
$(3)\ M' = \delta(M^0, \sigma_i),\ M'' = \delta(M^0, \sigma_j);$
$(4)\ M^0_{sp} = \emptyset,\ M'_{sp} \neq \emptyset,\ M''_{sp} \neq \emptyset;$
$(5)\ \exists ST' \in M'_{sp},\ \exists ST'' \in M''_{sp};$
$(6)\ CR(ST') = CR(ST'').$

Explanation: Property (1) denotes that there should exist two nontrivial transition sequences and they are disjoint each other. Property (2) denotes that the lengths of the two sequences σ_i and σ_j are not equal. Property (3) denotes that the marking M' is reachable from the initial marking M^0 by the sequence σ_i, and M'' is reachable from M^0 by the sequence σ_j. Property (4) denotes that no state token is deposited in the place p in the initial marking M^0. While in the markings M' and M'', there is at least one state token deposited in the place p. Property (5) denotes that there exists a state token ST', ST'' in the place p of the markings M' and M'', respectively. Property (6) denotes that these two state tokens ST' and ST'' have the same colour. In other words, together with properties (4), (5) and (6), it is indicated that the place p in both marking M' and M'' contains a state token with same colour, whereas no state token appears in that of M^0. Whereas properties (1), (2), (3) imply that these two markings M' and M'' are inferred from the initial marking via different paths, which are disjoint and with different lengths.

Since the redundancy of both two cases occurs as a result of the existence of inheritance relation among classes (i.e., if define a relation or property, which can be inferred via the inheritance relation, redundancy occurs), same state of the place p can be inferred via alternative paths with different lengths (containing a certain inheritance relation or not). Thus, the redundancy is detected by examining the alternative paths and markings generated from the initial marking.

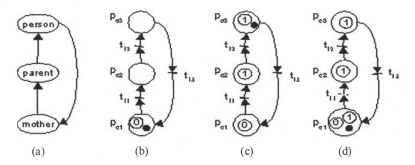

(a)   (b)   (c)   (d)

Fig. 16.7: Circularity

16.4.2 Circularity

For an ontology graph depicting the classes and their hierarchical relations, if multiple inheritances are allowed, the hierarchy would be a directed acyclic graph (e.g. the example shown in Fig. 1(a)), otherwise it is a tree. In other words, linking all classes via specialization relations, there cannot be circularity in the graph, since it is an anti-symmetric (partial order) relation. The circularity errors occur when a class is defined as a specialization of itself (or can be inferred via a chain of classes). For any two classes in a circularity, contradictory relations can be inferred between them that one class is a specialization of, and meanwhile a generalization of the other class.

An example of circularity and its mapping in SCCPN are shown in Fig. 7. Initially, if an instance token and a control token are presented in the place p_{c1}, the transition t_{11} is enabled (see Fig. 7(b)). After executing t_{11}, transition t_{12} will be consequently enabled. Via executing the sequence t_{11}, t_{12}, a state token with colour $CR = 1$ is created in the place p_{c3} (see Fig. 7(c)), and then transition t_{13} becomes enabled. After executing t_{13}, a state token with colour $CR = 1$ is created in the place p_{c1}, and the control token returns to p_{c1} (see Fig. 7(d)). Again, the transition t_{11} is enabled, and the circular loop continues.

Proposition 16.2. *For a given initial marking M^0, that minimally enables a nontrivial transition sequence σ, iff the ontology has circularity error as defined above, then $\exists j > i > 0$, $\exists p$ ($p \in P$, indicates a particular place), such that these sequences have the following properties:*

    $(1) M^i \in [M^0 >= \{M^0, M^1, \cdots, M^i, \cdots, M^j\}$;

    $(2) |M^0_{sp}|_{CR=1} = 0, |M^i_{sp}|_{CR=1} > |M^j_{sp}|_{CR=1} \geq 1$.

Explanation: Property (1) denotes that M^i is one of the markings which are reachable from M^0. Property (2) denotes that no state token with colour $CR = 1$ is deposited in the place p in the initial marking M^0. While in the marking M^i, there is at least one state token with colour $CR = 1$ deposited in the place p; and for M^j,

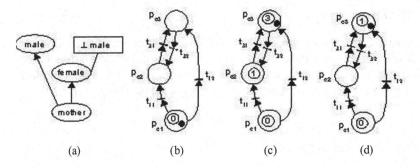

Fig. 16.8: Contradiction

the number of tokens with colour $CR = 1$ in the place p is more than that of M^i. It implies the accumulation of tokens while executing the circular loop.

16.4.3 Contradiction

In ontology, there usually are some classes being defined with exclusion relations among them. If a class or instance is defined (or can be inferred) as a subclass of more than one class which are exclusive, then contradiction occurs. An example is shown in Fig. 8. The places p_{c1}, p_{c2}, p_{c3} in SCCPN stand for the classes "mother", "female", and "male" respectively. Transitions t_{31} and t_{32} represent the exclusion relation between "male" and "female". Initially, the presence of an instance token and a control token enables the transition t_{11} and t_{12} (see Fig. 8(b)). If executing t_{11}, transition t_{31} will be consequently enabled. Via executing the sequence t_{11}, t_{31}, a state token with colour $CR = 3$ is created in the place p_{c3}, and the state of the net after executing the sequence is shown in Fig. 8(c). However, if executing t_{12} from the initial state, a state token with colour $CR = 1$ will be created in the place p_{c3}, as shown in Fig. 8(d). As discussed in the former section, colour $CR = 1$ can be explained as "true" whereas $CR = 3$ implies "false". Comparing Fig. 8(c) with (d), it is easy to see that contradictory states of the place p_{c3} are inferred from the same initial state.

Proposition 16.3. *For a given initial marking M^0, that minimally enables a nontrivial transition sequence σ_i, iff the ontology has contradiction as defined above, then $\exists \sigma_j, \exists p$ ($p \in P$, indicates a particular place), such that these sequences have the following properties:*

(1) $\sigma_i \cap \sigma_j = \emptyset$;
(2) $|\sigma_i| \neq |\sigma_j|$;
(3) $M' = \delta(M^0, \sigma_i), M'' = \delta(M^0, \sigma_j)$;
(4) $M^0_{sp} = 0, M'_{sp} \neq 0, M''_{sp} \neq 0$;
(5) $\exists ST' \in M'_{sp}, \exists ST'' \in M''_{sp}$;

$(6) CR(ST') \perp CR(ST'')$.

Explanation: The former Properties (1)-(5) have the same meanings with those in Proposition 1. Property (6) denotes that the colour of the token ST' has a contradictory meaning or exclusive relation with the colour of the token ST''. In other words, the two colours indicate contradictory states of the place p.

16.5 Performance Analysis

The analysis of modeling ontology by SCCPN is analyzed first. Then we focus on the complexity of ontology verification, which in the context of this chapter is defined to include the effort to map the ontology onto SCCPN, to derive the reachable markings, and to check the markings and the token colours for error examination.

In the following discussion, it is assumed that there are x classes and y relations among these classes are defined in the ontology. The amount of places and transitions in the SCCPN, which models the ontology, is denoted by x' and y', respectively.

16.5.1 Modeling Ontology by SCCPN

Via mapping ontology onto SCCPN, x class places are to be created to represent the corresponding classes. If each class in the ontology asserts a predicate (more facts or properties that a class holds can be combined into one predicate), there are x predicate places to be created. Thus, there is a maximum of $2x$ places in the Petri net, i.e. $x' \leq 2x$. To model these y relations defined in ontology, at most $2y$ transitions are to be created (in the case that each relation is modeled by two transitions with opposite directions linking to corresponding classes). Besides these transitions, there are still another transitions with a maximum of x to be created to link the predicate place. Therefore, $y' \leq x + 2y$. For the x' places in SCCPN, there are $2x'$ possible token facts (depicted by the presence of state tokens and control tokens). As a result, the total number of storage places for the computation is that $S = 2x' + y' \leq 5x + 2y$.

It should be noted that since the state tokens are coloured, each storage place for the state token will have a colour type, as defined in the colour set.

Moreover, for a special case that a concise ontology only consists of classes and their hierarchical relations (e.g. the example in Fig. 1), the upper bound for the amount of storage places will be decreased remarkably. In this case, it is easy to get that $x - 1 \leq y \leq \frac{1}{2}x(x-1)$. In other words, there exist at least $x - 1$ links representing the hierarchical relations among x classes, and it is upper bounded by $\frac{1}{2}x(x-1)$(while multiple inheritances are allowed and each pair of classes is linked by a relation). Thus, the storage places in this case hold that $S' = 2x' + y' = 2x + 2y$, $(x - 1 \leq y \leq \frac{1}{2}x(x-1))$.

16.5.2 Complexity Analysis of Ontology Verification

The complexity of ontology verification, in the context of this chapter is defined to include the effort to map the ontology onto SCCPN, to derive the reachable markings, and to check the markings and the token colours for error examination.

The reachable markings generated by transition firings in the Petri nets can be derived through a series of numerical computation. For the numerical computation, the multi-sets in M_s is to be represented by vectors spanned by the number of colours. It is similar with that being described by a formal sum of elements (here the element is a type of token with a particular colour) with a coefficient saying how many times it appears. Each element in the vector indicates the total number of tokens with a particular colour. It equals to the corresponding coefficient in the description by a formal sum. For example, the state marking for the place p_{c1} of M^0 in Fig. 4 (i.e. located at first row and first column) is $\{0\}$. It denotes the presence of a token with colour $CR = 0$ in the place p_{c1}. It also can be represented as a vector that $(1, 0, 0, 0, 0)$, in which the elements respectively indicate the number of tokens with colour $CR = 0, 1, 2, 3, 4$ (5 colours are considered in the example). With this representation, the marking (together with state marking and control marking) can be represented as a matrix consisting of non-negative integers. Taking M^4 in Fig. 4 for instance, it is represented as follows:

$$
\begin{array}{c}
(CR=) \quad 0\ 1\ 2\ 3\ 4\ M_c \\
M^4 = \begin{pmatrix}
1\ 0\ 0\ 0\ 0 & 0 \\
0\ 0\ 0\ 0\ 0 & 0 \\
0\ 1\ 0\ 0\ 0 & 0 \\
0\ 0\ 0\ 0\ 0 & 0 \\
0\ 0\ 0\ 0\ 1 & 1
\end{pmatrix}
\begin{array}{l}
p_{c1} \\
p_{c2} \\
p_{c3} \\
p_{c4} \\
p_{c1}
\end{array}
\end{array}
$$

As mentioned above, to reduce the complexity of computing, the generalization relation can be omitted and will not affect the ontology verification. Furthermore, for the purpose of detecting and verifying the three types of anomalies (i.e. redundancy, circularity and contradiction) discussed in the former section, only four colours that $CR = 0, 1, 3, 4$ should be in consideration. In other words, the three types of anomalies may occur while the inference involves instantiation relation, specialization relation, exclusion relation, and to assert a predicate. Thus, these four colours would contribute to the verification of the anomalies. Together with the control token, therefore, 5 different possible token facts (it is unfolded from the formerly mentioned 2 possible token facts, depicting state token and control token) are involved in the computation of reachable markings.

The numerical analysis of the SCCPN approach could be based on the matrix view of Petri nets. This is coupled by some heuristic operations to help simplify the mathematics involved in matrix calculation [5, 10]. Similar with the analysis in [16], it can be obtained that the complexity of numerical computation to derive the reachable markings (it is not allowed to span the immediate markings further, if any existence of a loop is detected) and to check different solutions for error examination is $O(5y'^3)$, where y' is the number of transitions in SCCPN.

16.6 Conclusion

In this study, a formal description technique for ontology representation and verification using a high level net approach is proposed. It is based on State Controlled Coloured Petri Net, and provides the capability of detection and identification of potential anomalies in ontology.

The approach of modeling ontologies by SCCPN contains the following main points. The concepts and their relationships are transformed as places and transitions linking to corresponding places in SCCPN, respectively. Besides the class places, another type of place, called predicate place, is adopted to represent the facts or properties asserted by some classes. Similarly, to distinguish different kinds of relations, the transitions are divided into different types. To maintain the state of class or predicate while inferring, each input place of a transition has a self-loop arc. Coloured tokens differentiate the dynamic knowledge inference by recording the transition type being fired. Control token is employed to control the firing or executing of transitions. A transition becomes active, just when at least one of its input places has a control token. If a transition is active and the transition condition is met (i.e., all its input places have the correct state tokens), then it is enabled. The transition condition is represented by different guard functions to specify the inference mechanisms for different relation types.

Via mapping ontologies onto SCCPN, formal technique for ontology verification using high level net approaches is proposed. The verification is done exhaustively by minimally initiating the sequence of transitions and closely examining the reachable markings. The reachable markings generated by transition firings in the Petri nets can be derived through a series of numerical computation. The complexity of numerical computation to derive the reachable markings and to check different solutions for error examination is $O(5y'^3)$, where y' is the number of transitions in SCCPN.

Our future work will focus on the further extension of the proposed approach. Although three types of anomalies, i.e. redundancy, circularity and contradiction, are discussed in this chapter, it is to be anticipated that other problems can also be verified by this technique. Furthermore, integrating the State Controlled Coloured Petri Net with fuzzy logic to model ontologies with uncertainty is also a promising and valuable direction.

Acknowledgements This chapter is supported by GRF grant (5237/08E), CRG grant (G-U756) of the Hong Kong Polytechnic University.

References

1. Bechhofer, S., Horrocks, I., Goble, C., Stevens, R.: OilEd: a reasonable ontology editor for the semantic web. In: Proc. KI 2001, 396–408 (2001)
2. Cimiano,P., Hotho, A., Staab, S.: Learning concept hierarchies from text corpora using formal concept analysis. Jour. Artif. Intel. Research, **24**, 305–339 (2005)
3. Farquhar, A., Fikes, R., Rice, J.: The Ontolingua Server: A tool for collaborative ontology construction. Jour. Hum.-Comput. Stud., **46(6)**, 707–727 (1997)
4. Gangemi,A., Catenacci, C., Ciaramita, M., Lehmann, J.: Modelling ontology evaluation and validation. Lect. Notes Comput. Sci., **4011**, 140–154 (2006)
5. Genrich, H. J.: Predicate/Transition nets. Lect. Notes Comput. Sci., **254**, 207–247 (1987)
6. Gomez-Perez, A.: Ontology Evaluation. Handbook on Ontologies, In: Staab, S., Studer, R. (eds.), pp. 251-273. Springer (2004)
7. Gomez-Perez, A., Fernandez-Lopez, M., Corcho, O.: Ontological engineering: with examples from the areas of knowledge management, e-commerce and the semantic Web. Springer-Verlag (2004)
8. Gruber, T. R.: A translation approach to portable ontology specifications. Knowl. Acqu., **5(2)**, 199–220 (1993)
9. Gruber, T. R.: Toward principles for the design of ontologies used for knowledge sharing. Jour. Hum.-Comput. Stud., **43(5-6)**, 907–928 (1995)
10. Jensen, K.: Coloured Petri nets: basic concepts, analysis methods, and practical use. **2**, Berlin; New York: Springer-Verlag (1995)
11. Jensen, K.: Coloured Petri nets: basic concepts, analysis methods, and practical use. **1**, Berlin; New York: Springer-Verlag (1996)
12. K. Wang, Liu, N. K., Ma, W. M.: Ontology Representation and Inference Based on State Controlled Coloured Petri Nets for Detecting Potential Anomalies. In: Proc. EJC 2010, Jyvaskyla, Finland (2010)
13. Lau, R. Y. K., Song, D. W., Li, Y. F., Cheung, T. C. H., Hao, J. X.: Toward a Fuzzy Domain Ontology Extraction Method for Adaptive e-Learning. IEEE Trans. Knowl. Data Eng., **21(6)**, 800–813 (2009)
14. Liu, N. K.: Formal description and verification of expert systems. Department of Computer Science and Computer Engineering, School of Mathematical and Information Sciences, La Trobe University, Bundoora, Victoria, Australia (1991)
15. Liu, N. K., Dillon, T.: Formal description and verification of production systems. Jour. Intel. Syst., **10(4)**, 399–442 (1995)
16. Liu, N. K.: Formal verification of some potential contradictions in knowledge base using a high level net approach. Appl. Intel., **6(4)**, 325–343 (1996)
17. Navigli, R., Velardi, P., Gangemi, A.: Ontology learning and its automated terminology translation. IEEE Intel. Syst., **18(1)**, 22–31 (2003)
18. Okeefe, R. M., Oleary, D. E.: Expert system verification and validation-a survey and tutorial. Artif. Intel. Review, **7(1)**, 3–42 (1993)
19. Petri, C. A.: Fundamentals of a Theory of Asynchronous Information Flow. In: Proc. 1962 IFIP cong., 386–390 (1962)
20. Pinto, H., Martins, J.: Ontologies: How can they be built?. Knowl. Info. Syst., **6(4)**, 441-464 (2004)
21. Protege. The Protégé ontology editor and knowledge acquisition System. Avaliable via DIA-LOG. http://protege.stanford.edu.
22. Shen, V. R. L.: Knowledge representation using high-level fuzzy Petri nets. IEEE Trans. Syst., Man, Cybern. Part A-Syst. Hum., **36(6)**, 1220–1227 (2006)
23. Shen, V. R. L., Juang, T. T. Y.: Verification of knowledge-based systems using predicate/transition nets. IEEE Trans. Syst., Man, Cybern. Part A-Syst. Hum., **38(1)**, 78–87 (2008)
24. Shiu, S. C. K., Liu, J. N. K., Yeung, D. S.: Formal description and verification of hybrid rule/frame-based expert systems. Expert. Syst. Appl., **13(3)**, 215–230 (1997)

25. Sridharan, B., Tretiakov, A., Kinshuk: Application of ontology to knowledge management in web based learning. In: Proc. ICALT 2004, pp. 663–665 (2004)
26. Strasunskas, D., Tomassen, S.: Web search tailored ontology evaluation framework. Lect. Notes in Comput. Sci., **4537**, 372–383 (2007)
27. Sure, Y., Erdmann, M., Staab, J. A. S., Studerr, R., Wenke, D.: OntoEdit: collaborative ontology development for the semantic web. Lect. Notes Comput. Sci., **2342**, 221–235 (2002)
28. Tadj, C., Laroussi, T.: Dynamic verification of an Object-Rule knowledge base using Colored Petri Nets. In: Proc. WMSCI 2005, **8**, 197–202 (2005)
29. Tartir, S., Arpinar, I.: Ontology evaluation and ranking using OntoQA. In: Proc. ICSC 2007, 185–192 (2007)
30. Wu, C., Lee, S.: Enhanced high-level Petri nets with multiple colors for knowledge verification/validation of rule-based expert systems. IEEE Trans. Syst., Man, Cybern. Part B-Cybern., **27**(**5**), 760–773 (1997)
31. Zhang, Z., Wang, S., Liu, S.: Dynamic knowledge inference, and learning of fuzzy Petri net expert system based on self-adaptation learning techniques. In: Proc. FSKD 2007, **1**, 377-381 (2007)

Chapter 17
A Reliable System Platform for Group Decision Support under Uncertain Environments

Junyi Chai, and James N.K. Liu

Abstract This chapter proposes a framework of Uncertainty-based Group Decision Support System (UGDSS). It provides a platform for multiple processes of decision analysis in six aspects including decision environment, decision problem, decision group, decision conflict, decision schemes and group negotiation. Based on knowledge engineering and multiple artificial intelligent technologies, this framework provides reliable support for the comprehensive manipulation of real applications and advanced uncertainty decision approaches through the design of an integrated multi-agents architecture.

17.1 Introduction

Nowadays, since companies are usually working in an uncertain and rapidly changing business environment, more timely and accurate information are required for decision-making, in order to improve customer satisfaction, support profitable business analysis, and increase their competitive advantages. In addition to the use of data and mathematical models, some managerial decisions are qualitative in nature and need judgmental knowledge that resides in human experts. Thus, it is necessary to incorporate such knowledge in developing Decision Support System (DSS). A system that integrates knowledge from experts is called a Knowledge-based Decision Support System (KBDSS) or an Intelligent Decision Support System (IDSS) [33]. Moreover, two kinds of situations significantly increase the complexity of de-

Junyi Chai
Department of Computing, The Hong Kong Polytechnic University, Hong Kong, SAR, China.
e-mail: csjchai@comp.polyu.edu.hk

James N.K. Liu
Department of Computing, The Hong Kong Polytechnic University, Hong Kong, SAR, China.
e-mail: csnkliu@comp.polyu.edu.hk

cision problem: (1) multiple participants involved in decision process; (2) decision-making under uncertainty environment.

In this chapter, we propose a framework of Uncertainty-based Group Decision Support System (UGBSS). Unlike existing DSS designs, this framework is based on multiagent technology and standalone knowledge management process. Through the adoption of agent technologies, this design provides an integrated system platform to address the uncertainty problem in group Multi-Criteria Decision Making (MCDM). Firstly, based on the literature review on MCDM researches, we analyze and provide a general model of group MCDM. Then, we carry out an analysis on uncertainty-based group MCDM, and present our designing basis of UGDSS. Thirdly, we propose the architectures and structures of UGDSS, including other two kinds of knowledge-related system components: (1) Decision Resource MIS and (2) Knowledge Base Management System (KBMS).

The rest of this chapter is organized as follows. Section 2 provides the general problem model of Group MCDM. Section 3 gives the uncertainty analysis of group decision environment. Section 4 presents the framework of UGDSS, including two knowledge-related system components. Section 5 shows our conclusion and outlines for future work.

17.2 Group Multiple Criteria Decision Analysis

17.2.1 Multiple Criteria Decision Making

Multiple Criteria Decision Making (MCDM) was derived from the Pareto Optimization. Many scholars contributed to this topic. Koopmans [25] introduced the Efficient Point in decision area. Kuhn and Tucker [26] provided the concept of Vector Optimization. Also, Charnes and Cooper [12] studied the model and application of Linear Programming in decision science. In 1972, the International Conference on MCDM held by Cochrane and Zeleny [15] remarked that the normative MCDM theory had been developed as the mainstream of decision science. More recently, many applicable MCDM approaches have been used to design Decision Support System for solving specific domain problems.

The MCDM with certain information or under certain decision environment is called classic MCDM. Major methods of classic MCDM can be roughly divided into three categories: 1) Multiple Criteria Utility Theory, 2) Outranking Relations, 3) Preference Disaggregation.

1. Multiple Criteria Utility Theory
   Fishburn [16] and Huber [21] provided very specific literature survey on Multiple Criteria Utility Theory. Besides, Keeney and Raiffa [24] published a monograph which deeply influences the future development.
2. Outranking Relations

The outranking relations approach aims to compare every couple of alternatives and then gets overall priority ranks, which mainly includes the ELECTRE method and the PROMETHEE method. ELECTRE was firstly proposed by Roy [29] in 1960s. Then, Roy [30], Hugonnard [22] extended its theory and applications. PROMETHEE method was initially established by Brans [9]. Xu [36] extended PROMETHEE with a Superiority and Inferiority Ranking (SIR) method which integrated with the outranking approach.

3. Preference Disaggregation

Jacquet-Lagreze et al. [23] provided a UTA method to maximize the approximation of the preference of decision makers by defining a set of additive utility functions. Zopounidis and Doumpos [40, 41] developed the UTADIS method as a variant of UTA for sorting problems, and extended the framework of UTADIS for involving multi-participants cases, which is called the MHDIS method.

17.2.2 General Problem Model of Group MCDM

The group MCDM problem involves multiple participants assessing alternatives based on multiple criteria. In order to facilitate the establishment and development of MCDM support system, we carry out an analysis of group MCDM to form a general model.

Fig. 1 shows our proposed general problem model for group MCDM. It generally contains three decision sets: alternative sets (Y_i), decision maker sets (e_k) and criterion sets (G_j). It involves two kinds of weights: decision maker weights (w_k) and criterion weights (ω_j). Decision makers provide their individual decision matrix $d_{ij}^{(k)}$ and the weights (ω_j) of every criterion. In this figure, individual decision information is represented with a decision-plane (P_k) including black points $(d_{ij}^{(k)})$ and grey points $(\omega_j^{(k)})$. Therefore, the group aggregation process can be shown as a plane-projection from individual decision plane P_k to group-integrated decision plane $P(k)$.

17.3 Uncertainty Multiple Criteria Decision Analysis

Although classic MCDM already has quite a complete theory in the past 50 years, it still cannot solve most MCDM problems in the real world. One main reason is that the decision information are not usually provided completely, clearly or precisely in reality. In most cases, people have to make decisions in uncertainty environment. Therefore, many researchers pay more attention to this new research branch-Uncertainty MCDM.

Uncertainty MCDM is non-classic, and can be treated as the extension and development of classic MCDM. We can generally divide the uncertainty problems into

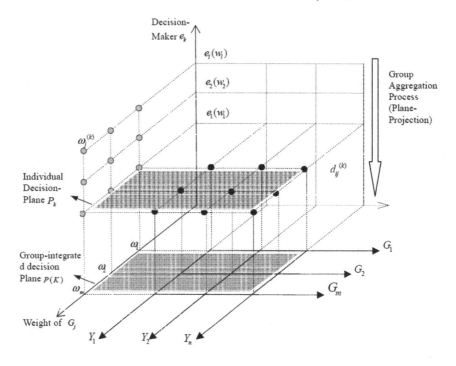

Fig. 17.1: General problem model of group MCDM

Table 17.1: The comparison in uncertainty types of decision problems

MCDM	Uncertainty objects	Research variable	Major approaches
Stochastic type	Possibility of decision results is uncertainty(not certain incidence)	Decision attributes in decision problem	Utility theory [4, 24], Probability aggregation [14], and Stochastic simulation [20]
Fuzzy type	The membership of objects is uncertainty (not clarity)	The value of decision attribute in decision problem	Fuzzy sets [1, 38] (Intuitionistic Fuzzy, Linguistic Fuzzy, ...)
Rough type	The granularity of objects is uncertainty (not accuracy)	Decision schemes	Rough sets [28, 17] (Variable Precision RSs, Dominance Based RSs, ...)

three categories: (1) Stochastic type (2) Fuzzy type (3) Rough type. A comparison of these uncertainty types is shown in Table I. Accordingly, Uncertainty MCDM also has three research directions: Stochastic MCDM, Fuzzy MCDM and Rough MCDM. Recently, many approaches have been developed to solve these problems (e.g. reference [10]). This study will adopt this classification method to establish the framework of UGDSS including its Subsystems, several intelligent agents and other function deployable applet.

17.3.1 Stochastic MCDM

Bayes theory is proposed for stochastic process which can improve the objectivity and veracity in stochastic decision making. Then, Bernoulli [6] introduced the concept of Utility and Expected Utility Hypothesis Model. von Neumann and Morgenstern [34] concluded the Expected Utility Value Theory, proposed the axiomatic of Expected Utility Model, and mathematically proved the results of maximized Expected Utility for decision maker. Wald [35] established the basis of statistical decision problem, and applied them in the selection of stochastical decision schemes. Blackwell and Girshich [8] integrated the subjective probability with the utility theory into a clear process to solve decision problems. Savage [31] extended the Expected Utility Model, and Howard [19] introduced the systematical analysis approach into decision theory and developed them from theory and application aspects.

Recently, many approaches have emerged for solving Stochastic MCDM. They can be generally divided into three directions:

1. Utility Theory based Approaches include Prospect theory, Cumulative Prospect theory [4].
2. Probability Aggregation based Approaches include Bayes method, Delphi method, Kaplan method [14], etc.
3. Stochastic Simulation based Approaches include Scenario Simulation, Monte Carlo method [20], etc.

17.3.2 Fuzzy MCDM

In 1965, Zadeh [38] proposed the Fuzzy Sets which adopted the membership functions to represent the degree of membership from elements to sets. Moreover, in 1978, Zadeh [39] proposed a theory of possibility to represent the difference of essence in stochastic problems and fuzzy problems. Atanassov and Gargov [1, 3] extended Zadeh's Fuzzy Sets concept into the Intuitionistic Fuzzy Sets (IFSs), and then as in the following, they extended IFSs into the Interval-Valued Intuitionistic Fuzzy Sets (IVIFSs), which are described by a membership degree and a nonmembership degree whose values are intervals rather than real numbers. Based on these pioneering works, theories of IFSs and IVIFSs have received much attention from researchers. Until recently, some basic theorems such as Calculation Operators and Fuzzy Measures, have just been founded for various applications [2, 37].

In Chai and Liu's earlier work [10], a novel Fuzzy MCDM approach was proposed based on the Intuitionistic Fuzzy Sets (IFSs) theory to solve real problems in Supply Chain Management (SCM). The theory firstly applied IFSs to define and represent the fuzzy natural language terms which were used to describe the individual decision values and the weights for criteria and for decision makers. And then six main steps of this approach were presented to solve uncertainty group MCDM problem. This work enriches the method base of solving fuzzy MCDM problem, and can be implemented in the proposed UGDSS.

17.3.3 Rough MCDM

Pawlak [27, 28] systematically introduced the Rough sets theory. Then, Slowin-ski [32] concluded the past achievements of Rough sets in theory and applications. Since 1992, the annual International Conference on Rough Sets has been playing a very important role in promoting the development of Rough sets in theory exten-sion and various applications. More recently, Greco [17] has proposed a Dominance based Rough Sets theory which produces the decision rules with stronger applica-bility. By now, Rough Sets theory can be applied in decision analysis, process con-trol, knowledge discovery, machine learning, pattern recognition, etc. In UGDSS, the rough MCDM approaches are mainly implemented by various subsystems with specific function modules, key intelligent agents, and other deployable applets.

17.4 UGDSS Framework

In this section, we propose the framework of Uncertainty Group Decision Support System (UGDSS). Here, the term "Knowledge" is a comprehensive concept, which includes data, model, human knowledge and other forms of information, so long as it can be used in uncertainty group decision making.

17.4.1 Uncertainty Group Decision Process and System Structure

In uncertainty group decision process, we mainly consider three factors which in-crease the complexity of decision-making in reality: (1) Uncertain decision envi-ronment, (2) Unstructured decision problem, (3) Complex decision group, and one issue in group decision making: Group unification of decision conflict. This process provides a mechanism to address the three kinds of complexities and group conflict, which consist of six analysis stages:

1. Decision Environment Analysis
2. Decision Problem Analysis
3. Decision Group Analysis
4. Decision Scheme Analysis
5. Decision Conflict Analysis
6. Group Coordination and Decision Analysis

From decision-makers' viewpoint, these stages have the basic sequence. Suppose there is a MCDM problem with complex internal structure involving multiple participants. We firstly need to analyze the existing internal and external environments, and figure out what are the decision conditions; whether the decision information is complete, certain and quantizable; what kind of uncertainty type it belongs to. Secondly, the specific decision problems need to be analyzed, including ontological investigation, problem representation and decomposition, etc. Thirdly, an ontological group analysis is required in order to reduce the complexity of human organizational structure. Fourthly, people need to establish problem-solving solutions which may be derived from various resources including previous problem-solving schemes in knowledge bases, decision schemes from domain experts, or results of group discussion, etc. Fifthly, we need to integrate those dispersive, multipurpose, individual or incomplete decision opinions into one or a set of applicable final decision results. Besides, the five stages mentioned above can momentarily be called Negotiation Support System in conflict analysis stage for possible decision conflicts.

From the viewpoint of system process, each stage consists of several subsystems with different functions. For example, we adopt the ontological problem analysis tools to represent, scrutinize and decompose the complex decision problem. These subsystems as the middleware are integrated in UGDSS platform with supports of interface technologies and intelligent agent technologies. In this design, parallel computation in subsystems and middleware is quite important, which can lead to better system efficiency.

17.4.1.1 Decision Environment Analysis

Decision environment is an important factor which significantly influences other decision stages. It may contain different aspects such as decision targets, decision principles, possible limitations, available resources, etc. More importantly, people need to analyze whether there are any uncertainty information. In this chapter, we define that the uncertainty decision information consists of the following situations:

1. Information deficiency
2. Information incompletion
3. Dynamic information
4. Unclarity information
5. Inaccuracy information
6. Multiple uncertainties

Although several MCDM approaches have been developed, it is not enough for solving complex uncertainty decision problem in reality. Therefore, one of our research directions aims to establish an Uncertainty Environment Analysis Subsystem (UEAS) to handle uncertainty information, and then extend its capability to solve other uncertainty MCDM problems.

17.4.1.2 Decision Problem Analysis

We can generally divide decision problems into three categories: 1) Structure, 2) Semi-structure, 3) Non-structure. To the first one, problems are well organized and represented for ontological analysis and decomposition. To another two, problems are usually represented in the form of text or interviewing dialogues. Therefore, these problems need to be ontological represented and described at this stage. Some useful analysis technologies can be adopted including ontological analysis in Ontobroker [42], natural language process, etc.

17.4.1.3 Decision Group Analysis

Many decision problems in reality (such as great strategic decision of government or industry, the organizational decision of large corporation, etc.), involve multiple participants with complex human relationship or organizational structure. A good group analysis can result in much efficient decision process and impartial decision results. Group Support System (GSS) is used for group analysis including decomposition, reorganization, character analysis, integration, etc. Some methods such as Double Selection Model [11] are a feasible approach to realize group analysis in GSS.

17.4.1.4 Decision Scheme Analysis

Decision schemes are the problem-solving solutions to specific decision problem. These schemes may be derived from previous decision schemes reorganized in Scheme Base; new problem-solving schemes established by domain experts; solutions produced in group discussion and negotiation; all kinds of information on Web or somewhere, etc. This stage is supported by Domain Expert System and corresponding Decision Resource MIS.

17.4.1.5 Decision Conflict Analysis

Decision conflict analysis is the core process in UGDSS. The conflicts may be derived at each stage of decision-making process. Therefore, the subsystem in each stage may call the programs of Negotiation Support System (NSS) for conflict analysis. Chai and Liu's earlier work [11] provided a Group Argumentation Model in order to solve complex decision conflicts. This model can be used to design and develop Negotiation Support System.

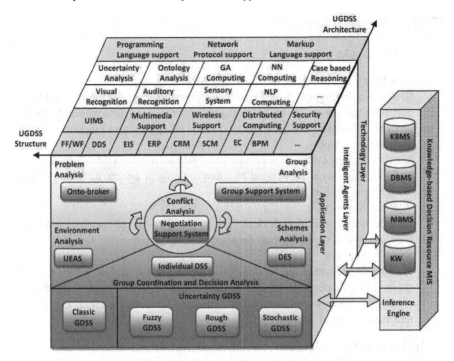

Fig. 17.2: UGDSS architecture

17.4.1.6 Group Coordination and Decision Analysis

This stage takes the responsibility for the integration of decision values provided by decision group. Many methods can be used to solve this problem including Vector Space Clustering, Entropy Weight Clustering, Intuitionistic Fuzzy Weight Average (IFWA) method [2], Weighted Group Projection method [10], etc. Besides, Individual Decision Support System is a helper of decision maker to develop their own opinion, and corresponds with Domain Expert Systems to form high quality individual decision schemes.

17.4.2 UGDSS Architecture

Unlike existing designs of DSS which mainly focus on specific problem domains, the UGDSS architecture provides an integrated system platform for complete decision analyses and comprehensive applications. The system architecture is shown in Fig. 2, which consists of three layers: the application layer, the intelligent agents layer, and the technology layer.

17.4.2.1 Application Layer

1. Basic Function Modules

   a. User Interface Management System (UIMS)

   UIMS, as a subsystem of UGDSS, is composed of several programs and functional interface components in intelligent agent layer such as natural language process, uncertainty analysis process, visual reorganization function, etc.

   b. Multimedia Support

   Multimedia technologies are comprehensively used in UGDSS. The interfaces in application layer are related to many intelligent agents including Visual recognition, Audio recognition, etc.

   c. Wireless Support

   Many mobile application devices such as PDA, mobile phone, wireless facilities are used to support group decision-making

   d. Security Support

   In order to guarantee the security of system and data transmission, security support is indispensible in system establishment. Some main technologies include internal control mechanism, firewall, ID authentication, encryption techniques, digital signature, etc.

2. Application Domain Modules

   The application domain modules aim to solve specific problems in different domains. For example, Chai and Liu's Fuzzy MCDM method [10] is used to solve the problem of supply chain partner selection. This application requires general domain knowledge of Supply Chain Management. These application modules as middleware of UGDSS can provide the necessary supports to various specific application domains. Several domains are shown as follows:

   a. Financial/Weather Forecasting (FF/WF)
   b. Director Decision Support (DDS)
   c. Enterprise Information System (EIS)
   d. Enterprise Resource Planning (ERP)
   e. Customer Relationship Management (CRM)
   f. Supply Chain Management (SCM)
   g. E-Commerce (EC)
   h. Business Process Management (BPM)

17.4.2.2 Intelligent Agent Layer

1. Sensory System

   Sensory systems, such as vision systems, tactile systems, and signal-processing systems, provide a tool to interpret and analyze the collected knowledge and to respond and adapt to changes when facing different environments.

2. Genetic Algorithm Computing Agent

Genetic Algorithms (GA) are sets of computational procedures, which learnt by producing offsprings that are better and better as measured by a fitness function. Algorithms of this type have been used in decision-making process such as Web search [13], vehicle routing [5], etc.

3. Neural Network Computing Agent

Neural Network (NN) is a set of mathematical models that simulate the functions of the human brain. A typical intelligent agent based on NN technology can be used in stock forecasting (i.e. [7]).

4. Uncertainty Analysis Agent

This agent is used to analyze the environment and conditions of decision problem.

5. Case Based Reasoning Agent

Case Based Reasoning (CBR) is the mean for solving new problems by using or adapting solutions of old problems. It provides a foundation for reasoning, remembering, and learning. Besides, it simulates natural language expressions, and provides access to organizational memory.

6. Natural Language Process Computing

Natural Language Process (NLP) technology provides people the ability to communicate with a computer in their native languages. The goal of NLP is to capture the meaning of sentences, which involves finding a representation for the sentences that can be connected to more general knowledge for decision making.

Besides, all of these intelligent agents with various group decision functions may consist of different kinds of Knowledge/Information bases which are united and embodied in Decision Resource Management Information System (MIS). This design can improve the efficiency of information processing and the robustness of system.

17.4.2.3 Technology Layer

This layer provides the necessary system supports to other two layers and Decision Resource MIS. It mainly includes (1) programming language support (VS.Net, C, Java, etc.) (2) network protocol support (HTTP, HTTPS, ATP, etc.) (3) markup language support (HTML, XML, WML, etc). Besides, the technology layer also provides various technology supports for constructing the four kinds knowledge-related systems (see section 4.3) and Inference engine, etc.

17.4.3 Knowledge-related System Designs

17.4.3.1 Knowledge-based Decision Resource MIS Framework

Fig. 3 shows the framework of Knowledge-based Decision Resource MIS. It mainly consists of four kinds of subsystem: KBMS, DBMS, MBMS, KW. In this system,

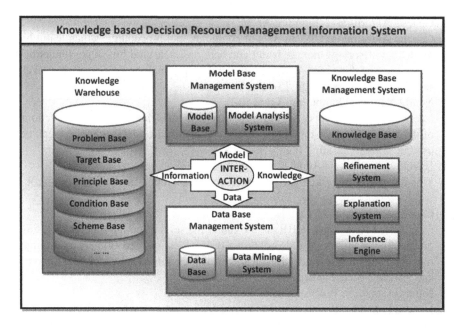

Fig. 17.3: Knowledge-based decision resource MIS framework

different kinds of information, knowledge, models and data interact together and provide the supports for the whole UGDSS.

1. Model Base Management System (MBMS)

   MBMS mainly includes Model Base and Model Analysis System. Model base contains routine and special statistical, financial forecasting, management science, and other quantitative models which provide the resources for Model Analysis System. Turban [33] divided the models into four major categories: Strategic, Tactical, Operational, and Analytical. In addition, there are model building blocks and routines. Based on these model resources, Model Analysis System is used to build blocks; generate the new routines and reports; update and change model; and manipulate model data, etc.

2. Knowledge Base Management System (KBMS)

   There are three kinds of knowledge which will be used in decision-making: 1) structure, 2) semi-structure, 3) non-structure. The structural knowledge is usually reorganized in available models and stored in model base. Most of the semi-structural and non-structural knowledge are so complex that they cannot be easily represented and reorganized. Therefore, more professional knowledge processing system called KBMS is required to enhance the capability of knowledge management. In next section, we present a detailed knowledge management process in KBMS.

3. Knowledge Warehouse (KW)

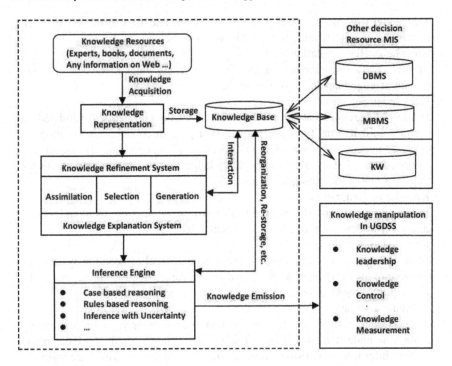

Fig. 17.4: Knowledge management process in KBMS

In UGDSS, KW mainly contains multiple bases for classified storage of decision knowledge including decision problems, targets, principles, conditions, schemes, etc. It is responsible for storage, extraction, maintenance, interaction and other knowledge manipulations.

17.4.3.2 Knowledge Management Process in KBMS

In this process, there are five basic classes of knowledge manipulation activities including: acquisition, selection, generation, assimilation, and emission [18]. These activities are the basis for problem founding and solving, as well as involved in the decision making process at each stage. In this chapter, we provide a knowledge management process in KBMS (see Fig. 4).

1. Knowledge Resource
   Some possible knowledge sources include domain experts, books, documents, computer files, research reports, database, sensors, and any information available on the Web.
2. Knowledge Acquisition

This activity is the accumulation, transmission, and transformation of documented knowledge resources or problem-solving scheme of experts.

3. Knowledge Representation

   The acquired knowledge is organized in this activity, which involves preparation of a knowledge map and encoding in the knowledge base.

4. Knowledge Selection

   In knowledge refinement and explanation system, the knowledge is validated and verified until its quality is acceptable. There are three activities to refine and explain the acquired knowledge: (1) selection, (2) generation, (3) assimilation. In selection activity, systems select knowledge from information resources and make it suitable for subsequent uses.

5. Knowledge Generation

   In this activity, knowledge is produced based on the decision incident by either discovery or derivation from existing knowledge.

6. Knowledge Assimilation

   In assimilation activity, this knowledge refinement and explanation system alter the state of the decision makers' knowledge resources by distributing and storing the acquired, selected, or generated knowledge [18].

7. Inference Engine

   In knowledge base, knowledge has been organized properly and represented in a machine-understandable format. The inference engine can then use the knowledge to infer new conclusions from existing facts and rules. There are many different ways of representing human knowledge, including Production rules, Semantic networks, Logic statement, and Uncertainty information representation, etc. Here, knowledge is recognized and restored in knowledge base which also conducts the communication with other decision resource MISs.

8. Knowledge Emission

   This activity embeds knowledge into the outputs of KBMS, and input the useful knowledge of specific decisional episode into UGDSS for further decisional knowledge manipulation activities including knowledge leadership, control and measurement.

17.5 Conclusion

This chapter proposes the framework of Uncertainty Group Decision Support System (UGDSS) and other two kinds of knowledge-related system components: Decision Resource MIS and Knowledge Base Management System (KBMS). We firstly provide a general problem model of group MCDM. And then, we carry out a brief analysis on uncertainty group MCDM problem, and present the basis of system design on handling the uncertainty decision-making. Finally, we propose a set of detailed designs of system architectures and structures for supporting a complete uncertainty group decision-making process including (1) environment analysis, (2) problem analysis, (3) group analysis, (4) scheme analysis, (5) group coordination analysis and (6) decision conflict analysis.

In future, we will make effort on two directions. In system aspect, we need to develop multiple intelligent agents, middleware or subsystems which are integrated in UGDSS. In decision theory aspect, we will consider how to develop more applicable uncertainty group decision-making approaches based on Fuzzy sets, Rough sets, Grey system theory and other uncertainty theories.

Acknowledgements The authors would like to acknowledge the partial supports from the GRF grant 5237/08E and CRG grant G-U756 of The Hong Kong Polytechnic University.

References

1. Atanassov, K: Intuitionistic fuzzy sets. Fuzzy Sets and Systems, 20, pp. 87-96 (1986)
2. Atanassov, K.: Operators over interval-valued intuitionistic fuzzy sets. Fuzzy Sets and Systems, 74, pp. 237-244 (1994)
3. Atanassov, K., Gargov, G.: Interval-valued intuitionistic fuzzy sets. Fuzzy Sets and Systems, 31, pp. 343-349 (1989)
4. Baucells, M., Heukamp, F.H.: Stochastic dominance and cumulative prospect theory. Decision Analysis, 52, pp. 1409-1423 (2006)
5. Bermudez, C., Graglia, P., Stark, N., Salto, C., Alfonso, H.: Comparison of recombination operators in panmictic and cellular GAs to solve a vehicle routing problem. Inteligencia Artificial, 14, pp. 34-44 (2010)
6. Bernoulli, D.: Exposition of a new theory on the measurement of risk. Econometrica, 22, pp. 23-36 (1954)
7. Bildirici, M., Ersin, O.O.: Improving forecasts of GARCH family models with the artificial neural networks: An application to the daily returns in istanbul stock exchange. Expert Systems with Applications, 36, pp. 7355-7362 (2009)
8. Blackwell, D., Girshick, M.A.: Theory of Games and Statistical Decisions. New York: Wiley (1954)
9. Brans, J.P., Vincke, Ph., Mareschal, B.: How to select and how to rank projects: The PROMETHEE method. European Journal of Operational Research, 24, pp. 228-238 (1986)
10. Chai, J.Y., Liu, J.N.K.: A novel multicriteria group decision making approach with intuitionistic fuzzy SIR method. Paper presented at the 2010 World Automation Congress, WAC 2010, Kobe, Japan, September (2010)
11. Chai, J.Y., Liu, J.N.K.: An ontology-driven framework for supporting complex decision process. Paper presented at the 2010 World Automation Congress, WAC 2010, Kobe, Japan, September (2010)
12. Charnes, A., Cooper, W.W.: Management Models and Industrial Applications of Linear Programming. New York: John Wiley and Sons (1961)
13. Chen, L., Luh, C., Jou, C.: Generating page clippings from web search results using a dynamically terminated genetic algorithm. Information Systems, 30, pp. 299-316 (2005)
14. Clemem, R.T., Winkler, R.L.: Combining probability distributions from experts in risk analysis. Risk Analysis, 19, pp. 187-203 (1999)
15. Cochrane, J.L., Zeleny, M.: Multiple Criteria Decision Making. University of South Carolina Press (1973)
16. Fishburn, P.C.: Lexicographic orders, utilities and decision rules: A survey. Management Science, 20, pp. 1442-1471 (1974)
17. Greco, S., Matarazzo, B., Slowinski, R.: Rough sets theory for multicriteria decision analysis. European Journal of Operational Research, 129, pp. 1-47 (2001)

18. Holsapple, C., Jones, K.: Exploring Primary Activities of the Knowledge Chain. Knowledge Process Management, 11, pp. 155C174 (2004)
19. Howard, R.A.: Decision analysis: applied decision theory. Proceeding in the 4th International Conference of Operational Research, New York: Wiley-Interscience (1966)
20. Huaser, D., Tadikamalla, P.: The Analytic hierarchy process in an uncertain environment: A simulation approach: European Journal of Operational Research, 91, pp. 27-37 (1996)
21. Huber, G.P.: Methods for quantifying subjective probabilities and multi-attribute utilities. Decision Science, 5, pp. 430-45 (1974)
22. Hugonnard, J., Roy, B.: Ranking of suburban line extension projects for the Paris metro system by a multicriteria method. Transportation Research, 16, pp. 301-312 (1982)
23. Jacquet-Lagreze, E., Siskos, Y.: Assessing a set of additive utility functions for multicriteria decision-making: the UTA Methods. European Journal of operational research, 10, pp. 151-164 (1982)
24. Keeney, R.L., Raiffa, H.: Decisions with Multiple Objectives: Preferences and Value Trade-offs, New York: Wiley (1976)
25. Koopmas, T.: Analysis of Production as an Effect Combination of Activities. New York: John Wiley and Sons (1951)
26. Kuhn, H., Tucker, A.: Nonlinear programming. University of California Press, pp. 481-492 (1951)
27. Pawlak, Z. Rough Sets: Theoretical Aspects of Reasoning about Data. Dordrecht: Kluwer Academic Publishers (1991)
28. Pawlak, Z., Skowron, A.: Rudiments of rough sets. Information Sciences, 177, pp. 3-27 (2007)
29. Roy, B.: Classement et choix en presence de point de vue multiples: Le methode electre. Revue Francaise dInformatique et de Recherche Operationnelle, 8, pp. 57-75 (1968)
30. Roy, B.: Partial preference analysis and decision aids: The fuzzy outranking relations concept. Conflicting Objectives In Decisions, D. E. Bell, R. L. Keeney, H. Raiffa, Eds., New York: Wiley (1977)
31. Savage, L.J.: The Foundations of Statistics. New York: John Wiley and Sons (1954)
32. Slowinski, R.: Intelligent Decision Support: Handbook of Applications and Advances of Rough Sets theory. Dordrecht: Kluwer Academic Publisher (1992)
33. Turban, E., Aronson, J.E., Liang, T.P.: Decision Support Systems and Intelligent Systems, 7th edition. Prentice Hall (2005)
34. Von Neumann, J., Morgenstern, O.: Theory of Games and Economic Behavior. Princeton University Press (1944)
35. Wald, A.: Statistical Decision Functions. New York: John Wiley and Sons (1950)
36. Xu, X.Z.: The SIR method: A superiority and inferiority ranking method for multiple criteria decision making. European Journal of Operational Research, 131, pp. 587-602 (2001)
37. Xu, Z.S.: Intuitionistic preference relations and their application in group decision making. Information Sciences, 177, pp. 2363-2379 (2007)
38. Zadeh, L.A.: Fuzzy Sets. Information and Control, 8, pp. 338-353 (1965)
39. Zadeh, L.A.: Fuzzy sets as a basis for a theory of possibility. Fuzzy Sets and Systems, 1, pp. 3-28 (1978)
40. Zopounidis, C., Doumpos, M.: Business failure prediction using UTADIS multicriteria analysis. Journal of the Operational Research Society, 50, pp. 1138-1148 (1999)
41. Zopounidis, C., Doumpos, M.: Building additive utilities for multi-group hierarchical discrimination: the M.H.DIS method. Optimization Methods and Software, 14, pp. 219-240 (2000)
42. Ontobroker. Avaliable via DIALOG. http://www.ontoprise.de/deutsch/start/produkte/ontobroker/

Index